ANSI C
PROGRAMMING

Steven C. Lawlor

FOOTHILL COLLEGE

WEST PUBLISHING COMPANY

Minneapolis/St. Paul   New York   San Francisco   Los Angeles

WEST'S COMMITMENT TO THE ENVIRONMENT

In 1906, West Publishing Company began recycling materials left over from the production of books. This began a tradition of efficient and responsible use of resources. Today, up to 95% of our legal books and 70% of our college texts and school texts are printed on recycled, acid-free stock. West also recycles nearly 22 million pounds of scrap paper annually—the equivalent of 181,717 trees. Since the 1960s, West has devised ways to capture and recycle waste inks, solvents, oils, and vapors created in the printing process. We also recycle plastics of all kinds, wood, glass, corrugated cardboard, and batteries, and have eliminated the use of Styrofoam book packaging. We at West are proud of the longevity and the scope of our commitment to the environment.

British Library Cataloguing-in-Publication Data. A catalogue record for this book is available from the British Library.

Production, Prepress, Printing and Binding by West Publishing Company.

TEXT IS PRINTED ON 10% POST CONSUMER RECYCLED PAPER

PRINTED WITH SOY INK™

COPYRIGHT © 1995 by   WEST PUBLISHING COMPANY
                      610 Opperman Drive
                      P.O. Box 64526
                      St. Paul, MN 55164-0526

All rights reserved
Printed in the United States of America
02 01 00 99 98 97 96 95   8 7 6 5 4 3 2 1 0

Library of Congress Cataloging-in-Publication Data

Lawlor, Steven C.

    ANSI C programming/ Steven C. Lawlor

    p.   cm.

    Includes index.

    ISBN 0-314-02830-7

    1. C (Computer program language)   I. Title

QA76.73.C15L39   1995

005.13'3--dc20   94-19251
                                                            CIP

CONTENTS

3 INTRODUCING DIRECTIVES AND STREAMS   55

7

POINTERS   *159*

8

ARRAYS   *177*

STRINGS   205

STRUCTURES   247

11 FILES   *279*

12 BITWISE OPERATIONS   *309*

13 THE PREPROCESSOR AND OTHER FEATURES *329*

A ASCII CODES *353*

B OPERATORS *355*

C FUNCTIONS 357

PREFACE

One of the greatest advantages of the C language is that it will let you do anything. On the other hand, one of the greatest disadvantages of the C language is that it will let you do anything. It is certainly one of the most powerful languages in existence, but its very power allows the undisciplined programmer any number of ways to get into trouble. To make the power accessible and avoid the trouble, *ANSI C Programming* integrates two very important parts of the programmer's art—fluency with the language and good programming habits.

ANSI C Programming is intended for use in a college-level programming course using C as its language. Its emphasis on structure, modularity, and good program design will satisfy the strict requirements of a computer-science course, while its easy accessibility make it applicable to a first course in programming for the CS major or non-CS major. For the traditional "C after some other language" course, it offers the complete ANSI implementation of C. For schools who have not yet installed ANSI C compilers, or for classes that teach the language but leave the implementation up to the student, non-ANSI implementations are addressed where applicable. For example, functions are introduced using ANSI prototyping but also shown in "K & R" or non-ANSI style.

APPROACH

ANSI C Programming is more than just a convenient title for the book. The objective is to give the student a solid foundation in the C language, especially according to the ANSI standards, while teaching and encouraging good programming habits.

From the Top Down

Modularity is a fundamental tool of program design and a fundamental indicator of a well designed program. The top-down, modular approach makes the process easier for the programmer and easier for anyone else who subsequently has to work with the program. This approach is not necessarily intuitive, however. Most of us have had its benefits imprinted on our minds by painful and unproductive experiences with the alternative.

One reason that new programmers fail to see the advantages of proper design is that they begin by writing simple programs—ones that can be successfully completed without much formal thought to design. A possible solution would be to have our students start out writing complicated programs, immediately impressing upon them that programming is not for the mental slacker. Our class dropout rates would be phenomenal.

Another solution is to introduce good practices when the students have learned enough about the language to write complicated programs. Unfortunately, by this time their sloppy habit patterns are established and many of them are almost beyond redemption.

Still another solution is to preface the course with a minicourse in structured, top-down, modular programming using some kind of strict pseudocode. Students often object to having to learn "another language" but usually that time is recovered later on in more efficient programming. Some professors have had success with this and indeed *ANSI C Programming* could be used with such a course.

In this text, however, we try to establish good program design habits as a natural part of programming. Design is not something "extra" but just part of putting together a program.

In many presentations, modularity revolves around the use of functions. In the C language especially, this is only natural. However, in the beginning when the students are writing simple programs, these functions tend to be trivial one- or two-liners leaving the students wondering "Why go to all this trouble; why don't we just stuff this into the in-line code?" Indeed, these programs would compile and execute more efficiently without the functions. Students, especially the more apt ones, tend to resist what they see as an artificial approach, viewing proper design at this stage as added burden on them. They want to sit down at the keyboard and start writing code.

ANSI C Programming in its philosophy and presentations shows tasks being laid out first in human terms using a loose pseudocode that is nothing more than a step-by-step process for performing the task. We stress the top-down approach by specifying the process in general terms or modules, and then expanding those modules into submodules, and so forth until the process is filled out in detail. The pseudoocode is simply plain English in outline form. The student's need to immediately attack the keyboard can be satisfied because the outline can be written in the text editor or C programming environment. The exercise will not be considered wasted because the outline as written will become the eventual program's comments. The top-down process is further solidified by showing it from start to finish in a "Putting It Together" section at the end of each chapter.

The modules in the program do not have to be divided into separate functions. Each of them is headed by the pseudocode comment and properly indented to be a visual as well as a procedural unit. By the time these modules become more complicated, or they can be thought of as standalone tasks that might be repeated within the same program or copied to some other program, the students will have been introduced to functions and the details of their operations, and can appreciate their use.

From the Bottom Up

"The best way to learn how to write programs is to write programs."

Anonymous, but fairly universal.

The learning process should be similar to the programming process; students should move from the simple to the more complex. The trick is to properly stage this flow so that basic concepts will prepare a foundation for the more advanced ones, which prepare a foundation for more advanced ones . . . and so on. In establishing concepts at each level we must give the students a complete understanding of that concept and its context in C programming, as well as an acceptance of it and an appreciation for it.

One of the most grievous errors we can make is "Notice that in this program listing the *whizbang()* function has been used. This function will be covered in detail in Chapter 147, Section 3.10.2.7." This leaves the students totally dissatisfied and frustrated. We should either be able to explain the function at this point in the learning process or pick another example. In most other languages, this credo is relatively easy to follow. In C it is not. Take functions for example. We want our students to write simple programs as quickly as possible, which requires use of at least the `main()` function if not `printf()` and `scanf()` as well. But to fully explain calls, formal arguments, parameter passing, the role of the stack, matching data types, returns, and so forth to raw beginners on the first day would not be productive.

So in C, there must be exceptions to this credo, but in *ANSI C Programming* those exceptions are rare and only found in the first three chapters and only for the purpose of getting the student up and running in C. Concepts are logically grouped to fit the bottom-up learning process and examples are chosen to illustrate those concepts. Concepts are never casually tossed in to be fully covered later (or covered apart from logically related concepts) simply to fit an expedient example.

Concepts must not only be introduced in the proper stages but also presented in a manner that will make them easy to absorb. In *ANSI C Programming,* each concept is fully presented, but in easy stages with constant reinforcement. For example, an individual function is introduced by establishing its need, showing its general form in ANSI prototype fashion, defining and explaining its arguments, and showing it in small examples designed to highlight just that function. Once the function is firmly established in the students' minds, it is used in larger examples to affirm its place in the language.

Nuts & Bolts

Is C a high low-level language or a low high-level language? Either way you look at it, one of the greatest advantages of C is its use in creating highly efficient programs. Much of its elegance comes from its simple relationship with the inner workings of the machine, especially main memory. A casual C programmer may understand that relationship on a conceptual level, but a serious C programmer must also grasp it on a guts-of-the-machine, nuts-and-bolts level. For example, arrays may be utilized by someone understanding them as "vectors" with "elements," but most efficient use of arrays, especially when pointers are involved, will come from understanding them as contiguous memory allocations with offsets from base addresses.

ANSI C Programming provides the students with both levels of understanding. Each topic is presented on a conceptual level, and *Nuts & Bolts* boxes throughout the text fill in the other level. The *Nuts & Bolts* boxes are optional. They are not required for the students' conceptual understanding of the material or for effective programming. For those who wish to pursue this more mechanical understanding, *ANSI C Programming* introduces the relevant parts of the machine, especially the characteristics of main memory, and is very careful to explain C operations in terms of these machine details. The necessity for matching data types in function calls, for example, becomes crystal clear when the role of the stack is understood.

In the *Nuts & Bolts* presentations, the students are required to know only those machine details that are directly utilized by the language and, rather than being bombarded with engineering facts, these details are introduced as natural features being used by the language. In this manner, students are made to feel comfortable with both the machine and the language.

TOPIC COVERAGE AND ORGANIZATION

ANSI C Programming covers all of the ANSI standard C language. It is not necessary to cover all of the text in a particular C course, however. Many sections or even chapters may be left out at the discretion of the professor. In keeping with the bottom-up approach, the first objective is to get the students comfortable with writing C programs. Chapter 1 establishes a common understanding of and vocabulary for hardware and software, introduces proper programming practices, and starts the students writing C programs, simple ones, immediately. Chapter 2 introduces data in its various forms, combining it together with expressions, and assignment to variables. Chapter 3 rounds out the first level by introducing simple input and output, and having the students write programs of some significance.

Chapters 4 and 5 solidify structured programming with the selection and iteration structures in their various implementations in C.

Chapter 6 begins the discussion of the special and more complicated features of the C language by introducing functions. The students have used `main()`, `scanf()`, and `printf()`, of course, but only to facilitate their learning of the rudiments and structure of the language. (Our exception to the bottom-up credo.) At this point they will be fully introduced to the workings of functions, examples of the ANSI mathematical functions, and making up their own. Modularity now begins to shift from comment-based to function-based.

Where to introduce pointers is always a difficult decision. Our bottom-up credo demands that the pointer concept be fully introduced but only when it can be appreciated and used. Human compassion demands that use of pointers be introduced in stages that can be reasonably assimilated by students. By Chapter 7 the students are deep enough into C to appreciate the language and see it as elegant rather than complex. They can handle the details of pointers, but will they be able to see enough practical application of pointers to really appreciate them?

Chapter 7 illustrates and reinforces the practical application of pointers by using them to pass values to functions. Once the concept of a pointer is established, it can be applied more easily in other applications to follow such as arrays, strings, structures, and so forth.

Some professors, however, will want to introduce arrays before pointers to make arrays less complicated and so that, when pointers are introduced, they will be able to show broader applications of them. These classes can move directly from Chapter 6 to the first part of Chapter 8, "Arrays, " which introduces the concept of arrays without using pointers. Then they can go back and pick up Chapter 7 and the last half of Chapter 8.

Once arrays and pointers are established, strings naturally follow as they do in Chapter 9.

Since structures and unions can be combinations of all data types, their introduction should come after other data including arrays and strings. For that reason they are included at Chapter 10. Since structures are often used in conjunction with files, that topic immediately follows structures. By shifting a few examples, these chapters could easily be reversed as the author actually does in his classes.

The bit-fiddling features of C make it an exceptional language, especially in writing low-level, high-efficiency programs. Chapter 12 covers C's bit-manipulation aspects. For many courses, however, this topic will be left out and, for that reason, Chapter 12 is entirely optional.

Chapter 13 is intended as a catch-all for the various parts and pieces of the language that we all put in different sections of our courses. This chapter is written in a modular fashion so that any or all parts of it can be included or not at the professor's discretion. Most will not cover it as a standalone chapter, but assign parts of it in conjunctuion with other chapters. The Chapter 13 "Preview" shows the chapter sections and the chapter with which that section might be introduced. For example, any of the sections on the preprocessor could be introduced concurrently with Chapter 3 or anytime thereafter.

CHAPTER APPARATUS

Each chapter begins with a **Preview** of the topics to be mastered in the chapter, giving the students an idea of what to look for and how the chapter is organized. Within each chapter, concepts are introduced in an orderly fashion, with new concepts building on the foundations created by the previous ones. As each concept is introduced, it is reinforced by program examples in structured form. New statements are always introduced using a general form and explanation, immediately followed by an example and a discussion of how the example operates.

To reinforce more difficult program code, I have included **Execution Charts** that follow the program step by step, showing the effect of each statement and how variables are affected at that point.

There are a number of sets of optional boxes throughout the book. **Nuts & Bolts** shows the student the inner workings of C concepts being discussed. **ANSI C Extra** shows material that is part of the ANSI standard, but may be skipped without lack of continuity. **Non-ANSI C** shows language components that are often treated differently in compilers that do not adhere to strict ANSI standards

Each chapter is capped with a comprehensive **Putting It Together** section using an example that illustrates that chapter's concepts and proper program development. This section follows a task from idea, through pseudocode development, to program, and even beyond with an explanation that includes an execution chart.

At the end of each chapter is a **Chapter Summary** and a list of **Key Terms** in the order of their appearance in the text.

There are three sets of activities at the end of each chapter. The first, **Review Questions**, tests the students' understanding of the material presented in the text. These can be used as written assignments, topics for class discussion, or for the students' own review of the materials.

Exercises provides questions about programs that require the students to use the concepts they have learned in the chapter. In this section, they show the output of program segments, debug program statements, pick correct code from incorrect, and so forth.

Programs are all programming assignments, giving the students and the professor ample opportunity to test the students' mastery of the use of the chapter materials. The programming problems are organized to follow the concepts as introduced within the chapter, with the earlier programs concentrating on single concepts and the later ones on combinations of concepts. Each problem gives a clear explanation of the task to be performed, suggested variables for use in the program, and samples of the output so that the students may check their results.

ANCILLARY MATERIALS

ANSI C Programming is not just a textbook, but an instructional package with a number of ancillaries to aid both the teaching and learning process.

Program Listings on Disk

All the program examples in the text are available on a disk packaged with the book. This allows the students to read about a concept and immediately reinforce the reading by running and experimenting with the example. In addition, listings for any programs in the "Exercises" section are included on the same disk. Since many of these are debugging exercises, this allows the students to quickly see the results of their changes.

Instructor's Manual with Test Bank

(Prepared by Rhoda Baggs, Florida Institute of Technology)

The Instructor's Manual with Test Bank contains for each chapter:

1. Answers to the end-of-chapter Review Questions and Exercises.

2. Listings for suggested solutions for each of the programming problems at the end of the chapter.

3. Test questions (60–75 per chapter). These questions include a mixture of different testing formats: multiple choice, true/false, fill-in-the-blank, short answer, program tracing, code debugging, and code segment writing.

ACKNOWLEDGMENTS

A package such as *ANSI C Programming* cannot be the product of only one mind. In this case it is the product of literally hundreds. All the folks at West, who are normally paid to do wonderful things, certainly earned more than their paychecks. I would especially like to thank Richard W. Mixter, the Sponsoring Editor, for his insight, encouragement, and perseverance; Keith Dodson, Developmental Editor, the guy who makes things happen and pulled together so many parts of the project; and Stefanie Reardon, Production Editor, who pounded the book through the production process, often doing the impossible—like making Macs and PCs *really* talk to each other.

ANSI C Programming was extensively reviewed. I felt that I was constantly on the hot seat, but the process was fruitful and made for a much more useful final product. For their thoughful reading and insightful comments, I wish to thank, in alphabetical order, professors:

Arun K. Agarwal	John B. Connely
Stephen J. Allan	Richard J. Easton
Michael P. Barnes	Mahmoud Fath El-Den
Niels K. Bauer	Rhonda Ficek
Michael Beeson	Jim Ford
A.T. Bell	Mike Holland
John Carroll	Joseph Hurley
Thomas Cheatham	Christopher G. Jones

Edward M. Keefe
Jeffrey A. Koenke
Robert D. Logcher
William A. Moy
Marc R. Parker
Suzanne Pawlan
William Perry
Lawrence Petersen
Joan Ramuta

Arline Sachs
Suzanne Sever
Susan Simons
Jeffrey A. Slomka
John Tappen
Mark Thomas
Donald Yee
Winnie Yu

One of the most important factors of the book was its extensive class testing, by the author and by many of his colleagues. I would like to thank professors John Berry, Elaine Haight, and Roberta Harvey for using it in their classes and providing invaluable feedback.

Perhaps most of all, I would like to acknowledge my debt of gratitude to the hundreds of students who suffered with amazing tolerance and good humor through the early test editions, and provided the most important commentary.

INTRODUCING C

Before you can write programs, you must know a little about the environment in which you are to program—the equipment that your program is to direct and how a program actually comes to be. In this chapter we shall examine:

1. The basic makeup of a computer system.

2. The equipment involved in a computer system and how its functional components work together.

3. The kinds of software used to direct the equipment.

4. The route software takes from an idea to an actual program capable of controlling a computer.

5. Programming design conventions in common use today.

6. Where the C language fits in the scheme of computer languages.

7. What a C program looks like and what its major components are.

In many ways the C language is as simple as its name, but that very simplicity gives it an elegance and efficiency available in very few other languages. Many languages take great pains to shield the programmer from the inner workings of the computer. They are designed to be "intuitive" and "user friendly." Because of this isolation, however, the programmer cannot take advantage of all the computer's inner mechanisms. Compromises must be made. The job gets done, but perhaps not in the most efficient manner.

C sets up few such barriers. You can dive right into the heart of the computer and manipulate its pieces directly and efficiently. This does not mean that you must be a computer hardware expert, but you do have to have an appreciation of its functional components and how they are manipulated using the C language. Once you gain this understanding, you will find that C becomes intuitive at a more elementary level and it, too, becomes user friendly.

THE COMPUTER SYSTEM

The word "system" is very important when we talk about computers. An effective computer system is an interconnected set of components working toward a common end. The system consists of two main categories—hardware and software. **Hardware** is the actual pieces of equipment—keyboards, screens, the stuff inside the boxes, printers, and so forth. To use a noncomputer example, a car, your Ferrari, is hardware.

Software is the instructions that direct the hardware—tell it how to perform tasks for us. One is not much good without the other. Take your Ferrari, for example. In order to use it for its intended purpose, getting from here to there, you must drive it—instruct it by pushing the pedals, turning the wheel, working the shifter, and pushing the buttons. Without those instructions, your Ferrari is nothing but a driveway ornament. Similarly, without software the computer is nothing but an expensive paperweight.

HARDWARE

Computers come in all sizes from pocket size to building size. The larger systems can process more data at a faster rate, but functionally, all computers are quite similar. They have the same categories of components that operate in the same way.

Access to Data

Almost any operation in the computer involves accessing data. There are two, and only two, types of data access: read and write. A computer **read**

▶EXHIBIT 1–1
Moving Data

A data move consists of a read and a write. The read copies the data from the location being read, and the write replaces the data at the location being written.

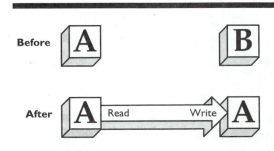

operation is similar to reading a book. You look at the words on the page and copy them to your mind but they are not removed from the page. Playing back an audio or video tape is a read operation. You may play it back as many times as you want; the data is not destroyed. A read access, then, simply makes a copy of the data while leaving the original intact.

A computer **write** operation is similar to writing on a paper, except that a computer write actually erases what was there before. Recording an audio or video tape is a more complete example of a write operation. The previous data is erased, and new data is recorded. A write access, then, replaces data where the write occurs.

Any movement of data in the computer involves a read and a write. Data is read from here and written there.

The CPU

The heart of any computer system is its **central processing unit** (**CPU**). The CPU has three main functions: control, arithmetic operations, and logical operations. In its **control** function the CPU takes your instructions, one at a time, and directs the rest of the computer system in following each of them. It is your foreman inside the system. You are the ultimate boss. You either write the instructions or load some other prewritten ones, but you give those instructions to the CPU and have it carry them out.

Once you give a set of instructions to the CPU and direct it to follow those instructions, you are no longer in control of the computer; the CPU is. Control will be returned to you only after those instructions are finished or some error condition forces the CPU to halt them. It is important to remember that the CPU is not some intelligent being but a brainless machine. It handles one instruction at a time, never looking forward or back, and never evaluating the propriety or outcome of the instruction. You would know to subtract deductions from an employee's paycheck; the CPU would just as happily add them if it was so directed. It would throw itself off a cliff if that was one of the instructions.

Obtaining proper results from the computer is, of course, up to you. You cannot expect any intelligent help from the CPU.

Many of the operations you do using the computer are actually performed within the CPU. For these operations, it directs itself. **Arithmetic operations**—addition, subtraction, multiplication, and division—for example, are performed within the CPU. Obviously a computer must perform arithmetic. Calculating a paycheck by multiplying the employee's hours by that employee's pay rate and subtracting various deductions is a typical example.

Logical operations—comparisons—are also performed within the CPU. Is this larger than that? Are these two items equal? You would probably use logical operations in producing a paycheck. To determine whether to pay overtime, you would compare the employee's hours to forty. To find the data on the employee's deductions, you would compare the employee's name to the names in our file of employees.

Main Memory

Having a CPU is a start, but you still need other components in your computer system as well. For example, where do the instructions come from that

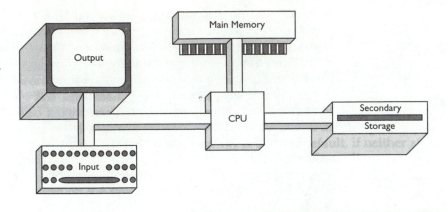

►EXHIBIT 1–2
A Computer System

A computer system consists of a number of functional components, all controlled by the CPU, which, in turn, follows program instructions.

the CPU is following? Where do you put the data that the CPU is processing or the results of its efforts? To the CPU you will connect a **main memory**—a temporary, working storage area. In the main memory you will store two types of things: the current set of instructions that the CPU is following, and the data that these instructions manipulate.

Main memory is wondrous stuff. It is all electronic, so it is very fast. A piece of data might be accessed in a twentieth of a millionth of a second. It is also individually accessible, meaning that any individual item, one letter, one number, or one instruction, can be accessed by itself. That sounds reasonable and, in fact, it is necessary to get anything done, but some other storage systems will not allow this individual access.

Physically, main memory is made up of thousands or millions of **locations**—sets of components that store these individual pieces of data. Each location has an **address**—a unique number that the CPU can use to refer to the location. This address is similar in concept to our street addresses. There is only one 45 Oak Street in town and there is only one location 721365 in the main memory.

Main memory has its limitations. It is relatively expensive and it is volatile, meaning that when the power is turned off, it forgets. Therefore you use main memory only for active, current storage—the program (or possibly a few programs with multitasking computers—those that can run more than one program concurrently) with which you are currently working, and data associated with it. When you finish with a program, you replace it in main memory with a new one.

►EXHIBIT 1–3
Main Memory

Main memory consists of individual locations, each of which has an address. In this example, the character *A* is stored in location 5008, 2 in 9003 and *Hello World!* in locations 7002 through 7013.

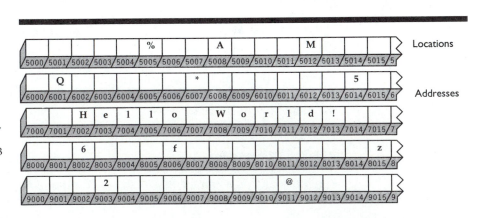

Secondary Storage

Disks, both hard and floppy, are the most common examples of **secondary storage**. Unlike main memory, secondary storage is permanent. You can change the data there any time you want, but unless you do, the data will remain forever. Secondary storage is also relatively cheap; therefore you typically have lots of it connected to the system, often hundreds of times the main memory capacity.

This sounds so good that perhaps you should forget main memory and work only with secondary storage. Secondary storage, however, is slow—hundreds of times slower than main memory. More importantly, secondary storage is only accessible in chunks called physical records, or sectors or blocks depending on the device. These physical records may be from about eighty to thousands of characters long. In order to work with data effectively you must be able to access individual characters, or numbers or instructions, which you can only do in main memory.

You use both storage systems, then, in the computer. You do your work using main memory. The data or instructions you need are loaded into main memory and processed. If you wish to save these things permanently, you read them from main memory and write them to secondary storage, typically hard or floppy disks. This then allows you to write the instructions and data for the next project into main memory and process them.

For example, if you had data in secondary storage that you wished to change, a payroll record perhaps, your instructions to the CPU would direct it to read the physical record or records containing that payroll record into main memory, write the change to the individual characters in the record (the copy in main memory, of course) and then write the physical record back to its original space in secondary storage, replacing the original physical record. Your change has now been made and is permanent.

Input and Output

Even with all this, the system still lacks some essential items—ways for us humans to communicate with it. The most common type of input device is the keyboard, although there are others such as the mouse, optical scanner, and so forth. Screens and printers are the most common types of output devices.

SOFTWARE

Hardware you can touch; software you can't. The software may be stored on various media, disks or paper perhaps, but the software is simply ideas—instructions to make the hardware perform for you. A set of instructions is called a **program**. Some programs figure out the payroll, others fly aircraft, still others assist you in writing reports or books. Software is divided into two categories: system and application. You are probably most familiar with **application software**—that written to perform specific tasks for individual users of the computer system. Some examples are accounting, spreadsheet, word-processing, and game programs. Most of the programs you write in C (and all that you will write from this text) will be applications.

System software provides services for all the users of the computer system. It has two main objectives. The first is to deliver the hardware's resources to you in a relatively simple manner. For example, to print some characters at the printer, the CPU must know to which wires the printer is connected, in what fashion and speed it should send the characters, whether the printer is currently busy printing characters previously sent to it and if so, to wait until it is free, and how to react to error conditions in the printer channel. All these things must be considered for each character printed and entail a bunch of computer instructions.

Since printing is such a common activity, you don't want to have to write those instructions into every program that uses the printer, so the system designers have written printing routines into the system software. Our application program designates a set of characters and passes them along to the system-software printing routine. When that routine is finished, it passes control back to our application program, which continues on with its task.

The second main objective is to provide compatibility between different hardware configurations. Computers within the same family often have different printers or screens, for example. A single configuring of the system software will allow the same set of application program instructions to accommodate the different hardware. This facilitates **portability** of application software—the ability to run the same application software on different hardware configurations.

Operating Systems

An **operating system** is a set of system software programs. Your application program will have to make use of, and be compatible with, the operating system in use on your computer. Unfortunately, there is not just one operating system. Life would be too simple if you could write application software that would run on any machine. Some of the popular operating systems are MS-DOS, Macintosh, and XENIX on microcomputers; and UNIX on micros, workstations, and midrange computers. Many manufacturers of midrange and mainframe computers supply their own operating systems. IBM, for example, has OS/400 for its AS/400 line of midrange computers.

Language Levels

Computers don't understand C. Or Basic or Cobol or Pascal or any of the common programming languages. Each CPU has a set of instructions manufactured into it. The instructions differ for different brands and models of CPUs but they all have two things in common: They all consist of sequences of offs and ons (because that is the internal alphabet of the computer); and each one doesn't do much. Displaying some characters on the screen is usually simple for you using a typical programming language, but it may require a dozen or more instructions to the CPU.

This built-in language is referred to as the computer's **machine language**, a term also used to describe the entire category of built-in CPU languages. It

►EXHIBIT 1–4
The Operating System

To make programming easier and to make systems more compatible, an application program sends general instructions to system-program routines in the operating system. These routines translate and expand the general instructions into the specific ones needed to drive the hardware.

is the lowest level of computer languages; easy for the computer but almost impossible for humans. When you write programs in high-level languages, like C, you can understand them, but they have to be translated to the computer's own machine language before the computer can execute them.

Writing a program in machine language might offer some advantages. Since it is the actual language of the computer, you could direct the computer to do anything it is capable of and in the most efficient manner. If a generalized language has to be translated into a specific machine language, compromises must be made. The job will get done but perhaps not with the greatest efficiency.

Nobody, however, programs in machine language. Trying to keep track of all those offs and ons (even if you use zero and one as symbols) would drive you nuts.

People can realize the advantages of machine-language programming by using **assembly languages**, the second level of languages. They are so called because a program called an assembler translates the assembly-language instructions into machine language to be executed. Simple assembly languages are merely symbolic machine languages. Instead of referring to an instruction as 0111010110110011, you use the word ADD, considerably easier on us humans. Programs must still be written in the same painstaking detail, though, because you are still dealing with the CPU's own instruction set. The trade-off between assembly and high-level languages is that a program in assembly executes as efficiently as possible, but takes a long time to write.

Assembly language is the second language level.

High-level languages are meant to be easy for humans to work with. They are similar to English (or some other human language), and one high-level-language instruction translates into many machine-language instructions, making high-level-language programs considerably shorter than machine-language programs. This does not mean that you can simply chat with the computer; strict vocabulary and syntax (construction of the instructions) are essential because the computer is nothing more than a machine and cannot understand our often relaxed and colorful way of speaking. Can you imagine what the very literal and precise computer would make of the expression "raining cats and dogs"?

From Source to Execution

A program written in C (or any other high-level language) is simply text—readable by humans but worthless to the computer. Let us follow the process of writing a C program and see how it turns into executable machine language.

You start by creating **source code**, the text program written in C. Since this is just text, you will use some kind of text-editing or word-processing program to aid you in the writing. Once it is completed, you will save (copy) the source program to secondary storage.

The next step is to create **object code**, the program translated to machine language. A **compiler** program performs this operation. You execute the compiler, tell it which source file you want translated, and the end result is an object program . . . or a batch of error messages. If there are errors at this stage, they must be corrected in the source code, so you must return to the previous stage—load up the text editor, make the changes, and then compile again.

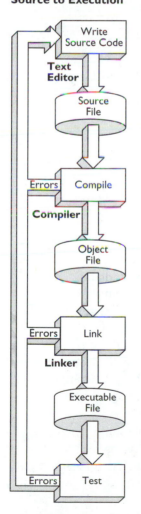

►EXHIBIT 1–5
Source to Execution

The compiled program is not ready to run yet. C, like most high-level languages, has libraries of prewritten routines that you as a programmer may use. You refer to them in the source code and the references are embedded with the object code. You must now **link** your object code with the object code for the prewritten routines. Similar to the compiling stage, you execute a linker program, tell it the object files (yours and the libraries') and it produces a file of **executable code**, the program that will actually run on the computer. Of course, if there are any errors at this stage, you must return to the source code for corrections and go through the process again.

The process is not finished yet. The computer only considers as errors things that it cannot execute. It has no understanding of what you want to do or whether an executing program will do it. You must test the program by running it and comparing it with known results. If there are errors here (referred to as logical errors) they must be corrected in the source code and the process repeated.

THE PROGRAMMING PROCESS

The purpose of a program is to instruct the computer to perform some task. In writing the program you must, of course, give the proper instructions so that the task is completed as required. But there are many ways to write a program and things to consider other than just completing the task. In your programming you should always keep these objectives in mind:

1. **Execution Efficiency**   Will the program execute in the least amount of time?

2. **Programming Efficiency**   Can you write, test, and complete the program in the least amount of time?

3. **Maintainability**   After the program is written and operating, can you or some other programmer easily make changes in it?

4. **Source for Future Programs**   Code lifted from previous programs is 93.86% (or thereabouts) of any new program. Is the code from this program written in such a way that it can be easily used in the future?

Often these objectives involve trade-offs. For example, it usually requires more programming effort to make a program that executes more efficiently. Since people time is much more expensive than computer time today, it might be economical to sacrifice some computational efficiency for ease of programming (except in time-critical applications such as screen updates, when waiting for the screen to fill would be frustrating). You will have to take extra care to ensure that your program is maintainable. Conditions and situations constantly change and your program will have to change to keep up. If your routines are to be suitable for future use, you will have to consider applications for them other than just the current one.

In any case, all these factors indicate the need for planning. There is a natural human tendency, when faced with a programming project, to sit down at the keyboard and start banging out code. Resist it! The time spent planning is more than made up for in the overall time required to successfully complete the project.

Modular Programming

The history of the world could be written in one long paragraph extending over thousands of pages. It might start with a bunch of coalescing gases and proceed chronologically to the present.

Nobody would read it.

If you were interested in the developments in Mesopotamia in 2000 B.C., you would first have to find the pages near that time period, and then scan through all the text, rejecting all the irrelevant stuff, gathering anything that had to do with Mesopotamia, or the Tigris River, or the Euphrates River, or any number of kingdoms, cities, rulers, and so forth and so on. Histories are not written that way. In an ancient history book, for example, there would be a chapter on Mesopotamia with all the relevant facts gathered together.

In other words, the history book would contain **modules**, self-contained sections with a complete treatment of a particular topic.

Computer programs should be similarly written. Rather than a long list of code, the code should be divided into modules, each performing specific, small tasks. By combining these modules together, you end up with a complete program that performs the overall task. For example, paying a company's employees is a complicated process but it really consists of several small, simple tasks. For each employee you must figure the federal income tax deduction, add the gross pay to the year-to-date figure, print the actual check, and so forth. Each of these tasks should be considered a module and programmed individually.

Each module should be **encapsulated**. It should be an entity within itself, not depending on other modules or data elsewhere in the program. Your program should send the required data to the module, which should do whatever it is supposed to and allow the program to go on to the next module. You should be able to insert a well-constructed module, without modification, in any program that requires the same task.

Modular programming offers a number of advantages:

❏ **Easier Programming**   Large, complicated programs are difficult to write but small ones are easy. If you treat your large program as a number of small, self-contained modules, the programming process will be much easier.

❏ **Easier Debugging**   A **bug** is some problem in a program. Often, and especially in C, these bugs are hard to pinpoint. A typical reaction to a program problem might be that the computer freezes up. Since each module is a self-contained programlet, it may be tested and debugged individually, significantly reducing the area in the code where you must look for problems. Once a module is debugged, you may combine it with other modules with confidence.

❏ **Easier Maintenance**   Making changes in programs is easier because you can isolate the module or modules that require changing and test them individually. New modules may be added to a program or existing modules deleted just as easily.

❏ **Easier Future Programming**   You can create new programs by extracting modules from old programs and combining them. There will always be something new that must be added, but these things can be inserted as new modules, or old modules may be modified to serve new purposes.

Top-Down Design

The modules are the individual pieces of the program, but what about the overall design? One does not build a house by constructing the individual rooms and then seeing how they might all fit together. You start with the house and then divide it into the rooms. This is the basic idea behind **top-down design**—starting with the overall project and then dividing it down into individual modules.

Top-down design is done in steps, the first being a statement of the objective of the undertaking—do the weekly payroll, for example. This is divided into the major tasks that will be required—gather timecard data, compute pay data, print checks, produce reports. These are major modules for the project. Each of these modules can be divided further. Producing reports should be divided into the individual report modules needed—payroll by department, benefits, expenses, and so forth. Each of these modules may be further divided.

When does it stop? When a module is a self-contained entity performing a specific task, small enough to be easily programmed but not so small that it would have no purpose except within a certain group of modules in this one undertaking. This may be five, fifty, or a hundred lines of code, depending on the task.

STRUCTURED PROGRAMMING

Even a well designed program may be difficult to write and even more difficult to communicate to others. Top-down design adds consistency to the design process and makes it easier. **Structured programming** does the same for the programming process by identifying three different types of programming patterns, called control **structures**, and building programs out of

➡EXHIBIT 1–6
Top-Down Design

A top-down design starts with an overall statement of the task (Weekly Payroll), breaks that down into individual modules (such as Compute Pay Data), and keeps breaking modules down until they become self-contained program segments.

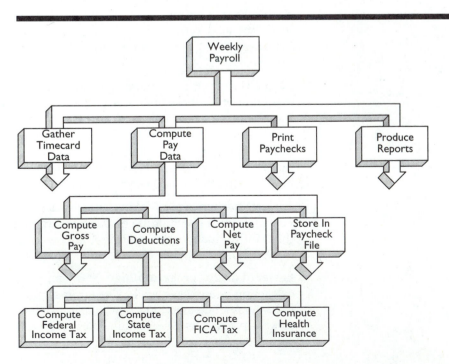

only those three standard patterns. By using them in various combinations you can write any (yes, any!) program, no matter how sophisticated. The individual structures are simple; they are the fundamental building blocks of programs. These building-block structures are combined to form useful, and sometimes quite complicated, programs. One structure may follow another; be put inside another; be put inside one that's inside another, following another, inside another; and so forth. These simple patterns can be combined any way you have to in order to get the job done. The end result may be a complicated program, but made of simple pieces.

A good structured programmer will outline the various structures in the program first in simple, human language (or in a more formalized **pseudocode**, literally false code, but still human instead of computer language). This outline is often done using the same text editor that the programmer will use to write the actual program source code. In fact, the outline will become part of the source code. A good structured outline looks like a well-ordered set of class notes. Major topics, in this case structures, are at the left margin; subsidiary topics, the structures inside, are indented within the major ones, and so forth. It is easy to see which structures are within other structures because they are indented within them.

There are numerous applications of each of these structures in our weekly payroll example and we shall use that to illustrate the structures and how an outline looks.

The Sequence Structure

The **sequence structure** is simply one operation after another. In the payroll example we gather timecard data, compute pay, write paychecks, and print reports in that order. Since the sequence is so simple, we don't have any special format or indenting for it. The sequence in our outline would be written like this:

```
Gather timecard data
Compute pay data
Write paychecks
Print reports
```

The Iteration Structure

Sometimes an operation or set of operations is repeated over and over. This repetitive pattern is called an **iteration structure** or a **loop**. Under the structured-programming guidelines, there must always be an end to the repetition—some condition set up that will tell the computer whether it should perform the operations again or go beyond the iteration to the rest of the program. This condition may be tested either before the individual operations are performed (at the beginning of the loop) or after (at the end of the loop).

In our payroll example, computing the pay must be done for each employee; the same operation must be done many times. Following the top-down modular procedure, we can expand the *Compute pay data* module with an iteration structure.

```
Begin loop
    Compute employee pay
End loop
```

This would not be good programming practice, however, because we have stated no conditions for continuing the loop or exiting it. The program would compute pay forever. In C, the test condition is always for continuing the loop—when the condition is true, the operations are repeated. If we choose to test at the beginning of the loop, we might write the outline this way:

```
While more employees
    Compute employee pay
End loop
```

Alternatively, we may wish to test at the end of the loop as follows:

```
Do
    Compute employee pay
While more employees
```

We have used the word *While* to state our test and, if the test was at the end of the iteration structure, the word *Do* to begin the loop. These are the same key words you will use later when you actually program the loop in C, so we might as well use them for our informal outline here.

Notice the difference between testing at the beginning of the loop (a **pretest** loop) and testing at the end (a **posttest** loop). There isn't much except for the first time through. In a pretest loop, if the conditions are not true when the program reaches the loop, the operations within the loop are never performed. Perhaps this section figures the pay for temporary employees and there might not be any in a particular week.

In a posttest loop, the operations are performed at least once no matter what the conditions are because the test is not made until the program reaches the end of the structure. Perhaps whether we have any employees or not we still must produce a check, even if it is void, to keep the bank happy.

Most of the time it doesn't make any difference whether you choose a pre- or posttest loop but you still must examine each situation carefully. If there is a possibility that you may not want the program to execute the operations

▶EXHIBIT 1–7
The Iteration Structure

The Iteration structure, or loop, repeats a process. The endless loop repeats forever; obviously not good programming practice because it allows no way to end the process. In a pretest loop the conditions are tested at the beginning of the loop. A posttest loop tests for the conditions at the end of the loop.

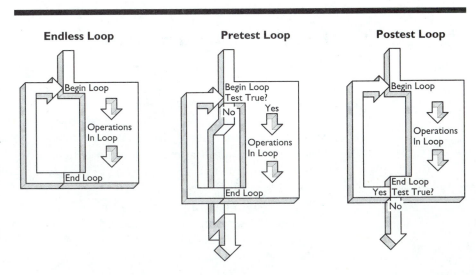

within the loop, you must choose a pretest loop. If the operations must be performed at least once no matter what, choose a posttest loop.

The top-down design is progressing. We will replace the single line, *Compute pay data*, with the structure above. We have kept the original line at the side to explain what the structure does.

```
Gather timecard data
Do                              [Compute pay data]
    Compute employee pay
While more employees
Write paychecks
Print reports
```

We now have an iteration structure within our sequence.

Computing the pay for a single employee consists of a number of tasks so we will expand the *Compute employee pay* line into a sequence, and include it within the iteration. Notice that the *Compute employee pay* line is at the top of the section as an explanation, with the sequence below it; and that the actual operations are at the left side of the outline while the comments are at the right. The operations and their indenting should clearly show the various structures in the program while the comments explain what they do. Neither Congress nor the International Association of Programming Gurus has passed a law mandating this style; it is the author's and others may differ. But this works and if you haven't already developed your own, try this one.

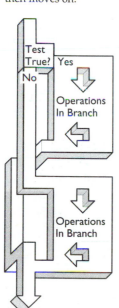

```
Gather timecard data
Do                              [Compute pay data]
                                [Compute employee pay]
        Compute gross pay
        Compute deductions
        Compute net pay
        Store in paycheck file
While more employees
Write paychecks
Print reports
```

The Selection Structure

As you might have suspected, this outline will be expanded further and further—top-down modular design at work. *Compute gross pay*, for example, is more complicated because we may either figure overtime pay or simply regular pay, one or the other. Each of these choices is a separate **branch** of the process—a particular path that the process may take. Notice that each time through the process, the program will follow only one of the two branches, overtime or regular pay, but no matter which branch is followed, the process will end up in the same place—gross pay will be figured. This last property, ending up in the same place, is extremely important to the modular programming process. We must be able to replace *Compute gross pay*, a simple "operation," with an entire structure but always continue on to *Compute deductions*.

The third and last of the structures, the **selection structure**, sets up this branching situation. There must be some reason to take this branch or that, pay overtime or regular pay, so the selection begins with some condition. If the condition is true (the hours are greater than 40), we will perform one

► EXHIBIT 1–9

Senseless
Pseudocode

Do
    Something
    If this is true
        Another thing
    While this exists
        Still another
    Else
        Yet another
    End If

branch (*Figure overtime pay*); if they are not, we will perform the other (*Figure regular pay*).

```
If hours > 40              [Compute gross pay]
    Figure overtime pay
Else
    Figure regular pay
End If
```

Again, notice the key words and the indenting. The structure starts with *If* followed by the condition. The branch that is performed if the condition is true is indented under *If*. In this example it is only one operation but it might be many, including other structures. The false branch is indented under the key word *Else*. Inserting this module in the outline, we end up with the following:

```
Gather timecard data
Do                        [Compute pay data]
                          [Compute employee pay]
    If hours > 40         [Compute gross pay]
        Figure overtime pay
    Else
        Figure regular pay
    End If
    Compute deductions
    Compute net pay
    Store in paycheck file
While more employees
Write paychecks
Print reports
```

There are some imperative key principles in top-down, modular, structured programming, without which the process breaks down.

❏ **One Entry, One Exit**   Each structure may have only one entry point and one exit point. This is important so that a single line can be replaced by an entire structure. Structures formed using the guidelines given above will follow this principle.

❏ **Proper Nesting**   To **nest** something is to enclose it entirely within something else. If, for example, a selection is put within an iteration, the selection structure must begin and end within the iteration. Something like the pseudocode in ►EXHIBIT 1–9 would be senseless. Try following it through. It doesn't work!

Programming the paycheck process will not end here, of course. More lines in the outline will be considered as modules and expanded into submodules until each submodule is a small but complete programmable entity. By following this top-down procedure, the design stage will be simpler and more manageable; and the programming stage will be equally simple and manageable because the final, complicated program may be built from simple, individual subprograms.

THE C LANGUAGE

The C programming language has had an explosion in popularity in the last few years. It seems to be the "fad" language of the day. But unlike other fads that have emerged, blossomed, and then withered, C seems destined to be around for a long time. It has a number of advantages. A major one is the ability to use it to write programs that execute quite efficiently. Many system programs and applications such as computer-aided design and screen-oriented word processing are written in C. Execution speed is extremely critical in these areas.

Another advantage is its portability. Much of this has been the result of C programmers themselves enforcing and demanding consistency in various implementations of the language. Yet another advantage is that C continues to grow with the advent of new techniques and greater demands on languages. A recent trend toward object-oriented programming, for example, has led to an extension of C called C++.

How did C get its name? Was there a B? An A?

There was no A. The seed language was the Basic Combined Programming Language (BCPL) developed in 1967. It was refined into a language called, simply, B, which Dennis Ritchie enhanced to form the original C language in 1972. In 1983, a group got together to set some official standards for C. They formed the X3J11 committee under the **American National Standards Institute** (**ANSI**) and by 1988, they had completed the standards for the C language. Before this standard, the *de facto* standards were contained in Appendix A of a book by Brian Kernighan and Dennis Ritchie called *The C Programming Language*. Their version is often referred to as **K&R** C.

ANSI C is, of course, based on this K&R C and so most current compilers will accommodate both versions. It is important to learn the ANSI version, however, because most C implementations (and virtually all new ones) adhere to the standards, and at some point, the few things that K&R did differently will disappear from the language.

It would be impossible for the ANSI standards to cover everything; there is too much that is nonstandard about the various hardware configurations in existence, for example. ANSI provides standard methods of displaying characters on the screen, for instance, but graphic screen controls differ so widely on various systems that graphics are not covered by the standard. The standard does, however, provide the solid core. Each compiler will add extensions to it to take advantage of the special capabilities of the hardware for which it is destined.

FORMING A C PROGRAM

C was designed to be a structured, modular language, and the format of the actual program supports these features. Actually, the C compiler is not very picky about the physical appearance of the program; but it allows you, through proper design and tradition, to make your programs neat, readable, and understandable by other programmers. For example, **whitespace**—spaces, tabs, line endings, and blank lines—is, for the most part, irrelevant to the compiler. You can add it in specific places to indicate the structure of your program, however.

Let us examine ➡➡Program 1–1 to see some of the characteristics of a properly formed C program.

➡Program 1-1

```
/* A Sample Program
   Meant to illustrate the format of a C listing */

#include <stdio.h>                                /* Compiler directive */

void main(void)                                  /* Beginning of function */
{  int quiz;                                      /* Declaration of a variable */

   quiz = 20;                                             /* Assignment */
   printf("A perfect quiz is %i points.\n",       /* Displays on screen */
        quiz);
   printf("Will I get perfect scores?\n");
}
```

Output

```
A perfect quiz is 20 points.
Will I get perfect scores?
```

Outline Form

The finished program should end up looking like the design we developed in the previous section—in outline form with main topics to the left and subordinate topics indented within the main topic. Here we have a number of main topics including void main(void), which has a number of subordinate topics within it, all of which are indented one level (three spaces in this example) to the right.

Line endings are mostly irrelevant, so the stuff inside the printf parentheses was continued on the next line. We clearly indicated that by starting the second line immediately below where the similar material was in the first line. Notice, however, that the line was not split within the quoted material. Line breaks are not allowed inside quotes.

Comments

Almost every language has a method of including **comments**—notations that appear in the program listing but do not become part of the final executable program. In C, everything between /* and */ is ignored by the compiler, and so becomes places to put comments. Line endings, as we said before, are ignored, so you may form multiline comments as shown in the first two lines of ➡Program 1-1.

Be careful to end your comments. If you should forget the final */ at the end of one, the compiler will keep searching for it, ignoring program elements all the time, until it finds it at the end of the next comment—or perhaps not at all, in which case the rest of the program is treated as a comment.

Since comments are ignored by the compiler, you may include anything there except, of course, */. There are no other restrictions.

Compiler Directives

Compiler directives do not become part of the compiled code. Instead, they direct the compiler to take some action before the actual compilation. The result may become part of the compiled code depending on the directive. The `#include` in the sample directs the compiler to insert the text found in the file stdio.h at this point in the source code before compilation.

Compiler directives always start with a # and end at the end of the physical line in the source code. Here is an exception to the "line endings make no difference" rule. Notice that the comment at the end of the first line is still ignored. Some non-ANSI compilers require that compiler directives begin at the left margin; ANSI C has no such restriction.

We will look at `#include` and a few other compiler directives in more detail later.

Statements

Some people call C a simple language because of the limited number of statements available. A **statement**, when compiled, becomes an instruction or group of instructions that performs a specific operation. The line `quiz = 20;` in the sample program is an assignment statement. It places the value 20 in the memory location labeled *quiz*. All single statements end with a semicolon and may be contained within the same physical line or may extend over many lines as with the first `printf()` in the sample.

Functions

Some people call C a complicated language (they use the euphemism "rich") because of all the functions available in it. What C lacks in statements, it more than makes up for in functions. A **function** is a set of instructions that performs an operation—often a much more complicated operation than is performed with a single statement. A function may include statements, other functions, machine-language instructions, and a host of other things. It may have been written by someone else and included with your compiler; or you may make it up yourself. Some preexisting functions are ANSI standard (you will concentrate on them in this book), others are peculiar to a particular compiler.

THE MAIN FUNCTION

By default, the `main()` function is an `int` function rather than a `void` function. We will see what all this means in Chapter 6, but your compiler may object to `void main(void)`. If it does, use `int main(void)` instead, but it still may object—something about returning values. If this happens, make the last statement of your program `return 0;` like the following:

```
int main(void)
{

    return 0;
}
```

When a function is used, it should set off some specific chain of events. Using the function should not require knowing the exact events that will take place, only the effects that those events produce. For example, in shifting your automatic transmission into drive, you don't know (nor do you even want to know) about all the gears, valves, and pumps that are operating, just that you may now go forward.

A function is defined (the operations within it are specified) either by you writing the definition in the program or in some library file that came with the compiler (or was purchased separately). The definition will include a name for the function. Once it is defined, it may be used or called (the operations in it performed) by including the name in a statement. The name is always followed by parentheses that contain the function's arguments (data that the function is to work with). Even if the function has no arguments, the parentheses are included.

The function `printf()` displays something on the screen. The material to be displayed is contained in the arguments in parentheses. The first argument determines the overall layout of what displays. If, as in the last `printf()`, it contains only normal characters in quotes, then those characters will be displayed exactly as they appear. The `\n` is called the newline character. It indicates that the output should drop to the beginning of the next line at that point. The end of the `printf()` function does not end a displayed line. Newline is seen as a single character by C, but, because it does not show as a distinct character symbol on the screen, we represent it with the two characters, backslash and *n*.

The `%i` in the first `printf()` indicates that there is some value to be inserted in the line at this point. In this case, it is the value of `quiz`, the next argument. Arguments in functions are separated by commas. Note that the `quiz` argument is on the next line. Remember, line endings and spaces make no difference in C. It is the semicolon that ends a statement.

C is designed to be a modular language, and modules are typically implemented in most languages by functions or procedures. A C program is written almost entirely in functions—one or more depending on the complexity of the program. When you execute a C program, it automatically starts by calling the `main()` function. In the sample program you see this function defined starting with `void main(void)` (more on the voids later). Note that there is no semicolon after this line—it is not a statement but the beginning of a function definition. The statements below it are the operations in the function.

Blocks

Modularity is also enhanced by allowing statements to be grouped into **blocks**. Any time a statement is called for in a program you can provide a single statement or a block of statements. The block begins with an open brace ({) and ends with a close brace (}). Notice that the statements in the `main()` function are within a block. The compiler doesn't care where it finds the braces; but you, being human and more visually oriented, will want to place them carefully. The open brace should be at the same indent level as the statement or definition of which it is a part; the statements within the block should be indented one level further; and the close brace should be directly below (in the same column as) the open brace.

This format has three advantages: (1) the structure is easy to see because of the indentation; (2) it is hard to forget the close brace because of its alignment with the open brace; and (3) many other C programmers follow the same pattern.

Declarations

In C, as in many other languages, before you use almost anything you must declare it. The **declaration** tells the compiler that a variable or a function can be a valid part of your program and how it may be used. Among other things, it allows the C compiler to check your source code for proper usage and spelling of variables and functions. In the sample program, the variable *quiz* is being declared as containing an integer (whole) number.

Although you do not see it in the source code, printf() is also declared. Its declaration is contained in the included file stdio.h. This is called a header file; it contains declarations and definitions that would normally be found at the beginning, or head, of a program. Except for main(), every function that you use must be declared whether you make an explicit declaration in your source code or include a file with the declaration in it. All ANSI-standard functions (and functions that are supplied with the compiler) are declared in various header files.

BASIC OUTPUT

We have introduced the various elements of a C program and will spend the rest of the book filling in the details, but in order for you to get used to your C compiler and practice with it, we shall introduce the simplest form of C's basic output function, printf(), so that you may write a program or two. Anything that you put in quotes within the parentheses following printf will be displayed at the standard output device (usually a screen) when the program is executed.

Notice in ▶▶Program 1–2 that since we are using the printf() function we have included the header file, *stdio.h*, near the beginning of the program. The three executable statements, each containing only a printf() function, are within the block (between the braces) that is the main() function. The newlines (\n) drop the cursor to the beginning of the next line. In the case of the second statement, the cursor was dropped two lines, leaving a blank line.

▶▶Program 1–2

```
/* A simple program */

#include <stdio.h>

void main(void)
{  printf("Hello world!\n");
   printf("I am now programming in C.\n\n");
   printf("I always knew I could!\n");
}
```

Output

```
Hello world!
I am now programming in C.

I always knew I could!
```

SUMMARY

A computer **system** consists of **hardware**, the physical pieces of equipment, and **software**, instructions that direct the hardware. The **central processing unit** is at the heart of the system and performs three main functions: **control** of the rest of the system, and **arithmetic** and **logical** operations. Much of a computer system's workload is moving data—**reading** and **writing**.

Main memory is used for temporary storage of the currently active program and its data. It consists of a number of storage **locations**, each of which has a unique **address**. Programs and data are kept permanently in **secondary storage**. To work on anything it must be transferred to main memory and, if changes are made, transferred back to secondary storage for permanent retention.

Software consists of sets of instructions called **programs**. We can divide software into **application software**, written to do specific tasks for specific people, and **system software**, which provides services to all the users of the computer. System software takes our relatively simple instructions and translates them into the detailed ones the CPU actually needs to operate. It also provides some compatibility between systems with different hardware configurations, facilitating **portability** of application software. An **operating system** is a set of system programs.

Machine language is the instruction set that is manufactured into the CPU. It consists entirely of offs and ons and so is very difficult for humans to use. **Assembly languages** use the same instructions but represent them with more human-oriented symbols. Programs in both languages tend to be long and difficult. **High-level languages**, such as C, are easier for people. One high-level instruction translates into several machine-language instructions.

Before it can control the computer, a C program must be translated to machine language. The **source code**, in C, is translated into **object code** by a program called a **compiler**. A **linker** program takes the object code and combines it with other pre-written object code to produce **executable code** that is now capable of controlling the computer.

There are four major objectives to keep in mind when writing a program: execution efficiency, programming efficiency, maintainability, and providing a source for future programming. Typically these objectives require trade-offs and the proper mix is a matter of careful planning. Most of our programs are written in modules—self-contained, encapsulated program sections. The idea is to treat a long, complicated program as a group of short, easy ones.

Most modular programs are designed according to the concepts of **top-down design**—dividing a large project down into various modules and those modules into submodules and so forth until each module at the lowest level is a small, self-contained unit.

Most such programs also incorporate the concept of **structured programming**, which says that even very complicated programs can be constructed with various combinations of only three different programming **structures**. Often these structures are outlined in **pseudocode** and translated to the desired programming language.

The **sequence structure** is the simplest—one operation after another. The **iteration structure (loop)** repeats a set of operations while certain conditions exist. The conditions can be tested for at the beginning of the loop (a **pretest**) or at the end (a

posttest). The **selection structure** allows a program to **branch** in one of two different directions depending on some conditions. Structures may be combined in any way required to do the job—added to the end of others or **nested** within others.

C was first developed in 1972 by Dennis Ritchie and its initial, *de facto*, standard was in a book by Kernighan and Ritchie (**K&R**). In 1988, the **American National Standards Institute** released the standard for **ANSI** C.

C lends itself to modular, structured design and by using **whitespace**, which is largely ignored by C, you can make your program visually represent its structure. Elements of a C program include **comments**, which are ignored by the C compiler; **compiler directives**, instructions to the compiler rather than the computer; **statements**, the instructions for the computer; **functions**, sets of statements that perform a particular task; **blocks**, groups of statements that can substitute for a single statement; and **declarations**, which inform C of your intent to use variables and functions. Declarations of functions provided by the compiler are provided in **header files**.

KEY TERMS (in order of appearance)

Hardware	Encapsulate
Software	Bug
Read	Top-down design
Write	Structured programming
Central processing unit (CPU)	Structure
Control	Pseudocode
Arithmetic operation	Sequence structure
Logical operation	Iteration structure
Main memory	Loop
Location	Pretest
Address	Posttest
Secondary storage	Branch
Program	Selection structure
Application software	Nest
System software	American National Standards Institute (ANSI)
Portability	K&R
Operating system	Whitespace
Machine language	Comment
Assembly language	Compiler directive
High-level language	Statement
Source code	Function
Object code	Block
Compiler	Declaration
Link	Header file
Executable code	
Module	

REVIEW QUESTIONS

1. Why is the term "system" so important with computers?

2. What are hardware and software and how do they differ? Why is one useless without the other?

3. What is the CPU? What are its three main functions?

4. Explain how data is moved from here to there using reads and writes. What data is erased and what is duplicated?

5. How does main memory differ from secondary storage?

6. What is the significance of individual locations and addresses in main memory?

7. Where does data or a program have to reside to be worked on? To be stored permanently?

8. What is a program?

9. How does application software differ from system software?

10. What is an operating system?

11. Of the three language levels, which is required by the computer? Which is easiest for humans?

12. Trace the process of going from a program that you write to a program capable of controlling the computer. Identify both the files produced along the way and the programs needed to produce them.

13. What are four important objectives to be considered in the programming process?

14. What is a module? Why is encapsulation of modules important?

15. What are some advantages of modular programming?

16. What is the process of top-down design?

17. Why does structured programming make the programming process easier?

18. Describe the three programming structures and how they differ.

19. What is the difference between a pretest and a posttest loop and why would you choose one or the other?

20. How may structures be combined in a program?

21. Define two key principles of top-down, modular, structured programming.

22. What are the two common versions of the C language?

23. Of what significance is whitespace in a C program?

24. How do we put comments in a C program?

25. What is the difference between a compiler directive and a statement?

26. What are functions and blocks?

27. What does a declaration tell the compiler?

EXERCISES

1. Examine a computer somewhere. (Please don't disassemble your school's mainframe.) See if you can identify the CPU, main memory, secondary storage devices, and various input and output devices.

2. Identify the operating system and the version of the C language available on your computer.

3. Make a top-down-design chart similar to the one in the text for reconciling and balancing your checkbook.

4. Write a structured program in pseudocode for the process in Exercise 3.

5. Make a top-down-design chart similar to the one in the text for a program that plays poker with the person at the keyboard.

6. Write a structured program in pseudocode for the process in Exercise 5.

PROGRAMS

1. Enter and execute the sample program given under *Forming a C Program* in this chapter.

2. Enter and execute the sample program given under *Basic Output* in this chapter.

3. Write a program to give some information about yourself. It should produce something like the following:

```
NAME:  your name
MAJOR:
OTHER COMPUTER COURSES TAKEN:
OCCUPATION:
HOBBIES AND ACTIVITIES:
REASONS FOR TAKING THIS COURSE:
COMMENTS:
```

VALUES AND VARIABLES

Before we can do any effective computer programming, we must understand how data is stored in the computer and something about how that data is interpreted and operated on by the language. In this chapter we shall examine:

1. How our normal human number system differs from that used by computers and the notational conventions we use in C to represent various systems.

2. How the computer stores characters and character representation in C.

3. The units of data storage in the computer.

4. The factors that differentiate data types and declaration of both values and variables in those data types.

5. Arithmetic operators and how arithmetic expressions are formed in C.

6. Differences in operations with different or mixed data types.

7. Assignment of values to variables.

NUMBER SYSTEMS: OURS AND THE COMPUTER'S

Our **decimal** number system is based on ten number symbols, 0 through 9. (*Decem* means ten in Latin.) We have all grown up with numbers like 6 or 49 or 3017, which are combinations of our ten basic symbols. It would be hard for us to imagine those values expressed in any other way. Our ten-symbol system developed quite naturally because our earliest counting machinery had only ten different elements, the ten fingers on a human's hands.

Each of the values 0 through 9 can be expressed with one symbol. To express numbers greater than 9 in the decimal system we use combinations of symbols and positional notation. A symbol's position determines its magnitude. In decimal, the first (rightmost) position tells how many ones, the second (to the left) tells how many tens, and so forth. The value twenty-four is two tens and four ones, written 24. Similarly, 4680 means four thousands, six hundreds, eight tens, and no ones.

Binary Numbers

The computer's basic counting machinery consists mainly of large sets or arrays of transistors acting as switches. These switches have only two possible states, off and on. Therefore, the computer is capable of working only with those states. We symbolize them with the digits zero and one. This means that instead of using the decimal system with ten digits, the computer must express numbers in a **binary** system—one with only two symbols, 0 and 1. Though humans express the value nine as 9, the computer must express it with a series of zeros and ones, 1001.

In decimal notation, the highest numeric value we can express with a single digit is nine (9). If we want to express the value ten, we have to start the current position over at zero (0), move to the next position, begin that with one (1), and write the value as 10. If we want to count beyond 99, we must start those two positions over and begin a third to give us 100.

In binary notation, the highest numeric value we can express with a single symbol is 1. To express values greater than 1, we also use positional notation, but we must use more number positions because we can express fewer numbers, only one of two, in each position. To express the value one, we would use the symbol 1, the same as in decimal, meaning one one. But since 1 is as high as we can go in binary notation, to express the decimal value two we would have to use the next binary position. Binary 10 (pronounced "one

The decimal number 712048

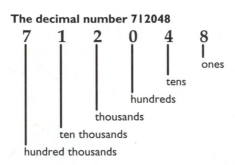

EXHIBIT 2–2
The Human's Versus the Computer's Counting Machinery

The computer's number system differs from the human's because of a fundamental difference in natural counting machinery. The human's has ten positions while the computer's has only two.

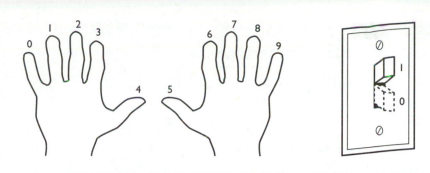

oh" or "one zero," never "ten") means one decimal two and no ones, the equivalent of decimal 2. Following this logic, we would express decimal three as binary 11, one two and one one. Decimal four would require yet another binary position, 100, meaning one four, no twos, and no ones. Decimal 9 would be 1001 (1 eight, no fours, no twos, 1 one) and decimal 87 would be binary 1010111. In the decimal system, each position is ten times the position to the right of it because there are ten symbols to use in each position. There are only two symbols in the binary system; therefore, each position is only two times the position to the right of it.

To work with large numbers, computers use large combinations of zeros and ones. This takes a lot of transistor switching, but what the computer loses in numerical efficiency, it more than makes up for in speed. A human can add 9 to 19 in perhaps half a second. The computer would have to add 1001 to 10011, but it can do it in about a millionth of a second.

Conversion Between Binary and Decimal

To convert a decimal number to binary, divide the decimal number by 2; the remainder becomes the rightmost binary digit. Repeat the process using the quotient, the next remainder becoming the next binary digit to the left. Keep this up until the quotient is zero. For example, 77 divided by 2 is 38 with a remainder of 1, so our rightmost binary digit is 1. The quotient 38 divided by 2 is 19 with a remainder of 0 so our next binary digit to the left is 0. (Our binary number is now 01.) Dividing 19 by 2 gives us 9 with a remainder of 1 (101). Dividing 9 by 2 gives us 4 with a remainder of 1 (1101). Our 4 divided by 2 gives us 2 with a remainder of 0 (01101). The 2 divided by 2 gives us 1

EXHIBIT 2–3
Binary Positional Notation

Positional notation works the same in binary as it does in decimal, except that each succeeding position is two times the position before it, rather than ten times as in decimal.

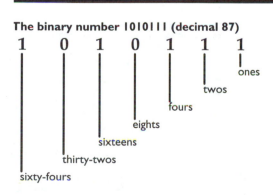

The binary number 1010111 (decimal 87)

| 1 | 0 | 1 | 0 | 1 | 1 | 1 |

ones
twos
fours
eights
sixteens
thirty-twos
sixty-fours

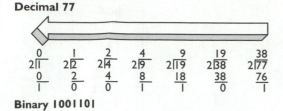

Decimal 77

Binary 1001101

Binary 1001101

Decimal 77

►EXHIBIT 2–4
Conversion Between Binary and Decimal

In the decimal to binary conversion, the rightmost bit is determined first, moving to the left with each subsequent calculation.

with a remainder of 0 (001101). Finally, 1 divided by 2 gives us 0 with a remainder of 1 (1001101). The process stops here because the quotient is 0. Decimal 77, then, is binary 1001101.

Going the other way, from binary to decimal, we add up the decimal values of the positions in the binary number that contain 1 digits. For example, from the right, 100110 has no 1, a 2, a 4, no 8, no 16, and a 32. Adding this up, 2 + 4 + 32, we end up with 38.

In C, decimal numbers are represented just as we do normally. There is no direct representation for binary numbers, although your decimal number will, of course, be internally translated to binary when it is stored in the computer.

Hexadecimal Numbers

One reason that there is no direct representation for binary numbers in C is that binary numbers tend to be long and cumbersome. The two-digit decimal number 99, for example, is binary 1100011. Still, in many applications, we must refer to the individual switch settings stored in the computer, in other words, to the individual binary digits. To do so, we typically use **hexadecimal** numbers, numbers with the base sixteen, because one hexadecimal digit represents exactly four binary digits.

A base-sixteen number requires sixteen number symbols, so we borrow 0 through 9 from the decimal system and add A, B, C, D, E, and F for the values above 9 (see ►Table 2–1). Decimal 10 in hexadecimal ("hex" for short), then, is A, and F is decimal 15. Decimal 16 would be hex 10.

To convert from binary to hex, group the binary digits in fours beginning from the right and convert each group to the appropriate hex digit. For example, we would separate binary 1101100 as 110 1100. The first group is decimal 6 or hex 6, and the second is decimal 12 or hex C. The complete hex number is 6C.

►EXHIBIT 2–5
Conversion Between Hex and Decimal

In the decimal to hex conversion, as in the decimal to binary conversion, the rightmost number is determined first, moving to the left with each subsequent calculation.

Decimal 19410

Hexadecimal 4BD2

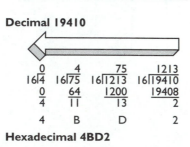

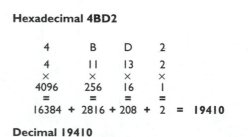

Hexadecimal 4BD2

Decimal 19410

Notice the extra digits it
takes to express a num-
ber using only the two
symbols available in the
binary system.

Decimal	Binary	Octal	Hex		Decimal	Binary	Octal	Hex
1	1	1	1		11	1011	13	B
2	10	2	2		12	1100	14	C
3	11	3	3		13	1101	15	D
4	100	4	4		14	1110	16	E
5	101	5	5		15	1111	17	F
6	110	6	6		16	10000	20	10
7	111	7	7		17	10001	21	11
8	1000	10	8		18	10010	22	12
9	1001	11	9		19	10011	23	13
10	1010	12	A		20	10100	24	14

Going from decimal to hex uses the same process as going from decimal to binary except that we divide by 16 and keep track of our remainder in hex digits. Hex to decimal follows the same pattern as binary to decimal except that the positions are powers of sixteen—1, 16, 256, 4,096, 65,536, and so forth.

Hexadecimal notation has direct representation in ANSI C; we precede the hex number with 0x. For example, decimal 46 would be hex 0x2E; decimal 25 would be hex 0x19.

Octal Numbers

The **octal** (base-eight) number system, using the symbols 0 through 7, is sometimes used in computers. Three binary digits make up one octal digit. The ANSI C representation is to precede the octal number with a 0 (zero). Decimal 9 would be octal 011, for example.

Conversion between octal and decimal follows the same processes as between hex and decimal except that you are dealing with eight number symbols and powers of eight—1, 8, 64, 512, and so forth.

CHARACTERS IN THE COMPUTER

A numeric value remains the same no matter which symbols we use to express it. A typical car has four wheels whether we call it 4 (decimal), 100 (binary), or IV (Roman). We saw that computers can handle numeric values easily with their two-symbol binary system. However, we know that computers work with more than just numbers. We have seen bills, advertising letters, and grade reports with As, Bs, and Cs on them. In fact, most computers can work with a set of at least 96 different printable characters.

How can computers work with 96 different character symbols when they can only store and understand two? They use various **coding schemes** that combine binary digits in definite patterns to represent different characters. One such scheme is the **American Standard Code for Information Interchange (ASCII**, pronounced ask'-key), shown in ▶ Table 2–2. A single ASCII code requires seven binary digits (zeros or ones) allowing 2^7 or 128 different combinations. It is used in almost all microcomputers, and many minicomputers and mainframes. An A in the ASCII coding scheme is 1000001, an N is 1001110.

Char	Decimal	Binary	Char	Decimal	Binary	Char	Decimal	Binary
Blank	32	0100000	A	65	1000001	a	97	1100001
,	44	0101100	B	66	1000010	b	98	1100010
.	46	0101110	C	67	1000011	c	99	1100011
;	59	0111011	D	68	1000100	d	100	1100100
?	63	0111111	E	69	1000101	e	101	1100101
			F	70	1000110	f	102	1100110
0	48	0110000	G	71	1000111	g	103	1100111
1	49	0110001	H	72	1001000	h	104	1101000
2	50	0110010	I	73	1001001	i	105	1101001
3	51	0110011	J	74	1001010	j	106	1101010
4	52	0110100	K	75	1001011	k	107	1101011
5	53	0110101	L	76	1001100	l	108	1101100
6	54	0110110	M	77	1001101	m	109	1101101
7	55	0110111	N	78	1001110	n	110	1101110
8	56	0111000	O	79	1001111	o	111	1101111
9	57	0111001	P	80	1010000	p	112	1110000

▶▶TABLE 2–2
Some ASCII Codes

The ASCII is a seven-bit coding scheme used by most micros, and many minicomputers and mainframes. See Appendix A for a complete table.

The **extended binary-coded-decimal interchange code (EBCDIC,** pronounced eb'-see-dick) uses eight bits, which allows 2^8 or 256 possible code combinations, about half of which are actually used. EBCDIC is used on many minicomputers and mainframes. Most computers could use either coding scheme; the choice really depends on the scheme for which the software was written. Since both schemes represent essentially the same group of characters, there is other software available to translate one code to the other so that ASCII computers can communicate with EBCDIC computers and vice versa.

The sets of binary digits that represent characters look to the computer just like binary numbers. For example, the characters *A* and *N* in ASCII are 1000001 and 1001110, which, if interpreted as binary numbers, would have the decimal values 65 and 78. If we could see inside the computer's memory we would find only offs and ons and we could not tell whether they were supposed to represent numeric values or characters. To use a human analogy, holding up a hand could mean "5," "Hi," or "Stop."

How does the computer know whether a given set of binary digits is a number or a character? It really doesn't. Our program will tell the computer what to do with the set of them and that will determine whether they are used as characters or numbers. If we instructed the computer to perform a mathematical operation, it would use the digits as numbers rather than as characters. If we instructed it to print text, those binary digits would be interpreted as characters.

Character Values

When we looked at number systems we saw three different ways of expressing numbers in C—decimal, octal, and hex. There is a fourth, ASCII (or EBCDIC if we happened to be using that type of computer). By enclosing a character in single quotes (apostrophes) we are really referring to its ASCII code. The notation 'A' is the same as 65 or 0101 or 0x41. The notation ' ' (a space) is the same as 32 or 040 or 0x20. We could add, for instance, 32 + 65 or ' ' + 0x41 or ' ' + 'A' or any combination of representations and, depending on how we wish to display the result, show 97 or 0141 or 0x61 or the character a (whose ASCII code is 1100001 or decimal 97). Remember, once it's stored, it's just a set of bits.

Some characters in either the ASCII or EBCDIC codes are not on the keyboard and so would be difficult to show in character notation. An example might be the form-feed code sent to a printer to tell it to go to the next page. In C we represent these characters with **special characters**, each of which consists of a backslash followed by a printable character. Even though two characters are shown within the quotes, it represents, and is stored as, just a single character. Here is the standard list:

\0	Null (absence of a character)	\t	Horizontal tab
\a	Audible alarm (bell)	\v	Vertical tab
\b	Backspace	\'	Apostrophe (single quote)
\f	Form feed	\"	Quote (double quote)
\n	Newline	\?	Question mark
\r	Carriage return	\\	Backslash

Notice that we need special characters to represent both the backslash and the apostrophe since we use those characters to create other special characters.

We can represent any character by putting its octal or hexadecimal value inside the apostrophes. For example, *A* could be represented by '\101' (octal) or '\x41' (hex) or, for that matter, 'A' or 65 (decimal). Note the difference between the character-value and the numeric-value representation for octal and hex. Remember, the numeric-value representation for decimal 65 was 0101 (octal) and 0x41 (hex). There is no special character-value representation in decimal notation; we simply used the decimal numeric value.

Octal or hex character-value notation is handy to represent characters that are not on the keyboard. For example, there are extended ASCII codes that add an extra binary digit, doubling the number of codes available (to 256). In one extended ASCII set, '\xA2' is the character ¢ while '\xDF' is ß.

UNITS OF DATA STORAGE

The Bit

We have called each symbol in a binary number a binary digit, or in computer terms, a **bit**. The number 11001110 (decimal 206) has eight bits (from

Nuts & Bolts

SPECIAL CHARACTERS

The use of special characters is a case in which ANSI C offers compatibility among various hardware configurations. Take the form feed (\f) for example. This is typically the ASCII code with a decimal value of 12, so we should be able to just use the number 12. But typically is a key word here; not all computer systems use the same codes to represent things. ANSI C has a list of special characters that represent certain functions that may be implementation dependent. The compiler will translate these to the proper code for that implementation. Newline (\n), for instance, is the character that returns the printer or cursor to the beginning of the next line. In some systems it is ASCII 10, but in others it is ASCII 13 followed by ASCII 10—actually two characters. It is still stored as one character but, depending on the implementation, it may represent the output of two.

right to left, no ones, 1 two, 1 four, 1 eight, no sixteens, no thirty-twos, 1 sixty-four, and 1 one hundred-twenty-eight). To store this value, the computer would use eight switches. The first two would be on; the second two, off; the next three, on; and the last one, off. The bit, the setting of one switch, is the smallest unit of computer storage. However, bits never sit alone in the computer but are grouped into larger units.

Bytes

Having the computer process data one bit at a time would be like putting sugar in your coffee one grain at a time; it is easier to use lumps. The computer processes bits in lumps called bytes, which saves computer instructions and time. Think about directing someone to put sugar in your coffee. It is much easier and faster to say, "Put in one lump," than "Put in one grain, another grain, another grain, another grain . . . ."

The **byte** is the smallest unit of computer operation. If you instruct the computer to move data from here to there, it will move at least one byte at a time. If you instruct it to add, it will add at least one byte to another to make up a resultant byte. The addition will be done a bit at a time in the CPU, but the single instruction will direct the computer to add all the bits in each byte involved.

In virtually all modern digital computers the byte contains eight bits, not because of some mysterious electrical property, but for convenience. It makes sense to process data a character at a time, and a character, in either ASCII or EBCDIC, will fit within eight bits. (EBCDIC is an eight-bit code. ASCII is seven bits, but by adding an extra, meaningless bit it will fill an eight-bit space.)

If our computer uses binary notation for numeric values, these binary values will be forced to fit within whole bytes. It would take only one bit to express the binary value zero (0), but when we store it in the computer we use at least an entire byte in memory (00000000). Decimal 23 would be stored as 00010111. In fact, all our memory circuits are organized in bytes. Numbers with values above 255 (eight bits, 11111111) require two or more bytes of storage and, depending on the computer, might take two or more sets of instructions to process. (We shall see later that there are instructions in C that refer to individual bits. These instructions still force the CPU to take in full bytes even though the operations are bit specific.)

Words

Even a small computer processes eight bits concurrently to save time and instructions. Larger machines process even more bits concurrently (16, 32, or 64, for example) for the same reasons. We call the number of bits a computer can actually process simultaneously a **word**. Since each character occupies eight bits (one byte), words are often multiples of eight. Even though many word lengths are multiples of whole bytes, they are always expressed in bits. We refer to a 32-bit rather than a 4-byte word.

VARIABLES

In any language, a variable represents a space in the computer's main memory. We put values in these spaces so that we may use the values elsewhere in the program. The space is "variable" because we may change the value stored there at any time. When we refer to that space, its current value is used.

Variable Names

To reasonably refer to that space in memory we must give it a **variable name** (or in ANSI C terms, a **variable identifier**). We are relatively free in naming variables in C. This allows us to use names that might have some meaning for us humans. For example, if we are going to store someone's pay in a variable, we would probably call it *pay* rather than *x* or *fp* or *iq*. There are, however, a few basic rules that we must follow:

1. We can use many characters in a variable name. How many depends on the compiler but ANSI C specifies that at least 31 will be significant. (Non-ANSI Cs may revert to the original C specification, which made only eight characters significant. Under these rules, *locomotive* and *locomotion* would be the same variable.)

2. We may use only alpha characters (*A* through *Z* or *a* through *z*), numeric characters (*0* through *9*), or the underscore (_) in variable names. Notice that a space in a variable name is not allowed. To specify a two-word variable name, for gross pay for example, we might use the underscore in place of the space: *gross_pay*.

3. Variable names must begin with an alpha character or an underscore, not a number. *Farley* and *_bluto* are valid names, *2bad* is not. Typically, application programmers do not start variable names with an underscore. These are traditionally reserved for variables or functions defined with the compiler or other libraries.

4. C is case sensitive; upper- and lowercase characters are not treated the same. *Total*, *total*, and *TOTAL* would be three different variables. It would not be considered good form to have in your program variables whose names differed only in case. By tradition, variable names in C were typically all lowercase but that tradition is falling away. Many C programmers capitalize the first character of each word in the variable and limit use of the underscore. They might have variables *Pay*, *GrossPay*, and *NetPay*.

5. The C compiler looks for certain key words, words with special meanings, when it compiles a program. They are treated as **reserved words**—reserved for use by the compiler. We will use them in program statements but we may not use them as variable names. ▶Table 2–3 shows the list of ANSI C's 32 reserved words. Your compiler will probably add some capability to the ANSI standards, so there will probably be extra reserved words that you will have to avoid.

▶**TABLE 2–3**
ANSI C Reserved Words

```
auto
break
case
char
const
continue
default
do
double
else
enum
extern
float
for
goto
if
int
long
register
return
short
signed
sizeof
static
struct
switch
typedef
union
unsigned
void
volatile
while
```

DATA TYPES AND DECLARATIONS

As in most other languages, data can be stored in various forms or **data types** in C. The major differences between data types are the size in bytes of each type, and whether or not it allows a decimal point. Which data type you choose depends on whether your value might have a fractional component and the size of the values you might use. With regard to size, your choice is often a trade-off between the amount of memory used and execution speed. Smaller data types take up less of your main memory and secondary storage but C often must convert small data types to larger ones to perform calculations and the extra conversion slows execution.

A single program may have many data types within it, and your operations may combine values of different types—for example, you may add values of two different types together for a meaningful result. We shall see, however, that there is a penalty to be paid for mixing data types that must be weighed against the advantages of storage size.

Declarations

Whenever we use a value or a variable, we will declare it and its data type. Variables must be explicitly declared before they are used. Values (or *literals* or *constants* as they are often called when they are written directly in a program) are implicitly declared wherever they appear in the program. C will know a value's data type by the manner in which we write it. A **declaration** performs a number of functions:

1. It directs C as to how to store the value, whether it can have a fractional component or whether it is allowed to be negative as well as positive, for example.

2. It automatically **defines** it, meaning that it allocates memory to the value or variable. The type of declaration tells the computer how much memory.

3. It may also **initialize** a variable—assign a meaningful value to that space in memory. Memory is never empty; there is always something lying about in it, which we colorfully refer to as "garbage" because we can't predict its value. A value used in a program will, of course, replace this garbage. A variable definition allocates memory to the variable, but it may or may not replace the leftover value. As part of our declaration and definition, we can assign a specific initial value to the variable.

Declarations follow this general form (the stuff in brackets, [ ], is optional):

```
datatype variable[ = initialization];
```

For example:

```
int frequency;
int StartValue = 14;
```

Notice the semicolons at the end of the declarations; they are statements and must end in semicolons.

We can declare more than one variable of a single type in one declaration statement by separating the declarations with commas.

```
int total, counter, interval;
int BeginRange = 0, EndRange = 100;
```

We can mix initialized and noninitialized declarations in the same statement (as long as they are of one type), but many consider it improper form. Notice that in the following declaration, *EndRange* is initialized to 100, but *BeginRange* is not initialized at all; it is garbage.

```
int BeginRange, EndRange = 100;
```

Integral Data Types

Integral data types allow only integer, or whole, numbers—no decimal points. The numeric values are stored in straight binary form, padded with leading zeros to fill the appropriate size defined by the data type. Decimal 65 would be stored as 1000001 with enough leading zero bits to make it the right size. There are two basic integral types: `char` for "character" and `int` for "integer."

The `char` data type is eight bits long. Some people pronounce it as in the first four letters of "charm," others as "care" like the beginning of "character." The basis for the name, "character," is somewhat misleading. Yes, we do store in it what we humans understand as characters, but we can also store numbers there. In fact, the computer can't tell the difference. Remember, a character is simply a set of bits just like a number.

In a single `char` space we can store the code for *A* or perhaps the number 65. Since the ASCII code for *A* consists of the same bits as the binary representation for decimal 65, exactly the same value, 01000001, will be stored. Note the leading zero bit to make up eight bits. Once that set of bits is established, we may instruct the computer to treat it as a character (print it out, for example) or a number (add it to another, for example).

Either integral data type may have one of two modifiers, `signed` or `unsigned`. The `signed` modifier means that the value may be either positive or negative. Under ANSI rules this is the default, so if there is no modifier, the `char` (or `int`) is assumed to be `signed`. The `unsigned` modifier means that the number may only be positive. An `unsigned char` may have values from 0 to 255, while (because it takes up one bit for the sign) `signed chars` may have values ranging from −128 to 127. By convention, we do not use signs with octal, hex, or character notation (such as 'A'); they may only be positive.

Some valid `char` declarations are:

```
char letter;
unsigned char index;
char TopGrade = 'A', BottomGrade = 'F';
char TopGrade = 65, BottomGrade = 70;
```

All of these declarations allocate 8 bits per variable but the second treats the stored value as only positive. The third and fourth declarations have exactly the same effect because the ASCII codes for *A* and *F* are 65 and 70. The two declarations could not exist in the same section of the program, of course, because we may not duplicate variable names.

The `int` data type has more bits than the `char` but its size is not precisely defined by ANSI. It is typically the word size of the machine for which the compiler is designed; however, there are a number of exceptions to that guideline. For example, PC-compatible computers have either 16- or 32-bit word sizes, but most C compilers for PCs use a 16-bit `int`.

The `int` data types may have a `signed` or `unsigned` modifier but it may also have `short` or `long` modifiers. ANSI tells us only that a `long int` will have at least as many bits as a `short int` but in most implementations a `short int` is 16 bits while a `long int` is 32. The default, if neither `short` nor `long` is specified, is either a short or long integer, depending supposedly on the word size of the machine, but that rule is so often violated that it could depend on the type of computer the compiler is designed for, the phase of the moon, whether Jupiter is in Capricorn, …. Know your compiler!

To enhance portability, being able to recompile unchanged source code for use on another type of machine, it a good idea to declare your `int`s as either `short` or `long`.

The data type `int` is the default. If a declaration has modifiers but no data type, it is assumed that it is an `int` of some kind. Here are some valid `int` declarations:

```
int current_page, last_page;
short age;                          /* Equivalent to short int age */
unsigned volts = 110;        /* Equivalent to unsigned int volts=110 */
unsigned volts = 'n';               /* Equivalent to declaration above */
unsigned long NationalDebt;
signed short Variance;       /* Modifier signed not needed under ANSI */
```

As mentioned, values are also declared when they are included in a program. If a value has no decimal point, it is integral. Character values such as `'A'` and hex and octal values such as `0x7F` and `074` have no decimal points so they are always integral. Unless otherwise stated, integral values default to type `int` (remember, that may be the same size as either `short` or `long` depending on your machine). Decimal-notation integers and character values are stored as `signed` (even though we would never state a character such as 'A' with a negative sign), and octal and hex as `unsigned`. In any case, if the value exceeds the size of a `short int`, it will be stored as a `long int`. For example, if the default `int` on your machine is 16 bits (with a maximum decimal value of 32767) and you put the number 145832 in your program code, the compiler will store it in a `long int`—32 bits.

Notice that character values, even though they fit within 8 bits, the size of data type `char`, are stored as `int`s.

We may also explicitly declare values by following the value with an `L` or a `U` (or `l` or `u`) or both. The postfix `L` forces the value to be stored as a `long` and `U` as `unsigned`. The value `56UL` would be stored as an `unsigned long`.

Floating-Point Data Types

Values with **floating-point data types** have decimal points and are stored not in simple binary notation but in a binary form of scientific notation (typically IEEE—Institute of Electrical and Electronic Engineers—floating-point notation). In scientific notation, we use a **mantissa** of significant digits multiplied by some power of ten. For example, 7146 might be expressed as 7.146×10^3. The two values are the same; 10^3 is 1000, and 7.146×1000 is 7146. In

	Signed	Unsigned		Signed
Integral	char short int [4 or 'A'] long [4L]	unsigned char unsigned short unsigned [4U] unsigned long [4UL]	**Floating Point**	float [4.2F] double [4.2] long double [4.2L]

➡**EXHIBIT 2–6**
Data-Type Designations

Here are the ANSI C data types (except enum) with their key words and examples of explicit declarations of values where such declarations are allowed.

our C program we can write the number as 7146.0 or 7.146E3, that is, a mantissa of 7.146 and a power-of-ten **exponent** of 3. The second form is referred to as **E notation**.

The IEEE notation that C uses for floating-point values is actually E notation—the computer stores the mantissa and the exponent. (Actually, since the computer works exclusively in binary, it stores a binary mantissa and the exponent of a power of two; but we shall look at it in decimal to keep it simple.) The memory space allocated to the number is fixed, depending on the data type we declare, and divided between mantissa and exponent. This means that there are limits on both the size of the mantissa and of the exponent. The data type we choose will take those limits into account.

There are three different floating-point data types: float, double, and long double. In terms of the size of each, all ANSI guarantees is that a double is greater than or equal to a float and a long double is greater than or equal to a double. In many microcomputer Cs, a float is 32 bits, a double is 64, and a long double 80. Unlike integral data types, floating-point data types always allow positive or negative values, and so cannot have the modifiers signed or unsigned.

Following are some examples of floating-point-variable declarations:

```
float WageRate = 12.75;
double Area, Volume;
long double humongous;
```

When declaring a long double, be sure to state long double, not just long, because that would default to a long int.

A value with a decimal point will normally be stored as a double. We may explicitly declare it as a float with F or f, or a long double with L or l. A number written as 3.806E-3F (or .003806F) would be stored as a float instead of a double. A value with a large number of significant digits or a large exponent will be stored as a long double.

String Data

A **string** is a set of characters. We include string values in a program by enclosing the characters in quotes; for example:

```
"This is a bunch of characters"
```

The quotes are not part of the string; they just serve to tell the C compiler where the string begins and ends. To include quotes as part of the string we must use the special character \". This is true of any of the special characters except the apostrophe and question mark, although the backslashes also work there.

```
"He said \"I\'m drowning in a sea of C!\""          /* \' not necessary */
```

would be stored as

```
He said "I'm drowning in a sea of C!"
```

(The \" must be used within double quotes, "\"", so that C can differentiate between the quotes that mark the beginning and end of the string, and
those that are meant to be within the string. There is no such problem with
the apostrophe. The \' is necessary when showing the single character value
apostrophe, '\'', because single character values are enclosed in
apostrophes.)

If you were to print the following,

```
"This thing cost\n49\xA2."
```

it would produce

```
This thing cost
49¢.
```

The character \n starts a new line and, assuming we are using the appropriate extended ASCII code, the ¢ symbol's value is hex A2.

The compiler will concatenate (connect together end to end) adjacent
strings. For example

```
"This is just "  "one string."
```

will be stored as

```
This is just one string.
```

Remember, whitespace, such as spaces, tabs, and line endings, is ignored
by the compiler (unless it is inside quotes), so this concatenation property is
often used to write a single long string using two lines in C code.

```
"This is just "
  "one string."
```

is stored the same.

Since we can't put line endings between quotes, the following wouldn't
work.

```
"This is just
  one string."
```

There are no string variables in C.

So how do we store variable sets of characters? As sets of individual character variables. We shall cover this in Chapter 9.

ARITHMETIC EXPRESSIONS

An **expression** is anything that can be reduced to a single value. Under this definition, a single value, 14, qualifies as an expression as does a single variable, *pounds*, which would have a value in memory. We are more interested in expressions that require some evaluation by the computer—they are made up of more than one value or variable, for example, 26 + 17. We have all done arithmetic and so have evaluated arithmetic expressions, but we must examine the strict rules that C applies to arithmetic expressions.

An arithmetic expression consists of values and/or variables connected by **arithmetic operators**, which tell the computer how to combine the values. The expression 26 + 17, for example, uses an operator, +, indicating that the values on either side, 26 and 17, are to be added together. The resultant value of the expression is 43.

Many expressions, such as 12 + 9 / 3, have more than one operator. A simple "chain" calculator would evaluate the expression by taking each of those operations in turn: 12 + 9 is 21, 21 / 3 is 7. C (or, for that matter, almost any other computer language) is not so simple. There are strict rules about which operation is to be done first no matter where it occurs in the expression. The rules involve **precedence**, a hierarchy of operations that dictate the types of operations that are to be performed before other types; and **associativity**, which dictates order if two operations have the same level of precedence. ➡️Table 2–4 shows the arithmetic operators in precedence, highest first, and their associativity. Appendix B shows all the operators.

The same calculation, 12 + 9 / 3 would have a different result in C. Since the division operation is higher in precedence than addition, it would be performed first—9 / 3 is 3, 3 + 12 is 15.

We can force calculations to be in any order we choose by enclosing some of them in parentheses. Inner parentheses will be evaluated before outer parentheses, before no parentheses. The same expression can be forced to the order that the simple calculator would follow by putting the addition operation in parentheses—(12 + 9) / 3.

The associativity rule applies when two operations are on the same precedence level. In the expression 12 / 6 / 2, the two division operations are on the same level but they associate from left to right so we have 12 / 6 is 2, 2 / 2 is 1.

The easiest way to make a C expression from a handwritten arithmetic expression is to spread the handwritten expression out in a straight line with

➡️**TABLE 2–4**
Arithmetic Operators in Precedence

Level	Type	Associativity	Operator	Symbol	Example
1	Unary	Right to left	Negate	-	-4
			Plus	+	+4
			Size	sizeof	sizeof x, sizeof (int)
2	Cast	Right to left	A data type	(type)	(int), (float), etc.
3	Multiplicative	Left to right	Multiply	*	6 * 4
			Divide	/	6 / 4
			Remainder	%	6 % 4
4	Additive	Left to right	Add	+	6 + 4
			Subtract	-	6 - 4
5	Assignment	Right to left	Equals	=	x = 4
			Accumulation	+=, -=, *=, /=, %=	x += 16, x %= 4

the proper operators and then, referring back to the original handwritten expression, add parentheses to ensure that the C expression will be evaluated in the same order as the handwritten one. Let us examine the following handwritten expression, translate it to C, and show how it will be evaluated by the computer. The first C expression was written without parentheses to illustrate precedence and to show that without parentheses many expressions will not evaluate as we had intended.

Handwritten Expression

$$\frac{\dfrac{6+4}{2} \times 4}{4 + \dfrac{3 \times 2}{2-1}} = 2$$

In C Without Parentheses   **In C With Parentheses**

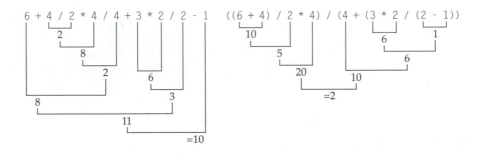

Note that in the second C expression (the one with parentheses), the inclusion of the parentheses around the top of the fraction, ((6 + 4) / 2 * 4), does not change the result. The parentheses are, indeed, unnecessary, but if they improve the readability or understandability of the program, they can certainly be included.

Integer Arithmetic

C performs its arithmetic according to the data types on which it is currently operating. If the data types in a particular operation are integer then the result will also be integer. This typically causes no problem except when the result exceeds the maximum capacity of an integer or when you are dividing. If you exceed the limits of an integer you will get a meaningless result. For example, 32000 * 10 (in a C that defaults to a short int) yields the result −7680.

When dividing an integer by an integer the result will be an integer—a truncated version of what a floating-point division would yield. The result of the expression 3 / 2 is 1, not 1.5. Since both 3 and 2 are integers (they have no decimal points) an integer calculation will be done yielding an integer result. Note that this is not a round-off but a truncation; the result is not 2, but 1.

The **remainder** (or *modulo* or *modulus*) operator deserves special attention. It is valid only with integers, and the result is the remainder after dividing the value before the operator by the value after the operator. The result of the expression 5 % 3 is 2 because 5 divided by 3 is one with a remainder of 2.

As the following long division shows, 762 % 35 is 27. Other examples are at the right.

$$35 \overline{)762}$$

```
      21
35 | 762
     70
     ---
     62
     35
     ---
     27
```

13 % 3 = 1

1 % 5 = 1

8 % 3 = 2

14 % 362 = 14

Be careful when using the remainder operator with negative numbers; the results vary with the particular implementation of C.

Mixed Arithmetic

In general, when data types are mixed in an expression, each operation will be performed at the highest data type involved in the expression—highest meaning the one that takes up the largest amount of memory. Since there is some overlap, floating-point types are considered higher than integral. It is important to recognize that the calculations are not all performed at the highest data type included in the expression; each operation is evaluated separately and performed at the highest data type involved in just that operation. Eventually the result will be of the highest data type in the entire expression but it may take a while to get there. For example:

```
8.3 + 5 / 2  [=10.3]
        |__|
          2 (int)
 |_____|
   10.3 (float)
```

The expression 5 / 2 was performed first and since both the 5 and the 2 are integers (they have no decimal points) 5 / 2 was performed as type int with a result of 2 (not 2.5). Compare that with this:

```
8.3 + 5 / 2.  [=10.8]
        |___|
         2.5 (double)
 |_____|
   10.8 (double)
```

Nuts & Bolts

MIXED ARITHMETIC

Most C compilers don't do arithmetic on all the standard data types; this would require too many built-in routines and conversions. Typically, for integers the smallest size for calculations is type int. Remember, this might be equivalent to short or long depending on your compiler. Chars are promoted to ints and, if the standard int is a long, shorts are also promoted. Long int calculations on a short int compiler are naturally done using long int calculations. For floating points, nothing less than double is calculated. Long doubles are, of course, calculated at long double size.

What does all this mean to you? Computing is a series of trade-offs. If you declare variables as type float rather than double (perhaps to save memory space), calculations on these floats will be done as double. In other words, the computer will have to go through extra conversions—floats to doubles and then back to float for the result. The trade-off is storage space versus execution speed.

In this case 2. is a floating-point value (actually a `double`; see the *Nuts &
Bolts: Mixed Arithmetic* box) so 5 / 2. was calculated as a floating-point
expression with a result of 2.5.

Casts

You don't have to be satisfied with the data type that C determines for an
expression; you can change it to anything you want by casting it. The **cast
operators** are simply the desired data-type key word enclosed in parentheses. For example:

```
(int)   (long double)   (unsigned short)   (float)
```

They may not look like it but they are operators, like + or − or *. They are
unary operators with right-to-left associativity, but fall on the precedence
level below negate and plus—level 2 in ➡Table 2–4.

Given these initialized declarations:

```
int x = 5, y = 2, z = 3;
```

the following expressions will evaluate as shown:

```
x / y * z [=6]    x / y * (float)z [=6.0]    x / (float)y * z [=7.5]
```

The resultant value of a floating-point number cast as an integer follows
the same rules as an integer division—only the whole-number part of the
value survives. If your program contained the declaration `float x = 2.7;`,
the value of the expression `(int)x` would be 2. Note that the value of the
variable x would not be changed; it would still be 2.7. Like any other operator, the cast operator only uses the values around it; it does not change them
any more than `4 + x` would change the value of x.

You must be careful with your casts. If you cast a value as a smaller data
type, a `long` as a `short`, for example, C will just copy as many bits as it can fit
and the result will be unrecognizable. The value of `(short)45612` in a typical
C implementation is −19924.

The `sizeof` Operator

The result of the `sizeof` operator is an integer equivalent to the number of
bytes required to store the object following it. This object can be either a data
type or an expression.

```
sizeof (datatype)            or        sizeof expression
```

The `sizeof` operator is unary and has the same precedence and associativity
as the other unary operators. If the object of `sizeof` is a *datatype*, then the
datatype must be in parentheses.

As we saw earlier, various Cs have different storage requirements for the
same data types. The expression

```
sizeof (int)
```

for example, typically yields 2 or 4 depending on the C. One way to find out the sizes of the various types would be to print out the `sizeof` each.

```
sizeof (char)
```

should produce 1 in every C.

The `sizeof` operator can be used in expressions just like any other unary operator. For example, given these declarations and initializations:

```
int a = 10;                          /* Assume a 2-byte int */
float b = 20.5;                      /* Assume a 4-byte float */
```

this expression,

```
sizeof a + b
```

would evaluate to the `float` value 22.5 (the `sizeof a`, 2 plus 20.5). Remember, `sizeof` is unary and higher in precedence than addition.

```
sizeof (a + b)
```

would evaluate to the integer value 4. Since the result of 10 + 22.5 would be `float`, `sizeof` would yield the number of bytes in the data type `float`.

ASSIGNMENT

Variables identify spaces in main memory. These spaces are variable because they can contain various and changeable values. Putting a value into one of these spaces is known as **assignment**. We usually refer to "assigning a value to a variable," but technically, we are writing a value into the memory space identified by the variable.

We have seen how initial assignments can be included as part of declarations, but we must also make assignments as part of our program. For example, we may wish to store the results of a calculation in a variable, or change the value of a variable we had assigned previously. There are many ways of assigning values to variables, but all ways follow this fundamental rule:

A variable may have only one value at a time.

We may assign many different values to a variable, but each time we do, we write to the memory space reserved for that variable, and, as we saw in Chapter 1, a write operation replaces data. If the variable *checkers* had the value 137.93, and you assign 6.2 to it, the 6.2 would overwrite, or replace, the 137.93, and the value of *checkers* would then be 6.2. What happens to the 137.93? Unless you specifically copied it somewhere else in memory beforehand, it is lost.

The standard assignment operator is the equal sign (=). Referring to Appendix B, we can see that its precedence is after all the arithmetic operators, which means that after all the arithmetic is done, the assignment is made. The general form of an assignment is

```
variable = expression
```

where *variable* identifies a space in memory, and *expression* evaluates to a single value.

Following are valid assignment statements:

```
x = 14;
y = (x + 15) / 12.7;
principal = interest * rate * time;
```

Notice that in each case, there is a single variable to the left of the equal sign—something to assign the value to. (The variable is often referred to in references as a *modifiable lvalue*—an identifier that can be legally used at the left of the assignment operator.) The spaces in the statements are not actually necessary in C, but they tend to make the statements a little more readable.

The resultant value of an assignment expression is the value of the assignment. Since the assignment operator's associativity is right to left, this allows more than one assignment to be made in a single statement. For example,

```
x = y = z = 17 + 9;
```

would calculate 17 + 9 and assign the value 26 to *z*. The value of the entire expression $z = 17 + 9$ is the assignment value 26, so that value would be assigned to *y*. The value of $y = z = 17 + 9$ is now also 26, so that value would be assigned to *x*.

Forced Conversions

Any value may be assigned to any type of variable. Whether that value is actually stored in its original form is essentially up to you and how you write the assignment. A value assigned to a variable will always be of the type of that variable. It has to be; there is a specific memory space allocated and a specific form (integer or floating point) to be followed. If a floating-point value is assigned to an integer variable, the decimal part will be dropped just as if it were cast. If a value is assigned to a data type that will not hold it, again just like a cast, as many bits as possible will be stuffed in, but the result will be unrecognizable.

Many C programmers get into the habit of explicitly declaring and casting their data types so that there are no forced conversions. Some variants of the language require this explicit typing and produce weird results if it is not present.

Accumulation

We can keep a running total, performing a process called **accumulation**, by using this kind of assignment statement:

```
total = total + new;
```

As an algebraic equation, that makes no sense at all, but this is a statement representing a sequence of instructions to the computer, not an equation. Let us suppose that the value of *total* is 100 and *new* is 5. Since addition (+) is higher in precedence than assignment (=) the addition expression is evaluated first. The computer will add the value of *total* (100) to the value of *new* (5), giving the result 105. The assignment operator is next, so the value 105 is assigned to *total*, replacing the 100.

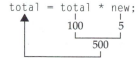

```
total = total + new;
          |       |
         100      5
          |_____|
              |
             105
```

We can use any arithmetic operator. In the previous example we accumulated by adding to the *total* variable. Below, starting with the same values, we will use the multiplication operator. The new value of *total*, of course, will be 500.

```
total = total * new;
          |       |
         100      5
          |_____|
              |
             500
```

Since accumulation is such a common operation, the designers of C gave us some shorthand notation for it: a set of **accumulation operators** formed by the arithmetic operator for the type of accumulation we are doing followed by an equal sign. For example, the statement just above could be rewritten

```
total *= new;
```

This operator does not represent some new kind of mathematical operation, it simply indicates two separate operations. During the compile process, the C compiler takes the variable before the operator (*total* in the example), copies it and the arithmetic operator following it to the other side of the equal sign, and then compiles the result. There is no execution advantage to the accumulation operator; it just saves a little typing in the source code.

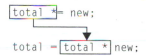

```
total *= new;

total = total * new;
```

The precedence and associativity of the accumulation operator are the same as the assignment operator—last on our list and right to left as the next example illustrates. If *total* was 100, *new* was 5, and *old* was 3, both *total* and *answer* would be 108.

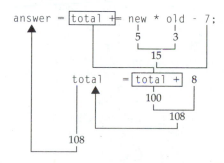

```
answer = total += new * old - 7;
                    |      |
                    5      3
                    |_____|
                       |
                      15

         total  = total + 8
                  100
                    |_____|
                       |
                      108

       108
```

Notice that the whole effect of the accumulation operator comes after the multiplication and subtraction. The copy of the *total* variable is not made before the expression is evaluated but during the evaluation when the accumulation operator is reached.

SIMPLE NUMERIC OUTPUT

To write useful programs we must have a way of printing out the results. In Chapter 1 we saw that, using the `printf()` function, we could print out strings and embed numbers—values of expressions—in those strings. We will discuss this much more fully in the next chapter, but for now we will use the code `%i` in a string to embed an integer, and `%f` to embed a floating-point number. ➡Program 2–1 shows both codes and the results of their use.

➡Program 2–1

```
#include <stdio.h>

void main(void)
{   int num = 25;
    float val = 2.5;

    printf("Here is the number: %i\n", num);
    printf("and the result of an expression: %f\n", num / val);
}
```

Execution

```
Here is the number: 25
and the result of an expression: 10.000000
```

Notice that each `%` code has a corresponding argument after the quoted argument in the `printf()`. In the second `printf()`, for example, the space reserved by the `%f` in the string is filled with the value of the expression `num / val` when the program is run.

PUTTING IT TOGETHER

Let us look at an example. The local bank has an odd incentive program going on. If you make a deposit for 180 days, they will give you 7% for the first third of that time, 8% for the second, and 9% for the last. The following program shows the results of a $100 deposit. The formula for the amount accumulated is

$$Amount = Amount + \frac{Rate}{100} \times \frac{Days}{365} \times Amount$$

In our program, the number of days will have to be divided by three for each period. Since this is a relatively simple program, our structured outline will also be simple.

Calculate and display value for first third
Calculate and display value for second third
Calculate and display value for last third

➡➡Program 2–2

(Note: The line numbers shown with this program are there only for reference in the following execution chart; they are not part of the code.)

```
#include <stdio.h>

void main(void)
1  {  int rate = 7, days = 180;
2     float amount = 100;

   /*********************** Calculate and display value for first third */
3        amount += rate / 100.0 * days / 3 / 365 * amount;
4        printf("After first third at %i percent:  %f\n", rate, amount);
   /*********************** Calculate and display value for second third */
5        rate += 1;
6        amount += rate / 100.0 * days / 3 / 365 * amount;
7        printf("After second third at %i percent: %f\n", rate, amount);
   /*********************** Calculate and display value for last third */
8        rate += 1;
9        amount += (rate / 100.0) * (((float)days / 3) / 365) * amount;
10       printf("After last third at %i percent:  %f\n", rate, amount);
   }
```

Execution

```
After first third at 7 percent:  101.150688
After second third at 8 percent: 102.480888
After last third at 9 percent:   103.997047
```

EXECUTION CHART

Line	Explanation	rate	days	amount
1	Allocate space and initialize *rate* and *days*. (Note that *amount* does not yet exist.)	7	180	----
2	Allocate space and initialize *amount*.	7	180	100.000
3	Calculate *amount* for the first third of the *days*. The *rate* is divided by the floating-point number 100.0 to force the result to a floating-point value. Since this will be part of all the other calculations, each will be forced to floating-point. The result of the expression will be added to *amount* and then assigned to *amount*.	7	180	101.150
4	Results are printed.	7	180	101.150
5	*rate* is increased by 1	8	180	101.150
6	Same as line 3.	8	180	102.480
7	Results are printed as in line 4.	8	180	102.480
8	*rate* is increased by 1	9	180	102.480
9	Same as line 5 except that in an attempt to make the expression more readable, we have put parentheses around the various sections. Because of the parentheses, the second section with *days* is calculated separately, so we had to force it to floating-point. We chose to cast *days* this time.	9	180	103.977
10	Final results are printed.	9	180	103.977

SUMMARY

While we humans typically use the **decimal** system to express numeric values, the computer cannot because its basic counting and storage machinery consists of two-state, on-off switches. This limits the computer to **binary** notation for everything. In C we cannot directly express binary numbers, but we can express **hexadecimal** numbers by preceding the hex digits 0–F with 0x, or **octal** numbers by preceding the octal digits 0–7 with 0. Both of these number systems, with single digits, express groups of binary digits—three for octal and four for hex.

Characters are also expressed with sets of binary digits within the computer. Which set represents what character is governed by the **coding scheme** in use, typically either **ASCII** or **EBCDIC**. To the computer, the set of binary digits that represents a character is the same as a number. We can put characters in our C code that do not exist on the keyboard by using special characters such as \t for tab or \n for newline, or by putting the octal or hex value of the character code after the backslash (\0xA2).

The smallest unit of data storage is the **bit**—a single off or on, or 0 or 1. The smallest unit we actually operate on, however, is eight bits—the **byte**. More efficiency is achieved by operating on larger units. The largest unit on which a computer can actually operate is the **word**.

A variable is a space in the computer's memory. **Variable names** (or **variable identifiers**) can be multicharacter combinations of alpha, numeric, or underscore characters and are case sensitive. None of ANSI C's 32 **reserved words** can be used as a variable name nor can a variable name begin with a numeric character.

When we use data, either as values or in variables, they must be declared as a specific **data type**. The **declaration** tells C whether the data is stored in straight binary fashion or IEEE floating-point notation; how many bytes to allocate to the data; and **defines** the value or variable by allocating memory to it. A variable may also be **initialized** in a declaration. The **integral data types** char and int use straight binary notation and may be signed or unsigned. The int data type may be short or long. The **floating-point data types** float, double, and long double use IEEE **E notation**. **Strings**, sets of characters, are not really data types but we may include string values in a program by putting the characters in quotes.

An **expression** is anything that reduces to a single value. Arithmetic expressions are made by combining values or variables together using **arithmetic operators**. The expressions must be carefully constructed because the order of operation is determined by the operators' **precedence** and **associativity**. The order of operations may be altered by enclosing operations in parentheses. Operators include not only the standard ones but also some special ones such as **remainder, cast,** and sizeof; and **accumulation** operators, which also make assignments.

The results of arithmetic operations are dependent on the data types. An operation on two integers produces an integer result, truncating any decimal places. Operations mixing integers and floating-point values will produce floating-point results. Generally speaking, in mixed arithmetic lower data types are promoted to higher before the operation is performed.

Assignment is the process of putting a value in a variable. A variable may have only one value at a time, so an assignment replaces any value that was there before. An assignment will always be of the data type of the assigned variable. C will perform conversions automatically if it needs to.

KEY TERMS (in order of appearance)

Decimal
Binary
Hexadecimal
Octal
Coding scheme
American Standard Code for Information interchange (ASCII)
Extended binary-coded-decimal interchange code (EBCDIC)
Special character
Bit
Byte
Word
Variable name
Variable identifier
Reserved word
Data type
Declaration
Definition
Initialize
Integral data type
`char`
`signed`

`unsigned`
`int`
`short`
`long`
Floating-point data type
Mantissa
Exponent
E notation
`float`
`double`
`long double`
String
Expression
Arithmetic operator
Precedence
Associativity
Remainder
Cast operator
`sizeof`
Assignment
Accumulation
Accumulation operator

REVIEW QUESTIONS

1. Why is the computer limited to a binary number system?

2. Can we directly represent numbers in binary notation in C?

3. Why are hexadecimal and octal notation often used to represent binary numbers?

4. How would the hex number 7C be written in C code? The octal number 406?

5. How are characters represented in the computer? Why?

6. In a C language using the ASCII code, how does storage of the values represented as `'A'` and 65 differ?

7. Why do we have special characters such as `\n` or `\a`? How do we represent the backslash?

8. In your C code, how would you represent an extended ASCII character whose hex code was D5?

9. What is the smallest unit of data storage?

10. What is the smallest unit of data we actually operate on? How many bits has it?

11. What is the unit of data that a CPU can actually operate on? How many bits has it?

12. Which characters can be used in C variable names? What can the name start with?

13. Are *books* and *BOOKS* the same variable?

14. What functions does a declaration perform in a program?

15. Which data types are integral? Which are floating-point? What is the difference between an integral and a floating-point data type?

16. What characters do we use at the end of numbers to declare values as `unsigned`? `long`? `unsigned long`? `float`? `long double`?

17. How do we put a quote mark in a string value?

18. How does precedence differ from associativity? Which is considered first?

19. Of the operators covered in this chapter, which are highest in precedence? Lowest?

20. What happens if an arithmetic operation involving two integers yields what we would think of as a fractional result (such as dividing 3 / 2)?

21. What is the result of a remainder operation?

22. If dissimilar data types are involved in an arithmetic operation, of what data type is the result?

23. How may we change the data type of an expression?

24. What is the purpose of the `sizeof` operator, and in what two ways is it used?

25. How many values may a simple variable have at one time?

26. Which of the operators covered perform assignments?

EXERCISES

1. What is the binary equivalent of these decimal numbers?

   a. 5   b. 21
   c. 42   d. 227

2. What is the decimal equivalent of these binary numbers?

   a. 1101   b. 10110
   c. 100011   d. 1101101

3. What are the octal and hexadecimal equivalents of these decimal numbers?

   a. 10   b. 51
   c. 147   d. 688

4. What are the decimal and binary equivalents of these hexadecimal numbers?

   a. B   b. 2C
   c. E84D   d. 143F

5. What are the decimal and binary equivalents of these octal numbers?

   a. 5   b. 61
   c. 474   d. 164436

6. In the ASCII coding scheme, P is binary 1011111. What are Q and R?

7. In an implementation of C using ASCII, to what character would the following expressions evaluate? (Refer to the complete table in Appendix A.)

   a. `'J' + ' '`   b. `'4' + '5'`
   c. `'p' - '?'`   d. `'~' # '<'`

8. All other things being equal, a CPU with a 32-bit word usually will not execute a typical program twice as fast as a 16-bit CPU. Why not?

9. Of the following, which are invalid variable names? Why are they invalid?

   a. gnash   b. union
   c. 9Times   d. too_many

10. Of the following, which are invalid declarations? Why are they invalid?

    a. `unsigned float zip = 46;`   b. `Double Dip;`
    c. `short stuff, pants = 12;`   d. `long double disaster`

11. In the C that you use, in what data types would the following values be stored? In what data types could they actually fit?

    a. 91   b. 40265

    c. 45.   d. 1657.39854

12. What are the values and data types of the following expressions?

    a. 7 / 4   b. 9 / 2. + 25 / 3

    c. 6 + 4.8 / 2 * 3   d. 25 % 5 + 12.5 * 2 / 5

13. If $x = 5$ and $y = 2$ and both are integers, what are the values of the following expressions?

    a. x % y + 14.6 / y   b. y = (float)x / 2 + 3.5

    c. y *= x   d. y = 16.2 * x / 3

14. Rewrite this program in proper form.

```
#include <stdio.h>
void main(void){int number;number = 2;printf("We had %i. ", number);num
ber *= 2;printf("Now we have %i.\n", number);}
```

15. Fill out an execution chart for the following program. (Note to future programmers: Wouldn't this program be a lot easier to understand if it were well structured and commented?)

Program

```
#include <stdio.h>

void main(void)
{  int bytes, code, dollars;
   float cost, per_byte = 1.42;

1     code = 3;
2     bytes = code * 17 * sizeof (int);
3     dollars = bytes * per_byte + .5;
4     printf("%i code segments cost %i dollars.\n", code, dollars);
5     code += 1;
6     bytes = code * 17 * sizeof (int);
7     cost = bytes * per_byte;
8     printf("%i code segments cost %f dollars.\n", code, cost);
9     printf("   This time we count the %i pennies.\n",
              (int) (cost * 100 + .5) % 100);
}
```

Execution

```
3 code segments cost 145 dollars.
4 code segments cost 193.119995 dollars.
   This time we count the 12 pennies.
```

PROGRAMS

1. The actual size in bytes of some data types is system dependent. Write a program that shows the size of various data types and operations on your system. You should not need any variables.

Execution (for a microcomputer C)

```
An int          is 2 bytes.
A  float        is 4 bytes.
A  double       is 8 bytes.
A  long double  is 10 bytes.
An integer value  is 2 bytes.
A  float value    is 8 bytes.
Integer arithmetic is 2 bytes.
Float arithmetic   is 8 bytes.
```

2. Find the value of each of these expressions. Be sure to pay attention to data type. Write a program that confirms your answers.

a.   `3.5 + 8 / 3`   b.   `4 * 11.5 / 2 + 16`

c.   `7.5 - 38 % 7 * 2 + 10`   d.   `25 / 2. + 13 / 3`

3. Write a program that assigns $a = 4$, $f = 9$, $b = -6$, $x = 4$, and $h = 7$ and prints out the results of the following expressions. All the variables are integers but the results should be as shown. Your output should have the same form and the same values as shown. (The last digit may vary according to your C.)

1. $a + f\dfrac{b^2 + h}{3}$

2. $x + 6f\dfrac{h + 9}{4 - b}$

3. $\dfrac{(a + b)^2}{f - \dfrac{x + 1}{h - 4}}$

4. $\dfrac{(1 + h)(1 - f)}{\dfrac{3f}{h^2 - x}}$

Execution

```
1 = 133.000000
2 = 90.400000
3 = 0.545455
4 = -106.666667
```

4. There are 12 inches in a foot. Write a program in which you initialize the integer variable *inches* to a value, say 46, assign the number of feet to *feet*, and print the result.

Variables

```
inches, feet
```

Execution

```
46 inches is 3.833333 feet.
```

5. Write a program to find the average of the four values 4, 42, 16.7, and .0045.

Variables

```
v1, v2, v3, v4
average
```

Execution

```
The four numbers are:
    4.000000 42.000000 16.700001 0.004500
The average is:
    15.676126
```

6. You are given a sphere with a radius of 25. Find the circumference, largest cross-sectional area, and the volume of the sphere.

Variables

pi	π (3.1416)
radius	25
circumference	($2\pi r$)
area	largest cross-sectional area (πr^2)
volume	$\left(\dfrac{4}{3}\pi r^3\right)$

Execution

```
Radius:              25
Circumference:       157.080002
Cross-sectional area: 1963.499878
Volume:              65449.996094
```

7. Rewrite the program in problem 6 to work with a radius of 14.

Execution

```
Radius:              14
Circumference:       87.964798
Cross-sectional area: 615.753601
Volume:              11494.066406
```

8. Write a program that produces a bill and coin breakdown for an amount of money. Initialize the amount in the float variable *dollars* and use the *pennies* variable to keep track of the amount not yet converted to bills and coins. You will have to use integer arithmetic and the remainder operator in this program.

Variables

```
dollars      float
pennies      int
```

Execution

```
The coin breakdown for 7.730000 dollars is:
Dollar bills: 7
Half dollars: 1
Quarters:     0
Dimes:        2
Nickels:      0
Pennies:      3
```

INTRODUCING DIRECTIVES AND STREAMS

3

PREVIEW

C may be considered a simple language, but its simplicity stems from the elegant way its simple pieces are integrated. To work in C, you must know a little bit about a lot of different things. In this chapter we shall briefly introduce some concepts to get our programming processes started. Later, these concepts will be revisited in greater detail. Here we shall discuss:

1. Instructions to the compiler itself.
2. ANSI C's method for standardizing input and output.
3. The most basic screen output function.
4. The most basic keyboard input function.

In Chapter 1 we discussed going from source code to executable code, including the role of the compiler. Now, we want to examine some of the capabilities of the compiler in a little more detail.

COMPILER DIRECTIVES

In a sample program in Chapter 1, we labeled one line as a **compiler directive**, an instruction to the compiler rather than a statement to be translated directly to machine language. When we compile a program, the compiler automatically invokes a **preprocessor**, which reacts to compiler directives. We shall look at the preprocessor more completely in Chapter 13, but two directives are used so frequently, even in the simplest programs, that they beg for at least partial attention now.

Notice that a compiler directive does not end in a semicolon. For the simple directives given here, be sure that they are each contained on a single line.

Including Source Code

The `#include` directive instructs the compiler to temporarily, at the beginning of the compile process, insert a file at that point in the source code.

```
#include <fileid>  or  #include "fileid"
```

The `fileid` is the identification of the file to be placed in the source code. In an MS-DOS system it might be something like *D:\SYSTEM\GOODIES.COD*, which includes not only the filename and extension but also the search path through disks and directories to find the file. For a UNIX system, make the backslashes (\) into slashes (/) and delete the reference to the disk drive (*D:*). Be sure to consult your system's reference manual for the correct format.

This difference in the two forms is the way in which the C compiler searches for the file to include. Both forms are system dependent, so you must find out the particulars of your system. The main difference, though, is that the first form, using the < >, searches a specific directory defined by the compiler (or in some cases, the operating system). This is typically the directory in which certain standard files, such as `stdio.h`, are stored. The other form uses the operating system's default search pattern, typically starting with the directory in which you are currently working. If it doesn't find the file there, it searches as if the `fileid` was enclosed in < >.

What can an include file include? Anything, really, but to be reasonable, it should make some sense to the C compiler. In other words, it should be C source code. **Header files**, of which `stdio.h` is an example, are C source code written for us by the makers of the compiler. They contain declarations and definitions, among other things. Try looking at one of them with a text editor or viewer (be careful not to make any changes!). You may have written source code that you want to put in a number of programs. Rather than typing or copying it into each program, you can put it in a file, for example, *MYSTUFF.INC* in an *INCLUDE* directory, and include it at the appropriate place in each program with the directive

```
#include "INCLUDE\MYSTUFF.INC"
```

Remember, the inclusion is only temporary, used only during the compile process. You will not see it in your source code. If you change the include file and then recompile your program, it will compile using the new code in the include file.

Character Replacements

The #define directive, among other things, establishes a character replacement for a program.

```
#define characters replacement
```

Following the directive, all occurrences of a specific set of *characters* in the source code are replaced by the characters in *replacement*. For example,

```
#define PI 3.14
```

will replace each PI in the source code with the characters 3.14. An instance of the specified characters in quotes, of course, will not be replaced (as we see in the printf() below). We will not see the replacement; like the #include directive, it works only during the compile process.

Source Code	Actual Compiled Code
`#include <stdio.h>`	[The entire stdio.h file here]
`#define PI 3.14`	`int main(void)`
`int main(void)`	`{  float radius = 25;`
`{  float radius = 25;`	`   float circ;`
`   float circ;`	
`   printf("The circumference "`	`   printf("The circumference "`
`           "formula uses PI\n");`	`           "formula uses PI\n");`
`   circ = 2 * PI * radius`	`   circ = 2 * 3.14 * radius`
`[and so forth]`	`[and so forth]`

By tradition, the *characters* are in all uppercase, as in PI. This makes the characters slated for replacement easy to spot in the source code, and reduces conflict with variables, which are traditionally in caps/lowercase or all lowercase. Remember, C is case sensitive.

Why not just put 3.14 in the source code? We usually use the *characters* as **defined constants**, symbols that represent specific values—PI representing the value 3.14, for example. One reason for putting them in the #define directive is to have them expressed at the beginning of the program where they may be easy to find if we want to change them. In our example, we may want our *circ* (circumference) or anything else based on π to be more accurate. All we have to do is to change the #define directive to, say,

```
#define PI 3.14159
```

and every occurrence of PI will reflect the change.

Another reason for using the #define directive is to enhance program readability. For example, our process may have a high limit of 849.325 and a low limit of -35.769. If someone read those two numbers buried in the source code, it might require some research to find out what they meant. But seeing the words HIGH and LOW would provide an instant clue.

DEFINED CONSTANTS VERSUS VARIABLES

Instead of using a defined constant, like

```
#define PI 3.14
```

why not use a variable, like

```
float pi = 3.14;
```

Either, of course, would do the job, but the defined constant is substituted during the compile stage, not during the program's execution. It requires no more memory in the executable code than a float value, and no execution time. A variable requires space in the executable code for the same float value plus the float variable *pi*, and it requires the execution time to make the initial assignment of the value to the variable as well as the time to read the variable's value each time it is used.

Moral: If a variable isn't variable, either use the value directly or define it as a constant.

STREAMS

Most computers have a number of input and output devices—keyboards, mice, screens, printers, communication devices—and access to these pieces of equipment is different depending on the computer hardware, the operating system, and the device itself. In other words, it's enough to drive a person charged with maintaining standards crazy. Therefore, specific access to many of these devices is not covered in the ANSI standard; it is left to individual implementations of C and/or supplemental libraries of C routines.

The ANSI standard does, however, provide for generalized input and output through a standard mechanism called a **stream**. ANSI C allows us to establish any number of streams to be used within a program but the standard itself provides three of the most used: stdin, stdout, and stderr. The stdin stream is normally associated with the keyboard, and stdout and stderr with the screen. The stderr stream is where C directs its error messages. In this chapter we will concentrate on stdin and stdout, the two that allow us to send data to the program through the keyboard, and have the program print data on our screen.

OUTPUT

Working with the ANSI standard output stream is straightforward; we send characters to the stream, and the stream sends them to the device attached to it, usually a screen. Although there are a number of C functions that do this, we shall concentrate at this point on the most basic and versatile—printf().

We have already seen that we can send character strings, characters enclosed in quotes, to the screen by putting the quoted string value within the parentheses. The statement

```
printf("This is an output line.\n");
```

when executed produces

```
This is an output line.
```

on the screen. The \n drops the cursor to the next line.

The name of the function comes from the fact that printf() performs formatted printing where we can specifically state how, and in what format, we want the result to appear. We can print numbers rounded to two decimal places, start or end values at specific character positions on the line, use many printf()s to create columns lined up on the decimal point, and so forth.

Formatted printing in most languages, C included, is a two-step process. First we design the line—show where things go and reserve space for values of various data types to print. Second, we state what values should be placed in the spaces reserved for them. Both steps are specified in the arguments to the function (the parameters between the parentheses).

```
printf("control string", argument, argument, ..., argument)
```

The first step, and the first argument to the function, is the line design, called a format or *control string*. This is a set of characters that we use to tell C what we want to go where in our output. The control string can contain two types of characters: printable characters and conversion codes. Printable characters just simply print at whatever position they happen to be in the format. Most characters are printable. In fact, all the printf() functions we have been using until now have consisted of only a single argument, the *control string*, and all the characters in the formats have been printable. (Remember, the special characters that were defined in Chapter 2, such as \" or \n, are used to represent single characters, and they are printable. Newline, of course does not print anything visible, but it does move the cursor to the beginning of the next line.)

Conversion Codes

Conversion codes are used to reserve space in the output for some other values to print—the value of a variable or expression, for example—and to show how those values should be converted to characters and printed. All conversion codes begin with a % and end with a **type specifier**, a character indicating the data type of the value that will be displayed at that location. For example, this program segment,

```
void main(void)
{   int dollars = 150;

    printf("I have %i dollars in my pocket.\n", dollars);
}
```

when executed displays

```
I have 150 dollars in my pocket.
```

All the characters in the format are printable except the conversion code %i which reserves space for an integer value to print. The format requires a value to fill in that space, so C takes the value of the next argument, dollars, and puts it there. Given this format there must, of course, be a next argument. Notice that our first uses of `printf()` did not require any further arguments because there was nothing to fill in.

Since the `%` character is used as the beginning of a conversion instead of a printable character, to print a `%`, use `%%`.

```
void main(void)
{  float yours = 126.4, mine = 17.5628;

   printf("You have %f and I have %f, %f%% of that.\n",
          yours, mine, mine / yours * 100);
}
```

when executed will display

```
You have 126.400002 and I have 17.562799, 13.894620% of that.
```

Why aren't the values exactly as we initialized them? Remember that the computer stores the numbers in binary E notation. The `%f` format prints with six decimal digits, so when C made the conversion, that was the closest approximation it could come up with. The arguments for the conversion codes can, of course, be any valid expression, anything that can be reduced to a single numeric value—a number, variable, or, as in the last argument, a formula.

The various type specifiers, `i`, `f`, `e`, and so forth, are listed in ➡️Table 3–1.

➡️**TABLE 3–1**
Data Type Specifiers
for `printf()`

Specifier	Data Type	Explanation	Sample	Output
c	char	A single character.	"%c",65	A
d	int	PreANSI version of i. Still valid in most ANSI implementations.	"%d",-4725 "%d",4725	-4725 4725
E	float or double	Signed E notation.	"%E",462.58	4.625800E+02
e	float or double	Signed E notation with small e.	"%e",462.58	4.625800e+02
f	float or double	Standard signed decimal notation with six digits after the decimal point. Negative signs print, positive signs don't.	"%f",462.58 "%f",-1.7225	462.580000 -1.722500
g	float or double	Either e or f format, whichever outputs fewer characters. Trailing zeros or trailing decimal points are not printed.	"%g",1.25 "%g",4.0	1.25 4
G	float or double	Same as g except that a capital E will be used in E-format outputs.	"%G",.0000476234	4.76234E-05
i	int	Signed integer with negative but not positive signs printing.	"%i",-4725 "%i",4725	-4725 4725
n	pointer to int	Nonprinting. Used to store a character count. More on this later.		
o	unsigned int	Octal digits	"%o",327	507 [Octal]
p	pointer to void	An address in memory. More on this later.		
s	string	Prints an entire set of characters. We shall look at strings later.		
u	unsigned int	Decimal digits.	"%u", 123 "%u",-23456	123 42080 [Garbage]
x	unsigned int	Hex digits with abcdef.	"%x",334	14e
X	unsigned int	Same as x except using ABCDEF.	"%X",735	2DF

Size Modifiers

Some data types may optionally have **size modifiers** that further define the type. The size-modifier character appears just before the type specifier; remember, the conversion code must end with the type specifier. The size modifiers h, for short, and l, for long, may modify any of the integral types, d, i, o, u, x, or X. The conversion code %li, then, indicates that a long int value will print here.

The L modifier may modify any of the floating-point type specifiers to indicate a long double value. Notice that the uppercase L is used for floating-point data types, whereas the lowercase l is used for integral data types. The conversion code %LE indicates a long double value will be printed in E notation.

Width and Precision

Again as an option, we may set the minimum **width** of a print field by putting a number before the type specifier or size modifier, if one exists. This is useful in printing values in columns; each printf() function used to print in the columns should start the conversion code at the same character position, and then use conversion codes with the same width. Beware, the width parameter is the *minimum* width. If the value to be printed has more characters (including signs and so forth) than the minimum, the entire value will print, ruining the neat column. By default, fields with specified widths will be right justified, that is, lined up on the right side. In other words, padded with leading spaces.

▶**Program 3–1**

```
#include <stdio.h>

void main(void)
{   long eastville = 322536, westport = 643, gotham = 6445821;

    printf("Eastville has %6li people.\n", eastville);
    printf("Westport has  %6li people.\n", westport);
    printf("Gotham has    %6li people.\n", gotham);
}
```

Output

```
Eastville has 322536 people.
Westport has     643 people.
Gotham has   6445821 people.
```

The value of *gotham* required seven characters so when it printed in a field with a minimum of six characters it overflowed by one character.

In addition to the width of a field we may also, optionally again, state the **precision**. The precision parameter comes after the width if there is one, before the size modifier if there is one, and always starts with a decimal point. This parameter means different things for different data types. For floating-point types except for the g (or G) type specifier, it specifies the number of digits after the decimal point; the value will be rounded to that number of digits.

```
#include <stdio.h>

void main(void)
{  float yours = 126.4, mine = 17.5628;

   printf("You have %.2f and I have %.2f, %5.1f%% of that.\n",
          yours, mine, mine / yours * 100);
}
```

Output

```
You have 126.40 and I have 17.56,  13.9% of that.
```

With the exception of the formats, this ➤➤Program 3–2 is exactly the same as ➤➤Program 3–1, but forcing a roundoff to a specific number of decimal digits cleaned up the conversion approximation problems. There are two spaces in this output instead of one between the comma and the 13.9%. The format was %5.1f, a minimum width of five, and 13.9 has four characters, so a leading space shows as part of the output field. Remember that the width is the minimum width of the entire field. Don't forget to count signs, decimal points, and digits after the decimal point.

For the g or G type specifiers, the precision parameter defines the maximum number of significant digits to be output; leading zeros do not count.

For integral data types the precision parameter defines the minimum number of digits. Leading blanks are added to fill in.

The width or precision parameters, or both, may be represented by an asterisk (*), which means that the value of that parameter will be provided by the next argument in the argument list. Arguments for the * parameters must be of integral data types.

➤➤Program 3–3

```
#include <stdio.h>

void main(void)
{  int characters = 5, places = 2;
   float x = 1.2345;

   printf("The value of x is %*.*f\n", characters, places, x);
}
```

Execution

```
The value of x is  1.23
```

Flags

There are a number of other things we might specify in a conversion code by means of various **flags** (see ➤➤Table 3–2). These characters go immediately after the % before any other parameters that might exist.

Flag	Explanation	Sample	Output
-	Left justify.	`"X%-5.1fX",2.65`	`X2.6  X`
+	Print a + or -. Normally only negative signs print.	`"%+i",25`	`+25`
space	Put a space in front of positive values. (Ignored if + flag also present.)	`"X% iX",25`	`X 25X`
		`"X% iX",-25`	`X-25X`
#	For o, x, or X types: Output values prefixed with 0, 0x, or 0X.	`"%#x",63`	`0x3f`
	For e, E, f, g, or G types: Forces printing of decimal point.	`"%#4.0f",38.`	`38.`
	For g or G types: All trailing zeros are printed.	`"%#g",3.126`	`3.12600`
0	For d, i, o, u, x, X, e, E, f, g, or G types leading zeros printed. (Ignored if - flag also present.)	`"%05i",42`	`00042`

The complete format of a conversion code, then, is as follows (the items in brackets are optional):

`%[flags][width][.precision][size]type`

INPUT

The `printf()` function takes data in all kinds of forms, converts it to characters, and displays those characters in whatever format you desire. The `scanf()` function does the opposite. It takes a series of characters in a specific format, converts the characters to data in various forms, and assigns the data to spaces in memory. In the case of the `scanf()`, the data comes from the input stream `stdin`, typically associated with the keyboard.

The form of the `scanf()` function is similar to `printf()`. The first argument is a *control string* with conversion codes. Subsequent arguments define the locations in the computer's memory where the results of the conversions will be stored.

`scanf("control string", location, location, ..., location)`

To design the *control string*, we must know how the input will look. Is there an integer number followed by space followed by a decimal number and a slash and another decimal number? Once we know the input format, we may design the *control string* to take the input characters, and divide them into sets of characters to convert to the appropriate data types for the locations. For example, given the keyboard input

`45.87 12`

the statement

`scanf("%f %i", &x, &y);`

will assign the value 45.87 to the variable *x* and the value 12 to the variable *y*.

Notice the ampersands (&) in front of the variables *x* and *y*. Remember, the `scanf()` function arguments after the *control string* are not variables, but the locations of the variables in main memory—their memory addresses. We will discuss addresses in more detail later on, but C gives us a simple notation to refer to the address of a specific variable—preceding the variable name with an ampersand. The notation &x means the address of the variable *x*.

Conversion Codes

The conversion codes for scanf() are similar to, but not exactly like, those for printf(). They are listed in ▶▶Table 3–3.

When the scanf() function executes, it matches the characters in the input stream with the characters in the *control string*. A single conversion code in the *control string* will match input characters following these steps:

1. Leading whitespace characters (spaces, tabs, and newlines) are skipped (except for type specifiers c, n, or [).

2. Subsequent characters will be taken for conversion and assignment up to the first character that is inappropriate for the data type.

For example, if the input characters were ^^^46.8 (the ^ indicates a space), a %i conversion code would skip the three spaces and assign the value 46 to the variable, leaving the characters .8 for the next match. The conversion stopped there because a decimal point is not an appropriate character for an integer conversion. In ▶▶Program 3–4 (and subsequent ones in this chapter), keyboard inputs are shown in boldface.

▶▶Program 3–4

```
#include <stdio.h>

void main(void)
{  float food, drink, tip, total, tax, bill;

   printf("Food total: ");
   scanf("%f", &food);
   printf("Beverages:  ");
   scanf("%f", &drink);
   printf("Tip:        ");
   scanf("%f", &tip);
   total = food + drink + tip;
   tax = total * .06;
   printf("Tax:        %6.2f\n", tax);
   bill = total + tax;
   printf("Please pay: %6.2f\n", bill);
}
```

Execution

```
Food total: 34.82
Beverages:  16.75
Tip:        6
Tax:           3.45
Please pay:  61.02
```

Specifier	Data Type	Explanation	Code	Sample Input	Assignment
c	char	A single character. Whitespace characters (space, tab, or newline) will be assigned, not skipped.	%c	ABC	'A' [65]
d	int	PreANSI version of i. Still valid in most ANSI implementations.	%d	025pieces [Octal notation]	21 [decimal]
e, f, g	float	Decimal value in either standard or E notation.	%f	^^^62.15^ [^ is a space]	62.15
i	int	Integer value in decimal, octal, or hex notation.	%i	025pieces [Octal notation]	21 [decimal]
n	int	Scanf() assigns the number of characters read so far to this variable.	%n	12 34 56	8
o	int	Octal digits.	%o	42	34 [decimal]
p	pointer	An address. More about them later.			
s	string	More about those later.			
u	unsigned int	Decimal digits.	%u	3740	3740
x	int	Hex digits.	%x	BA	186 [decimal]
[É]	string	More about those later.			

▶ TABLE 3–3
Type Specifiers for scanf()

Prompts

The printf()s before each of the scanf()s in this example are called **prompts**. They exist to display something on the screen to tell the person at the keyboard what to type in. Can you imagine the previous program running without those printf()s? In almost every conceivable case a scanf() should be preceded by a prompt.

Matching Characters

Characters other than conversion codes in the control string are matched with like characters in the input stream, and are discarded—that is, not assigned.

▶ Program 3–5

```
#include <stdio.h>

void main(void)
{  float weight, height;

   printf("Enter \"Subject is {weight} kg and {height} cm\"\n     ->");
   scanf("Subject is %f kg and %f cm", &weight, &height);
   printf("     Subject is %.2f pounds and %.2f inches.\n",
          weight * 2.2, height / 2.54);
}
```

Execution

```
Enter "Subject is {weight} kg and {height} cm"
     ->Subject is 75 kg and 185 cm
       Subject is 165.00 pounds and 72.83 inches.
```

In ➡Program 3–5, Subject is was matched and discarded, 75 converted and assigned to *weight*, kg and matched and discarded, 185 converted and assigned to *height*, and cm matched and discarded. This particular property of scanf() has little use in keyboard input—why make the input operator type all that extra stuff verbatim?—but later on we shall use a variation of scanf() to access data files, and those files may have a lot of characters that we may wish to discard in a particular application.

In both the *control string* and the input stream, all contiguous whitespace characters are treated as a single whitespace character. In other words, one whitespace character in the control string would match and discard 47 contiguous whitespace characters in the input stream and vice versa.

Size Modifiers

Like printf(), the scanf() conversion codes can have size modifiers to further define the data type of the assignment. The size modifiers h, for short, and l, for long, may modify any of the integral types, d, i, o, or x. The conversion code %ho, then, indicates that a set of octal digits will be assigned as a short unsigned int.

Under printf(), floats and doubles use the same conversion code, %f. When an assignment is made by scanf() we must differentiate between the two, so the lowercase l modifier is pressed into double duty. When it modifies a floating-point specifier, e, f, or g, it indicates a double. The uppercase L modifier still indicates a long double assignment. The conversion code %lf indicates a double assignment will be made.

Width Parameters

A width parameter tells scanf() the maximum number of characters that it should read to make the current conversion. The conversion stops, then, at the first inappropriate character or when the maximum number of characters is reached. Any characters beyond the maximum are left for the next conversion. For example (the keyboard input is in boldface):

➡Program 3–6

```
#include <stdio.h>

void main(void)
{  float x, y;

   printf("Enter two numbers: ");
   scanf("%4f %f", &x, &y);
   printf("Your numbers are: %f %f\n", x, y);
}
```

Execution

```
Enter two numbers: 12.3456 99
Your numbers are: 12.300000 456.000000
```

The first conversion, %4f, took the first four characters from the input stream, 12.3, and assigned them to the variable *x*. The input stream then contained 456 99. The second conversion, %f, skipped whitespace (there was none) and converted characters to the next inappropriate one, the space; so 456 was assigned to *y*. This left 99 in the input stream and some unexpected assignments to the variables. To correct this situation, the width parameter would have to be at least 7 or simply left out.

Flags

There is a single flag that can be used with a scanf() conversion code: the *. This flag does not change the reading and conversion of characters from the input stream, but the resultant value is not assigned, and there should be no variable in the argument list corresponding to this conversion. This, like matching characters, has limited value in keyboard input but greater value in some of the other functions derived from the scanf().

The complete form of a conversion code for scanf() is (items in brackets are optional):

```
%[*][width][size]type
```

Flushing the Input Stream

If the person at the keyboard is not careful to give responses that fit the control string in the scanf(), there is a chance that extra characters will be left in the input stream waiting to be converted by the next scanf(). For example, the first execution of ➡Program 3–7 shows how it should operate. In the second execution, 1.23 was typed in as the integer. The scanf() converted to the first inappropriate character, the decimal point, and assigned the value 1 to the variable *i*. At that point, the input stream contained .23. The next scanf() found characters in the stream. They were appropriate for a float; so without waiting for any further input, it converted them and assigned the value 0.23 to *f*.

➡Program 3–7

```
#include <stdio.h>

void main(void)
{   int i;
    float f;

    printf("Enter an integer: ");
1   scanf("%i", &i);
    printf("Enter a float: ");
3   scanf("%f", &f);
4   printf("Integer: %i. Float: %f\n", i, f);
}
```

Execution

```
Enter an integer: 1
Enter a float: 2.34
Integer: 1. Float: 2.340000
```

Execution

```
Enter an integer: 1.23
Enter a float: Integer: 1. Float: 0.230000
```

EXECUTION CHART

Line	Explanation	Stream Before Statement	Stream After Input	Stream After Statement	i	f
1	Input value for *i*.	- - - -	1.23	.23	1	- - - -
3	Input value for *f*.	.23	No input	- - - -	1	.23
4	Print values of *i* and *f*.	- - - -		- - - -	1	.23

The `fflush()` function,

```
fflush(stream)
```

will **flush**, in other words, empty, the *stream* given as its argument. In this case we want to flush the input stream, `stdin`; so if we add an `fflush(stdin)` function following the first `scanf()`, it will empty the stream of any characters that might have been left there.

➡Program 3–8

```
#include <stdio.h>

void main(void)
{  int i;
   float f;

   printf("Enter an integer: ");
1  scanf("%i", &i);
2  fflush(stdin);
   printf("Enter a float: ");
3  scanf("%f", &f);
4  printf("Integer: %i. Float: %f\n", i, f);
}
```

Execution

```
Enter an integer: 1.23
Enter a float: 4.56
Integer: 1. Float: 4.560000
```

EXECUTION CHART

Line	Explanation	Stream Before Statement	Stream After Input	Stream After Statement	i	f
1	Input value for *i*.	- - - -	1.23	.23	1	?
2	Empty the stream	.23		- - - -	1	?
3	Input value for *f*.	- - - -	4.56	- - - -	1	4.56
4	Print values of *i* and *f*.	- - - -		- - - -	1	4.56

In our listing of the ANSI functions in Appendix C, the `fflush()` function is listed under files because, as we shall see, streams are used with files as well as the keyboard and the screen.

PUTTING IT TOGETHER

Gleam and Glitter Jewelers make jewelry out of gold and diamonds. They have a program to estimate the cost of a piece by inputting the various materials and labor. They have put the cost of gold, diamonds, and labor in defined constants because these change from time to time, and they want to make modifications to the program easy. Their salespeople must know the cost of a piece in order to wheel and deal with potential customers, so G and G uses an ingenious cost code that only the salespeople, who are all computer freaks and are intimately familiar with hexadecimal numbers, will understand.

Their program follows this overall structure:

Input materials
Figure values of materials
Print value report
Print cost code

▶ **Program 3–9**

```c
#include <stdio.h>

#define GOLD_COST 312
#define DIAMOND_COST 1640
#define HOURLY_COST 55

void main(void)
{  float gold, gold_value, diamonds, diamond_value;
   float creation, creation_value;
   int carats, grade;

   /***************************************************** Input materials */
   printf("Gold - weight (oz), carats: ");
1  scanf("%f, %i", &gold, &carats);           /* Comma matches comma in input */
2  fflush(stdin);                        /* In case someone enters decimal value */
   printf("Diamonds - weight (carats), grade: ");
3  scanf("%f, %i", &diamonds, &grade);
   printf("Design and creation time (hours): ");
4  scanf("%f", &creation);

   /***************************************** Figure values of materials */
5  gold_value = gold * GOLD_COST * carats / 24;
6  diamond_value = DIAMOND_COST / 2 * (1 + grade / 5.);        /*Force float*/
7  creation_value = creation * HOURLY_COST;

   /************************************************* Print value report */
   printf("\nValue Analysis\n");
8  printf("  Gold:    %8.3f oz  @ %4i (%-3i carats) $%8.2f\n",
          gold, GOLD_COST, carats, gold_value);
9  printf("  Diamonds:%8.3f cts @ %4i (%-3i grade)   %8.2f\n",
          diamonds, DIAMOND_COST, grade, diamond_value);
10 printf("  Creation:%8.3f hrs @ %4i              %8.2f\n",
          creation, HOURLY_COST, creation_value);
11 printf("     Total value:                        $%8.2f\n\n",
          gold_value + diamond_value + creation_value);
```

—Continued

```
                                                              Print cost code */
12    printf("Cost code: %X\n",              /* Cost to the nearest dollar in hex */
            (unsigned) (gold_value + diamond_value + creation_value));
    }
```

Execution

```
Gold - weight (oz), carats: 1.864, 18.5
Diamonds - weight (carats), grade: 2.33, 4
Design and creation time (hours): 12.5

Value Analysis
  Gold:      1.864 oz  @  312 (18  carats) $  436.18
  Diamonds:  2.330 cts @ 1640 (4    grade)   1476.00
  Creation:  12.500 hrs @   55                687.50
     Total value:                          $ 2599.68

Cost code: A27
```

EXECUTION CHART

Line	Explanation	Input Stream	*gold*	*carats*
1	Enter line at keyboard.	1.864, 18.5\n	?	?
	Skip any whitespace and convert to inappropriate float character (%f).	, 18.5\n	1.864	?
	Match comma and whitespace (,).	18.5\n	1.864	?
	Convert to inappropriate integer character (%i).	.5\n	1.864	18
2	Flush input stream.		1.864	18
			diamonds	*grade*
3	Enter line at keyboard.	2.33, 4\n	?	?
	Convert to inappropriate float character (%f).	, 4\n	2.33	?
	Match comma and whitespace (,).	4\n	2.33	?
	Convert to inappropriate integer character (%i).	\n	2.33	4
			creation	
4	Enter line at keyboard.	\n12.5\n	?	
	Skip any whitespace and convert to inappropriate float character (%f).	\n	12.5	
			gold_val	*diam_val* *creat_val*
5	Calculate gold value.	\n	436.176	? ?
6	Calculate diamond value. Since *grade* is integer, must force division to float.	\n	436.176	1476.0 ?
7	Calculate creation value.	\n	436.176	1476.0 687.5
8	Output gold information.	\n	436.176	1476.0 687.5
9	Output diamond information.	\n	436.176	1476.0 687.5
10	Output creation information.	\n	436.176	1476.0 687.5
11	Output total value.	\n	436.176	1476.0 687.5
12	Output total value in hex.	\n	436.176	1476.0 687.5

SUMMARY

A number of instructions available to us in C are **compiler directives** rather than instructions to be executed as part of the program. The #include directive instructs the computer to insert a file of source code at the point of the directive. Typical files to include are the header files that come with the compiler and other source code files that we or someone else may have written that are useful to the current program.

Another commonly used directive is #define, which allows us to specify a set of characters and a replacement string. At compile time, the compiler substitutes the replacement string for all occurrences of the defined characters. The specified characters are typically used as **defined constants**. Putting them at the beginning of the program makes them easy to find if we want to change them, and using words rather than numbers can make the program more readable.

ANSI C provides for standardized input and output using **streams**. Three that are automatically established by C are stdin, stdout, and stderr. The printf() function directs characters to the standard output stream, stdout. This function's first argument is a **control string**, which defines the format for the output. In addition to printable characters, the control string contains **conversion codes** that specify the format for various values. These values must be supplied in additional arguments to the printf() function.

Conversion codes begin with a % and end with a **type specifier**, which defines the data type of the conversion. An optional **size modifier** further defines the type. The optional **width** specification defines the minimum width of a field, and the optional **precision** specifier defines the number of decimal places for floating-point numbers or the minimum number of digits printed (with zero fill) for integral data types. A * for width and/or precision means that the parameter will be supplied by the next argument in the list.

The optional **flags** specify the printed value's justification in the field, whether or not positive signs print, leading zeros, leading spaces for positive numbers, special formats, and so forth.

The scanf() function gets values from the stdin stream in almost the opposite way that printf() puts characters in the stdout stream. A major difference is that the arguments to scanf() must be addresses rather than variables. The ampersand in front of a variable name refers to the variable's address.

Input stream values (except for single-character input) are converted by skipping any leading whitespace and converting characters up to the next character inappropriate for the data type. Noncode characters in the control string are matched and discarded by scanf(). A keyboard input is typically preceded by a **prompt**, a screen output informing the user of the kind of data expected.

The scanf() function uses size modifiers similar to printf(). The width parameter specifies the maximum number of characters to be taken from the input stream. There is no precision parameter, and the only flag is the asterisk, which tells scanf() that this conversion will be made, but the result will not be assigned. There should not be an address in the argument list for it.

The fflush() function will **flush** (empty) a stream, including stdin.

KEY TERMS (in order of appearance)

Compiler directive	stdout	Precision
Preprocessor	stderr	Flag
#include	printf()	scanf()
Header file	Control string	Prompt
#define	Conversion code	fflush()
Defined constant	Type specifier	Flush
Stream	Size modifier	
stdin	Width	

REVIEW QUESTIONS

1. What is the difference between a compiler directive and a program statement? At which point in the process does each one act?

2. Are the things in an include file source code or object code? Can you see the actual instructions put in your program by an #include directive?

3. What is the difference between " " and < > in an #include directive on your system?

4. What does the #define directive do?

5. Why would you use defined constants in your program?

6. Why does ANSI C utilize streams for input and output rather than simply going directly to the input and output devices?

7. What three standard streams are provided for in ANSI C? What devices are they usually associated with? What are they used for?

8. What is the first argument to the printf() function? What are the subsequent arguments?

9. What is the purpose of a conversion in either printf() or scanf()?

10. What character begins a conversion code?

11. What are the possible characters that end conversion codes for printf() and scanf() and what do they mean?

12. What is a size modifier in a conversion code, and what are the possible ones for printf() and scanf()?

13. What is a width parameter in a conversion code, and what does it mean for printf() and scanf()?

14. What is the precision parameter in a conversion code, and what does it mean for printf() and scanf()?

15. What are flags in a conversion code, and what are the possible ones for printf() and scanf()?

16. What are the conditions that stop a conversion in a scanf()?

17. What is a prompt, and how do we display them?

18. How do matching characters work in a scanf()?

19. To what use do we put the fflush() function?

EXERCISES

1. Write the proper directive to put the source file *GOODIES.INC* in your program, assuming that:

   a.   the file is in the default directory.
   b.   the file is in an include directory specified by your compiler.

2. Write the proper directive to change each instance of METERS_TO_INCHES to 39.37.

3. Why does ANSI C use input and output streams? How does the stream's use of a particular computer's operating systems facilitate compatibility between different types of computers?

4. Write the printf() conversion codes to provide the proper output from the values given. The vertical bars (|) show the whole field including spaces (^ denotes a space). If vertical bars are not given, no width should be specified.

a.	46	|46^|	b.	8.046	|^^8.05|
c.	73.28	|+73.3|	d.	86425	|^086425|
e.	214	326 (Octal)	f.	214	D6 (Hex)
g.	67	C	h.	35.6	|3.560E+01^^|

5. Show the output of these values given the printf() conversion codes (use ^ to denote a space).

a.	'A'	%3i	b.	'A'	%c
c.	4.26	%-6.1f	d.	.00000425	%g
e.	38.567	%12.2E	f.	16	%x
g.	1.2345	%+.2f	h.	52	%03i

6. Show the assignments made from these keyboard inputs given the scanf() conversion codes (^ denotes a space).

a.	^^A	%c	b.	^29.6	%i
c.	14.62	%f	d.	1D	%x
e.	1234	%3i	f.	2.653E3	%f

PROGRAMS

1. Using printf() with control strings that contain only whitespace (including newlines) and %*c conversion codes, write a program that prints the following pattern. You need no variables; your arguments after the control strings will be specific values.

Execution

```
 >
  > >
  >   >
>>>     >
  >   >
  > >
  >
```

2. Write a program that accepts two numbers from the keyboard and prints the following information.

Variables

```
first
second
```

Execution

```
First number?  7
Second number? 2
The second goes into the first 3 times
with a remainder of 1.
The quotient is 3.5.
```

3. Write a program to print out a customer bill for Ajax Auto Repair. The parts and labor charges are input and a 6 percent sales tax is charged on parts but not on labor. Be sure to line up the output as shown.

Variables

```
Parts
Labor
SalesTax
Total
```

Execution

```
PARTS? 104.50
LABOR? 182.15


     AJAX AUTO REPAIR
     SERVICE INVOICE
PARTS            $ 104.50
LABOR              182.15
SALES TAX            6.27
TOTAL            $ 292.92
```

4. The Ajax Company would like a program to compute an employee's paycheck. The employee's gross pay is the hours worked times the hourly pay. Income tax withholding, FICA tax, payroll savings plan, retirement, and health insurance are subtracted from the gross pay. From time to time the various rates (all variables that end in _RATE) for these deductions change, so the values should be put in #define directives.

Constants

FIT_RATE	15% of gross pay
FICA_RATE	6.2% of gross pay
SAVINGS_RATE	3% of gross pay
RETIREMENT_RATE	8.5% of gross pay
HEALTH_INS	$3.75 per employee

Variables

Hours	
HourlyPay	
GrossPay	
FIT	Federal income tax withholding
FICA	Social security tax withholding
Savings	Payroll savings
Retirement	
NetPay	Gross pay less deductions

Execution

```
HOURS? 40
HOURLY PAY? 7.50

GROSS PAY:          $ 300.00

FEDERAL INCOME TAX: $  45.00
FICA:               $  18.60
PAYROLL SAVINGS:    $   9.00
RETIREMENT:         $  25.50
HEALTH INSURANCE:   $   3.75

NET PAY:            $ 198.15
```

5. Write a program to figure out interest on a loan. It should allow input of principal, rate in percent, and time in days. Use the following variables. Don't add any variables, don't leave any out. Your output should look like the one below.

$$interest = principal \times \frac{rate}{100} \times \frac{time}{365}$$

Variables		Execution
principal		PRINCIPAL? 1450
rate		RATE, TIME? 14.5 250
time	Integer	
interest		INTEREST: $144.01

6. Write a program to figure out the circumference, cross-sectional area, and volume of a sphere, given a radius. The radius should be input and the rest printed out as shown.

Variables

		Execution
pi	(3.1416)	RADIUS: 25
radius		
circum	$(2 \times pi \times radius)$	CIRCUMFERENCE: 157.080
area	$(pi \times radius^2)$	CROSS-SECTIONAL AREA: 1963.500
volume	$(^4/_3 \times pi \times radius^3)$	VOLUME: 65449.996

7. Write a program that will accept keyboard input of various coins and return the total value.

Variables

input	Value from keyboard
total	To accumulate the value of the inputs

Execution

```
Half dollars? 3
Quarters?    3
Dimes?       2
Nickels?     3
Pennies?     7
Your total is $2.67.
```

8. Write a program that accepts a number of seconds from the keyboard and converts it into days, hours, minutes, and seconds. Use integer arithmetic and the remainder operator.

Variable

seconds

Execution

```
How many seconds? 106478
Days:     1
Hours:    5
Minutes: 34
Seconds: 38
```

THE SELECTION STRUCTURE

We talked about structured programming and the three control structures in Chapter 1, but up to this point we have used only one, the sequence structure. We now know enough programming to use the other two effectively. First we will examine the selection structure, including:

1. Setting up conditions for choosing one branch or another.
2. Types of operators we use in these conditions.
3. The principal statement used to create a selection.
4. Extending our selection to more than two branches.
5. C's special, multibranch structure.
6. An expression that includes a selection.

Here we are at the fork in the road. We have to get to the place beyond, but should we take the high route or the low route? If it's cold, the high route might be blocked with snow. If it's warm, the low route might be uncomfortably hot. It's decision time. If the temperature is over 60 degrees Fahrenheit, we'll take the high route. Otherwise, it's the low.

But so far we have worked only with the sequence structure—one operation after another. Using only that simple sequence, we would have difficulty with this type of operation. This situation is the basis for the second of our structures, the **selection structure**. We have two possible paths, or **branches**, and based on some condition, we will take one branch or the other. No matter which branch we take we will end up in the same place.

CONDITIONS

There must be some condition set up to tell the computer to take one branch or the other. This condition will evaluate to either true or false, and typically is some kind of comparison. The condition in the example above is based on the temperature. It is either over 60 degrees, true, or it isn't, false.

A **condition** in C typically consists of one or more comparisons that compare one value to another. A comparison has the form

```
expression comparison_operator expression
```

For example:

```
x + 4 > 9
```

where we compare the value of the expression $x + 4$ with the value 9. An expression, remember, is anything that reduces to a single value; so in essence, a comparison always compares two values. The *comparison_operator*, > in our example, tells the computer how the comparison should be made. If the value of x is 7, then $7 + 4$ is 11, 11 is greater than 9, and the comparison is true.

Relational and Equality Operators

The *comparison_operator* comes from one of two categories: **relational operators** and **equality operators**. The operators differ, of course, in function, but the categories also differ in precedence with the relational operators being higher than the equality operators. Both sets of operators are shown in ➡Table 4–1. (The entire set of operators is shown in Appendix B.) Be sure to notice that the equal operator (==) is not the same as the assignment operator (=).

Operators of both categories have left-to-right associativity. In precedence, of the operators we have examined so far, all the arithmetic operators are first, followed by the relational operators, followed by the equality operators, and ending with the assignment operators. This order of evaluation is convenient because the arithmetic expressions are reduced to values first, and then the values are compared according to the comparison operators.

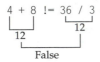

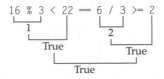

Operator	Explanation	Symbol	Example
Arithmetic — Discussed in Chapter 2			
Relational — Left-to-right associativity			
Greater	First greater than second?	>	`x+y > z-19`
Less	First less than second?	<	`cost < maximum-100`
Greater or equal	First greater than or equal to second?	>=	`load >= limit`
Less or equal	First less than or equal to second?	<=	`TestValue <= Norm`
Equality — Left-to-right associativity			
Equal	First equals second?	==	`Count+1 == EndCount`
Not equal	First not equal to second?	!=	`CheckSum != NewSum`
Logical AND — Left-to-right associativity			
	First and second true?	&&	`day > 28 && month != 2`
Logical OR — Left-to-right associativity			
	First or second or both true?	||	`Score > 90 || Grade == 'A'`
Conditional — Right-to-left associativity			
	If test true, perform first expression, otherwise perform second.	? :	`x > 4 ? p + 9 : p - 14`
Assignment — Discussed in Chapter 2			

▶▶TABLE 4–1

Relational, Equality, Logical, and Conditional Operators

Logical Operators

Our conditions can consist of more than one comparison. We can tie multiple comparisons together with **logical operators**, of which we have two—**AND** (&&) and **OR** (||). Using the AND operator, if the comparisons on both sides are true, then the whole condition is true. If even one comparison is false, then the whole condition is false.

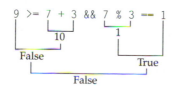

Using the OR operator, if either or both of the comparisons are true, then the whole condition is true. Both comparisons would have to be false for the whole condition to be false.

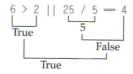

Many comparisons can be combined together using many ANDs and ORs. The AND operator is higher in precedence than OR. Both of them are lower than the comparison operators, but higher than assignment, as you can see in ▶▶Table 4–1. This means that comparisons are evaluated first and then combined by the logical operators. Order of evaluation can, of course, be adjusted any way we want by using parentheses.

WHAT'S TRUE AND WHAT'S FALSE

Could you lie to a computer? Easily. The computer, being a nonthinking machine, has no idea what is true or false, good or bad, or nice or nasty. Our human concepts of true and false are translated into strictly numeric terms for the computer. In C anything that evaluates to true is assigned the value one; false is assigned zero. The statement

```
printf("%i %i\n", 6 == 6, 3 > 9);
```

would produce

```
1 0
```

on the screen.

When trying to decide true versus false, C interprets any nonzero value as true and zero as false. The value of

```
7 > 3 && 14
```

is true, or one.

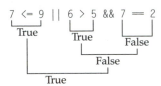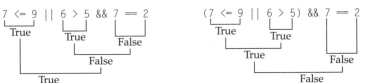

The **NOT** operator (!) is a logical operator, but it is also unary, acting on only one expression. In precedence and associativity, it falls with the other unary operators. The logical NOT operator makes what was true false, and what was false true.

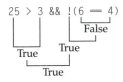

THE if STATEMENT

In C, the selection structure is implemented by the if statement, which has this general form:

```
if (condition) statement;
```

We can, and usually do, substitute a block of statements for the single *statement* in the general form, giving us the more common form

```
if (condition)
{   statement;
    statement;
      . . .
    }
```

The *condition* in the `if` statement is as we have described earlier and, of course, will evaluate to either true or false. If the condition is true, the statements within the block will be executed; otherwise, they won't. Notice that the condition is enclosed in parentheses, and there is no semicolon after the condition. To put a semicolon there would end the entire structure at that point.

To illustrate, let us assume that the Ajax Company has an automatic apple scale that weighs each apple and labels it accordingly. Unfortunately, the input interface is broken so an operator will have to type the weights into a keyboard. Apples are normally priced at 20¢ each, but if one weighs over 10 ounces, it is a premium apple and worth another 10¢. ➡Program 4–1 shows how we price our apples.

➡Program 4–1

```
#include <stdio.h>

void main(void)
{  float weight, price = .2;

   printf("Enter weight of apple: ");
   scanf("%f", &weight);
   printf("Ajax ");
   if (weight > 10)
   {  printf("Premium ");
      price += .1;
   }
   printf("Apple. $%4.2f.\n", price);
}
```

Execution

```
Enter weight of apple: 11.3
Ajax Premium Apple. $0.30.
```

Execution

```
Enter weight of apple: 7.8
Ajax Apple. $0.20.
```

The else Clause

Like all selections, the one in the apple program above has two branches. One is to add ten cents to the price of the apple and print "Premium" on the label; the other is to do nothing. In most cases, though, the second branch, the false branch, involves some action. To accommodate this we can add an **else** clause to the if statement.

```
if (condition) statement; else statement;
```

or more commonly

```
if (condition)
{  statement;
   statement;
    ...
}else
{  statement;
   statement;
    ...
}
```

The Ajax people don't want to call their apples just "Ajax Apples" even if they are only normal apples; so an apple weighing ten ounces or less will be called an "Ajax Juicy Apple." ➡Program 4–2 is the new, improved program.

▶▶Program 4–2

```
#include <stdio.h>

void main(void)
{  float weight, price = .2;

   printf("Enter weight of apple: ");
   scanf("%f", &weight);
   printf("Ajax ");
   if (weight > 10)
   {  printf("Premium ");
      price += .1;
   }
   else
   {  printf("Juicy ");
   }
   printf("Apple. $%4.2f.\n", price);
}
```

Execution

```
Enter weight of apple: 9.2
Ajax Juicy Apple. $0.20.
```

Execution

```
Enter weight of apple: 10.1
Ajax Premium Apple. $0.30.
```

Bowing to market pressures, the Ajax people now have set up four grades of apples. Premium apples still weigh more than 10 ounces and cost an extra 10¢. Juicy apples are the normal grade at a normal price but they have to weigh more than 8 ounces. Those weighing more than 6 ounces but up to 8 are called snack apples and cost 5¢ less. All others are cooking apples selling for 10¢ less. This leaves us with four branches to deal with, but our selection structure only has two.

The solution, as shown in ▶▶Program 4–3, is to branch one of the branches. In the Ajax case, if the weight is not more than 10 ounces, our program will test to see if it is more than eight. The first else clause contains a complete selection structure with two branches and the condition weight > 8. The else clause within that selection structure will also contain a complete selection structure with two branches and the condition weight > 6.

▶▶Program 4–3

```
#include <stdio.h>

void main(void)
{  float weight, price = .2;

   printf("Enter weight of apple: ");
   scanf("%f", &weight);
   printf("Ajax ");
   if (weight > 10)
   {  printf("Premium ");
      price += .1;
   }
```

—Continued

```
    else
    {  if (weight > 8)                                /* Brace necessary? */
       {  printf("Juicy ");
       }
       else
       {  if (weight > 6)                             /* Brace necessary? */
          {  printf("Snack ");
             price -= .05;
          }
          else
          {  printf("Cooking ");
             price -= .1;
          }
       }                                              /* Brace necessary? */
    }                                                 /* Brace necessary? */
    printf("Apple. $%4.2f.\n", price);
}
```

Executions

```
Enter weight of apple: 12
Ajax Premium Apple. $0.30.


Enter weight of apple: 9.2
Ajax Juicy Apple. $0.20.
```

Executions

```
Enter weight of apple: 7.5
Ajax Snack Apple. $0.15.


Enter weight of apple: 5.9
Ajax Cooking Apple. $0.10.
```

The else if **Construct**

If you examine the sets of braces with the comments Brace necessary? beside
them you will see that these brace sets are really not necessary. Each of them
encloses the material within an else clause, but that material in each case
consists of only an if statement. Granted, the if statements contain statements within their clauses, but still they are single if statements. This section of the program could be rewritten as shown in ➡️Program 4–4.

➡️Program 4–4

```
if (weight > 10)
{  printf("Premium ");
   price += .1;
}
else
   if (weight > 8)                                    /* Brace not necessary */
   {  printf("Juicy ");
   }
   else
      if (weight > 6)                                 /* Brace not necessary */
      {  printf("Snack ");
         price -= .05;
      }
      else
      {  printf("Cooking ");
         price -= .1;
      }
```

Branching of `else` clauses with `if` statements is so common that the `else` followed by the `if` is often written on one line almost as if it was one key word, `else if`. It is not, but the indenting that results outlines a very clear multibranch structure that is actually made of multiple two-branch `if else` statements. This section could be rewritten as in ▶Program 4–5.

▶**Program 4–5**

```
if (weight > 10)
{  printf("Premium ");
   price += .1;
}
else if (weight > 8)
{  printf("Juicy ");                              /* Brace necessary? */
}                                                 /* Brace necessary? */
else if (weight > 6)
{  printf("Snack ");
   price -= .05;
}
else
{  printf("Cooking ");
   price -= .1;
}
```

You might have also noticed that the set of braces commented are not necessary either. There is only one statement, `printf("Juicy ")`, within them. These braces could be eliminated, but to maintain consistency, we probably should retain them.

THE `switch` STATEMENT

The C language includes a multibranch alternative to the `if` statement called the `switch` statement. It has some severe limitations, but within these limitations, it can be very handy.

```
switch (integral_expression) {statement block}
```

The *statement block* is a number of statements within the various branches. The beginnings of the branches are distinguished by case identifiers, all beginning with the key word `case`.

```
switch (integral_expression)
{  case integral_value:
      statement;
      statement;
   case integral_value:
      statement;
      statement;
   case as many as are necessary:
      ...
   default:
      statement;
      statement;
}
```

The *integral_expression* following the switch key word must evaluate to some integral data type, char or int; floating point results are not allowed. The value of the expression becomes a case value to be matched to the possible case identifiers within the statement block following the switch. For example, if the *integral_expression* evaluated to 6, the switch would look for case 6.

Each of the cases within the block following switch has an *integral_value*, which, along with case and a following colon, becomes the identifier. For example, two of the cases might be case 9: and case 6:. The switch causes the program to jump directly to the matching identifier; in other words, the next code to be executed will be that immediately following the identifier. In the example, that would be the code following case 6:. If there is no matching label, the jump is to the default label. The default label is not absolutely necessary and, if it appears, may be in any position within the block, but it may appear only once. In practice, there is usually a default label, and it is typically the last one.

In ➡Program 4–6, the Ajax Company, with their usual tendency toward hyperbole, have modified their apple-labeling program.

➡Program 4–6

```
#include <stdio.h>

void main(void)
{   float price = 0;
    char grade;

    printf("Enter grade of apple: ");
    scanf(" %c", &grade);
    printf("Ajax ");
    switch (grade)
    {   case 'P':
        case 'p':
            price += .1;
            printf("Super ");
        case 'J':
        case 'j':
            price += .05;
            printf("Excellent ");
        case 'S':
        case 's':
            price += .05;
            printf("Delicious ");
        default:
            price += .1;
    }
    printf("Apple. $%4.2f.\n", price);
}
```

Executions

```
Enter grade of apple: p
Ajax Super Excellent Delicious Apple. $0.30.

Enter grade of apple: J
Ajax Excellent Delicious Apple. $0.20.
```

Executions

```
Enter grade of apple: s
Ajax Delicious Apple. $0.15.

Enter grade of apple: q
Ajax Apple. $0.10.
```

Notice that a jump to a case identifier continues execution from that point on. Subsequent case identifiers in the code are ignored. In other words, a jump to one branch will execute all the code in the switch block from that point on, not just the code between that identifier and the next.

In our example, to allow for either capital or lowercase letters in the input, two cases are put together. If the value of *grade* is *j*, execution will continue from case 'j':. If *grade* is *J*, execution will continue from case 'J': passing right by case 'j':. If *grade* is *P*, of course, execution will flow from case 'P': down through the entire block, passing all of the other identifiers.

As we stated in Chapter 2, character values such as 'P' are integral numeric values—the ASCII codes for those characters. The program would have run the same had we substituted case 80:, using the ASCII value for *P*, for case 'P':.

A little review of punctuation is in order here. Notice that the *integral_expression* following switch is enclosed in parentheses and that there is no semicolon after the statement. All the statements within the following structure are contained within one set of braces. There need not be separate sets of braces in each branch, although there certainly could be if the structure warranted it. Each case identifier is followed by a colon, which tells C that it is a case identifier.

The break Statement

The switch statement as demonstrated above is not a very effective multi-branch structure because the branches are not separated. One branch flows through all the subsequent branches including default:. The break statement can solve that problem. The break statement causes an immediate jump to the statement following a switch structure. If we put break statements at the end of each of the branches, C will execute the statements after the case, but jump to the statement after the closing brace when it encounters the break.

A less effusive C programmer has used break to modify the Ajax program.

▶ Program 4-7

```
#include <stdio.h>

void main(void)
{  float price;
   char grade;

   printf("Enter grade of apple: ");
   scanf(" %c", &grade);
   printf("Ajax ");
   switch (grade)
   {  case 'P':
      case 'p':
         price = .3;
         printf("Super ");
         break;
      case 'J':
      case 'j':
         price = .2;
         printf("Excellent ");
         break;
```

—*Continued*

```
        case 'S':
        case 's':
            price = .15;
            printf("Delicious ");
            break;
        default:
            price = .1;
    }
    printf("Apple. $%4.2f.\n", price);
}
```

Executions

```
Enter grade of apple: p
Ajax Super Apple. $0.30.


Enter grade of apple: J
Ajax Excellent Apple. $0.20.
```

Executions

```
Enter grade of apple: S
Ajax Delicious Apple. $0.15.


Enter grade of apple: e
Ajax Apple. $0.10.
```

The vast majority of switch structures use breaks at the end of each branch.

THE CONDITIONAL EXPRESSION

We have been examining ways of forming two-branch or multibranch structures using sets of statements. C also gives us the **conditional expression**, using the operators ? and :, which allows us to set up a two-branch situation within an expression. The general form of a conditional expression is

```
condition ? true_expression : false_expression
```

C first evaluates the condition to true or false. If the condition is true then C will evaluate the true_expression, which becomes the value of the entire conditional expression. Otherwise C will evaluate the false_expression. For example, if the value of x is 150 then the value of this expression,

```
x > 100 ? x * 1.1 : x * .9
```

is 165, the value of the true_expression.

This is not like an if statement where the value of the condition allows the program to go to one set of statements or another. A conditional expression, like any other expression, reduces to a single value. As an example, let us say that salespeople are paid their salary plus a commission of 10% on all sales if they sell up to and including $1000, but 12% on all sales plus a bonus of $100 if they sell over $1000.

```
pay = salary + (sales > 1000 ? sales *.12 + 100 : sales * .1);
```

If *sales* was $2000 then the value of the entire conditional expression, everything within the parentheses, would be $340—*sales* × .12 + 100.—which would be added to *salary* and the result stored in *pay*.

The parentheses are important in the example above because the precedence of the conditional operators is very low, just above the assignment operators. Its associativity is right to left. Again, refer to ➡Table 4–1 or Appendix B.

The data type of the entire conditional expression is determined by both of the expressions contained within it, not by which one is eventually chosen. The usual promotion rules apply. If the true expression evaluates to `int` and the false to `float`, then the type of the whole expression is `float` even if the condition is true.

PUTTING IT TOGETHER

Each computer that comes into the warehouse has a product code that tells something about that particular machine. The following program deciphers that product code. A valid product code starts with an uppercase alpha character. If that is not present, the program prints an error message and quits. The overall structure is:

```
Input product code
If code not in range
    Print error message
Else
    Decipher code
End if
```

Deciphering the code is a bit more complicated, so we can expand that part of the pseudocode.

```
Input product code
If code not in range
    Print error message
Else
                    [Decipher code]
    Country of origin
    Type of CPU
    Size of hard disk
    Size of floppy disk
End if
```

The rest of the expansion of the process is done directly in the code in ➡Program 4–8. Notice that the `scanf()` function is set up to assign the values to the proper variables given a product code with this format:

Characters	Conversion Code	Data Type	Variable
1	`%c`	`char`	*Country*
1	`%li` (one i, not el i)	`int`	*Processor*
3	`%3f`	`float`	*HardDrive*
Any number	`%f`	`float`	*Floppy*

```
#include <stdio.h>

void main(void)
{  char Country;
   int Processor;
   float HardDrive, Floppy;

   /************************************************** Input product code */
   printf("Enter product code: ");
1  scanf("%c%1i%3f%f", &Country, &Processor, &HardDrive, &Floppy);
2  if (Country < 'A' || Country > 'Z')                    /* Not alpha start */
3     printf("   Invalid product code.");
   else                                            /* Decipher good product code */
   {                                                     /* Country of origin */
      printf("Made in ");
4     switch (Country)
5     {  case 'U':                        /* Both U and A (America) mean U.S. */
6        case 'A':
7           printf("United States\n");
8           break;
9        case 'J':
10          printf("Japan\n");
11          break;
12       case 'S':
13          printf("Singapore\n");
14          break;
15       case 'K':
16          printf("Korea\n");
17          break;
18       default:
19          printf("<Country invalid>\n");
      }
      /***************************************************** Type of CPU */
      printf("Processor: ");
20    switch (Processor)
21    {  case 3:
22          printf("386\n");
23          break;
24       case 4:
25          printf("486\n");
26          break;
27       case 5:
28          printf("Pentium\n");
29          break;
30       default:
31          printf("<Invalid processor>\n");
      }
      /********************************************** Size of hard disk */
            /* Hard drives for Pentium computers stated in gigabytes in */
            /* product code and must be converted; all others in megabytes */
32    printf("Hard disk: %g MB\n",
            Processor == 5 ? HardDrive * 1000 : HardDrive);
```

—Continued

```
          /******************************************  Size of floppy disk */
          printf("Floppy: ");
33        if (Floppy == 360)
34            printf("360 KB\n");
35        else if (Floppy == 720)
36            printf("720 KB\n");
37        else if (Floppy == 1.2)
38            printf("1.2 MB\n");
39        else if (Floppy == 1.4)
40            printf("1.44 MB\n");
          else
41            printf("<Invalid floppy>\n");
      }
  }
```

Execution

```
Enter product code: S53.61.8
Made in Singapore
Processor: Pentium
Hard disk: 3600 MB
Floppy: <Invalid floppy>
```

EXECUTION CHART

Line	Explanation	Input Stream	Country	Processor	HardDrive	Floppy
1	Enter line at keyboard.	S53.61.8\n	?	?	?	?
	Assign first character.	53.61.8\n	S	?	?	?
	Convert one character to int.	3.61.8\n	S	5	?	?
	Convert three characters to float.	1.8\n	S	5	3.6	?
	Convert to inappropriate float character.	\n	S	5	3.6	1.8
2	See if *Country* out of range *A – Z*. It isn't.	\n	S	5	3.6	1.8
4	Look for case S:. Find it in line 12.	\n	S	5	3.6	1.8
13	Print *Singapore*.	\n	S	5	3.6	1.8
14	Jump beyond end of switch structure.	\n	S	5	3.6	1.8
20	Look for case 5:. Find it in line 27.	\n	S	5	3.6	1.8
28	Print *Pentium*.	\n	S	5	3.6	1.8
29	Jump beyond end of switch structure.	\n	S	5	3.6	1.8
32	Print hard-drive size. *Processor* equals 5, so execute expression after ?.	\n	S	5	3.6	1.8
33	See if *Floppy* equals 360. It doesn't.	\n	S	5	3.6	1.8
35	See if *Floppy* equals 720. It doesn't.	\n	S	5	3.6	1.8
37	See if *Floppy* equals 1.2. It doesn't.	\n	S	5	3.6	1.8
39	See if *Floppy* equals 1.4. It doesn't.	\n	S	5	3.6	1.8
41	Print *Invalid floppy*.	\n	S	5	3.6	1.8

SUMMARY

The **selection structure** contains two **branches**. Which branch the execution will take depends on a **condition** consisting of one or more **comparisons**. Comparisons are made of expressions connected by **relational operators** or **equality operators**. Comparisons can be tied together with the **logical operators and** and **or**. The **not operator** is a unary operator that makes what was true false, and vice versa.

The `if` statement implements the selection structure. It may contain only one true branch, in which case the false branch is to do nothing; or it may have an `else` clause where the false branch is stated. To form a multibranch structure, one branch of an `if else` statement may contain another complete `if else` statement. It is so common to branch the `else` branch of the selection structure that most programmers treat that construct as a single multibranch structure.

The `switch` statement sets up a more limited multibranch structure by allowing the program to jump to any of a number of case identifiers. The integral expression following switch is evaluated, and C searches for a corresponding value following any number of `case` statements. If it finds no match, it looks for a `default` label. Execution resumes at the appropriate label.

A `break` statement causes the execution to transfer to the statement following the end of the `switch` structure. These `break`s are often used to separate the `switch` structure into individual branches.

A **conditional expression** allows us to put a limited kind of selection within an expression. C evaluates the condition before the question mark and if it is true will evaluate the expression before the colon; otherwise, it will evaluate the one after.

KEY TERMS (in order of appearance)

Selection structure	Or
Branch	Not operator
Condition	`if`
Relation	`else`
Relational operator	`switch`
Equality operator	`case`
Inequality operator	`default`
Logical operator	`break`
And	Conditional expression

REVIEW QUESTIONS

1. What is meant by "branches" in a program?

2. To what two values may a condition evaluate? How is each represented numerically?

3. What is the typical, general form of a comparison?

4. Name the two classes of comparison operators and list the members of each class. Which class has a higher precedence?

5. What are the three logical operators and how do they fall in precedence?

6. Outline the typical structure of an `if else` pattern.

7. Outline the typical structure of a multibranch process using the `else if` construct.

8. Outline the general form of a multibranch structure using `switch`.

9. How does `switch` use case identifiers?

10. What is the purpose of a `break` statement in a multibranch structure using `switch`?

11. Show the general form of the expression that allows us to put a selection in an expression.

EXERCISES

1. In mathematics, we might state a range for x as $1 < x < 5$. Show how we should write the expression in C.

2. Correct the errors in this program segment:

```
if y > 25
    x = 2;
    printf("x is %i\n", x);
else
    y = 19
```

3. Write the condition that is true if $6 \leq x \leq 25$.

4. If $a = 1$, $b = 2$, and $c = 3$ are the following conditions true or false?

   a.   `a >= c - b`   b.   `b / 2 == a || c < 3`

   c.   `b < c -2 || a * 3 >= c && b > a`   d.   `5 || !b && c`

5. The following code segment compiles without error, but it prints *that's it* no matter what the value of x is. What's wrong?

```
if (x = 4)
    printf("That's it\n");
else
    printf("Wrong number\n");
```

6. Put the following program segment in proper structured format using the `else if` construct.

```
if (p >= 6) {x = 25; printf("High p value\n");} else if (p >= 2) {x = 50;
printf("Minimal p value\n");} else {x = 100;
printf("p below minimum\n");}
```

7. Do the same for the program segment in Exercise 6, but use the nested `if`s instead of the `else if` construct.

8. With traffic lights, R (for red) means "Stop," Y means "Caution," and G means "Go." Any other color letter means "Weird." Given the statements below, write the program segment that prints what the color letter means. Use the `else if` construct.

```
printf("Color letter: ");
scanf(" %c", &color);
```

9. Do the same for the program segment in Exercise 8 using the `switch` statement.

10. What is wrong with the following program segment?

```
float p, x, y;

Switch p + 14 / y
    case 12.6
        printf("1\n");
    case x
        printf("2\n");
    else
        printf("0\n");
```

11. What is the difference in these two program statements? What value of x is produced if its initial value is 2?

```
if (x > 0)                  if (x > 0)
    x += 2;                     x += 2;
else if (x > 2)             if (x > 2)
    x += 4;                     x += 4;
```

12. Replace the following program segment with one statement using a conditional expression.

```
if (x > 10)
    x += y + 150;
else
    x += y + 50
```

PROGRAMS

1. Write a program to compare two numbers with executions similar to the following.

   Variables

   ```
   number1, number2
   ```

   Executions

   ```
   Enter two numbers separated by a comma 37.589,24
   37.589 is greater than 24.

   Enter two numbers separated by a comma 26.3354,47.2
   47.2 is greater than 26.3354.

   Enter two numbers separated by a comma 84,84
   They are equal.
   ```

2. Adams County (county code *A*) has a 7 percent sales tax rate while the rest of the state has a 6 percent rate. Write a program to print out the amount owed on a purchase including sales tax given the amount of the purchase and the county.

   Variables

Purchase	Amount of purchase
County	
TaxRate	Determine using selection

   Execution

   ```
   AMOUNT OF PURCHASE? 15
   COUNTY? B
   TOTAL BILL: $ 15.90
   ```

   Execution

   ```
   AMOUNT OF PURCHASE? 26
   COUNTY? A
   TOTAL BILL: $ 27.82
   ```

3. Write a program that changes 12-hour, a.m.-p.m. time into 24-hour time. It should execute like the samples.

   Variables

   ```
   hours
   minutes;
   suffix    a - am; p - pm; n - noon; m - midnight
   ```

   Executions

   ```
   Enter time (H:Mx): 6:42p
   1842 hours

   Enter time (H:Mx): 9:5a
   0905 hours

   Enter time (H:Mx): 12:00m
   2400 hours

   Enter time (H:Mx): 12:0n
   1200 hours
   ```

4. A truth table shows the results of values when combined in certain ways. Write a program to show truth tables for combining true and false values using the and operator and or operator. Print out the results as the values of the and or or expressions (0 or 1).

Variables

T	Variable with true value
F	Variable with false value

Execution

```
AND Truth Table    OR Truth Table
    T  F               T  F
T   1  0           T   1  1
F   0  0           F   1  0
```

5. The Ace Courier Service charges $10 for the first pound or fraction thereof and $6 per pound for anything over one pound. Write a program that figures the charges for the packages.

Variable

```
weight
```

Execution

```
WEIGHT? .7
CHARGE: 10
```

Execution

```
WEIGHT? 2.5
CHARGE: 19
```

Execution

```
WEIGHT? 4.2
CHARGE: 29.2
```

6. Social Security (FICA) tax is currently 7.65% of earnings up to $50,400 for the year. Write a program that accepts earnings for the current week and previous cumulative earnings up to the current week, and returns the amount of FICA tax to be withheld.

Variables

```
CurrentEarnings
PrevEarnings
```

Execution

```
This week's pay? 700
Previous pay? 12600
FICA to withhold: $ 53.55
```

Execution

```
This week's pay? 1850
Previous pay? 50200
FICA to withhold: $ 15.30
```

7. Write a program to assign grade points according to a letter score. An *A* is 4 grade points; *B* is 3; *C*, 2; *D*, 1; and *F*, 0. Use the else if construct.

Variables

```
grade
grade_points
```

Executions

```
Letter grade: B
Grade points: 3

Letter grade: a
Grade points: 4
```

Executions

```
Letter grade: F
Grade points: 0

Letter grade: Q
Grade points: 0
```

8. Rewrite the program above using the switch statement.

9. The HiRisq Insurance Company determines auto insurance rates based on a driver's age, number of tickets in the last three years, and the value of the car. The base rate is 5 percent of the value of the car. Drivers under 25 years old pay 15 percent more and drivers from 25 through 29 pay 10 percent more. A driver with one ticket pays 10 percent over the rates already figured. Two tickets draws a 25 percent extra charge; three tickets adds 50 percent; and drivers with more

than three tickets are refused. Write a program to show a driver's insurance premium.

Variables

car   Value of car
age
tickets
premium   Total cost of the insurance

Executions

```
DRIVER'S AGE? 35
NUMBER OF TICKETS? 1
VALUE OF CAR? 10000
PREMIUM: $ 550

DRIVER'S AGE? 29
NUMBER OF TICKETS? 2
VALUE OF CAR? 15000
PREMIUM: $ 1031.25
```

Executions

```
DRIVER'S AGE? 19
NUMBER OF TICKETS? 3
VALUE OF CAR? 850
PREMIUM: $ 73.3125

DRIVER'S AGE? 81
NUMBER OF TICKETS? 4
VALUE OF CAR? 12500
COVERAGE DENIED
```

THE ITERATION STRUCTURE

5

PREVIEW Iteration is the last of our three structures and completes our knowledge of the control patterns. In this chapter we will look at:

1. How to set up the basic iteration structure.

2. Two different places in the loop to put conditions for staying in the structure.

3. Some common concepts usually applied within the iteration structure.

4. The special case of controlling the iteration structure with a counter.

5. Putting iterations within iterations.

6. Shortcut, but unstructured, methods of modifying the structure.

One major reason for using a computer rather than doing things by hand is that many of our tasks are repetitive. With only the two structures we have covered so far, to repeat a set of operations we would have to either execute the program a number of times or rewrite the same code over and over in the same program. Neither solution sounds entirely satisfactory, so in this chapter we shall introduce the programming mechanism for directing the computer to repeat a set of operations—the **iteration structure**.

We saw in Chapter 1 that the iteration structure, the **loop**, performs a single set of statements more than once. We also saw that, while it is possible to repeat a set of statements forever (an infinite loop), it is not only bad programming form but also rarely productive. We will always have some condition for the computer to test to see whether it should continue with the same operations or go on to whatever is next.

In Chapter 4 we looked at conditions—those expressions that evaluated to either true or false. The conditions we use for the iteration structure will be formed in the same way.

LOOPS

In C, the iteration structure condition is always that for continuing rather than exiting the loop. When the condition is true, C will repeat the statements in the loop. As mentioned in Chapter 1, this test for the condition can be either before the statements in the loop are executed, a **pretest**, or after the statement is executed, a **posttest**.

EXECUTION CHART: ➡➡Program 5–1

Line	Explanation	price	quantity	answer
1	Prompt for input. Notice that the values for the variables at this time are undetermined.	?	?	?
2	The %c will take one character from the input stream. The space before the conversion code will match any whitespace that might have been left in the input stream. This is not terribly important here, for the first input, but it will be important in the similar statement in line 8.	?	?	y
3	The beginning of the loop and also the test. Since this is a pretest, there must be something to test; this was provided by line 2. As with all pretest loops, the condition might be such that we would never execute the loop at all but go directly beyond the closing brace to line 10. In this case, however, the value of *answer* is y. Because of the or operator (||), the condition will be true with either upper- or lowercase Y.	?	?	y
4	Another input prompt.	?	?	y
5	This input control string has a comma to be matched between the conversion codes. The person at the keyboard will have to be certain to separate the values with a comma. (A "%f%hi" would only require a space.)	1.98	6	y
6	Prints out the result in dollars and cents.	1.98	6	y
7	Yet another input prompt.	1.98	6	y
8	This input gives the program something to test when it goes back to the beginning of the loop. The space in front of the conversion code will match the newline left at the end of the stream by the previous scanf() and request that the system wait for a new input. Without the space, the %c assigns the existing newline to answer and continues without waiting.	1.98	6	Y
9	End of the block that makes up the body of the while loop. The program will go back to the test in line 3.	1.98	6	Y
3	Condition true, continue with loop.	1.98	6	Y
4,5	Input new values.	4.29	15	Y
6	Print result.	4.29	15	Y
7,8	Ask the question.	4.29	15	n
3	Neither relation is true, so the condition is false.	4.29	15	n
10	The program is now beyond the loop and, since this is the last statement, it finishes.	4.29	15	n

Pretest Loops

A pretest loop begins with the keyword `while`. The general form of this form of the iteration structure is:

```
while (condition) statement;
```

For the `statement` referred to above, we can substitute a block of statements—a group of statements enclosed in braces—which leads us to the most common form of the structure:

```
while (condition)
{  statement;
   statement;
     . . .
}
```

Notice the punctuation and indenting. The `condition` is enclosed in parentheses; each statement in the block is indented one level and ends with a semicolon, and there is no semicolon after the condition or after the block's closing brace. The punctuation is required by the C compiler. The indenting and line endings are for us; they make the program more readable.

The ➡Program 5–1 allows a customer to type in the price of an item and the quantity being purchased, and get the total amount for that item. The customer can do this over and over again until there are no more items. Again, the numbers preceding some of the lines are not part of the program; they are only there so that we may refer to those lines in the discussion.

➡Program 5–I

```
#include <stdio.h>

void main(void)
{  float price;
   short quantity;
   char answer;

1     printf("Do you wish to enter a purchase (Y/N)? ");
2     scanf(" %c", &answer);
3     while (answer == 'Y' || answer == 'y')/* Upper or lowercase Y */
4     {  printf("Enter 'price,quantity': ");
5        scanf("%f,%hi", &price, &quantity);
6        printf("The total for this item is $%6.2f.\n", price * quantity);
7        printf("Another (Y/N)? ");
8        scanf(" %c", &answer);
9     }
10    printf("Thank you for your patronage.\n");
}
```

Output

```
Do you wish to enter a purchase (Y/N)? y
Enter 'price,quantity': 1.98,6
The total for this item is $ 11.88.
```

—Continued

```
Another (Y/N)? Y
Enter 'price,quantity': 4.29,15
The total for this item is $ 64.35.
Another (Y/N)? n
Thank you for your patronage.
```

Posttest Loops

We could have set this up as a posttest loop if we assumed that a person who did not wish to make a purchase would not have run the program. In other words, the body of the loop would be executed once no matter what. The posttest loop begins with a do statement and has this general form:

```
do statement while (condition);
```

with our usual implementation of it looking like this:

```
do
{   statement 1;
    statement 2;
        . . .
}while (condition);
```

There was no semicolon after the closing brace in the pretest loop but there is, and must be, one at the end of the *condition* in the posttest loop.

▶▶Program 5–2

```
#include <stdio.h>

void main(void)
{   float price;
    short quantity;
    char answer;

    printf("Enter 0,0 to quit.\n");
    do
    {   printf("Enter 'price,quantity': ");
        scanf("%f,%hi", &price, &quantity);
        printf("The total for this item is $%6.2f.\n", price * quantity);
        printf("Another (Y/N)? ");
        scanf(" %c", &answer);
    }while (answer == 'Y' || answer == 'y');
    printf("Thank you for your patronage.\n");
}
```

Output

```
Enter 0,0 to quit.
Enter 'price,quantity': 2.45,12
The total for this item is $ 29.40.
Another (Y/N)? y
```

—*Continued*

```
Enter 'price,quantity': .99,4
The total for this item is $  3.96.
Another (Y/N)? n
Thank you for your patronage.
```

Sentinel Values

In the previous program we asked the person at the keyboard a separate question about whether to continue or not. We could eliminate that question by interpreting special responses to the other question about price and quantity not as normal data but as a signal to the program to do something different. We call the value of this special response a **sentinel value**. The sentinel value must be something that would not occur in the normal course of operations—for example, a price and quantity of zero. The sentinel value must be tested for immediately; we would not want the following situation:

```
Enter 'price,quantity': 0,0
The total for this item is $  0.00.
That's all for that customer.
```

One structured solution is the following:

➡Program 5–3

```c
#include <stdio.h>

void main(void)
{  float price;
   short quantity;

   printf("Enter 0,0 to quit.\n");
   printf("Enter 'price,quantity': ");
   scanf("%f,%hi", &price, &quantity);
   while (price != 0)
   {  printf("The total for this item is $%6.2f.\n", price * quantity);
      printf("Enter 'price,quantity': ");
      scanf("%f,%hi", &price, &quantity);
   }
   printf("Thank you for your patronage.\n");
}
```

Output

```
Enter 0,0 to quit.
Enter 'price,quantity': 3.75,2
The total for this item is $  7.50.
Enter 'price,quantity': 10.59,6
The total for this item is $ 63.54.
Enter 'price,quantity': 0,0
Thank you for your patronage.
```

The `printf()` and `scanf()` functions are repeated, but that is necessary so that the `while` has something to test and we don't print a meaningless result.

Combining Expressions

We can combine two or more expressions into a single one to make programs more compact or, as we shall see here, execute and evaluate a number of expressions where a language element allows only one.

If, for example, we were assigning three different but related variables,

```
length = 14;
width = 6;
height = 2;
```

we could use the **comma operator** to combine the three expressions into one:

```
length = 14, width = 6, height = 2;
```

The comma operator is absolutely last in precedence, has left to right associativity, and discards the result of the expression to the left of it. In an expression such as the one above, the value of the entire expression will be the value of the last assignment, 2. Notice that the comma operator does not discard the execution of all the component expressions. All the assignments in the example above are made, but remember from Chapter 2 that the value of an assignment expression is the value of the assignment. It is these values that are discarded.

If we wanted *height* and *depth* assigned the same value, we could write a single expression as follows:

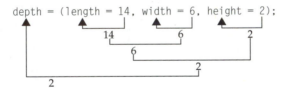

We have used the above expression for illustrative purposes only. Although the expression is correct, we do not advocate such an expression—it's a bit complicated. But let us see how we can apply the comma operator to a sentinel-value controlled loop. In our previous example, the `printf()` and `scanf()` functions had to be repeated because the loop needed something new to test each time through. We can write those statements only once if we include them as expressions in the while loop condition. The `main()` function from that program can be rewritten as follows:

```
void main(void)
{  float price;
   short quantity;

   printf("Enter 0,0 to quit.\n");
   while (printf("Enter 'price,quantity': "),          /* Prompt */
          scanf("%f,%hi", &price, &quantity),          /* Input */
          price != 0)                                  /* Test */
   }  printf("The total for this item is $%6.2f.\n", price * quantity);
   }
   printf("Thank you for your patronage.\n");
}
```

The prompt, input, and test expressions are all contained within the parentheses following `while`. Each time the program gets to the `while` statement, whether from above or being sent back from the end of the loop, the condition expression, with all its component parts, is executed. Here, the `printf()` is executed first and, since it is followed by a comma, its return value (24 because it printed 24 characters) is discarded. Then the `scanf()` is executed, assigning the values to *price* and *quantity*. It is followed by a comma, so its return value, 2, is also discarded. Finally, the test expression is evaluated. It will be either 0 or 1 (false or true) depending on the value of *price* just assigned. That value is not discarded, and becomes the value of the entire expression within the `while` parentheses. In other words, it is that last value that determines whether to stay in the loop or exit it.

This use of the comma operator is not universally accepted in structured environments because of its propensity toward abuse. Can you imagine a `while` condition with 47 statements separated by commas? If you use it, use it carefully. Do not make it too long (three expressions is almost too long), and only use it to avoid writing a statement twice in a loop situation.

Accumulating and Counting

Accumulation, adding (or multiplying, or whatever) values to a variable to keep a running result, is a common operation in loops. We saw how the accumulation operators worked in Chapter 2, so let us put one to use to keep track of the total bill and print out its value after finishing the loop.

▶▶Program 5–4

```
#include <stdio.h>

void main(void)
{   float price;
    float total = 0;
    short quantity;

    printf("Enter 0,0 to quit.\n");
    printf("Enter 'price,quantity': ");
    scanf("%f,%hi", &price, &quantity);
    while (price != 0)
    {   printf("The total for this item is $%6.2f.\n", price * quantity);
        total += price * quantity;
        printf("Enter 'price,quantity': ");
        scanf("%f,%hi", &price, &quantity);
    }
    printf("Your total is $%6.2f.\n", total);
}
```

Output

```
Enter 0,0 to quit.
Enter 'price,quantity': 6.35,8
The total for this item is $ 50.80.
Enter 'price,quantity': 2.50,10
The total for this item is $ 25.00.
Enter 'price,quantity': 0,0
Your total is $ 75.80.
```

In order to work correctly, the accumulator variable, *total*, was initialized to zero at the time of its declaration. Without that initial assignment the first value of *total* would have been whatever was lying around in memory. Accumulating on top of that would not have been very productive.

The accumulation statement `total += price * quantity` is exactly equivalent to `total = total + price * quantity`, so *price* and *quantity* are multiplied and that figure added to *total*, replacing the previous value of *total*.

Counting is specialized, simplified accumulation. Instead of adding a different value to the accumulation variable each time the statement is executed, the counting process adds the same value—1 or 9 or 2.8 or whatever we are counting by. The statement

```
count += 5;
```

would count by fives.

If we wanted to know how many purchases were made, we could count by one at each purchase and, after exiting the loop, print out that total.

➡Program 5–5

```
#include <stdio.h>

void main(void)
{  float price;
   float total = 0;
   short quantity, items = 0;

   printf("Enter 0,0 to quit.\n");
   printf("Enter 'price,quantity': ");
   scanf("%f,%hi", &price, &quantity);
   while (price != 0)
   {  printf("The total for this item is $%6.2f.\n", price * quantity);
      total += price * quantity;
      items += 1;
      printf("Enter 'price,quantity': ");
      scanf("%f,%hi", &price, &quantity);
   }
   printf("Your total is $%6.2f for %hi different items.\n", total, items);
}
```

Output

```
Enter 0,0 to quit.
Enter 'price,quantity': 22.95,3
The total for this item is $ 68.85.
Enter 'price,quantity': 7.29,8
The total for this item is $ 58.32.
Enter 'price,quantity': 15,4
The total for this item is $ 60.00.
Enter 'price,quantity': 0,0
Your total is $187.17 for 3 different items.
```

COUNTER-CONTROLLED LOOPS

In some cases we want to execute a set of statements a certain number of times—10, 100, 416, or whatever—or we want to look at, for example, every fifth instance of an event. We will use a counter to control our loop. The following program prints out the numbers one through three. We will use it to illustrate the elements needed for a **counter-controlled loop**.

➡Program 5–6

```
#include <stdio.h>

void main(void)
{  int count;

   count = 1;                                    /* Initialization */
   while (count <= 3)                            /* Test */
   {  printf("%i\n", count);                     /* Body */
      count += 1;                                /* Counter */
   }                                             /* End */
   printf("Finished, but why is the count %i?\n", count);
}
```

Output

```
1
2
3
Finished, but why is the count 4?
```

The following elements are necessary for a successful counter-controlled loop:

❑ **Initialization**   A counter, like any accumulator, must start with some initial value.

❑ **Test**   This is a pretest. The loop will continue until the counter is greater than 3.

❑ **Body**   The statement(s) that the loop was set up to repeat.

❑ **Counter**   Adds one to the counter variable each time through the loop.

❑ **End**   Sends the program back to the test at the beginning.

Since counting and counter-controlled loops are so common in programming, C, like many other languages, has a special form for them, the for statement:

```
for (initialization; test; counter) statement;
```

or more commonly

```
for (initialization; test; counter)
{  statement 1;
   statement 2;
      . . .
}
```

➡Program 5–7 will execute exactly as did ➡Program 5–6.

➡Program 5–7

```
#include <stdio.h>

void main(void)
{  int count;

   for (count=1; count <= 3; count += 1)
   {  printf("%i\n", count);                          /* Braces not required */
   }
   printf("Finished, but why is the count %i?\n", count);
}
```

Output

```
1
2
3
Finished, but why is the count 4?
```

To answer the question at the end of the program, when the count was less than or equal to three, the loop continued. The counter had to go beyond three (to four) to make the loop condition false and exit the loop.

For the most part, the actions caused by a statement occur at the location of the statement within the program. The for statement is the exception; its actions are spread around the loop. The first action, the initialization, occurs only once before the repeating parts of the loop. The second, the test, is the first repeated action in the loop. The third, the counter, actually occurs after the body of the loop, in some cases hundreds of statements away from the for statement.

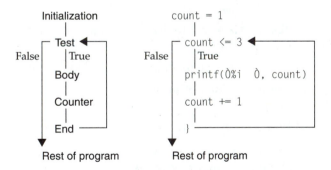

Increment and Decrement Operators

Counting, especially by one, is a common computer operation. We can add one to a variable by the process of accumulation as used above. For example,

whatever = whatever + 1;   **or**   whatever += 1;

adds one to the value of *whatever*. C provides us with the ++ operator to add one to, **increment**, a variable and the -- operator to subtract one from,

MORE ON for

We have identified the parameters of the `for` statement as an initialization, a test, and a counter. Internally, C makes no such distinctions. Any statements can be used in the initialization and counter positions, and any expression in the test position. C will simply execute whatever statement is in the initialization position, test whatever expression is in the test position, perform any statements in the body, execute whatever statement is in the counter position, and then go back to the test position.

C is very loose about what we put in these various positions, but we probably should not be. If we are not specifically writing a counting loop—with initialization, test, and counter—we should probably use a `while` or `do` loop.

decrement, a variable. These are classed in precedence and associativity with the unary operators, but they actually perform assignments—change the values of variables. They can only be used with variables—it wouldn't make sense to change a constant value or the value of an expression—and they can only add one to or subtract one from the variable—not 2, 9, or 46. If *rabbit* was 17, it would be 18 after this statement:

```
++rabbit;
```

The increment and decrement operators become more interesting because they can be used in arithmetic expressions, changing the values of the variables they are attached to as the expression is being evaluated. The operator may appear as a prefix, before the variable it changes, or as a postfix, after the variable. If it appears before, then the variable is changed before its value is used in the expression. If it appears after, the value of the variable is used in the expression, and then the variable is changed.

In this example, if *Quantity* was 2 and *Price* was 3.5, after the following statement was performed, *TotalSales* would be 7.0 and *Quantity* would be 3.

If the increment operator was put in front of the variable, *Quantity* would still end up being 3 but *TotalSales* would be 10.5.

One common place to find increment and decrement operators is in counter-controlled loops incrementing or decrementing the loop counter variable. In our previous loop example, our `for` statement looked like this:

```
for (count=1; count <= 3; count += 1)
```

It could have just as easily been written like this:

```
for (count=1; count <= 3; ++count)
```

Or, for that matter, this:

```
for (count=1; count <= 3; count++)
```

In this case, it doesn't matter whether we increment *count* before we use it in the expression or after, because we are not using it, only changing it.

NESTED LOOPS

Any valid statement or set of statements may be included within a loop. For example, the following program segment is a loop that prints the numbers 1 to 4.

Program

```
for (x = 1; x <= 4; ++x)
{ printf("%i ", x);
}
```

Output

```
1  2  3  4
```

There is no reason why this could not be part of another loop.

Program

```
for (y = 1; y <= 3; ++y)
{ printf("Line %i: ",y);
   for (x = 1; x <= 4; ++x)
   { printf("%i ", x);
   }
   printf("\n");
}
```

Output

```
Line 1:  1  2  3  4
Line 2:  1  2  3  4
Line 3:  1  2  3  4
```

A loop within another loop is referred to as a **nested loop**. Nesting may be as deep as needed—a loop within a loop within a loop within . . . as long as you make sure of two things:

1. An inner loop must be entirely contained within an outer one. With proper indenting, as in the example above, violation of this rule will be obvious.

2. If the loops are counter controlled, each loop that is operating simultaneously (nested within another) must have a different loop counter variable, such as *x* and *y* above. If you violate this rule, one loop will be modifying the other loop's counter, yielding a mess!

➡Program 5–8 keeps track of $100 deposited at the beginning of 1995 in an account compounded (interest is added back to the amount in the account) four times a year.

➡Program 5–8

```
#include <stdio.h>

void main(void)
{  int year, quarter;
   float amount = 100;

   printf("Deposit of $100 at 10%% compounded quarterly\n");
   printf("                     Quarter\n");
   printf("Year        1       2       3       4\n");
   for (year = 1995; year <= 2000; ++year)
   {  printf("%4i  ", year);
      for (quarter = 1; quarter <= 4; ++quarter)
      {  amount += amount * .1 / 4;                    /* 10% for one quarter */
         printf("%8.2f", amount);
      }
      printf("\n");
   }
}
```

Output

```
Deposit of $100 at 10% compounded quarterly
                 Quarter
Year     1       2       3       4
1995   102.50  105.06  107.69  110.38
1996   113.14  115.97  118.87  121.84
1997   124.89  128.01  131.21  134.49
1998   137.85  141.30  144.83  148.45
1999   152.16  155.97  159.87  163.86
2000   167.96  172.16  176.46  180.87
```

PUTTING IT TOGETHER

Harley Honda, David's son, is looking into alternative interest-bearing investments. He has written a program to compare $1000 compounded quarterly (the interest figured and added back to the balance four times a year) over three years at whatever interest rate he chooses to enter. Overall his program should:

Enter interest rate
Print chart

Since he wants to perform many analyses, the program should be in a loop.

Do while new analysis desired
    Enter interest rate
    Print chart
End loop

He feels that he should not consider any rate under 5 percent nor will he be offered any over 20. If any input is outside that range, the program should ask for another input.

Do while new analysis desired
    Enter interest rate
    If input out of range
        Print error message
    Else
        Produce chart
    End If
End loop

He wants his chart to show each quarter's activity with a yearly summary of the balance and total interest. Expanding the Produce chart section, we get:

                    [Produce chart]
Initialize balance and total interest
Do yearly for three years
    Initialize yearly interest
    Do quarterly for four quarters
        Print quarter and beginning balance
        Figure interest and add to yearly interest and balance
        Print interest and new balance
    End Loop
    Add year's interest to total
End Loop
Print final totals

➡️Program 5–9

```
#include <stdio.h>

void main(void)
{   float rate, balance;
    float interest;                         /* Interest for the quarter */
    float yearly_interest;          /* Accumulated interest within year */
    float total_interest;                  /* Total accumulated interest */
    int year, quarter;

    printf("Enter interest rate (zero to quit): ");
    scanf("%f", &rate);
    while (rate != 0)
    {   if (rate < 5 || rate > 20)              /* If input out of range */
            printf("   Out of the reasonable range.\n");
        else
```

—Continued

Program 5-9 —*Continued*

```
          {  printf("\n          Start Interest        End\n");
             balance = 1000;
             total_interest = 0;                   /* Initialize for new chart */
             for (year = 1; year <= 3; ++year)
             {  printf("Year %i\n", year);
                yearly_interest = 0;               /* Initialize yearly interest */
                for (quarter = 1; quarter <= 4; ++quarter)
                {  printf("      %i  %7.2f", quarter, balance);
                   interest = balance * rate / 100 * .25;
                   yearly_interest += interest;
                   balance += interest;
                   printf("  %7.2f  %7.2f\n", interest, balance);
                }
                printf("    Total interest for the year: $%.2f\n",
                       yearly_interest);
                total_interest += yearly_interest;            /* Accumulate */
             }
             printf("\nEnding balance: $%.2f.  Interest earned: $%.2f.\n\n",
                    balance, total_interest);
          }
          printf("Enter interest rate (zero to quit): ");
          scanf("%f", &rate);
       }
}
```

Output

```
Enter interest rate (zero to quit): .125
   Out of the reasonable range.
Enter interest rate (zero to quit): 12.5

          Start Interest        End
Year 1
      1  1000.00   31.25  1031.25
      2  1031.25   32.23  1063.48
      3  1063.48   33.23  1096.71
      4  1096.71   34.27  1130.98
   Total interest for the year: $130.98
Year 2
      1  1130.98   35.34  1166.33
      2  1166.33   36.45  1202.77
      3  1202.77   37.59  1240.36
      4  1240.36   38.76  1279.12
   Total interest for the year: $148.14
Year 3
      1  1279.12   39.97  1319.09
      2  1319.09   41.22  1360.32
      3  1360.32   42.51  1402.83
      4  1402.83   43.84  1446.66
   Total interest for the year: $167.54

Ending balance: $1446.66.  Interest earned: $446.66.
Enter interest rate (zero to quit): 0
```

SUMMARY

The **iteration structure**, or **loop**, repeats a set of statements. The condition for repeating the statements is given in a `while` statement. If it is a **pretest** loop, the `while` appears at the beginning of the loop. If it is a **posttest**, the loop starts with a do statement and the `while` appears at the end of the loop.

Often, the condition for a loop involves a **sentinel value**, a special value for a variable that is being used in the loop, and such loops require repetition of statements. To avoid this situation we may use the **comma operator**, which allows us to combine expressions into single ones, discarding the value to its left. Two other concepts that are commonly used with loops are **accumulating**, keeping a running total, and **counting**, adding some fixed value to a variable each time through the loop.

In many cases we use the counter in a **counter-controlled loop**. This loop has five important ingredients: an **initialization** of the counter; a **test** to determine if the loop should repeat; a **body** of statements to repeat; a **counter** statement that adds to the counter; and an **end** of the loop that sends the execution back to the test. The parameters for these various elements can all be stated in a `for` statement. **Increment** and **decrement** operators, which also make assignments, are often used in counting loops.

Since any valid statement or structure can be included within any other, we often encounter **nested loops**, one loop within another.

KEY TERMS (in order of appearance)

Iteration structure	Counter-controlled loop
Loop	Initialization
Pretest	Test
Posttest	Body
`while`	Counter
`do`	End
Sentinel value	`for`
Comma operator	Increment
Accumulation	Decrement
Counting	Nested loop

REVIEW QUESTIONS

1. What is the purpose of an iteration structure?

2. When the condition in a C iteration structure is true, does the execution of the loop continue or stop?

3. What is the difference between a pretest and a posttest loop? How are each implemented in C?

4. How are sentinel values used to control loops?

5. How is the comma operator used in C?

6. How does accumulation work and why is initialization of an accumulator variable important?

7. How does counting differ from accumulation? How are they the same?

8. What five elements are necessary in a counter-controlled loop? What does each do?

9. Outline the general form of a `for` statement.

10. At what point in the loop does each parameter of a `for` statement execute?

11. What is the difference between ++x and x++ when used in an arithmetic expression?

12. What is a nested loop?

13. What two rules must be followed for the correct formation of a nested loop?

EXERCISES

1. Rewrite the following program statements using proper, readable form.

```
printf("Input a number ");scanf("%f", &numb);while (numb != 0){
printf("That's not zero. Another ");scanf("%f", &numb);}
printf("Finally a zero.\n");
```

2. Fill in an execution chart for the following program segment with the given execution.

```
int quiz, total = 0, quizzes = 0;         Quiz score? 16
                                          Quiz score? 19
printf("Quiz score? ");                    Quiz Score? -1
scanf("%i", &quiz);                        Average quiz: 17.5
do
{  total += quiz;
   ++quizzes;
   printf("Quiz score? ");
   scanf("%i", &quiz);
}while (quiz > 0);
printf("Average quiz: %.1f\n", (float) total / quizzes);
```

3. Rewrite these `while` loops using the `for` statement.

```
x = 14;                      y = 6.5;
while (x >= 3)               while (y <= 8.5)
{  printf("%i\n", x);        {  printf("%f\n", y);
   x -= 5;                      y += .05;
}                            }
```

4. Rewrite these `for` statements using `while` loops.

```
for (x = 250; x >= 100; x -= 50)
    printf("%i\n", x);


for (y = 122.6; y <= 142.6; y += .2)
    printf("%f\n", y);
```

5. What will the output be from the following program segment?

```
for (x = 16; x >= 4; --x);
    printf("Hello\n");
```

6. What will the output be from this program segment?

```
for (a = 1; a <= 5; ++a)
{  printf("%i", a);
   for (b = a; b >= 1; --b)
      printf(" %i", b);
   printf("\n");
}
printf("%i %i\n", a, b);
```

PROGRAMS

1. Write a program that gives the smallest of five numbers input. Use an `if` statement to see if the new number input should replace the current minimum.

   Variables

input	Number input at keyboard
min	To keep track of smallest
count	Loop counter

   Output

   ```
   Enter number 1: 59.2
   Enter number 2: -3.789
   Enter number 3: 42.5
   Enter number 4: -28
   Enter number 5: 12.6
   The smallest is -28
   ```

2. Rewrite the program in Problem 1 to use a conditional expression to assign the value to the `min` variable each time.

3. You have found some cockroaches in your apartment. Rather than call the exterminator, you decide to perform an experiment. You count the number of roaches and then wait a week and count them again to determine their breeding rate. Print out the estimated roach population from that point on, assuming that the breeding rate remains constant. Stop at the week that shows over a million roaches. You need not actually continue the experiment to validate your computer results—call the exterminator.

   Variables

   ```
   initial_roaches
   roaches
   breeding_rate
   week
   ```

   Output

   ```
   Roaches at beginning of week: 6
   Roaches at end of week: 38
   ```

Week	Roaches
2	38
3	240
4	1520
5	9626
6	60964
7	386105
8	2445331

4. A Pythagorean triple is three integers that make up the sides of a right triangle; for example, 3, 4, and 5. The sides may be calculated according to the formulas given as long as a is greater than b. Write a program that shows possible triples for a and b varying from 1 to 5.

   Formulas

   $$side1 = a^2 - b^2$$

   $$side2 = 2ab$$

   $$hypotenuse = a^2 + b^2$$

Variables

```
a, b
side1, side2, hypotenuse
```

Output

Side1	Side2	Hypotenuse
3	4	5
8	6	10
5	12	13
15	8	17
12	16	20
7	24	25
24	10	26
21	20	29
16	30	34
9	40	41

5. The game Totals can be played by any number of people. It starts with a total of 100 and each player in turn makes an integer adjustment between -20 and 20 to that total. The winner is the player whose adjustment makes the total equal to 5. Use only the three variables given.

Variables

```
total
adjustment
counter        Number of adjustments
```

Output

```
WE START WITH 100. WHAT IS
YOUR ADJUSTMENT? -20
    THE TOTAL IS 80
YOUR ADJUSTMENT? 4.6
    NOT AN INTEGER BETWEEN -20 AND 20
YOUR ADJUSTMENT? -35
    NOT AN INTEGER BETWEEN -20 AND 20
YOUR ADJUSTMENT? -20
    THE TOTAL IS 60
YOUR ADJUSTMENT? -15
    THE TOTAL IS 45

    . . .

    YOUR ADJUSTMENT? -6
    THE TOTAL IS 5
THE GAME IS WON IN 14 STEPS
```

6. Write a program to assign a letter grade given a numeric score: 90 or above is an A; 80, B; 70, C; 60, D; and below 60, F. The program should continue to accept values until a negative number is input. The program should print how many of each letter grade were assigned after the input is completed. Use the `else if` construct in your program.

Variables

```
score                       Score input
a_s, b_s, c_s, d_s, f_s     Counters for letter grades
```

Output

```
SCORE? 92
   THE GRADE IS A
SCORE? 70
   THE GRADE IS C

 . . .

SCORE? -1

 2 A'S
 2 B'S
 4 C'S
 0 D'S
 1 F'S
```

7. Modify the program in Problem 6 to use the `switch` statement.

8. Specific points on a compass may be expressed in general directions. For example, $130°$ is in an easterly direction. Write a program that will take directions in degrees and give them one of four general-direction titles: $315°$ up to but not including $45°$ is north, $45° - 135°$ is east, $135° - 225°$ is south, and $225° - 315°$ is west. The program should end when a negative compass reading is input.

Variable

degrees   Direction in degrees input at keyboard

Output

```
COMPASS READING? 104
   EAST
COMPASS READING? 370
INVALID, ENTER ANOTHER COMPASS READING? 242
   WEST
COMPASS READING? -1
```

9. Write a program that converts feet to meters. Use a for loop. It should go from one to ten feet in half-foot steps. One meter equals 3.28083 feet.

Variable

feet   Loop counter

Output

```
FEET TO METERS CONVERSION TABLE
FEET    METERS
 1.0    0.30480
 1.5    0.45720
 2.0    0.60960
        .
        .
        .
 9.0    2.74321
 9.5    2.89561
10.0    3.04801
```

10. Write a program to show the area of a circle (πr^2) and the volume of a sphere ($\frac{4}{3}\pi r^3$) for all radii between 100 and 150 cm in increments of 5 cm. ($\pi = 3.1416$).

Variable

```
radius
```

Output

RADIUS	AREA	VOLUME
100	31416.0	4.18880E+06
105	34636.1	4.84906E+06
110	38013.4	5.57530E+06
115	41547.7	6.37064E+06
120	45239.0	7.23825E+06
125	49087.5	8.18125E+06
130	53093.1	9.20280E+06
135	57255.7	1.03060E+07
140	61575.4	1.14941E+07
145	66052.1	1.27701E+07
150	70686.0	1.41372E+07

11. Write a program to create a multiplication table for all combinations of two numbers from 1 to 8.

Variables

```
multiplier
multiplicand
```

Output

	1	2	3	4	5	6	7	8
1	1	2	3	4	5	6	7	8
2	2	4	6	8	10	12	14	16
3	3	6	9	12	15	18	21	24
4	4	8	12	16	20	24	28	32
5	5	10	15	20	25	30	35	40
6	6	12	18	24	30	36	42	48
7	7	14	21	28	35	42	49	56
8	8	16	24	32	40	48	56	64

12. Write a program that allows you to input a desired total and prints all the possible combinations of three nonnegative integers that add up to that total. Set up nested loops to generate the three numbers and then test each combination to see whether its total equals the input total. The individual numbers never have to be greater than the desired total.

Variables

`total`	The desired total
`c1, c2, c3`	Counters to generate the three numbers
`count`	To count the number of valid combinations

Output

```
Desired total: 4
 0  0  4
 0  1  3
   . . .
 3  1  0
 4  0  0
15 number combinations total 4.
```

13. Write a program to produce the following output. Use nested `for` loops.

Output

```
1
1  2
1  2  3
1  2  3  4
1  2  3  4  5
1  2  3  4  5  6
1  2  3  4  5  6  7
1  2  3  4  5  6  7  8
1  2  3  4  5  6  7  8  9
1  2  3  4  5  6  7  8
1  2  3  4  5  6  7
1  2  3  4  5  6
1  2  3  4  5
1  2  3  4
1  2  3
1  2
1
```

FUNCTIONS

PREVIEW   C is a modular language and most of its modularity comes from a structure based on functions. In this chapter we will closely examine the principles of function use and learn how we can create functions for our own purposes. Here you will be exposed to:

1. The differences in the accessibility of variables—where we can use them and where we can't.

2. Various classes of variables, how they are declared, and when they are accessible.

3. How functions are set up and used in programs.

4. Sending values to functions to be processed.

5. Getting processed values back from functions.

6. Some of the functions that exist in ANSI C.

The elegance and sophistication of the C language is largely due to its free use of, and indeed virtual dependence on, functions. The language itself has very few statements, but included with your C compiler, you will undoubtedly receive a wealth of different functions—not only the standard ANSI set but also others besides, many of which address the unique capabilities of your particular hardware. If the language still doesn't do what you want it to, you can make up your own functions.

In fact, making up your own functions is a desired objective. Top-down, modular designs are easily implemented by translating each module into a separate function. If you encapsulate these modules carefully, being sure they are totally self-contained, you can use the modules you have designed for one program as modules in another.

We have already used two of the standard ANSI functions, `printf()` and `scanf()`. When we included the name of the function, `printf`, for example, in a program statement and gave it something to work with such as (`"The num ber is %i\n", value`), it performed its intended operation at that point in the program. Here we will look at the mechanisms by which these functions operate.

STORAGE CLASSES

We have examined data types and seen how storage differs from data type to data type. At this point we will examine the accessibility of the data—can we use it or can't we? Accessibility is not determined by data type but by **storage class**, and a variable of any data type can belong to almost any storage class depending on how and in which part of the program we declare it.

Lifetime and Visibility

Storage class affects two important properties of data: its lifetime and its visibility. The **lifetime** of a variable is the part of the program's execution during which the variable exists; in other words, space for the variable is allocated in memory. As we said in Chapter 2, a variable is defined—space allocated for it—when it is declared, so the lifetime of a variable begins upon declaration. It ends when C frees that memory for some other use—deallocates it. The value of a variable will continue to exist during its lifetime. We can, of course, assign and reassign that value, but we can be sure that its value will always be the one we last assigned.

The **visibility** (or *scope*) of a variable is the part of the program's execution in which we can access, read from or write to, the variable by using the variable's name. We may have found out where it is in memory and be able to access that location directly, but unless we can refer to the variable by name, it is not visible. A variable can never be visible outside its lifetime, but it may not be visible at times within its lifetime. Visibility always starts with the variable's declaration, but it may be ended or interrupted by a number of factors, as we shall see.

We use the terms local and global to refer to the duration of visibility or lifetime. **Global** lifetime or visibility extends from the variable's declaration to the end of the program. A variable with global visibility must have global lifetime but the reverse is not necessarily true. There are many instances of variables that exist, but in a certain part of the program we cannot access them. Even if a variable has so-called global visibility, we shall see cases where it might be covered up, **superseded**, by another variable with the same name.

Local lifetime or visibility is existence or access only within a segment of the program, a particular function or block of statements, perhaps. A variable might have global lifetime but only local visibility. In no case could a variable have local lifetime but global visibility.

Internal versus External

An **internal** declaration is one made within a function. All of the variables we have used to this point have been internal because they have been declared within the `main()` function. An **external** declaration is outside of any function, typically before the `main()` function. In this program fragment, *away* and *trouble* are declared externally, and *ernal* and *isma* are declared internally.

```
#include <stdio.h>

float away;
double trouble;

void main(void)
{   int ernal;
    char isma;

}
```

Storage class will depend on, among other things, whether the declaration was made internally or externally.

External Variables

An **external variable** is one declared outside of any function with no other storage-class key words. The variables *away* and *trouble* in the program above are both external variables. All external variables have global lifetimes. There are cases in which external variables do not have global visibility, however.

Longer programs are often created by combining two or more shorter program segments. These shorter programs may be written in separate source files, compiled individually, and their object code combined in the linking process. One advantage of this strategy is that the shorter programs may be tested individually; another is that these pretested shorter programs can be combined with other programming projects. Of course, there can be only one `main()` function in the combined source files; the execution has to start in some specific place.

An external variable declared in one source file is not visible in another source file unless we **reference** it in that source file. The reference is the same as the declaration except that it is preceded by the key word `extern`.

```
extern type identifier;
```

For example, the following two source files shown side by side use the integer variable *freebus*:

```
Source File 1          Source File 2

#include <stdio.h>     #include <stdio.h>

int freebus;           extern int freebus;                 /* Legal */

extern double what;    double what;                        /* Legal */
char is;               long it;   /* Legal, different from internal it */

void main(void)        void some_function(void)
{  long it;            {  char is; /* Legal, different from external is */
   Rest of program        Rest of program
```

The line in Source File 1, `int freebus;`, declares the variable *freebus* to be an integer and defines storage space for it. The line in Source File 2, `extern int freebus;`, announces that Source File 2 will use a variable, *freebus*, that was declared and defined externally elsewhere. In this case, the elsewhere was in Source File 1, but might have been in some other source file that was eventually linked to Source File 2. In fact, the declaration could even have been some time later in Source File 2. The declaration of *freebus* could not have been internal and still be referenced by extern.

The declaration, `int freebus;`, defines *freebus*, establishing storage space for the variable. The reference, `extern int freebus;`, only announces the intention to use the variable. If Source File 2 did not have the reference, *freebus* would not be visible to any of the code in Source File 2. Furthermore, if Source File 2 had a declaration, `int freebus;`, instead of the reference, another variable with the same name (*freebus*) would be set up whose visibility would supersede that of the *freebus* from Source File 1. Both *freebus* variables would exist in different places in memory with independent values, but while executing code from Source File 2, the Source File 1 *freebus* would be superseded—not visible.

Automatic Variables

By default, any variable declared internally (within a function) with no other storage-class key word is an **automatic** variable. We may use the key word `auto` but it is not necessary. All of the variables we have used previous to this chapter have been automatic. Both of the variables in the following program code are automatic.

```
#include <stdio.h>

void main(void)
{  int contents;
   auto float dilution;
```

An automatic variable must be declared at the beginning of the program block in which it will be used. That could be the beginning of a function, as above, or any other block of statements set off by braces, as below.

```
    if (t > 10)
    {   short count = 0;
        for ( ; t > 0; t = t / 2)
        {   ++count;
        }
        printf("%hi iterations.\n", count);
    }
```

The automatic variable has local lifetime and local visibility. Both start at the time of declaration, like any other variable, but both end at the end of the block in which the variable was declared. In the example just above, the variable *count* lasts only until the end of the if statement.

If a local variable has the same name as a global variable, the local variable will supersede the global variable—hide it. The global variable will continue to exist, but access by name will be to the local variable, as ➡Program 6–1 shows.

➡Program 6–1

```
#include <stdio.h>

int test = 10;

void main(void)
{
    printf("Before the block, test is %i\n", test);
    {   int test = 5;

        printf("Within the block, test is %i\n", test);
    }
    printf("After the block, test is %i\n", test);
}
```

Output

```
Before the block, test is 10
Within the block, test is 5
After the block, test is 10
```

Local variables have two main advantages. First, the variable ceases to exist when the program leaves the block in which it was declared. This means that the memory space allocated to it can now be used for some other purpose. Second, it enhances encapsulation and data abstraction. Local variables are not visible outside their block (nor do they even exist), helping to isolate the internal workings of the block from the outside world. A side benefit of this is that by using local variables in our modules, we need not concern ourselves about the variable names we have chosen conflicting with those of other modules or even global variables.

Static Variables

Declaring a variable static gives it global lifetime but limited visibility. It exists from the time it is declared until the end of the program, but its visibility is limited to only a part of the program.

```
static type identifier;
```

For example,

```
static float bubbles;
```

If the static variable is declared internally, it is visible only within the block in which it is declared. When the program moves out of that block, the variable continues to exist and maintains its value, but it is no longer accessible. "Great," you might say, "now I've created a variable that has a value and takes up memory, but I can't get to it."

But you can get to it if and when the program reenters that block. You could do the same thing with an external variable, but the external variable would be visible all the time. If you were making up a program out of segments of other programs, as we so often do, you would have to be sure that the other program segments did not use the same variable name. The static variable is accessible in the section where it is needed and retains its value throughout the program, but will not interfere with, or be modified by, other variables of the same name in the rest of the program.

▶▶Program 6–2

```
#include <stdio.h>

void main(void)
{  int i;                                    /* Automatic variable */

    for (i = 1; i <= 12; ++i)
    {  printf("%2i ", i);
       if (i % 3 == 0)
       {  static int i = 1;                  /* Static internal variable */

          printf("  Sets of three: %i\n", i);
          ++i;
       }
    }
}
```

Output

```
 1  2  3   Sets of three: 1
 4  5  6   Sets of three: 2
 7  8  9   Sets of three: 3
10 11 12   Sets of three: 4
```

In this program we have declared the variable *i* twice . . . or have we? There is one declaration at the beginning of the main() function and another just after the if statement. The first declared *i* as automatic and therefore of local lifetime and visibility, but its lifetime and visibility should extend throughout the function in which it was declared. The second declaration declared *i* as a static internal variable—global lifetime but local visibility.

Is there a conflict?

No, because the declarations set up two different variables. Each is named *i* but they are stored in different memory locations and maintain different values. The automatic *i* should be visible throughout the function, but its visibility is superseded, hidden, by the static *i* in the block within the `if` statement.

In this case both *i* variables maintain their separate values; the automatic *i* because the program never leaves the block in which it was declared (the `main()` function), and the static *i* because, even though the program leaves its block several times, it has a global lifetime.

The static *i* was initialized to 1 in its block, but it did not go back to 1 when we reentered the block. The initialization of a static variable is done only when it is allocated, and the allocation will actually be made at the beginning of the program's execution. Subsequent entries into the block will not reallocate the static variable.

If the static variable is declared externally, its lifetime is, of course, global, but its visibility is limited to the source file in which it was declared.

For example,

Source File 1	**Source File 2**
`#include <stdio.h>`	`#include <stdio.h>`
`static float whatsis;`	`extern float whatsis;` `/* Forget it! */`
`void main(void)`	Rest of program
`{   Rest of program`	

The variable *whatsis* has a global lifetime because it was declared externally, but it is visible only from the code in Source File 1 because we have declared it `static`. An `extern float whatsis;` reference in another source file would not work.

One principle of encapsulation and modular programming is to create abstract data objects, ones that can be manipulated only by the methods specifically supplied by the creator of the object within the object itself. In order to implement this abstraction, the inner workings of the object and its internal variables must be hidden from the outside world. If we consider a C source file in a program containing many source files, or a C function or program block, as a single object, then we must hide its global variables from other source files or functions. The `static` declaration gives it this kind of global lifetime but local visibility.

Register Variables

The central processing unit contains a number of data-holding circuits called **data registers**. There are very few of them (from two to about a dozen, depending on the CPU) and each holds only a few bytes of data, typically a word. Small and few though they may be, this is where most of the work gets done. When we perform an operation on some data, typically that data must be moved from main memory to one of these registers, the operation performed, and the result written back to main memory—three distinct procedures for each operation.

By declaring a variable as **register** we direct C to attempt to store the variable in a data register in the CPU instead of in main memory. An operation on it, then, would execute in less time because it would not require moving it from main memory to a register and back again.

Just declaring it as `register` does not guarantee that it will be stored in a register; they are too precious and often must be used for other processes. C will make the attempt and if a register is free, will succeed; otherwise the variable will be stored as automatic.

A `register` variable must be declared within a block and must be of type `int` (or be a pointer that will fit within the space allocated for an `int`; more about pointers in the next chapter). This means that `register` variables have local lifetime and visibility, like automatics.

Normally, we would declare only a very few `register` variables and even those only in a small block of the program. (Recall the discussion of blocks from Chapter 1. A block is the section between an open brace and a close brace.) Loop counters are often good candidates for register variables.

```
{                                                      /* Begin block */
    register int count;

    for (count = 1; count <= end; ++count)
    {
        statements in the body of the loop
    }
}                                                      /* Count is dead */
```

As soon as the program exits the block, *count*'s lifetime will be over and the register will be free.

Since `int` is the default data type, the declaration

```
register count;
```

would do just as well.

Initializations

We may give any variable an initial value when we declare it. But what if we don't? We saw that the variables that we have used until now simply retained any bits that were left around in their section of memory whether they made any sense or not—and usually they didn't. We gave this the wonderfully descriptive term "garbage."

This is true of automatic and `register` variables—any variables with local lifetime. Global lifetime variables—`static` and external—are initialized by C to zero at the time of their declaration unless we explicitly state otherwise.

Type Qualifiers

ANSI has added two qualifiers to variable declarations that are generally not available in non-ANSI compilers. The `const` qualifier declares that a variable is not variable but constant. It will retain its initial value and anything that tries to reassign it should be rejected by C.

```
const float zap = 56.234;            /* zap's value may not be changed */
blam = pow + zap;          /* No problem. zap is being read, not assigned */
blam = pow + zap++;        /* Error! Incrementing attempts to change zap */

const int i;                         /* Ridiculous. There is no initial value */
```

The `volatile` qualifier warns the compiler that the variable may be modified by actions external to the C program. Perhaps the program is linked to some other non-C program that modifies memory in unspecified (to C) ways.

```
volatile int vapor;                    /* May be changed outside of C */
```

The two qualifiers, `const` and `volatile`, are not related in any way; one is certainly not the opposite of the other. In fact, they can both be used in the same declaration.

```
const volatile long system_clock;
```

In this case `volatile` indicates that the *system_clock* variable will be modified by something outside of C, presumably the operating system, and `const` indicates that C should never write to it. C can, of course, read it.

HOW FUNCTIONS WORK

Now that we know something about how variables react inside and outside of functions, let us concentrate on the functions themselves. The following program computes an employee's net pay from the number of hours worked, the hourly pay rate, and the number of the employee's dependents. The program consists of a sequence of three modules:

> Input data
> Calculate net pay
> Display net pay

Expanding these three modules into C code we have what follows in ➡Program 6–3:

Nuts & Bolts

OPTIMIZING COMPILERS

Many compilers, in an effort to reduce the size of the executable code and/or make a program execute more efficiently, try to optimize the code during compilation. This may come in the form of taking shortcuts in assembling the object code or utilizing system resources that may be temporarily available at one point in a program. When a variable is declared as `const`, the compiler may not need to generate object code to load the value from memory. Instead it can put the value directly in the object code, saving a few instructions in the executable program.

Another optimization trick is to cache the last variable or two accessed, presuming that they might be used again immediately. Caching means that the value is stored closer to the process, perhaps in a CPU register. Declaring a variable as `volatile` warns the compiler that the contents of the memory location of a variable may be modified by something outside of C and that the compiler shouldn't cache it. If the memory contents were changed while the value was cached, when the cached value was written back to that location the other change would be wiped out.

➡Program 6–3

```
#include <stdio.h>

void main(void)
{ float hours, rate;
  float gross, tax;
  double net_pay;
  int dependents;

  /*********************************************************  Input data */
  printf("Hours: ");
  scanf("%f", &hours);
  printf("Pay rate: ");
  scanf("%f", &rate);
  printf("Dependents (other than self): ");
  scanf("%i", &dependents);
  ++dependents;                             /* Include self in dependents */

  /***************************************************  Calculate net pay */
  gross = hours * rate;
  tax = (.16 - .02 * dependents) * gross;
  net_pay = gross - tax;

  /****************************************************  Display net pay */
  printf("Pay is: %8.2f\n", net_pay);
}
```

The second module, Calculate net pay, calculates the net pay based on the total number of deductions, including the one for the employee; so the first module must adjust the value of *dependents* before turning over the data to the second. Why not simply adjust the second module to accommodate? The Calculate net pay module might be an object used in a number of other programs and, following our objective of encapsulation, it must be the same in each.

Let us firmly establish Calculate net pay as a data object by encapsulating it into a separate function, *pay()*. This function will have to receive the data it needs from the main() function—the values of *hours*, *rate*, and *dependents* + 1—and give back the result, which will then be assigned to the variable *net_pay*.

➡Program 6–4

```
#include <stdio.h>

double pay(float hrs, float rt, int dep);          /* Function declaration */

void main(void)
{ float hours, rate;
  double net_pay;
  int dependents;

  /*********************************************************  Input data */
  printf("Hours: ");
  scanf("%f", &hours);
```

—Continued

```
    printf("Pay rate: ");
    scanf("%f", &rate);
    printf("Dependents (other than self): ");
    scanf("%i", &dependents);

    /************************************************  Calculate net pay */
    net_pay = pay(hours, rate, dependents + 1);          /* Function call */

    /************************************************   Display results */
    printf("Pay is: %8.2f\n", net_pay);
}

/*****************  Calculates net pay given hours, rate, and dependents */
double pay(float hrs, float rt, int dep)          /* Function definition */
{  float gross, tax;

    gross = hrs * rt;
    tax = (.16 - .02 * dep) * gross;
    return gross - tax;
}
```

Output

```
Hours: 30
Pay rate: 12.5
Dependents (other than self): 2
Pay is:   337.50
```

These two programs, ▶▶Program 6–3 and ▶▶Program 6–4, will give equivalent results, but let us see how the second one, with the function, works.

Function Calls

We **call** a function—that is, set it into operation—by including its name in a statement such as

```
net_pay = pay(hours, rate, dependents + 1);
```

The function call is of the general form

```
function_name(arguments)
```

The *function_name* is any valid C identifier. The naming rules are the same as those for variables, but even though it might be possible in some cases, you should avoid giving a function the same name as a variable. The *argu ments* are expressions that specify the values to be sent to the function. In our example we are sending the values of *hours*, *rate*, and *dependents* + 1, that is, 30, 12.5, and 3, to the function *pay()*.

The function call, then, passes values to the function and transfers execution to the statements in the function.

Not all functions have values passed to them. If we had moved the "Input data" section from the main() function into our *pay()* function, there would have been no need to pass it values. The function call still must have the parentheses following the function name; for example,

```
net_pay = pay();
```

We shall use this statement in an example shortly.

The Function Definition

The **function definition** is the function itself. It is the object, including declarations and statements, that describes the job performed by the function. The first line of the function definition contains information about the function and follows this form:

```
return_type function_name(parameter declarations)
```

Notice that there is no semicolon at the end of this line.

The *function_name*, of course, is the identifier that will be used to call the function from elsewhere in the program. The *parameter declarations* declare the variables that will be initialized by the values that are passed as a result of the function call. Since the values in the call are assigned to the variables declared in the first line of the definition, the values of the expressions in the call should agree with parameter declarations in number, data type, and order. Actually, the ANSI C compiler will convert arguments to the data types in the parameter declarations, but older C compilers won't, nor will some of the offshoots of the C language, so most programmers are somewhat fussy about this.

Extracting from the example above, we can see that those requirements are met.

```
float hours, rate;
int dependents;

net_pay = pay(hours, rate, dependents + 1);          /* Function call */

double pay(float hrs, float rt, int dep)       /* Function definition */
```

The parameter declarations in the function definition set up automatic variables that are local to the function in both lifetime and visibility. In the same function in our example we see other declarations,

```
{ float gross, tax;
```

within the function block (inside the braces). These, too, set up automatic variables local to the function. The only difference is that variables declared as function parameters are initialized to the values passed from the call. When the program enters the function, *hrs*, *rt*, and *dep* will have valid values; *gross* and *tax*, because they have no initialization, will be garbage.

If the function is designed so that it has no values passed to it, as in our modified *pay()* function, then the first line of the definition will declare the parameters as void. This statement:

```
net_pay = pay();
```

contains the proper call to this function:

```
double pay(void)
```

The `main()` function, as we have used it thus far, has had no values passed to it.

Function Returns

Most functions, *pay()* included, perform some kind of operations and send some value, a **return value**, back to the calling point in the program. The return value becomes the value of the call and the program continues from that point. Every value in C, including the return value of a function, has a data type. The *return_type*, the first parameter in the first line of the function definition, declares this data type. We refer to it as the function's data type but it is really the data type of the function's return value. Our *pay()* function has the data type `double`.

```
double pay(float hrs, float rt, int dep)          /* Function definition */
```

The return value is established by a `return` statement with the form,

```
return expression;
```

An example is the one at the end of the *pay()* function,

```
return gross - tax;
```

The `return` statement performs two operations: It passes the return value back to the calling point, substituting it for the function call; and it sends execution of the program back to this point, thereby exiting the function.

In our example, the value of *gross − tax*, 337.5, is passed back to the calling point in the statement

```
net_pay = pay(hours, rate, dependents + 1);
```

where it substitutes for the function call. In essence, then, the statement becomes

```
net_pay = 337.5;
```

The statement continues with the assignment of that value to *net_pay* and the program moves on.

A function does not necessarily need to return a value. Many functions perform some self-contained operation; for example, printing a page heading on each page of output. No value is required by the program so none is returned. The function's *return_type* is declared `void` and the `return` statement will have no expression in it. The only purpose for the `return` statement in such a function is to send execution back to the calling point. The call to a `void` function could not be included in an expression because no value would be substituted for it. Typically, it would be the only thing in a statement.

```
    page(number);                           /* Function call */

    void page(int PageNo)                    /* Function definition */
    {   .

        .

        .

      return;
    }
```

Again, our use of `main()` is an example of using a function with no return value.

In a function with no return value, the `return` statement is not even necessary. When there are no more statements in the function, the program will return to the calling point.

Nuts & Bolts

THE ROLE OF THE STACK

The stack is a set of contiguous memory locations that C establishes and maintains for many of its internal operations. C puts things on the stack (assigns them to some of those locations) and takes them off (reads them and assigns them elsewhere). Use of the stack is on a last in, first out (LIFO) basis—the last item put on the stack will be the first taken off. The best way to visualize it is to imagine a stack of coins. When you add to the stack, the coins go on top. When you remove from the stack, you also remove from the top.

One purpose for which C uses the stack is passing values to and from functions. In the use of the *pay()* function in the text, the call placed two `float`s (assume four bytes each) and one `int` (assume two bytes) on the stack at the current (beginning) level. The function must use those values to initialize its parameters. To maintain the proper order, the function takes things off the stack in the reverse order of its declarations. It takes the first two bytes and assigns them to the `int` variable *dep*, the next four to the `float` variable *rt*, and the next four to the `float` variable *hrs*. The ending level of the stack is now below that last four bytes—at the original beginning level.

(Actually, some C compilers turn this around by putting things on the stack in reverse order and taking them off in the order of the parameter declarations in the function definition. Either way achieves the same overall result, but don't get fancy in your programming and write something that depends on the order, because another C may reverse the order.)

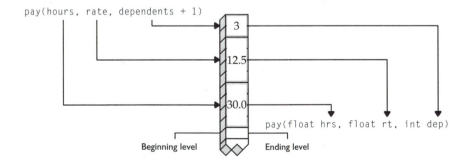

Knowing how the stack works, you can see the importance of the data types in the call agreeing with those in the definition. Can you imagine if your call put a four-byte `float` on the stack and the function pulled a two-byte `int` off? The first two bytes of a `float` would make no sense at all interpreted as an `int`!

A function may have more than one `return` statement. Only one will execute, of course, but you could set up a branching situation in which `return`s might be in more than one branch. The following two program segments will execute equivalently:

```
int GradePoints(char LetterGrade)      int GradePoints(char LetterGrade)
{  int GradePoints;                     {  switch LetterGrade
                                           {  case 'A':
   switch LetterGrade                           return 4;
   {  case 'A':                             case 'B':
         GradePoints = 4;                      return 3;
      case 'B':                            case 'C':
         GradePoints = 3;                      return 2;
      case 'C':                            case 'D':
         GradePoints = 2;                      return 1;
      case 'D':                            default:
         GradePoints = 1;                      return 0;
      default:                           }
         GradePoints = 0;              }
   }
   return GradePoints;
}
```

Although these examples are possible and legal in C, some do not consider the second example good structured-programming practice because the `switch` structure has more than one exit point.

➡️Program 6–5 is a variation on our earlier example. We have moved essentially all of the program's processes to the *pay()* function so that it needs neither arguments nor a return value. Although this is an impractical example merely to show these concepts, it might actually be practical if this function were used in a larger program with other functions performing other operations.

➡️Program 6–5

```
#include <stdio.h>

void pay(void);                                          /* Function declaration */

void main(void)
{
   /************************************************** Calculate net pay */
   pay();                                                /* Function call */
}

/***************** Calculates net pay given hours, rate, and dependents */
void pay(void)                                           /* Function definition */
{  float hrs, rt, gross, tax;
   int dep;
   double net_pay;
```

—Continued

```
/*********************************************************** Input data */
printf("Hours: ");
scanf("%f", &hrs);
printf("Pay rate: ");
scanf("%f", &rt);
printf("Dependents (other than self): ");
scanf("%i", &dep);

/***************************************************** Calculate net pay */
gross = hrs * rt;
tax = (.16 - .02 * (dep + 1)) * gross;
net_pay = gross - tax;

/***************************************************** Display results */
printf("Pay is: %8.2f\n", net_pay);
}
```

FUNCTION DECLARATIONS

Before anything can be used in C it must be declared. This is true of variables and it is true of functions. Some compilers will allow the first line of the definition to act as a declaration, but this means that definitions of the functions that are called in main() must appear before the main() function; and typical structured, modular programming puts the control module first, always main() in C, and other modules afterward.

FUNCTION DEFINITIONS AND DECLARATIONS

The ANSI method of declaring parameters in a function definition often is not accepted in non-ANSI compilers. For those compilers we use just the parameter variable names in the first line of the definition and declare them immediately below, before the opening brace. Any variables declared after the opening brace are treated the same as under ANSI—ordinary variables to be used by the function.

The first few lines of the *pay()* function in a non-ANSI C would be written as follows:

```
double pay(hrs, rt, dep)    /* Function definition */
    float hrs, rt;
    int dep;
{   float gross, tax;
```

The declaration, to appear above in the code, still must state the return type, but often it would be just

```
double pay();
```

If your compiler accepts either, use the ANSI style for future compatibility.

A major objective of declarations is to define the objects being used in a program so that the compiler can verify that they are being used correctly. To this end, ANSI has introduced the function **prototype**, a very complete declaration of a function. The prototype has this form:

```
return_type function_name(parameter types);
```

Using our example:

```
double pay(float, float, int);                    /* Function declaration */
```

Like other declarations, this is a statement and must be followed by a semicolon. Unlike other declarations, no memory space is allocated by the function declaration. When the function is called, the variables declared in the definition will be allocated, but the declaration of the function itself only tells the compiler about the data types used by the function.

ANSI allows variable names to follow the types in the prototype. The compiler actually ignores them but at least they are allowed. Using variable names can give us a better idea of what a function does when we look at the declaration, and it allows us to simply copy the first line of the definition to create our declaration. Don't forget to add the semicolon to the declaration.

```
double pay(float hrs, float rt, int dep);         /* Function declaration */
```

An advantage of prototyping is that the values passed to the function do not necessarily have to agree in data type with the parameter declarations in the function. Since the compiler knows the types in both places, it can include the code to make the conversion. Don't try this with your non-ANSI compiler! In fact, to be proper, you shouldn't take advantage of this property of your ANSI compiler either.

Like variables, functions may be declared externally or internally. An external declaration gives the function visibility in the entire program—it can be called from any function within the program. If the function is declared internally, it is only visible in that block of the program. In other words, it can only be called from that block. A function declared as static is visible only from the source file containing the declaration.

EXTERNAL VARIABLES AND FUNCTIONS

Passing values to a function and assigning them to the parameter variables of the function takes both executable instructions and time. The same can be said of return values. Why bother with all these local variables and returns? Why not declare external, global variables in the first place and have them directly accessed by the function? We could rewrite our pay-computing program this way and have it produce the same results in less time.

▶▶Program 6–6

```
#include <stdio.h>

void pay(void);                                    /* Function declaration */

float hours, rate;                                    /* Global variables */
double net_pay;
int dependents;

void main(void)
{
    /*********************************************************** Input data */
    printf("Hours: ");
    scanf("%f", &hours);
    printf("Pay rate: ");
    scanf("%f", &rate);
    printf("Dependents (other than self): ");
    scanf("%i", &dependents);
    ++dependents;

    /*********************************************** Calculate net pay */
    pay();                                            /* Function call */

    /*********************************************** Display results */
    printf("Pay is: %8.2f\n", net_pay);
}

/****************** Calculates net pay given hours, rate, and dependents */
void pay(void)                                   /* Function definition */
{   float gross, tax;

    gross = hours * rate;
    tax = (.16 - .02 * dependents) * gross;
    net_pay = gross - tax;
}
```

Output

```
Hours: 30
Pay rate: 12.5
Dependents (other than self): 2
Pay is:    337.50
```

Although there may be some advantages to this approach, there are significant disadvantages. The *pay()* function is no longer an encapsulated object; it depends not only on data from another function but also on specific variable names. Making a change in one part of your program may lead to unexpected changes in other parts and modifications and debugging become difficult. The price in execution for using local variables is small compared to the benefits in programming and maintainability. Do yourself and other C programmers (who might have to look at your program) a favor and keep your code as clean and encapsulated as possible.

SOME EXISTING FUNCTIONS

An ANSI C compiler will come with a complete stock of functions—certainly all those defined in the ANSI standard and usually a bunch that work with the specific target computer. To this group you may add an unlimited number of functions that you can buy from third-party vendors and those that you write yourself.

Header Files

Under ANSI, all functions should be prototyped—explicitly and completely declared—typically near the beginning of the program. When we use the ANSI functions and usually all the functions provided by third-party vendors, we don't have to write the declarations; they are already written in separate files called **header files**. These files, by convention, have the extension *.h* and are usually kept in some specific directory on the system. The file `stdio.h` is one such file; it stands for "standard input and output headers." These files are source code, readable by you and me, and we put them in our source code using the `#include` directive.

```
#include <stdio.h>
```

We never see the source code because the compiler, when it reaches that directive in our source code, shifts to the header file and takes lines from it. When it runs out of lines from the header file, it returns to where it left off in our source file and continues on.

We can, however, see the code in the header file by using a text editor and calling up the header file. If you try this, be sure not to make any modifications! You would find that the header files contain prototyped function declarations (among other things) but not function definitions. The definitions are in **libraries** of object code waiting to be combined with your program, if they are needed, during the linking process.

Header files also contain definitions of many constants that are used in ANSI C as well as other things that are system dependent. For example, the return value of the `scanf()` function might be `EOF`, a constant defined in `stdio.h`. The value of this constant will be different for different implementations of C. We don't have to know the actual value of `EOF` because its value is defined for us in each implementation of ANSI C. We can just refer to `EOF` in our program.

When you use a library function, then, you must `#include` the proper header file for it; otherwise, C will not recognize the function name. When we introduce a library function in this book, we will always put the header-file name in angle brackets out to the right of the description.

`printf()` and `scanf()` Revisited

We have used the `printf()` and `scanf()` functions since almost the beginning of the book. Now let us examine them more closely in light of what we know about functions. The declaration of the `printf()` function is as follows:

```
int printf(control_string, arguments)                          <stdio.h>
```

This declaration (in slightly different form) is in the header file stdio.h, which is why

```
#include <stdio.h>
```

has been at the beginning of all our programs.

The first function we chose to examine happens to contain exceptions to many of the standard traditions. The control_string, which we have already described, we will examine in more detail once we have tackled strings (Chapter 9). The printf() function has a variable number of arguments, the types and number controlled by the conversion codes in the control_string.

We have not used it so far, but printf() returns an integer value equal to the number of characters printed. In case of some error, it returns a negative value.

```
if (printf("Class: %5i\tMembers: %5i\n", class, members) == 28)
    success = 1;
else
    success = 0;
```

If everything works right, the return value of the printf() above should be 28; note that the tab and the newline each count as one character. If the return value is not 28, either there has been an error (setting the return value negative) or perhaps one of the values exceeds the minimum width of five characters set in the conversion codes. The function still executes, of course, even though it is part of a condition in an if statement; the line will be printed.

The scanf() declaration is also in stdio.h. We will represent it by

```
int scanf(control_string, arguments)                           <stdio.h>
```

Again, we will discuss the control_string more fully when we discuss strings, but, like the printf(), the types and number of arguments are determined by the control_string.

The return value of scanf() is the number of items that have been successfully converted and assigned. Usually, that is the number of conversion codes in the control string, with three possible exceptions. If you included an asterisk flag in a conversion code, meaning to skip a value in the stream, that value will not have been assigned and will not be counted in the return value. If there is an error in the input—something that the scanf() cannot handle—the return value will be different. If the scanf() encounters an end-of-file condition, it will return the value of the defined (in stdio.h) constant EOF. This should not occur if we use the scanf() for normal keyboard input.

The return value of scanf() can be used for a number of purposes. In the following example, it is the test value in a while loop.

```
#include <stdio.h>

void main(void)
{  int i1, i2, i3, total=0;

   printf("Enter three integers or 'q' to quit: "),
   while (scanf("%i %i %i", &i1, &i2, &i3) == 3)
   {  int subtotal;

      subtotal = i1 + i2 + i3;
      printf("These three total   %4i\n", subtotal);
      total += subtotal;
      printf("Enter three integers or 'q' to quit: "),
   }
   printf("The grand total is %5i\n", total);
}
```

Output

```
Enter three integers or 'q' to quit: 1 2 3
These three total      6
Enter three integers or 'q' to quit: 4 5 6
These three total     15
Enter three integers or 'q' to quit: q
The grand total is    21
```

The condition for our `while` loop compares the return value of the `scanf()` to three, the value we expect to get if three integers are input. When the relation is evaluated, the `scanf()` is called (and of course, executed) and its return value compared to three. An invalid character in the input stream will halt the `scanf()` and the return value will be the number of assignments to that point. A *q*, or any other nonnumeric character, is invalid; so in our example, an input of *q* stops the function and returns zero—a value not equal to three.

Be aware that the *q* remains in the input stream. If there was another `scanf()` later in the program, it would not wait for more keyboard input, but would use the characters currently in the stream. An `fflush(stdin)` would take care of the problem.

Terminating a Program

When C runs out of statements, the program quits; this is the normal way of terminating a program. But what if something unexpected happens? The program might receive erroneous or meaningless data; it could get stuck in a loop; the person in the office next to yours could stick his finger in a light socket, causing your computer to cough. You may want to build other exit points into your program to give the program a "normal" termination instead of printing 147 pages of gibberish and dying.

Most operating systems are capable of reacting to a termination of a program that has run successfully versus one that has run unsuccessfully. In order to do that, however, the operating system must receive a signal from the program as it terminates, indicating success or failure. The `exit()`

function provides both the termination and the indicator to the operating system.

```
void exit(int status)                                    <stdlib.h>
```

The *status* can be any value or expression, but in order for the operating system to recognize it, we should use the constants EXIT_SUCCESS or EXIT_FAILURE, also defined in stdlib.h, to send the proper signal to the operating system.

```
if (result < 0)
    exit(EXIT_FAILURE);
else
    exit(EXIT_SUCCESS);
```

The return value is void because there is no program left to which to return a value!

ANSI C has a number of other functions dealing with program termination, cleaning up loose ends, and communicating with the operating system. They are beyond the scope of this book, but as you become more sophisticated in your C programming, you will want to look them up.

Some Mathematical Functions

ANSI C contains over two dozen mathematical functions and most ANSI C implementations even more. We will not discuss all of them, but a few examples should give you enough to tackle most tasks and the understanding to research other available functions.

The absolute value of a number is the magnitude of the number irrespective of sign; in other words, expressed without a sign. The absolute value of 5 is 5. The absolute value of −5 is also 5. Three functions, abs(), labs(), and fabs(), return absolute value. The choice of function depends on the data type you are working with.

```
int abs(int expression)                                  <stdlib.h>

long labs(long expression)                               <stdlib.h>

double fabs(double expression)                           <math.h>
```

C has no exponentiation operator, no way of directly raising a number to a power. Raising values to integer powers can be accomplished by successive multiplication—2^3 is $2 \times 2 \times 2$—but that is certainly insufficient for general exponentiation. C's pow() function handles the task for us.

```
double pow(double expression, double exponent)           <math.h>
```

The *exponent* can, of course, be any expression. The return value will be the *expression* raised to the power of the *exponent*, that is, $expression^{exponent}$.

The pow() function follows the usual rules of exponentiation. The *expression* and *exponent* cannot both be zero. If the *exponent* is zero then pow() returns one. If the *expression* is negative, the *exponent* must be a whole number.

➤Program 6–8 prints the volume of a sphere of any radius.

➤**Program 6–8**

```
#include <stdio.h>
#include <math.h>

#define PI 3.1416

void main(void)
{  double radius;

   printf("Enter the radius: ");
   scanf("%lf", &radius);
   printf("Volume: %12.2f\n", 4 / 3. * PI * pow(radius, 3));
}
```

Output

```
Enter the radius: 6.28
Volume:      1037.45
```

If you want a square root, you can either raise something to the 0.5 power or use the sqrt() function:

```
double sqrt(double expression)                                    <math.h>
```

which returns the square root of the *expression*.

In addition to pow() and sqrt() there is a full set of logarithmic functions.

The **trigonometric functions** are straightforward in C. For example, to get the sine of an angle,

```
double sin(double angle)                                          <math.h>
```

The *angle* in C is represented in radians, not degrees. The following function call would return the sine of *degrees* expressed in degrees.

```
sin(degrees * 3.1416 / 180)
```

There are also functions for the arc sine and hyperbolic sine as well as those for cosine and tangent. All require double arguments and return double values.

```
sin          asin          sinh
cos          acos          cosh
tan          atan          tanh
```

For a summary of all the ANSI C mathematical functions, refer to Appendix C.

Random Numbers

C has three functions that, when used together, generate random numbers (or more properly, pseudorandom numbers—mathematically generated random numbers). The first, rand(), mathematically generates a pseudoran-dom number by taking a seed number and applying some monstrous algo-rithm to it so that the result looks nothing like the seed.

```
int rand(void)                                                    <stdlib.h>
```

There is no argument; not even a seed. C maintains the seed number within the system. We don't know where it is but C does. The value of the pseudorandom number is always positive and between zero and RAND_MAX, a constant defined in stdlib.h. To illustrate random numbers let us run ➡Pro-gram 6–9 three times.

➡Program 6–9

```
#include <stdio.h>
#include <stdlib.h>

void main(void)
{
    printf("Three random numbers:\n %i %i %i\n",
           rand(), rand(), rand());
}
```

Output   **Output**   **Output**

```
Three random numbers:   Three random numbers:   Three random numbers:
 10982 130 346           10982 130 346           10982 130 346
```

All three series of random numbers are exactly the same!

If you start with the same seed (the default seed is 1) and apply the same formula to it, you are bound to get the same results. We must use the srand() function to set another seed.

```
void srand(unsigned seed)                                         <stdlib.h>
```

Modifying our program we now get this:

➡Program 6–10

```
#include <stdio.h>
#include <stdlib.h>

void main(void)
{
    srand(10);
    printf("Three random numbers:\n %i %i %i\n",
           rand(), rand(), rand());
}
```

Output   **Output**   **Output**

```
Three random numbers:   Three random numbers:   Three random numbers:
 10345 30957 3463        10345 30957 3463        10345 30957 3463
```

At least the series is different from the earlier one, but we still get the same thing each time we run the program. It's the same problem: same seed, same series. We must have a way of changing the seed with each execution. One way is through the computer system's clock. The time() function gives us the computer clock's current time and date. The form of the time and date varies from system to system but at least its value will be different each time we run the program.

```
time_t time(time_t NULL)                                              <time.h>
```

The data type time_t is defined in the header file time.h, but it is compatible with the unsigned integer required for srand(). As well as returning the time and date, time() will also store it in a memory location of our choosing. The NULL argument directs the function to just return the value and not store it anywhere else in the system.

Let's try our program again.

➡Program 6–11

```
#include <stdio.h>
#include <stdlib.h>
#include <time.h>

void main(void)
{
    srand((unsigned) time(NULL));
    printf("Three random numbers:\n %i %i %i\n",

        rand(), rand(), rand());
}
```

Output   **Output**   **Output**

```
Three random numbers:    Three random numbers:    Three random numbers:
 3288 27551 25218          12653 22807 69          527 19141 5956
```

Success! Be sure to set the seed (srand()) before calling the rand() function.

RECURSION

One function may call another function by including the function name in its code. In an earlier example, the main() function called the *pay()* function. Control passed to the *pay()* function, which returned a value that substituted for the function call in the main() function. C places no limits on which functions can call which other functions as long as the called function is visible from the calling function. In fact, a function may call itself—a situation known as **recursion**. For purposes of analysis, a recursive call can be treated the same as one function calling another—as if there were two separate functions. In a recursive situation, though, the "two" functions do exactly the same thing.

Many processes lend themselves to recursive solutions, especially those that repeat an operation as some factor moves toward an ending condition. The classic example, and probably the best, is calculating the factorial of a number. The factorial of a number is the number times the number minus one, times the number minus one, and so forth until the number becomes one. For example, four factorial (4!) is

$$4 \times 3 \times 2 \times 1 \text{ or } 24$$

We could also say that 4! was $4 \times 3!$

$$4 \times (3 \times 2 \times 1) \text{ or } 4 \times 6 \text{ or } 24$$

and 3! was $3 \times 2!$ and 2! was $2 \times 1!$. The sequence ends when the number gets back to one, which has a defined factorial of one.

Summing up:

$$4! = 4 \times 3! = 4 \times 3 \times 2! = 4 \times 3 \times 2 \times 1!$$

A number factorial, then, is that number times the factorial of the number minus one. It sounds as if we are defining the term in terms of itself—and we are. If we had the proper, preexisting *factorial()* function, we could say that

$$4! = 4 \times \text{factorial}(3) \quad \text{or} \quad n! = n \times \text{factorial}(n-1)$$

Let us set up that function, then.

```
int factorial(int n)
{
    return n * factorial(n - 1);
}
```

This, of course, would be infinite; the function would continue to call itself. We need some ending condition. The mathematical definition of the factorial provides us with one: 1! is defined as 1. Therefore, if we send the *factorial()* function a value of 1, we will have it return 1 instead of calling itself again.

```
     int factorial(int n)
     {
f1       if (n <= 1 )/* <= to account for zero and negative arguments */
f2           return 1;

         else
f3           return n * factorial(n - 1);
     }
```

To analyze the execution of this function, it is convenient to treat each call as a call to a separate instance of the function, as if there were many, many functions with the name factorial. In essence, that is what C does. Let us look at the values passed by each call and each return. In the execution chart on the following page we show which instance of the function is being examined.

EXECUTION CHART

Line	Instance	Explanation	n	Pass	Return	Diagram
f1	1	n not <= 1.	4			
f3	1	Call *factorial()*.	4	3		
f1	2	n not <= 1.	3			factorial(4)
f3	2	Call *factorial()*.	3	2		24
f1	3	n not <= 1.	2			4 * factorial(3)
f3	3	Call *factorial()*.	2	1		6
f1	4	n is <= 1.	1			3 * factorial(2)
f2	4	Return 1.	1		1	2
f3	3	Return 2 * 1.	2		2	2 * factorial(1)
f3	2	Return 3 * 2.	3		6	1
f3	1	Return 4 * 6.	4		24	1

Recursion or Iteration?

Any situation that could be described recursively could also be described iteratively, that is, using a loop. For example, the *factorial()* function could be rewritten as

```
    int factorial(int n)
f1  {  int fact = n;      /* An accumulator to build up the factorial value */

f2, f3, f4    for (--n; n > 1; --n)
f5              fact *= n;
f6          return fact;
    }
```

If we pass the function a value of 4, it executes as follows:

EXECUTION CHART

Line	Explanation	n	*fact*
f1	Declare and initialize the factorial accumulator.	4	4
f2	Decrement n.	3	4
f3	n is > 1, execute loop.	3	4
f5	Multiply n into the *fact* accumulator.	3	12
f4	Decrement n.	2	12
f3	n is > 1, execute loop.	2	12
f5	Multiply n into the *fact* accumulator.	2	24
f4	Decrement n.	1	24
f3	n not >1, exit loop.	1	24
f6	Return the value of the *fact* accumulator.	1	24

Which is better? Each could be said to describe the calculation of a factorial. The first follows the theoretical basis of a factorial; the second, the typical hand calculation of it. In general, though, recursive solutions tend to be less efficient. There is a great deal of overhead in a function call. Each call must assign the passed value somewhere in memory and then to the function variable to which it is passed. In addition, the call must store the memory address at which the program will resume when it returns. The return must perform similar operations with the return value as well as finding out where to return. See the Nuts & Bolts box on "The Role of the Stack" for more information.

Use recursive algorithms with care. If it makes the program more understandable and the difference in efficiency is not too great, the recursive function may be worth it.

PUTTING IT TOGETHER

The Lucky 13 Casino and Car Wash would like us to write a computer twenty-one (blackjack) program for them. We are a little busy now, but we said that we will give them a start. Our program will deal just the first hand for the house (the dealer) and the player. It will be set up the way a casino would like it—with an infinite number of decks of cards, making it possible to deal more than one card of the same number and suit. Overall the program will be organized like this:

```
Deal for house
Deal for player
```

The deal for the house will consist of one card showing and one not. The player's hand will consist of two cards showing. Each card has a suit, a face (two, five, jack, queen), and a value (face value except for jack, queen, and king, which count 10; and ace, which can count as either 1 or 11). For each hand, we should print out the face and suit for the card or cards and, for the player, the total for the hand. Since the house may take more cards later, we may as well also keep track of the house's hand total.

Expanding the modules above, then, we have:

```
[Deal for house]
    Show first card face
    Add to hand total
    Show first card suit
[Deal for player]
    Show first card face
    Add to hand total
    Show first card suit
    Show second card face
    Add to hand total
    Show second card suit
    Print hand total
```

Three card faces and three suits are being shown, and three times the card value is being added to the hand total. Instead of writing this code three times, let's write one set of functions and call them three times. We can create one function, *Card()*, to print out a random card face and add to a hand total passed to it.

```
[Card]
    Pick random card
    Show face
    Add to hand total
```

Since aces can count 11 or 1, we count them 11 if the resultant total is not over 21, or 1 otherwise. If a hand has an ace that is being counted as 11, we can denote that by keeping the hand total negative. A 19 made up of an ace and an eight would be carried as −19.

Another function, *Suit()*, can print out a random suit.

[Suit]
    Pick random suit
    Show suit

The overall design, then, is:

[Deal for house]
    [Card]
    [Suit]
[Deal for player]
    [Card]
    [Suit]
    [Card]
    [Suit]
    Print hand total

The individual functions are expanded in the ➡Program 6–12 code.

➡Program 6–12

```
#include <stdio.h>
#include <stdlib.h>
#include <time.h>

int card(int total);              /* Prints random card and adjusts hand total */
void suit(void);                             /* Prints a random suit */

void main(void)
{  int player, house;                        /* Hand totals for both sides */

1     srand(time(NULL));                      /* Set a varying seed */

      /*****************************************************  Deal for house */
      printf("House has a ");
2     house = card(0);                        /* Start with zero total for hand */
      printf(" of ");
3     suit();
      printf(" and a down card\n");

      /*****************************************************  Deal for player */
      printf("You have a ");
4     player = card(0);                       /* Start with zero total for hand */
      printf(" of ");
5     suit();
      printf(" and a ");
6     player = card(player);                  /* Add to previous hand total */
      printf(" of ");
7     suit();
8     printf(" for %i\n", abs(player));       /* Player's hand total */
}

   /***************************** Prints random card and adjusts hand total */
   int card(int total)
   {  int value;

c1    value = rand() % 13 + 1;                /* Random number between 1 and 13 */
c2    switch (value)
```

—Continued

Program 6-12 —*Continued*

```
c3      { case 1:                    /* Ace is 11 unless hand over 21, then it is 1 */
c4          printf("Ace");
c5          value = 11;                           /* Default to 11, may change later */
c6          if (total >= 0)                                             /* First Ace */
c7            total = -total;                            /* Make total negative */
c8          break;
c9        case 11:
c10         printf("Jack");
c11         value = 10;
c12         break;
c13       case 12:
c14         printf("Queen");
c15         value = 10;
c16         break;
c17       case 13:
c18         printf("King");
c19         value = 10;
c20         break;
c21       default:                                          /* 2 through 10 */
c22         printf("%i", value);
        }
c23     total += (total >= 0) ?                          /* If total not negative */
c24           value :                                       /* add value */
c25           -value;                                /* Otherwise, subtract it */
c26     if (total < -21)                   /* If Ace in hand and total over 21 */
c27       total = abs(total) - 10;         /* Make Ace 1, drop negative flag */
c28     return total;                                /* Total with new card */
      }


      /*************************************************  Prints a random suit */
      void suit(void)
      {
s1      switch (rand() % 4 + 1)                  /* Random number between 1 and 4 */
s2      { case 1:
s3          printf("Spades");
s4          break;
s5        case 2:
s6          printf("Hearts");
s7          break;
s8        case 3:
s9          printf("Diamonds");
s10         break;
s11       default:
s12         printf("Clubs");
        }
s13     return;
      }
```

Outputs

```
House has a 5 of Spades and a down card
You have a King of Hearts and a Ace of Diamonds for 21

House has a Queen of Diamonds and a down card
You have a Jack of Hearts and a 3 of Spades for 13
```

EXECUTION CHART

Line	Explanation	player	house	total	value
1	Set seed for later random numbers.	?	?		
2	Call *card()*, pass 0.	?	?		
c1	Generate random number between 1 and 13.	(?)	(?)	0	5
c2	Look for `case 5:`. Doesn't exist so look for `default:` at c21.	(?)	(?)	0	5
c22	Print card face.	(?)	(?)	0	5
c23	Total not negative, so evaluate the true expression (c24), and accumulate in *total*.	(?)	(?)	5	5
c26	No ace in hand	(?)	(?)	5	5
c28	Return *total*.	(?)	(?)	5	5
2	Assign return value to *house*.	?	5		
3	Call *suit()*.	?	5		
s1	Expression evaluates to 1; look for `case 1:`. Find at s2.	(?)	(5)		
s3	Print "Spades".	(?)	(5)		
s4	Jump beyond end of structure.	(?)	(5)		
s13	Return.	(?)	(5)		
4	Call *card()*, pass 0.	?	5		
c1	Generate random number between 1 and 13.	(?)	(5)	0	13
c2	Look for `case 13:`. Find at c17.	(?)	(5)	0	13
c18	Print "King".	(?)	(5)	0	13
c19	Set *value* to 10.	(?)	(5)	0	10
c20	Jump to end of structure.	(?)	(5)	0	10
c23	Total not negative, so evaluate the true expression (c24), and accumulate in *total*.	(?)	(5)	10	10
c26	No ace in hand	(?)	(5)	10	10
c28	Return *total*.	(?)	(5)	10	10
4	Assign return value to *player*.	10	5		
5	Call *suit()*, print "Hearts".	10	5		
6	Call *card()*, pass *player*.	10	5		
c1	Generate random number between 1 and 13.	(10)	(5)	10	1
c2	Look for `case 1:`. Find at c3.	(10)	(5)	10	1
c4	Print "Ace".	(10)	(5)	10	1
c5	Set *value* to 11.	(10)	(5)	10	11
c6	*total* not negative, first ace.	(10)	(5)	10	11
c7	Make total negative.	(10)	(5)	-10	11
c8	Jump to end of structure.	(10)	(5)	-10	11
c23	Total negative, so evaluate the false expression (c25), and accumulate in *total*.	(10)	(5)	-21	11
c26	Ace in hand but not over 21.	(10)	(5)	-21	11
c28	Return *total*.	(10)	(5)	-21	11
6	Assign return value to *player*.	-21	5		
7	Call *suit()*, print "Diamonds".	-21	5		
8	Print absolute value of *player*.	-21	5		

The *suit()* function neither accepts values from the calling function nor does it return anything. All of what it does is contained within the function. The *card()* function accepts a value, changes it, and returns the changed version; as well as performing other operations. Near the end of this function, we adjust the total by adding to a positive total or subtracting from a negative one.

This program is, of course, only the start of a complete blackjack game, which, with your current knowledge of C, you could finish.

SUMMARY

Whether we can access a variable in a program depends on that variable's **storage class** and the particular point in the program at which we attempt the access. Storage class determines a variable's **lifetime** and **visibility**—either **global**, from declaration to the end of the program; or **local**, from declaration to the end of the block in which it was declared. Even though a variable might normally have visibility, it can always be **superseded** by another variable of the same name.

External variables, the default storage class if a variable is declared outside a function, have global lifetime and visibility. If they are to be accessed by code from another source file, however, they must be **referenced** using an extern key word. An external variable declared as static, however, has its visibility limited to the source code file in which it is declared.

Variables declared **internally** default to **automatic** with local lifetime and visibility. An internal variable declared as static has a global lifetime but is visible only when the program is in the block in which the declaration was made. Internal variables declared as register are local in both senses, can only be integers, and C will store them in CPU **data registers** if possible. If variables have the same name, the last one made visible will supersede the other until its visibility ceases.

Global lifetime variables are automatically initialized to zero at declaration; local variables are garbage at the time of declaration. Any variable, however, may be explicitly initialized in the declaration. An internal static variable is declared and initialized only the first time it is encountered in the code. The const qualifier declares that a variable may not be changed from its initialized value. The volatile qualifier declares that a variable is subject to change from forces outside the C program.

The inclusion of a function name in code **calls** the function. The call may pass values to the function, which will use those values to initialize variables declared in the **function definition**. The function code will then execute, and the return statement will pass a **return value** back to the calling point, which then substitutes for the call. It is important that the values in the call agree in number, order, and type with the values declared in the first line of the function definition and that the return value of the function agrees with its use at the calling point. A function that expects no values to be passed to it will have the key word void in place of the parameter declarations. If the function returns no value, it will be declared as type void. In ANSI C a very specific function **prototype** is used to declare the function.

Instead of passing values to functions, external variables might be used, but the practice tends to make a program less modular and its functions less encapsulated.

Most existing functions are in object-code libraries with their declarations in source-code **header files**, which we must #include if we are to use them. The functions printf() and scanf() both have return values. The first is the number of characters printed and the second is the number of assignments made. Other functions reviewed were exit(), to terminate a program; abs(), labs(), and fabs(), to return absolute values; pow() to raise values to powers; sqrt(), to take the square root; various **trigonometric functions** with their arguments all stated in radians; rand() and srand() to generate pseudorandom numbers and time() to provide a constantly varying seed value.

Functions can call not only other functions but also themselves in a process called **recursion**. Most recursive processes could also be performed iteratively, and often there is a choice to be made between the efficiency of the process and its understandability.

KEY TERMS (in order of appearance)

Storage class
Lifetime
Visibility
Global
Superseded
Local
Internal
External
External variable
Reference
extern
Automatic
static
Data register
register
const
volatile
Call

Function definition
void
Return value
return
Prototype
Header file
Library
exit()
abs()
labs()
fabs()
pow()
sqrt()
Trigonometric function
rand()
srand()
time()
Recursion

REVIEW QUESTIONS

1. Differentiate between the terms lifetime and visibility.

2. Differentiate between the terms local and global.

3. What does it mean to supersede a variable with another?

4. Differentiate between the terms internal and external.

5. What does the extern key word do?

6. What are the lifetime and visibility of an external variable?

7. What are the lifetime and visibility of an automatic variable?

8. What are the lifetime and visibility of a static variable?

9. What are the lifetime and visibility of a register variable?

10. What extra limitations are there on register variables?

11. Variables of which storage classes are automatically initialized to zero?

12. How does the const qualifier change a variable?

13. How does the volatile qualifier change a variable?

14. How do local variables lead to better encapsulation within programs?

15. What actions does a function call initiate?

16. What is the purpose of the parameter declarations in the first line of a function definition?

17. What does the parameter declaration void mean?

18. What is a return value? How is it generated and how is it used?

19. Why is ANSI prototyping advantageous?

20. What is the purpose of a header file?

21. What is the return value of printf()? scanf()?

22. How is the exit() function used?

23. How are random numbers made really random?

24. What makes recursive function calls special, and how can we treat them so that they do not appear special?

EXERCISES

1. Fill in the following table concerning the storage classes of variables.

Storage Class	Lifetime	Visibility	Value
External			
Static (external)			
Automatic			
Static (internal)			
Register			

2. State the lifetime and visibility (global or local) and values (or garbage) of the variables in the following program segment.

```
short a;
static float b;

void main(void)
{  double c;
   static long d;
   register int e;
```

Variable	Lifetime	Visibility	Value
a			
b			
c			
d			
e			

3. What will the following program segment produce on the screen?

```
int x = 100;

void main(void)
{  int x = 10;

   printf("%i\n", x);
   for (x = 1; x <= 5; ++x)
   {  static int x = 20;

      printf("%i ", x);
      ++x;
   }
   printf("\n%i\n", x);
}
```

4. Given the following main() segment, fill in the first line of the function definition. How would the prototyped declaration appear?

```
double t;                        _____ func(_____ x, _____ y)

float a;
int f;
   . . .
t = func(f, a);
```

5. Given the following function, write a proper call statement to send it the value 16, and the values of a and $b + c$. The result of the function should be stored in d.

```
void main(void)          double func(float x, double y, float z)
{  float a;              {
   int b, c;                return (x + y) / z;
   long double d;        }
```

6. Modify the following program so that the marked code is executed in a *miles_per_gallon()* function. The `main()` function should have no *gallons*, or *miles_per_gallon* variables, and the function should be called directly from the last `printf()` function.

```
#include <stdio.h>

void main(void)
{   int beg_miles, end_miles;
    float odo_adjust, gallons, miles_per_gallon;

    beg_miles = 296;
    end_miles = 513;
    odo_adjust = 1.15;

                                        /* This stuff should be in a function */
    printf("How many gallons? ");
    scanf("%f", &gallons);
    miles_per_gallon = (end_miles - beg_miles) * odo_adjust / gallons;
                                                 /* End of function stuff */

    printf("Miles per gallon: %.2f\n", miles_per_gallon);
}
```

7. Show an execution chart for the following program that prints a two-decimal-place random number in a given range.

```
#include <stdio.h>
#include <stdlib.h>
#include <time.h>

float two_place(float bottom, float top);

void main(void)
{   float low, high;

    srand((unsigned) time(NULL));
    printf("Enter low high for range: ");
    scanf("%f%f", &low, &high);
    printf("Number: %.2f\n", two_place(low, high));
}

float two_place(float bottom, float top)
{   int range, begin, rnd_num;

    range = (int) ((top - bottom) * 100);
    begin = (int) (bottom * 100);
    rnd_num = rand() % (int) range + begin;
    return rnd_num / 100.0;
}
```

8. Rewrite the *two_place()* function in the program in Exercise 7 so that it has no variables other than those declared in the formal parameters, and it has only a `return` statement.

9. Rewrite the *total()* function on the next page so that it works recursively rather than iteratively. Don't change `main()`.

```
#include <stdio.h>

int total(int cur, int end);

void main(void)
{  int beg, end;

   printf("Enter beginning ending: ");
   scanf("%i%i", &beg, &end);
   printf("Total: %i\n", total(beg, end));
}

int total(int cur, int end)
{  int count, tot = 0;

   for (count = cur; count <= end; ++count)
      tot += count;
   return tot;
}
```

PROGRAMS

1. Create a function whose job is to print a page heading. It should print the next page number each time it is called. Use the following driver (main() function segment) to test your function.

Driver

```
void main(void)
{  int p;
   for (p = 1; p <= 5; ++p)
      page();
}
```

Function and Variable

```
page()
   page_no
```

Output

```
Major Document     Page 1

Major Document     Page 2

Major Document     Page 3

Major Document     Page 4

Major Document     Page 5
```

2. Write a program that accepts any number from the keyboard and tells you whether it is a nonnegative integer. The number should be sent to the function *int_test()*, which returns either the integer value, or −1 if the number is negative, or zero if it is nonnegative but not an integer. Inputs should continue until a zero is input.

Functions and Variables

```
Main()
    input        From keyboard
    integer      Return from function
int_test()
    value        From main()
    result       Value to return
```

Output

```
Your number: 48
The number is 48.
Your number: -14.3
The number is negative.
Your number: 12.345
The number is not an integer.
Your number: 0
```

3. Write a program that will show the maturity value (principal plus accumulated interest) on a deposit at interest rates of 4, 5, 6, and 7 percent. The formula should be calculated in a separate function.

Formula

$$maturity\_value = p\left(1 + \frac{r}{100}\right)^y$$

Functions and Variables

```
main()
    y            number of years
    r            interest rate (percent)
    p            principal
mat_val()        maturity value function
    any local variables needed for function
```

Output

```
AMOUNT? 1000
NUMBER OF YEARS? 5

MATURITY VALUES AT VARIOUS INTEREST RATES
4% 1216.65    5% 1276.28    6% 1338.22    7% 1402.55
```

4. The formula for determining the number of possible combinations of N things taken K at a time is:

$$C = \frac{N!}{K!\,(N-K)!}$$

Write a program to use this formula. $N!$ means "N factorial." The factorial of a number is the number times the number minus 1, times that number minus 1, and so forth until the multiplier is 1. For 5! (five factorial) $= 5 \times 4 \times 3 \times 2 \times 1 = 120$. The factorial calculations should be done in a separate function and should be done iteratively. N and K must be positive integers with $N >= K$ for the formula to work.

Functions and Variables

```
main()
    c            Combinations
    n            Number of things
    k            Number taken at a time
factorial()
    counter
    fact         Accumulator for factorial
```

Output

```
HOW MANY THINGS? 7
HOW MANY AT A TIME? 4
NUMBER OF POSSIBLE COMBINATIONS IS 35
```

5. Write a program that allows input of two sides of a right triangle and calculates the hypotenuse according to the Pythagorean theorem (*Hypotenuse*^{2} = *side1*^{2} + *side2*^{2}). Use no multiplication; use the pow() function instead. Use only the variables given.

Variables

side1, side2, hypotenuse

Output

```
Enter first, second side: 3,4
Hypotenuse: 5
Enter first, second side: 24.75, 38.2
Hypotenuse: 45.5171
```

6. Write a program to determine the sides and angles of a right triangle given one side and the adjacent angle. Remember that the angles in the trig functions are expressed in radians.

Variables		**Formulae**
side	given side	Hypotenuse = side / cosine
op_side	opposite side	Opposite side = side × tangent
hypotenuse		Other angle = 90 − given angle
angle	given angle	Radians = degrees × π / 180
op_angle	opposite angle	π = 3.1416

Output

```
ENTER ANGLE? 30
ENTER ADJACENT SIDE? 10
OPPOSITE SIDE= 5.77352
HYPOTENUSE= 11.547
OPPOSITE ANGLE= 60
```

7. The pseudorandom numbers generated by C should be pretty good, statistically. Write a program to see how good. Generate 1000 integers between 1 and 5, and keep track of how many of each were produced. Try it with a million. (Don't forget to use longs for your accumulators.) Save as *RANDOM* for modification later.

Functions and Variables

```
main()
   ones, twos, three, fours, fives   Accumulators
   count                             Loop counter
rnd()                                Integer between 1 and 5
```

Sample Output

Ones	Twos	Threes	Fours	Fives
220	211	197	204	168

8. Write a guessing game for the computer in which the computer generates a random whole number between 1 and 100 and the player tries to guess that number. The program should allow only ten guesses, and it will tell the player whether the guess is too low, too high, or right.

Functions and Variables

```
main()
    secret      The number to be guessed
    guess       The players guess
    guesses     The number of guesses
rnd()           Function for random number between 1 and 100
```

Output

```
THE SECRET NUMBER IS BETWEEN 1 AND 100.

WHAT IS YOUR GUESS? 5
TOO LOW, GUESS AGAIN? 45
TOO LOW, GUESS AGAIN? 92
TOO HIGH, GUESS AGAIN? 46

RIGHT! IT TOOK YOU 4 TRIES.
```

Output

```
THE SECRET NUMBER IS BETWEEN 1 AND 100.

WHAT IS YOUR GUESS? 7
TOO LOW, GUESS AGAIN? 46
   .
   .
   .
TOO HIGH, GUESS AGAIN? 71

YOU LOSE, THAT WAS YOUR LAST GUESS. THE NUMBER WAS 74
```

9. Write a simple calculator so that you can input an expression with two values separated by an operator and the computer will print out the proper result. Your calculator should include the ^ operator for exponentiation. All calculations should be done in an appropriate function (the functions will be small) and the results printed in main().

Functions and Variables

```
main()
    op          Operator
    x, y        Values for calculation
add()
subtract()
multiply()
divide()
exponentiate()
    a, b        Local variables for each function
```

Output

```
Enter expression (q to quit): 34.7+23.5
  58.2
Enter expression (q to quit): 5.27 * 32.6
  171.802
Enter expression (q to quit): 1.41414 ^ 2
  1.99979
Enter expression (q to quit): 657.82 / 0
  Can't divide by  0
Enter expression (q to quit): 534 & 26
  Invalid operator
Enter expression (q to quit): q
```

10. Write a program to make change in coins. The main() function should accept input of the purchase and the amount tendered, and the *change()* function should print the number of quarters, dimes, etc.

Functions and Variables

```
main()
   purchase

   tendered
change(amount)
   cents           Convert the float amount to the int cents
```

Output

```
Purchase: 3.08
Amount tendered: 4
Quarters: 3
Dimes   : 1
Nickels : 1
Pennies : 2
```

11. In the kids' game "Paper, Rock, Scissors" each player chooses one of the three and the winner is determined by the relationship between the two choices. "Paper covers rock," so paper wins; "rock breaks scissors," so rock wins; and "scissors cuts paper," so scissors wins. If both choose the same it is a tie and no one wins. Write a program to play the game against the computer until the player enters *q* instead of a choice.

Functions and Variables

```
main()
   machine              The machine's choice: p, r, or s
   player               The player's choice
   result               Win, lose, or tie
   score                Accumulated score
char MachineChoice(void)  Prints paper, rock, or scissors
   choice               Random choice
```

Sample Output

```
Choose (p)aper, (r)ock, (s)cissors or (q)uit: p
   The machine chooses scissors.   You lose!    Your score: -1
Choose (p)aper, (r)ock, (s)cissors or (q)uit: s
   The machine chooses scissors.   Its a tie!    Your score: -1
Choose (p)aper, (r)ock, (s)cissors or (q)uit: p
   The machine chooses rock.    You Win!    Your score: 0
Choose (p)aper, (r)ock, (s)cissors or (q)uit: r
   The machine chooses scissors.    You Win!    Your score: 1
Choose (p)aper, (r)ock, (s)cissors or (q)uit: q
```

POINTERS

7

One of the advantages that C has over other languages is its access to the internal parts of the computer, particularly main memory. Any language can access variables by name in main memory, but in C we often access them by referring directly to where they are stored. This is such an important and useful concept in C that it is imperative that it be fully understood. This chapter is short because its object is simply to build a foundation for this concept without too much added complication. In subsequent chapters we will use the concept in a number of different applications. After reading this chapter you should understand:

1. The data type that stores memory addresses rather than other data.
2. How variables of that data type are declared.
3. How memory can be accessed, read or written, by referring to memory locations stored in these variables.
4. The use of these data types in working with functions.
5. Overcoming the limitation of returning only one value from a function.

Let us examine C's facility for reaching into main memory.

VARIABLE ADDRESSES

Back in Chapter 1 we saw that main memory was made up of thousands or millions of individual storage spaces, or **locations**, each of which has a distinct numeric **address**. When we declare a variable, C finds an available contiguous set of locations large enough to accommodate that data type, and allocates it to the variable. For example,

```
float grinch;
```

might result in memory allocation like this:

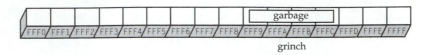

grinch

Assuming that this was an internal declaration, *grinch*'s value would be garbage.

C allows us to access the variable by name because it keeps track of the address of the first location allocated to the variable. The address of *grinch* is FFF9 (we have used hex notation here as a convenience so that we can identify numbers being used as addresses as opposed to those used as other data values). Unless we demand it, C does not let us know the addresses of variables we declare; it simply uses its own mechanisms to access them.

If we knew where the variable was, instead of referring to the variable's name, we could tell the computer to access the variable that was in the location with the address 7115 or 24236 or FFF9 or whatever. We call this **pointing** to a variable.

The address of a variable, whether we use hex or decimal notation, is just a numeric value, and like any other numeric value, it can be stored in another variable. A variable that contains an address value, rather than a value we would normally think of as regular data, is a pointer variable or simply a **pointer**.

THE POINTER DATA TYPE

Every stored value is of one data type or another, and the variables that store these values must be of the same type. We are familiar with data types such as short int or double and know that types are distinguished by the number of bytes allocated for them and the type of notation—straight binary or exponential. A memory address has its own data type. Although ANSI does not give it an official title, we shall refer to it as type pointer.

The pointer data type is integral, similar to int. Its size, however, depends on your particular implementation of C. In most Cs the size is the number of bytes in which the target computer stores a memory address. For the sake of discussion, let us assume that a pointer has three bytes. It probably doesn't in your C, but since no other common data type has three bytes it will help us to distinguish pointers from others.

We have already had some experience with addresses. The scanf() function requires addresses rather than variables for its arguments. Remember, the symbol & in front of a variable name means "the address of" that variable rather than the value stored in the variable. Using the conversion code %p in printf() we can actually print out the address contained in the pointer data type. For example:

➠Program 7–1

```
#include <stdio.h>

void main(void)
{   long number = 12345;

    printf("Number's value is %li. Its address is %p.\n", number, &number);
    printf("Number's size is %i bytes. The address' size is %i bytes.\n",
           sizeof number, sizeof &number);
}
```

Output

```
Number's value is 12345. Its address is FFF4.
Number's size is 4 bytes. The address' size is 3 bytes.
```

number

The value of the address is printed in hexadecimal notation, and the size of the address is three bytes in our imaginary C. The address is of the location where the variable starts. Here the variable starts at FFF4 (actually FFFFF4, but that many characters won't fit on the diagrams) and spans four bytes, FFF4 through FFF7. Why the specific address FFF4? That address was chosen by C; we had no control over it. When we declared *number* as a long, C found an empty four bytes somewhere in memory and allocated it to *number*.

Pointer Variables

We can declare a variable as type pointer, but in a slightly roundabout fashion. The pointer points to something—it contains the address of something—so in addition to declaring it of type pointer we also state the data type to which it points. An asterisk (*) in front of a variable name in a declaration indicates that it is of type pointer, and the type to which it points is declared in the usual way. In the following declaration *data* is a float and *ptr* is a pointer that we usually describe as being "pointer to float."

```
float *ptr, data = 100;
```

This declaration allocates four bytes (in a typical C) for *data* and three bytes (in our imaginary C) for *ptr*. Assuming the declaration was internal, *ptr*'s value is garbage. In other words, it points to a memory space somewhere in the system, but you don't know where it is or what value is stored there—garbage pointing to garbage.

A pointer variable may be assigned and used in the same way that any other variable can, but we must remember that its data type is pointer, and its value is an address, not usual data. Saying

```
ptr = 26;
```

is valid in some non-ANSI Cs (ANSI recognizes that 26 is data type int, not pointer), but using the value could be hazardous because who knows what is stored at memory location 26 (or 1A in hex)? We now have something valid pointing to garbage.

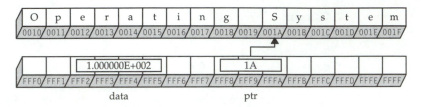

If, however, we assign a valid address to *ptr*, an address whose contents we know, then we have something useful.

```
void main(void)
{   float *ptr, data = 100;

    ptr = &data;
```

Now the value of *ptr* is an allocated address, the address of *data*, and it points to a valid value, 100.

This statement,

```
printf("%p %p\n", ptr, &data);
```

will produce this output:

```
FFF2 FFF2     (Actually FFFFF2 FFFFF2 for a three-byte address.)
```

The addresses are, of course, the same, but notice that we used the conversion code %p for printing &data. The variable *data* is type float but &data is a pointer.

INDIRECTION

Often we use pointer variables to access the locations to which they are pointing—a process we refer to as **indirection**. The **indirection operator**, *,

162   POINTERS

in front of a variable directs the computer to interpret the value of the variable as an address, go to the location defined by that address, and access the value starting there. Declaring the pointer variable as a pointer to a particular data type is important so that C will know how many bytes beyond the address to access and whether the storage is in straight binary or E notation.

The indirection operator (*) looks suspiciously like the symbol we used to declare a variable as a pointer (*). Though the two symbols look the same, their functions are totally different depending on where we find them in the program. In a declaration, the * means pointer variable; in any other statement it means indirection—the contents at the address contained in the variable.

Both the indirection operator and the address operator are unary like the negate (!), unary minus (-), and increment (++), and have the same precedence (the highest except for the expression operators such as parentheses) and the same associativity (right to left).

We can access the value 100 in three ways:

▶ Program 7–2

```
#include <stdio.h>

void main(void)
{   float *ptr, data = 100;

    ptr = &data;
    printf("%p %p\n", ptr, &data);
    printf("%f %f %f\n", data, *ptr, *&data);
}
```

Output

```
FFF2 FFF2
100.000000 100.000000 100.000000
```

The variable *ptr* is, of course, type pointer, but the notation *ptr is type float because it refers to the value stored at FFF2, the floating point value of *data*. As we saw, &data is type pointer but *&data is float because it refers to the value (*) stored at the location (&) of the variable *data*. To summarize, the value of data is equal to the value of *ptr, which is equal to the value of *&data. All are of type float.

The indirection operator can also be used in assignments. If we added these statements to the end of the previous program:

```
*ptr = 200;
printf("%f %f %f\n", data, *ptr, *&data);
```

our output would become

```
FFF2 FFF2
100.000000 100.000000 100.000000
200.000000 200.000000 200.000000
```

Our statement told C to assign the value 200 to the memory location pointed to by *ptr*. In other words, C evaluated the variable *ptr*, found that its value was FFF2, and assigned the value 200 at the location FFF2.

POINTERS AND FUNCTIONS

All this makes for a diverting mental exercise but how can we use it? One valuable way is with functions. Instead of passing data values to functions, we can pass addresses. Once the function knows the address of a variable, the function can change the contents at that location. In other words, without knowing a variable's name, we can change its value.

In ➡Program 7–3 we pass the address of the variable *cost* to the function *inflate()* and allow the function to change the value stored there. That address is assigned upon entry to the function to the pointer variable *value*. Within the function, we multiply the contents at the location pointed to by *value*.

➡Program 7–3

```
#include <stdio.h>

void inflate(double *value, double inflator);

void main(void)
m1  {   double cost, inflation = 1.3;

        printf("Enter the project's cost: ");
m2      scanf("%lf", &cost);
m3      inflate(&cost, inflation);
m4      printf("Cost adjusted for inflation is %.2f\n", cost);
    }

i1  void inflate(double *value, double inflator)
    {
i2      *value *= inflator;                    /* *value = *value * inflator */
i3      return;
    }
```

Output

```
Enter the project's cost: 100
Cost adjusted for inflation is 130.00
```

Passing a variable address rather than a value is often referred to as a **pass by reference** as opposed to a **pass by value**. This program combined both in one call. Accessing the location whose address is stored in a pointer variable is **dereferencing** the variable.

The address of *cost* is used more in this program than the variable itself—in both the scanf() and the *inflate()* calls. Why not just declare the variable *cost* as a pointer in the first place, and rewrite the program as in ➡Program 7–4 on the next page?

Line	Explanation	cost	inflation	value	inflator
m1	Declare variables in main(). *value* and *inflator* don't exist yet.	?	1.3	----	----
m2	Input *cost*.	100	1.3	----	----
m3	Call function, pass FFF0 (address of *cost*) and 1.3.	100	1.3	----	----
i1	Allocate and initialize function variables. Variables in main() still exist but are not visible.	(100)	(1.3)	FFF0	1.3
i2	Multiply the value at FFF0 by 1.3, store result at FFF0.	(130)	(1.3)	FFF0	1.3
i3	Transfer execution back to m3.	130	1.3	----	----
m4	Print inflated *cost*.	130	1.3	----	----

▶▶Program 7–4

```
void main(void)
{  double *cost, inflation = 1.3;

   printf("Enter the project's cost: ");
   scanf("%lf", cost);                          /* This won't work */
   inflate(cost, inflation);
   printf("Cost adjusted for inflation is %.2f\n", *cost);
}
```

The problem is that although *cost* is allocated, it is never assigned a value—where it points, no one knows. If we write a value at the location pointed to by *cost*, as we would in the scanf() function, it might end up in the middle of the operating system, change critical instructions, and crash the computer!

Returning More Than One Value

You can't!

A function can return only one value, but we can effectively get more than one value back to the calling function by putting addresses in the call, having the called function change the values at those locations, and returning to the calling function.

Let us swap the values of two variables as an example. A swap is a common operation done in sorts, inserting into lists, and many other tasks. In a swap, we want the value that was in *a* to end up in *b* and the value that was in *b* to end up in *a*. To do it we will have to use a temporary variable, *t*, to hold one of the values while we move the other.

```
int a = 125, b = 37, t;
```

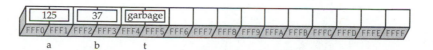

t = b;

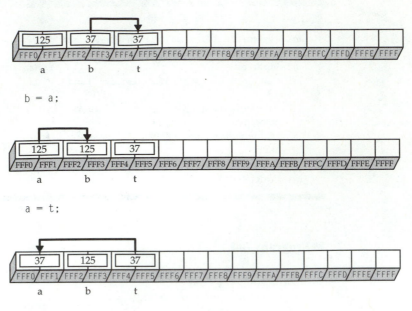

b = a;

a = t;

Since we do swaps so frequently, we want a function, *swap()*, that we can call whenever we need it—*swap(a, b)*. But we want the values of both *a* and *b* in the calling function to change and we cannot return two values from the *swap()* function, so let us pass the addresses of *a* and *b* and have *swap()* manipulate the values at those addresses.

▶▶Program 7–5

```c
#include <stdio.h>

void swap(int *x, int *y);

void main(void)
{   int a = 125, b = 37;

    printf("Before swap  a: %3i    b: %3i\n", a, b);
    swap(&a, &b);
    printf("After swap   a: %3i    b: %3i\n", a, b);
}

void swap(int *x, int *y)
{   int t;

    t = *y;
    *y = *x;
    *x = t;
    return;
}
```

Output

```
Before swap  a: 125    b:  37
After swap   a:  37    b: 125
```

Let us examine the *swap()* graphically.

```
void swap(int *x, int *y)
{  int t;
```

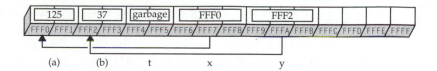

The first line of the definition allocates the variables *x* and *y* and initializes them with the addresses passed from the `main()` function. The variables *a* and *b* still exist, but they are not visible at this time. The local variable *t* is allocated but has no value yet.

```
t = *y;
```

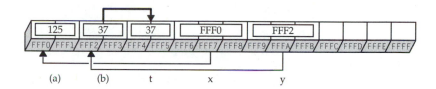

We follow the address stored in *y*, FFF2, to find the value 37. This value is assigned to *t*. The data type of *t* is int as is the data type of **y*.

```
*y = *x;
```

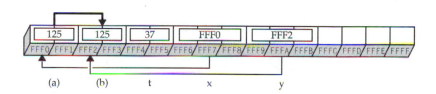

Following the address stored in *x*, FFF0, we find the value 125. This is assigned to the location whose address is stored in *y*, FFF2. The data types of both **x* and **y* are int.

```
*x = t;
```

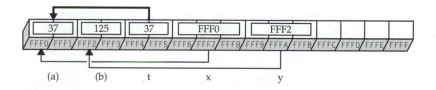

The value of *t* (37) is assigned to the location whose address is stored in *x*, FFF0.

When the function returns, *x*, *y*, and *t* disappear, and *a* and *b* are once again visible but with their values swapped.

USING RETURNS AND REFERENCES

The Mobile Mud Concrete Company, as part of its sales-invoice program, figures the price of an order and how many trucks it will take to fill the order in the function *price()*. The main() function then prints out the results. The price is figured at $75 per yard plus $50 per truck, and a truck can carry a maximum of 4 cubic yards. The main() function needs both the price and the number of trucks from the *price()* function. One value, in this case the price, can be returned by the function. The other value, the number of trucks, is calculated in the function and assigned at the address contained in the pointer variable *vehicles*. The value of *vehicles* (the address stored there) was initialized in the function call to the address of *trucks*, a variable visible in the main() function. Assigning a value at the location pointed to by *vehicles*, then, assigns a value to *trucks*.

➡Program 7–6

```
#include <stdio.h>

float price(float yds, int *vehicles);

void main(void)
{  float yards;
   int trucks;

       printf("How many yards? ");
m1     scanf("%f", &yards);
m2     printf("  Price:  %.2f  \n", price(yards, &trucks));
m3     printf("  Trucks: %i\n", trucks);
   }


p1 float price(float yds, int *vehicles)
   {
p2     *vehicles = (yds - .001) / 4 + 1;        /* .001 adjusts for any */
p3     return yds * 75 + *vehicles * 50;        /* possible rounding error */
   }
```

Output

```
How many yards? 4
   Price:  350.00
   Trucks: 1
```

Output

```
How many yards? 8.2
   Price:  765.00
   Trucks: 3
```

EXECUTION CHART

Line	Explanation	yards	trucks	yds	vehicles
m1	Assign value at address of *yards*.	4	garbage	----	----
m2	Evaluate printf() argument, call *price()*, pass value of *yards* (4) and address of *trucks* (FFF2).	4	garbage	----	----
p1	Allocate *yds* and initialize as 4. Allocate *vehicles* and initialize as FFF2.	(4)	(garbage)	4	FFF2
p2	Evaluate expression, assign result at location pointed to by *vehicles*.	(4)	(1)	4	FFF2
p3	Evaluate return expression (350) and pass back to calling point.	(4)	(1)	4	FFF2
m2	Pass return value of *price()* to printf() and execute printf().	4	1	----	----
m3	Print value of *trucks*.	4	1	----	----

PUTTING IT TOGETHER

Following is a checking-account reconciliation program. You enter your checking-account balance according to the bank statement and the balance according to your checkbook, and all your outstanding (uncleared) checks and deposits, then have the program print out a summary of the number of outstanding checks and their total, as well as the number of outstanding deposits and their total. Finally, the program tells you whether you are in balance or, if not, how far off you are. The overall process is:

```
Input bank and book balances
Input uncleared checks
Input uncleared deposits
Calculate balance
Print summary and balance
```

If we expand the Input uncleared checks and Input uncleared deposits modules, we would have

```
Input bank and book balances
Input uncleared checks
    WHILE more checks
        Input check amount
        Accumulate amount in reconciliation balance
        Count check
    END LOOP
Input uncleared deposits
    WHILE more deposits
        Input deposit amount
        Accumulate amount in reconciliation balance
        Count deposit
    END LOOP
Calculate balance
Print summary and balance
```

PECULIARITIES OF THE STACK

It would be tempting to combine the printing of the price and the number of trucks in the same `printf()` function:

```
printf("  Price: %.2f  Trucks: %i  \n",
       price(yards, &trucks), trucks);
```

Since the call to the *price()* function is before the use of the variable *trucks* in the `printf()` function, *trucks* should have a valid value. It seems reasonable, but remember in the previous Nuts & Bolts box on the "Role of the Stack" we said that values are taken off the stack in the reverse order that they are put on. The order of argument evaluation is not defined by the ANSI standard, but, at least in the C used here, the reversing of the order is accomplished when the values are taken off the stack. The address of the *price()* function is first on the stack during the call to `printf()`, but last off, meaning that it is last to be evaluated. In other words, `printf()` looks up the value of *trucks* first, when it is garbage, and then calls the *price()* function, which would have given *trucks* a real value.

In order to print both values in the same line, we would either have to reverse their order in the `printf()` function (but that might not work in another C), or call the *price()* function beforehand and assign its return value to another variable to be used in `printf()`.

The two modules we just expanded are almost alike. The process is the same, but one works with deposits and the other with checks. Since the process is the same, let us have a function (*InData()*) that performs the process and gives the results to the main program. We can return the balance produced in the function and assign it to either a check amount (*ChecksOut*) or deposit amount (*DepositsOut*). To count the checks or the deposits we will pass the function the address of either the check counter (*NoOfChecks*) or deposit counter (*NoOfDeposits*), and have the function modify the contents at those addresses.

➡Program 7–7

```
#include <stdio.h>
double InData(short *Number);            /* Input, accumulate checks, deposits */

void main(void)
{   short NoOfChecks = 0, NoOfDeposits = 0;                    /* Counters */
    double BankBalance, BookBalance;           /* Bank statement & checkbook */
    double Balance;                 /* Checkbook balance after reconciliation */
    double ChecksOut, DepositsOut;                   /* Amounts outstanding */

    /****************************           Input bank and book balances */
    printf("Bank statement balance: ");
1   scanf("%lf", &BankBalance);
    printf("Checkbook balance: ");
2   scanf("%lf", &BookBalance);

    /*********************************            Input uncleared checks */
    printf("Enter outstanding checks\n");
3   ChecksOut = InData(&NoOfChecks);

    /***********************************          Input uncleared deposits */
    printf("Enter outstanding deposits\n");
4   DepositsOut = InData(&NoOfDeposits);

    /*********************************************        Calculate balance */
5   Balance = BookBalance + ChecksOut - DepositsOut;

    /************************************************         Print summary */
    printf("Outstanding: Number    Amount\n");
6   printf("    Checks: %6i%9.2f\n", NoOfChecks, ChecksOut);
7   printf("   Deposits: %6i%9.2f\n", NoOfDeposits, DepositsOut);
8   if (Balance == BankBalance)
9      printf("You are in balance.\n");
10  else if (Balance > BankBalance)
11     printf("You think you have $%.2f more\n"
              "than the bank thinks you have.\n", Balance - BankBalance);
    else
12     printf("The bank thinks you have $%.2f\n"
              "more than you think you have.\n", BankBalance - Balance);
}
/***********************        Enter data for either checks or deposits */
double InData(short *Number)
            /* Return total amount of checks or deposits. Number is count */
{   double Amount, Balance = 0;

    printf("  ('q' to quit)\n");
    printf("  Amount: ");
```

—Continued

Program 7-7   *—Continued*

```
i1    while (scanf("%lf", &Amount) != 0)
i2    {  Balance += Amount;
i3       ++*Number;
         printf("  Amount: ");
      }
i4    fflush(stdin);
i5    return Balance;
   }
```

Output

```
Bank statement balance: 842.39
Checkbook balance: 377.12
Enter outstanding checks
   ('q' to quit)
   Amount: 149
   Amount: 23.87
   Amount: 106.33
   Amount: 305.44
   Amount: q
Enter outstanding deposits
   ('q' to quit)
   Amount: 119.37
   Amount: y
Outstanding: Number    Amount
      Checks:     4     584.64
      Deposits:   1     119.37
You are in balance.
```

Output

```
Bank statement balance: 465.78
Checkbook balance: 284.22
Enter outstanding checks
   ('q' to quit)
   Amount: 182.56
   Amount: 80.35
   Amount: stop
Enter outstanding deposits
   ('q' to quit)
   Amount: 50
   Amount: 31.34
   Amount: q
Outstanding: Number    Amount
      Checks:     2     262.91
      Deposits:   2      81.34
You think you have $0.01 more
than the bank thinks you have.
```

EXECUTION CHART

Line	Explanation	NoOf Checks (FFF0)	NoOf Deposits (FFF2)	Number (InData)	Amount (InData)	Balance (InData)
1	Enter bank balance (842.39).	0	0			
2	Enter book balance (377.12).	0	0			
3	Call *InData*, pass address of *NoOfChecks*.	0	0			
i1	Enter *Amount*. It is valid, so go into loop.	(0)	(0)	FFF0	149.00	0.00
i2	Accumulate *Amount* into *Balance*.	(0)	(0)	FFF0	149.00	149.00
i3	Add 1 to location pointed to by *Number*.	(1)	(0)	FFF0	149.00	149.00
i1–i3	Continue entering *Amounts*, accumulating in *Balance*, and incrementing *Number*, until invalid input *q* makes scanf( ) return value zero.	(4)	(0)	FFF0	305.44	584.64
i4	Flush input stream.	(4)	(0)	FFF0	305.44	584.64
i5	Return *Balance*.	(4)	(0)	FFF0	305.44	584.64
3	Assign return to *ChecksOut*.	4	0			
4	Call *InData*, pass address of *NoOfDeposits*.	4	0			
i1	Enter *Amount*. It is valid, so go into loop.	(4)	(0)	FFF2	119.37	0.00
i2	Accumulate *Amount* into *Balance*.	(4)	(0)	FFF2	119.37	119.37
i3	Add 1 to location pointed to by *Number*.	(4)	(1)	FFF2	119.37	119.37
i1	Invalid input *y* makes scanf( ) return value zero.	(4)	(1)	FFF2	119.37	119.37
3	Assign return to *ChecksOut*.	4	0			
4	Call *InData*, pass address of *NoOfDeposits*.	4	0			
i4	Flush input stream.	(4)	(1)	FFF2	119.37	119.37
i5	Return *Balance*.	(4)	(1)	FFF2	119.37	119.37
4	Assign return to *DepositsOut*.	4	1			
5–12	Complete program.	4	1			

There could be any number of ways of handling this input while accumulating numbers and balances. The *InData()* function, however, encapsulates the operation and allows it to be used in any application requiring that type of task. We don't have to worry about the variables in the application conflicting with those in the function or, indeed, how the function actually operates once it is tested and debugged. *InData()* has become an abstract data object.

Before we move on, let us examine the way in which we exit the `while` loop in the *InData()* function. When we type an inappropriate character for the `float` variable *Amount*, the `scanf()` stops, returning the value zero, indicating no assignments were made. It works fine as we don't access the input stream again, because the inappropriate character, *q* or whatever we type in, is left in the stream. Whatever accesses the stream next, the next call to the `scanf()`, will be faced with the same character, again inappropriate for a `float`, stopping the next input loop before we even have a chance to type anything.

The `fflush(stdin)` function call at the end of the *InData()* function empties the input stream, leaving it ready for the next input. The next call to `scanf()` will find an empty stream and wait for us to type something.

SUMMARY

Main memory consists of a number of **locations**, each of which has an **address**. Variables are store in sets of these locations and so have addresses. We can refer to the variable by name or by **pointing** to its address. Since the address of a variable is a numeric value, we can store it in a variable, one with a **pointer** data type.

When we declare a pointer variable we also declare the data type to which it points. Three symbols are used with pointers: the ampersand (&), meaning "the address of"; the asterisk (*) used in a declaration, meaning that the variable following it is a pointer; and the asterisk, the **indirection operator**, used in a statement other than a declaration, meaning **indirection**—to access the contents at the address in the variable.

When a pointer variable is declared, its value is garbage; it points to some unallocated location. One way to give it a valid location is to assign to it the address of another variable. The location being pointed to can be accessed like any other variable by using the indirection operator in front of the pointer variable.

Pointers are often used in conjunction with functions. By passing a pointer to a function, the called function can change the value at an address that is visible in the calling function, enhancing encapsulation and data abstraction. This is a **pass by reference** rather than a **pass by value**. The value being pointed to is **dereferenced** by following the pointer back to where it points. Passing by reference is also a way of overcoming the limitation of a function being able to return only one value. The one value may be returned but other values may be communicated to the calling function by changing values at locations whose addresses are passed by the calling function.

KEY TERMS (in order of appearance)

Location
Address
Pointing
Pointer
Indirection

Indirection operator
Pass by reference
Pass by value
Dereferencing

REVIEW QUESTIONS

1. What is a memory location? An address?

2. How is a variable's declaration reflected in locations and addresses?

3. What does pointing to a variable refer to?

4. What do we call a variable that contains an address?

5. Why might we consider a pointer as its own data type?

6. In the imaginary C referred to in the text, how many bytes would be allocated to a pointer to `short`? A pointer to `long double`?

7. Why is it important that a pointer be declared as a pointer to a specific data type?

8. An asterisk in front of a variable name can mean two things. What are they and how do we tell which it means? Give an example of each use.

9. What does the ampersand in front of a variable name mean?

10. What `printf()` conversion code will allow us to print out an address?

11. Differentiate between a pass by value and a pass by reference.

12. What does the term dereference mean?

13. How can we return more than one value from a function?

14. How can a function be made to access a variable that is not visible in that function?

EXERCISES

1. Given the declarations and statements below, what are the data types (if it's pointer, don't forget *pointer to what*) and values of the expressions? Mention any problems that might arise.

```
char *c, *b, a = 'A';
float d, *e;

*c = a;
b = c;
e = &d;
d = 1.5;
```

Expressions:

&a _____

*c _____

*b _____

e _____

*e _____

*&d _____

2. If C would allow us to make such an assignment (which it won't) what would be the result of the first assignment below? What about the second, which is a legal assignment?

```
float x = 123.45;
int *y;

y = &x;
*y = x;
```

3. Fill in the effects of the following statements with values and arrows on the following memory diagram.

```
c = &a;
*b = a;
```

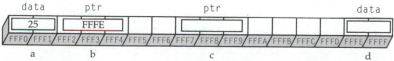

4. Finish the function call and the function that squares both *x* and *y* in the `main()` function.

```
square(___x, ___y);                                      /* Function call */


void square(_____a, _____b)                      /* Squaring function */
{  ____ *= ____;
   ____ *= ____;
}
```

5. Show an execution chart and the output for the following program.

```
#include <stdio.h>

float miles_per_gallon(int m, float g, float *c);

void main(void)
{  int miles = 400;
   float mpg, gallons = 20.0, cost = 1.0;

   mpg = miles_per_gallon(miles, gallons, &cost);
   printf("The cost of this trip was %.2f at %.1f mpg.\n",
          cost, mpg);
}

float miles_per_gallon(int m, float g, float *c)
{
   *c = g * *c;
   return m / g;
}
```

PROGRAMS

1. Write a program that will figure the average of any number of integer values input into the computer. The value zero should be used to signal the end of input. For the main body of the program use only the three pointer variables given. To ensure that they point to usable places in memory, assign them the addresses of the first three variables below. For example, val = &value;. That statement (and the declaration) is the only time the variable *value* should appear in the program.

Variables

		Output
value		VALUE? 28
counter		VALUE? 92
total		VALUE? -15
*val	number to input	VALUE? 0
*count	number of values to average	THE AVERAGE IS 35
*tot	sum of all the values	

2. Write a program that shows the volumes of all cubes with lengths, widths, and heights varying from one to three. For the main body of the program use only the three pointer variables given. To ensure that they point to usable places in memory, assign them the addresses of the first three variables below. Treat these variables the same as those in Problem 1.

Variables

```
length
width
height
*len
*wid
*hgt
```

Output

LENGTH	WIDTH	HEIGHT	VOLUME
1	1	1	1
1	1	2	2
1	1	3	3
1	2	1	2
1	2	2	4
. . .			
3	3	3	27

3. Write a program that generates five random numbers between 25 and 50 and keeps track of the smallest, largest, and the sum of the numbers. A *rnd()* function should generate each random number in the proper range, and a *stats()* function should be used to update the smallest, largest, and sum with each new random number. All printing should be done from `main()`.

Variables and Functions

```
main()                              rnd()   Returns random number in range
    count
    number   The random number      stats()
    min, max, sum                        num, smallest, biggest, total
```

Output

Numbers	Minimum	Maximum	Sum
42	42	42	42
35	35	42	77
50	35	50	127
37	35	50	164
27	27	50	191

4. Write a program to write an employee's paycheck stub. You should type in the employee's hours, pay rate, and tax rate. All calculations should be done in the function *PayCheck()* but the resultant information should be printed out in the `main()` function.

Functions and Variables

```
Main():             PayCheck():
    Hours               Hrs
    PayRate             PRate
    TaxRate             TRate
    GrossPay            GPay
    Tax                 Tx
    NetPay              NPay
```

Output:

```
Hours, pay rate: 30.5, 12.60
Tax rate (%): 15.2

Gross Pay      $384.30
Taxes           58.41
Net Pay        $325.89
```

5. Design a function that calculates the roots of a quadratic equation. The formula is given below. Since there are two roots, have the function return one, and pass the function an address where it can place the second. Test the function by calling it with *a* set to 1, *b* to 5, and *c* to 4. It should produce the given output.

Quadratic Formula

$$\frac{-b \pm \sqrt{b^2 - 4ac}}{2a}$$

Output

```
The roots are -1 and -4.
```

6. Write a program that accepts three integers form the keyboard, puts them in order and prints out the ordered set as well as the total. The function *order()* should put the values in order. One way is to compare the first to the second; if it is larger, swap the two. Do the same with the second and third; then with the first and second again. The *swap()* function should perform the swap.

Functions and Variables

```
main()              order()            swap()
   n1, n2, n3          i1, i2, i3         a, b
   total                                  temp
```

Outputs

```
Enter three integers: 35 27 52
27, 35, and 52 add up to 114.

Enter three integers: 9 8 7
7, 8, and 9 add up to 24.

Enter three integers: 16 314 72
16, 72, and 314 add up to 402.
```

ARRAYS

PREVIEW

In this chapter we will look at data in groups called arrays, and learn how we can most easily manipulate these arrays in C. After reading this chapter you should understand

1. What arrays are and about the individual variables they are made of.

2. How arrays are stored in memory.

3. How we declare and initialize arrays.

4. The relationships that arrays have to pointers.

5. How we pass arrays to functions.

6. Using arrays of arrays of variables.

7. Some common applications for arrays.

Data often does not come one piece at a time, but in sets—groups of tens, hundreds, or thousands of values to be processed. We could, possibly, think of tens, hundreds, or even thousands of different variable names, but keeping track of them and processing them one after another would require a lot of C code. Using arrays, we can designate a set of variables with a name for the set and use a number to designate individual members of the set. We will still have tens, hundreds, or thousands of variables with as many names, but the names will be easier to keep track of.

SUBSCRIPTED VARIABLE NAMES

In algebraic notation, we use variables such as X and Y. We can also use **subscripted variables** such as X_1, X_2, and X_3 (the subscript is the number following the letter). Subscript notation is typically used for grouping sets of variables. For example, the values of ten samples in a chemical analysis might be stored in S_1, S_2 on up to S_{10}. Each of the variables is completely separate and has its own value, but we can see that they are all part of a set because we have given them names with the same prefix, S. We refer to a set of subscripted variables as an **array**. In our example all the analyses can be referred to collectively as the array S. Remember, however, that the set is made up of individual variables, and even though we may refer to the set, we must access each of those individual variables.

We can also use subscripted variables in C. Algebraic notation will not work for us because, with most equipment, we cannot write source code with the subscript subscripted—dropped down half a line. So we put the subscript in brackets [ ]—*S[1]*, *S[2]*, *S[10]*. In algebra, we can choose whatever subscripts we want. In C, we cannot. The first subscript is always zero, and the rest go up from there.

A subscripted variable may be used like any other variable; remember, it is only a different kind of name. For example, if *S[4]* is an `int`, it can be treated like any other `int`.

```
S[4] = 25;
printf("The value is %i\n", S[4]);
```

This program segment will, of course, print out the value 25.

ARRAY DECLARATIONS

Like anything else in C, array variables must be declared. They can be of any data type and any storage class except register. Since registers are limited, it would not make sense to declare a set of register variables. A single declaration declares and defines an entire set of subscripted variables. The statement

```
short sales[7];
```

declares a set of variables all with the prefix *sales*. The number in brackets represents the number of variables to be declared. It must be a constant expression; variables are not allowed here. This declaration, then, allocates space in memory for seven variables, *sales[0]*, *sales[1]*, *sales[2]*, on up to *sales[6]*. There is no space allocated for *sales[7]*. (In some other languages the value in the declaration is the highest subscript, but not in C. Here it is the number of subscripts. The highest subscript will be one less than this.)

HOW MANY VARIABLES IN YOUR ARRAY?

You have declared your array as `float apples[3]`, and C has allocated space in memory for three floats, *apples[0]*, *apples[1]*, and *apples[2]*. Is that all the variables you have in your array? Yes and no. Yes, that is all the space allocated for the variables in this array, but no, you can access *apples[35]* if you want to. C does not keep track of the number of variables in your array, so you are free to use any subscripts you want. You are also free to shoot yourself in the foot with your own gun!

When you refer to a subscripted variable, such as *apples[1]*, C uses the subscript to count variable spaces away from the beginning of the array; *apples[1]*, then, is one `float` from the beginning of the *apples* array. The variable *apples[35]*, then, would be 35 variables away from the beginning of the *apples* array. You can actually assign a value there—C won't stop you—but the place in memory was not allocated for that variable, and may have been allocated for some totally different purpose. What will happen? If you're lucky and the space was unallocated, the program might work. Or it may crash miserably, wiping out everything you've worked on all day.

The moral here is that it is up to you to keep your subscripted variables within the allocated bounds. C won't do it for you.

Initializations

Since subscripted variables are like any other variables, we can assign them in statements such as

```
sales[5] = 47;
sales[0] = 3806;
```

Also, like other variables, we can initialize them at the time of their declaration. Any global lifetime variables, including array variables, have a default initialization to zero. We can declare them explicitly by putting their values, separated by commas, in braces. Remember, an array declaration establishes a number of variables, so we will have to have a number of values to assign to them.

```
short sales[7] = {3806, 28, 4522, 476, 1183, 47, 12};
```

We do not necessarily have to initialize the entire array. If we initialize any of the variables, the rest will automatically be set to zero by C, even if they are local variables. For example,

```
short sales[7] = {3806, 28, 4522};
```

assigns those values to *sales[0]*, *sales[1]*, and *sales[2]*, and C will initialize *sales[3]* through *sales[6]* to zero.

We can easily initialize an `auto` array to all zeros like this:

```
short sales[7] = {0};
```

The variable *sales[0]* will be explicitly set to zero, and all the rest will be set to zero by default.

If we initialize the array, we can even leave the space within the brackets blank. The C compiler will figure out the number of subscripted variables to allocate. The declaration

```
short sales[] = {3806, 28, 4522, 476, 1183, 47, 12};
```

will allocate and initialize seven variables, *sales[0]* through *sales[6]*.

THE VARIABLY DEFINED VARIABLE

A major advantage of subscripted variables is that we can change the variable name by changing the subscript. To make that easier, we can put any expression, anything that reduces to a numeric value, within the brackets. For example, all of the following are valid:

```
sales[4]
sales[x]
sales[b + q * pow(d, f / 2)]
```

The subscript will be determined by the value of the expression within the brackets. The subscript must be an integer value, so if the expression evaluates to a floating-point value, it is truncated to an integer. The notation sales[4.9] refers to the variable *sales[4]*. Be careful of floating-point subscripts, however. Something that evaluates to what looks to be 4.0 may actually be stored in the binary version of 3.99999999, which would truncate to 3.

It is up to you to see that the subscripts are within the range allocated in the declaration of the array. The notations sales[-1] and sales[10] will lead to two values, the first located in the 2 bytes before the array, and the second 20 bytes after the beginning of the array, which is 6 bytes past the array. What is there? Who knows? (See the Nuts & Bolts section "How Many Variables in Your Array?")

The ▶▶Program 8–1 prints out the values stored in each variable of the *sales* array. The value of *count* becomes the subscript, which in turn determines the variable name.

▶▶**Program 8–I**

```
#include <stdio.h>

void main(void)
{   short sales[] = {3806, 28, 4522, 476, 1183, 47, 12};
    short count;

    for (count = 0; count < 7; ++count)
        printf("Variable sales[%hi] =%5hi\n", count, sales[count]);
}
```

Output

```
Variable sales[0] = 3806
Variable sales[1] =   28
Variable sales[2] = 4522
Variable sales[3] =  476
Variable sales[4] = 1183
Variable sales[5] =   47
Variable sales[6] =   12
```

ARRAY APPLICATIONS

Inserting

An **insert** begins with a list of values in order, and adds one more to the list. The new value is added so that the list remains in order after the addition. We will store the list of values in an array, which will have to be one variable larger than the number of values in the original list, because we are going to add one. If we are going to insert a value into a list of 100 values, our array will have to consist of at least 101 variables.

We know that the new value should be inserted in the list where it is greater than the number before and less than the number after. Now all we have to do is explain that to the computer. Let us consider a list of four values—2, 4, 6, and 8—to which we want to add one—5. We will declare an array of five variables *data[5]*, assign the values to the first four variables in the array, and assign the value we wish to insert to *insert*. We will consider each position in the array as a possible insert position using the variable *position* to keep track of the possible insert position. The variable in that position would be *data[position]*. We will either assign our insert value (*insert*) to that variable or go on to the next position.

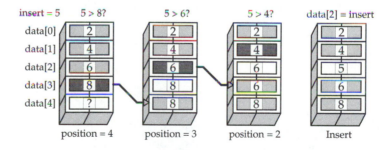

There will already be a blank position at the end of the array, so let's use that as our first possible insert position. (In the graphic example, the possible insert position is represented by a clear area.) If our insert value is greater than the value in the position before our possible insert position (*data[position - 1]*), then it must belong in this position (*data[position]*). (The darker shaded area is the position before the possible insert position.) If it is not greater, then it must belong somewhere above, so let's begin to make space for it by moving a value down one position—assigning the value in *data[position - 1]* to *data[position]*. Then we can move our possible insert position up one variable by decrementing *position* and repeat the process.

The process will stop when we have either found the proper insert position or considered all the positions back to the second. If it doesn't belong in the second position, it must belong in the first. In either case, if we have decremented our *position* correctly, we can simply insert—assign *insert* to *data[position]*.

➤Program 8–2

```c
#include <stdio.h>

void main(void)
{  int data[5] = {2, 4, 6, 8};
   int insert = 5;
   int position;

   /********************************************* Print list before insert */
   printf("Before: ");
   for (position = 0; position < 4; ++position)
      printf("  %i", data[position]);
   printf("\nInsert:   %i\n", insert);

   /*************************************************************** Insert */
   position = 4;                 /* Start from empty variable at end of list */
   while (insert < data[position - 1] && position >= 1)
   {  data[position] = data[position - 1];         /* Move next value down */
      --position;                                  /* Go up the list */
   }
   data[position] = insert;                        /* Add insert value to list */

   /********************************************* Print list after insert */
   printf("After : ");
   for (position = 0; position < 5; ++position)          /* One more added */
      printf("  %i", data[position]);
   printf("\n");
}
```

Output

```
Before:   2  4  6  8
Insert:   5
After :   2  4  5  6  8
```

Try the program above with the *insert* values 1 and 9. In fact, it is a good idea to test the boundary conditions when testing any code.

Sorting

A sort arranges a list of values in order. Unlike an insert, the values in a list to be sorted do not have to start out in any particular order, and no new value is added to the list. There are a number of different sort routines, some more efficient at sorting certain types of data, some extremely complicated, some quite specialized. We will use one called a **selection sort** here, not because of its great efficiency, but because it works in all situations and is one of the least complicated.

In the selection sort, the program makes a number of passes through the list. With each pass, the smallest value is "selected"—moved to the top of the list. We will call this position in the list the *select* position. At the end of the pass, then, the smallest value is in the *select* position.

The program now makes another pass but, since the value in the *select* position is already in the proper place, we shall move the *select* position down to the second position and select the smallest number from there down. We will continue to move the *select* position down and select the smallest number from that point downward until we have selected values into all but the last position in the list. If all the others are in their proper place, the last one must be also.

When we move a value to the *select* position, what happens to the value that was there before? The two values are swapped. The one originally in the *select* position moves to where the other value was and vice versa.

In this graphic example (slightly simplified; it doesn't show all the intermediate swaps) we sort a list of five values. The lightly shaded areas show the *select* positions and the lines show the swaps at each pass. The darker areas show values in their final, ordered positions. After four passes, the entire list is in order.

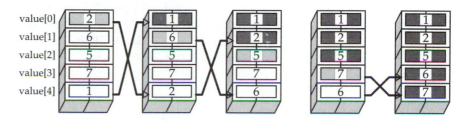

To effect the selection sort, we will put the values in an array; call it *value* for this example. Then we will have our program set up *select* positions from 0 to 3—remember, we don't have to select the last one. This can be done with a for loop.

```
for (select = 0; select <= 3; ++select)
```

Our select variable, then, will be *value[select]*.

To make a pass through the list, we will have our program compare the value of *value[select]* (the value in the select position) with the value in each position below it; we will call these unselected positions. If we use the variable *unselected* to keep track of our unselected position, then our unselected variable will be *value[unselected]*.

We want to start our *unselected* positions one below our *select* position (*select* + 1) and go to the end of the list (4, in this example). We can do this with a for loop also. Since the set of unselected positions changes with each new select position, the unselected loop will be nested within the select loop.

```
for (select = 0; select <= 3; ++select)
                              /* 1 less than number of values to sort*/
{   for (unselected = select + 1; unselected <= 4; ++unselected)
                              /* select+1 to end */
    {
       ×
    }
}
```

This set of nested loops would set *select* to zero and proceed to the *unselected* loop, starting it with one. We would make our comparison between *value[select]* and *value[unselected]* and swap if needed. The program would set *unselected* to two, and we would make the comparison again. It would do the same with *unselected* being three and four. After exiting the *unselected* loop, the program would make *select* one and begin the *unselected* loop again, this time at two.

The comparison should test to see whether the value of *value[unselected]* is smaller than that of *value(select)*.

```
if (value[unselected] < value[select])
```

If so, we should swap those two values to get the smaller one in *value[select]*.

```
temp = value[select];
value[select] = value[unselected];
value[unselected] = temp;
```

We will perform the test, and possibly swap, with each new unselected value; therefore, the statements should be inside the *unselected* loop. The following program includes the declarations and initializations, as well as a printout of the sorted array.

➡Program 8–3

```
#include <stdio.h>

void main(void)
{   short value[] = {2, 6, 5, 7, 1};
    short select, unselected, temp;

    /**************************************************************** Sort */

    for (select = 0; select < 4; ++select)
                                        /* 1 less than number of values */
    {   for (unselected = select + 1; unselected <= 4; ++unselected)
                                                    /* Select+1 to end */
        {   if (value[unselected] < value[select])        /* Lower value? */
            {   temp = value[select];                           /* Swap */
                value[select] = value[unselected];
                value[unselected] = temp;
            }
        }
    }
    /**************************************************** Print result */
    for (select = 0; select <= 4; ++select)
        printf("%hi ", value[select]);
    printf("\n");
}
```

Output

```
1 2 5 6 7
```

ARRAYS AND POINTERS

Like any other declaration, an array declaration allocates memory space for the variables. For array variables, this memory space is guaranteed to be contiguous—one variable follows the next. For our declaration of the *sales* array we used earlier, C would have to find 14 bytes of free memory, say at address FFF0, and allocate them to the variables *sales[0]* through *sales[6]*. The variable *sales[0]*, then, would occupy FFF0 and FFF1; *sales[1]*, FFF2 and FFF3, and *sales[6]*, FFFC and FFFD.

```
short sales[] = {3806, 28, 4522, 476, 1183, 47, 12};
```

You could easily find the address of the beginning of the array, the **base address**, thusly:

```
printf("The sales array starts at %p\n", &sales[0]);
```

and the statement would print out FFF0. In C, however, the array prefix, without any subscript, is also the base address of the array. It can be used as type pointer, or more specifically, since we declared *sales* as an array of shorts, **pointer to** short.

```
printf("The sales array starts at %p\n", sales);
```

would do exactly the same thing.

The prefix *sales*, however, is not a variable but a constant. Once declared, it cannot be changed. This makes a certain amount of sense. Changing the base address of the array would make all the variable names refer to some other locations. Unfortunately, their values would remain at the old addresses! We can assign values, then, to the variable *sales[0]*, but not to the constant prefix *sales*.

Offsets from the Base Address

We humans can think of *sales[0]*, *sales[1]*, and *sales[2]* as different variables with different names. The concept holds true in C, but C's way of implementing the concept is both simple and elegant. The variables *sales[0]*, *sales[1]*, and *sales[2]* are still different variables with different values, but to C the only identifier is the variable's prefix or base address, *sales*. The subscript, the number in brackets, is an **offset** from that base address. C interprets *sales[3]* as an offset of 3 from the base address *sales*, FFF0.

But three what? Certainly not bytes because *sales[3]* does not begin at FFF3. The offset is the number of variables from the base address. In bytes it is the subscript times the size of an individual variable. The variable *sales[3]* begins at FFF0 + (3 × 2) or FFF6. The variable *sales[0]* begins at FFF0 (FFF0 + (0 × 2)).

C keeps track of the base address of an array, but it does not keep track of the highest declared subscript. We could actually assign a value to *sales[7]* and C would put that value at memory locations FFFE and FFFF (FFF0 + (7 × 2)). This may well be a location that C has allocated for some other purpose, so our assignment will mess things up. Again, it is up to us to see that we do not go out of the bounds of our array.

Pointer Notation

We saw that the prefix for an array is really the base address of the array. Using pointer notation we could refer to the variable *sales[0]*, the first variable of the array, by *sales, the contents of the location at the address *sales*. The statement

```
printf("%hi\n", *sales);
```

would print the number 3806, the value of *sales[0]*.

To print out all the values in the array, as above, could we simply add two to sales at each step, having it point to a different location each time? No, because *sales* is not a variable; it is constant. We could, however, use *sales* in an expression such as *sales* + 4 and use indirection to reference the contents at other addresses. The statement,

```
printf("%hi\n", *(sales + 4));
```

would print out the number 1183, the value of *sales[4]*.

We have illustrated this pointer notation for accessing array variables and it is certainly valid, but in most cases, it is not considered good form to mix notations. If you have declared an array using subscript notation, stick with subscript notation unless there is some overriding reason to use pointer notation.

Pointer Arithmetic

If *sales* is FFF0, doesn't *sales* + 4 evaluate to FFF4? And why should *sales* + 4 refer to *sales[4]* whose address is FFF8? It does indeed refer to the address FFF8 because of **pointer arithmetic**. We declared *sales* as an array of shorts, which means we can use *sales* as a pointer to short. Any time we do arithmetic with pointers, the values refer to the number of variables, not the number of bytes. We saw this same phenomenon in calculating offsets from base addresses using bracket ([]) notation. The expression *sales* + 4, since *sales* is a pointer to short, is evaluated as *sales* + (4 × 2) or FFF8. If x was declared as a long double array and allocated the address 7000, then x + 3 would be interpreted as x + (3 × 10) (assuming 10 bytes for a long double) or 7030.

The parentheses in the expression *(*sales* + 4) are important. The indirection operator (*) is higher in precedence than the addition operator. Given the values stored in the *sales* array, look at the difference in evaluation with and without parentheses:

3806	28	4522	476	1183	47	12	

| FFF0 | FFF1 | FFF2 | FFF3 | FFF4 | FFF5 | FFF6 | FFF7 | FFF8 | FFF9 | FFFA | FFFB | FFFC | FFFD | FFFE | FFFF |

sales[0] sales[1] sales[2] sales[3] sales[4] sales[5] sales[6]

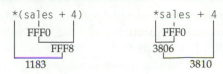

Without the parentheses, the indirection operator is applied to *sales*. The address there is FFF0 and the value at that location is 3806. To this we add the four, not 4×2, because we are not dealing with pointers any more, yielding the result 3810, hardly what we were looking for.

The notation `*(sales + 4)`, then, is equivalent to `sales[4]`. Both are offsets from the same address. The `for` loop in the program above could be rewritten

```
for (count = 0; count < 7; ++count)
    printf("Variable sales[%hi] =%5hi\n", count, *(sales + count));
```

Since *sales* is a pointer, could we not just increment *sales* and rewrite the for loop this way?

```
short *end;

end = sales + 6;
for (; sales <= end; ++sales)
    printf("Variable sales[%hi] =%5hi\n", count, *sales);
```

The new variable *end* keeps track of the address of the end of the array. Its value would be *sales* + (6×2) or FFFC. The only problem with this approach is that *sales* is constant, it cannot be changed. The expression ++sales would cause the compiler grief.

We could, however use a pointer variable and increment it.

```
short *ptr;

ptr = sales;
for (; ptr <= sales + 6; ++ptr)
    printf("Variable sales[%hi] =%5hi\n", count, *ptr);
```

The increment operator (++), which normally adds one to the value of a variable, is being applied to a pointer to `short`; therefore it adds two each time, bringing us to the next variable.

ARRAYS AND FUNCTIONS

Let us write a function *sum_array()* that returns the sum of the values of all the variables in an array. Our call must pass the array to the function, and the function definition must declare variables to accept the array. One possible call would be

```
sum_array(sales[0], sales[1], sales[2],

          sales[3], sales[4], sales[5], sales[6])
```

meaning that the definition would have to have seven short variables to accept those values.

```
short sum_array(short value0, short value1, short value2,
                short value3, short value4, short value5, short value6)
```

Possible, but ugly.

Instead of passing all the values in the array, let us instead pass the base address of the array, and allow the function to access those addresses. The call will be simpler,

```
sum_array(sales)
```

as will the first line of the definition,

```
short sum_array(short value[])
```

The declaration in this function definition appears to allocate an array, a set of contiguous variables. But notice that there is no value in the brackets, nor should there be one. The declaration does not allocate an array, only a pointer to short—in this case, the address of *sales*.

Where does the *value* array in the *sum_array()* function end? First of all, the function does not recognize *value* as an array, only as the address of a short. But even if it did, C does not keep track of the end of allocated arrays, only their base addresses. We repeat, keeping track of the end of the array is up to you.

Let us add a *sum_array()* function to ▶▶Program 8–3 to print out the total sales. The result is ▶▶Program 8–4.

▶▶Program 8–4

```
#include <stdio.h>

short sum_array(short value[]);

void main(void)
{   short sales[] = {3806, 28, 4522, 476, 1183, 47, 12};
    short count;

    for (count = 0; count < 7; ++count)
        printf("Variable sales[%hi] =%5hi\n", count, sales[count]);
    printf("Total sales =      %hi\n", sum_array(sales));
}

short sum_array(short value[])
{   short count, sum = 0;

    for (count = 0; count < 7; ++count)
        sum += value[count];
    return sum;
}
```

Output

```
Variable sales[0] = 3806
Variable sales[1] =   28
Variable sales[2] = 4522
Variable sales[3] =  476
Variable sales[4] = 1183
Variable sales[5] =   47
Variable sales[6] =   12
Total sales =     10074
```

The `sizeof` an Array

In this program, the function was written specifically for a seven-variable array. To make it more general, we would also have to pass the number of variables from the calling function as well as the base address. To make the call even more general, let us have the call figure out how many variables are in the array. We can use the `sizeof` operator to find the number of bytes in the entire array.

```
sizeof sales[0]
```

gives us the number of bytes in the variable *sales[0]*, 2. But

```
sizeof sales
```

gives us the number of bytes in the entire *sales* array, 14.

We previously stated, however, that C does not keep track of the number of variables in an array. How, then, can the `sizeof` operator do this? It is handled at compile time when the compiler itself can see the declaration, not at execution time. If we pass the address of the array somewhere else, such as to a function, `sizeof` will not give us the expected result. The `sizeof` operator will only give us the number of bytes in the entire array in the block in which the array was declared.

If we divided the `sizeof` the array by the number of bytes in a single variable, 2, we would get the number of variables in the array.

```
sum_array(sales, sizeof sales / 2)
```

In fact, we could make it still more general if we figure the number of bytes in a variable right in the function call.

```
sum_array(sales, sizeof sales / sizeof sales[0])
```

(This way, if instead of `short` we were using `int`, which can be a different size on different machines, the call would still work.)

The function could be changed to the following. Note that *number* is declared as `int`. The result of the `sizeof` calculation will be compatible with `int`, so we matched that data type in the function.

```
int sum_array(short value[], int number)
{   short sum = 0;

    for (--number; number >= 0; --number)
        sum += value[number];
    return sum;
}
```

We got rid of *count* and used *number* to keep track of our subscript, counting backward down to zero. We began *number* at one less than its passed value because for variables 7 through 1, our subscripts would be 6 through 0.

In the function, *value* is a pointer to short. We could also declare it as a pointer to short using the asterisk notation, and vary the pointer instead of varying an offset to the base address. The function would be rewritten this way:

```
1  short sum_array(short *value, int number)
2  {   short *end, sum = 0;

3      end = value + number - 1;
4      for (; value <= end; ++value)
5      {   sum += *value;
6      }
       return sum;
   }
```

Let us follow it through:

3806	28	4522	476	1183	47	12		
FFF0/FFF1	FFF2/FFF3	FFF4/FFF5	FFF6/FFF7	FFF8/FFF9	FFFA/FFFB	FFFC/FFFD	FFFE/FFFF	
sales[0]	sales[1]	sales[2]	sales[3]	sales[4]	sales[5]	sales[6]		

EXECUTION CHART

Line	Explanation	value	number	end	sum
1	*value* and *number* initialized.	FFF0	7	---	---
2	Declare *end* as pointer to short and *sum* as short.	FFF0	7	?	0
3	Starting address of last variable in array. Remember, any time a pointer is involved in a calculation, it is pointer arithmetic, so it is FFF0 + (7 × 2) − (1 × 2) or FFFC.	FFF0	7	FFFC	0
4	No initialization because *value* is the counter and it is already pointing to the beginning of the array. Test for that pointer being <= to *end*.	FFF0	7	FFFC	0
5	Add contents at location pointed to by *value* to *sum*.	FFF0	7	FFFC	3806
6	Increment *value*; remember, this is pointer arithmetic.	FFF2	7	FFFC	3806
4–6	Keep going until *value* not <= to *end*.	FFFE	7	FFFC	10074

Passing the address of an array to a function allows us not only to read the values of the variables in the array but also to write to them, just as we have been able to do when we pass the pointer to an individual variable. For example, let us say that the boss wants us to double our sales. We can create a function *double_it()*, which will double each value of the array passed to it, the *sales* array in this case. Since the variable *value[2]*, for example, in the *double_it()* function refers to the same address as *sales[2]* in the main() function, changing *value[2]* also changes *sales[2]*.

To ➧Program 8–4, we have also added another function, *show_sales()*, which prints the current values in the array passed to it—*sales* again. The result is ➧Program 8–5.

➧Program 8–5

```
#include <stdio.h>

void double_it(short value[], int number);
void show_sales(short value[], int number);

void main(void)
{   short sales[] = {3806, 28, 4522, 476, 1183, 47, 12};

    printf("True sales:\n   ");
    show_sales(sales, sizeof sales / sizeof sales[0]);
    double_it(sales, sizeof sales / sizeof sales[0]);
    printf("Desired sales:\n   ");
    show_sales(sales, sizeof sales / sizeof sales[0]);
}

void double_it(short value[], int number)
{   short count;

    for (count = 0; count < number; ++count)
        value[count] *= 2;
}

void show_sales(short value[], int number)
{   short count;

    for (count = 0; count < number; ++count)
        printf("%hi  ", value[count]);
    printf("\n");
}
```

Output

```
True sales:
   3806  28  4522  476  1183  47  12
Desired sales:
   7612  56  9044  952  2366  94  24
```

MULTISUBSCRIPTED VARIABLES

Subscripted variables may have more than one subscript. No matter how many subscripts, however, we can still view them as separate variables with separate values, but with slightly more complicated names. The following are possible declarations:

Nuts & Bolts

ARRAY NOTATION IN FUNCTIONS

In ANSI C, a declaration in the formal parameters of a function to receive the base address of an array can be expressed equivalently in subscript notation or pointer notation. The function definitions

```
void func(float x[])  and  void func(float *x)
```

are exactly equivalent. In other words both xs are variables. Actually, both are declared as pointers to float, and both can be varied within the function. Also, both can be accessed using either subscript or pointer notation.

The notation you use in defining your function and accessing the array within the function is largely a matter of style. Many C programmers think that you should stick with the notation you started with. In other words, if your formal parameters express the base address of the array using subscript notation, you should try to use subscript notation for that array in the rest of the function, and likewise with pointer notation.

```
float axle[7][100], bearing[20][12][25];
int flexus[200][2][4][2];
```

As an example, let us say that our major product, the Finortna, comes in any combination of two models, standard and deluxe, and three colors, red, green, and puce. This gives us six possibilities, but two different criteria, model and color. If we allowed the first subscript to represent the model and the second the color, we could store the inventories of Finortnas in a double-subscripted array *inv[2][3]*.

```
short inv[2][3];
```

inv	[0]	[1]	[2]	
[0]	46	12	122	(Standard)
[1]	62	20	88	(Deluxe)
	(Red)	(Green)	(Puce)	

The typical way of viewing a double-subscripted array is as a two-dimensional table. The inventory of deluxe, red Finortnas would be stored in *inv[1][0]*, standard, puce ones would be in *inv[0][2]*.

A convenient way to view this is an array of arrays. In fact, this gives us a good insight into how C actually allocates space for it. There are three variables in the *inv[0]* array and three in the *inv[1]* array. Since C guarantees us contiguous storage, if the base address, *inv*, is FFF0, then storage would be like this:

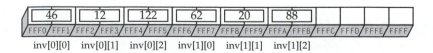

We have contiguous storage of two arrays with contiguous storage of the variables in each array. In essence, the second subscript (or last subscript, if there are more than two) varies first.

We saw that the prefix of an array was a pointer to the base address of the array. This also holds true for multisubscripted arrays. The prefix *inv* is a constant with the value FFF0, the equivalent of the notation &inv[0][0]. But if this is an array of arrays, then *inv[0]* must be the prefix of the first three-variable array and *inv[1]* the prefix of the second. This is indeed the case with *inv[0]* being a constant pointer to the base address of the first, FFF0 (the equivalent of &inv[0][0]) and *inv[1]* a constant pointer to the base address of the second, FFF6 (the equivalent of &inv[1][0]).

Initializing Multisubscripted Arrays

We could initialize the *inv* array as we did our one-subscript ones—by putting enough values in braces in the declaration.

```
short inv[2][3] = {46, 12, 122, 62, 20, 88};
```

Since we are dealing with an array of arrays, the values will be assigned to each major array in turn. In other words, 46, 12, and 122 will be assigned to *inv[0][0]*, *inv[0][1]*, and *inv[0][2]*, and 62, 20, and 88 will be assigned to *inv[1][0]*, *inv[1][1]*, and *inv[1][2]*.

C also allows us to separate the arrays-within-the-array by nesting braces,

```
short inv[2][3] = {{46, 12, 122}, {62, 20, 88}};
```

which we would probably write more illustratively like this:

```
short inv[2][3] = {{46, 12, 122},
                   {62, 20, 88}};
```

maintaining the tablelike view of the array.

If we do not supply enough values, the rest of the variables will be initialized to zero. But, if we use nested braces, this applies to each of the subarrays. For example,

```
short inv[2][3] = {{46, 12},
                   {62}     };
```

is equivalent to

```
short inv[2][3] = {{46, 12, 0},
                   {62, 0, 0}};
```

If we supply enough values, we can leave the rightmost subscript blank, and leave it to the compiler to fill it in.

```
short inv[2][] = {46, 12, 0, 62, 0, 0};
```

is equivalent to the previous declaration.

Accessing Multisubscripted Arrays

We could print out the values in the *inv* array by using nested for loops; the outer one controls the first subscript, the row, and the inner one controls the second subscript, the column.

▶▶Program 8–6

```
#include <stdio.h>

#define MODELS 2
#define COLORS 3

void main(void)
{   short inv[MODELS][COLORS] = {{46, 12, 122},
                                 {62, 20,  88}};
    int model, color;

    printf("             RED   GREEN   PUCE\n");
    for (model = 0; model < MODELS; ++model)
    {  if (model == 0)
          printf("STANDARD ");
       else
          printf("DELUXE   ");
       for (color = 0; color < COLORS; ++color)
          printf("%6hi ", inv[model][color]);
       printf("\n");
    }
}
```

Output

```
            RED   GREEN    PUCE
STANDARD    46     12      122
DELUXE      62     20       88
```

Passing Multisubscripted Arrays to Functions

As we know, passing the base address of an array to a function does not tell the function how many variables are in the array. Nor, of course, would it tell the function how many subscripts are in the array or the organization of those subscripts.

In our declaration of the formal parameters of the array in the function, however, we can fill in some of that information by showing how many subscript positions there are and the number of subscripts in each position but the first. The function still will not know the overall size of the array, but its pattern, at least, is evident.

▶▶Program 8–7 is ▶▶Program 8–6 rewritten to print out the inventory in a function. The output is exactly the same.

Program 8-7

```c
#include <stdio.h>
#define MODELS 2
#define COLORS 3
void print_inv(short inv[][COLORS]);

void main(void)
{  short inv[MODELS][COLORS] = {{46, 12, 122},
                                {62, 20,  88}};
   print_inv(inv);
}
void print_inv(short inv[][COLORS])
{  int model, color;

   printf("           RED  GREEN   PUCE\n");
   for (model = 0; model < MODELS; ++model)
   {  if (model == 0)
         printf("STANDARD ");
      else
         printf("DELUXE   ");
      for (color = 0; color < COLORS; ++color)
         printf("%6hi ", inv[model][color]);
      printf("\n");
   }
}
```

PUTTING IT TOGETHER

Professor Fassbinder maintains a strict seating chart in her class; her students are known only by their row and seat numbers. For some time, she has suspected that students in the window seats perform less well than those in the other seat positions, so in her grade reports she prints out the averages of all the students in each seat position. Her program for inputting scores and printing results follows this pattern:

Enter scores
Print report

Expanding those modules we have:

[Enter scores]
While row not zero
    Enter row and seat
    Enter score
End loop

[Print report]
For each row
    For each seat
        Print scores in seat grid
        Accumulate score in seat-position total
        Count score in seat-position count
    End loop
End loop
For each seat
    Calculate and print average
End loop

▶▶Program 8–8

```
#include <stdio.h>
#define ROWS 4                                           /* Number of rows */
#define SEATS 3                                    /* Number of seats per row */
void input(int scores[][SEATS], int rows);               /* Enter scores */
void output(int scores[][SEATS], int rows);              /* Print report */

void main(void)
{   int grades[ROWS][SEATS] = {{20},{18},{16}};        /* grades[row][seat] */
       /* Seat 1 for rows 1, 2, and 3 initialized for illustration purposes */
                              /* Also initializes everything else to zero */
1      input(grades, ROWS);                                /*Enter scores*/
2      output(grades, ROWS);                               /*Print report*/
}
/***************************************** Enter scores by row and seat */
void input(int scores[][SEATS], int rows)
{   int row, seat;

    printf("Enter row, seat: ");
i1  while (scanf("%i, %i", &row, &seat),
i2         row != 0)                                  /* Input til zero row */
i3  {   if (row <= rows && seat <= SEATS)            /* Within valid ranges */
        {   printf("Enter score: ");
i4          scanf(" %i", &scores[row - 1][seat - 1]);
i5      }else
i6          printf("Invalid row or seat.\n");
        printf("Enter row, seat: ");
    }
}
/*************************** Print report showing seat-position averages */
void output(int scores[][SEATS], int rows)
{   int row, seat;
    int total[SEATS] = {0};           /* Accumulator for each seat position */
    int count[SEATS] = {0};           /* Count scores in each seat position */
    /*************************************************** Print seat grid */
o1  printf("\nSeat      1     2     3\nRow");
o2  for (row = 0; row < rows; ++row)                /* Go through each row */
o3  {   printf(" %i ", row + 1);                    /* Zero subscript is row 1 */
o4      for (seat = 0; seat < SEATS; ++seat)        /* Seats in each row */
o5      {   if (scores[row][seat] == 0)             /* Don't print zeros */
o6              printf("      ");
            else
o7          {   printf("  %4i", scores[row][seat]);
o8              total[seat] += scores[row][seat];        /* Total for seat */
o9              ++count[seat];                           /* Count for seat */
            }
        }
o10     printf("\n   ");
    }
    /*************************************************** Print averages */
o11 printf("\nAvgs   ");
o12 for (seat = 0; seat < SEATS; ++seat)            /* For each seat total */
o13     if (count[seat] != 0)              /* Don't print average if no scores */
o14         printf("  %4.1f", (float) total[seat] / count[seat]);
        else
o15         printf("      ");
o16 printf("\n");
}
```

EXECUTION CHART

Line	Explanation	grades[4][3]

| 1 | Call *input()*, pass address of *grades* array and number of rows. The latter could have been calculated by dividing the number of bytes in the entire array (`sizeof grades`) by the number of bytes in one array variable (`sizeof grades[0][0]`), and then dividing by the seats per row (`SEATS`). Since we defined the number of `ROWS` at the beginning of the program, we use that instead. | 20 0 0
 18 0 0
 16 0 0
 0 0 0 |

Line	Explanation	rows	row	seat	scores[][3]
i1	Input row and seat; dump `scanf()` return.	4	1	3	20 0 0 18 0 0 16 0 0 0 0 0
i2	Continue while *row* not equal to zero.	4	1	3	Same
i3	Check for valid range.	4	1	3	Same
i4	Input score into *scores[0][2]*.	4	1	3	20 0 17 18 0 0 16 0 0 0 0 0
i1, i2	Input *row* and *seat*; continue while *row* not equal to zero.	4	4	2	Same
i3	Check for valid range.	4	4	2	Same
i4	Input score into *scores[3][1]*.	4	4	2	20 0 17 18 0 0 16 0 0 0 19 0
i1–i4	Continue until 0, 0 input. Return.	4	0	0	20 0 17 18 0 0 16 20 15 0 19 0

Line	Explanation	grades[4][3]
2	Call *output()*, pass address of *grades* array and number of rows.	20 0 17 18 0 0 16 20 15 0 19 0

Line	Explanation	rows	row	seat	total[3]			count[3]			scores[][3]
o1	Print heading.	4	?	?	0	0	0	0	0	0	20 0 17 18 0 0 16 20 15 0 19 0
o2	Loop through rows.	4	0	?	0	0	0	0	0	0	Same
o3	Print side heading for each row.	4	0	?	0	0	0	0	0	0	Same
o4	Loop through seats.	4	0	0	0	0	0	0	0	0	Same
o5	Value of *scores[0][0]* not zero.	4	0	0	0	0	0	0	0	0	Same
o7	Print score.	4	0	0	0	0	0	0	0	0	Same
o8	Accumulate *scores[0][0]* in *total[0]*.	4	0	0	20	0	0	0	0	0	Same
o9	Add one to *count[0]*.	4	0	0	20	0	0	1	0	0	Same
o10	Drop to next line and indent.	4	0	0	20	0	0	1	0	0	Same
o2–10	Continue through nested loop.	4	4	3	54	39	32	3	2	2	Same
o11	Drop to next line, print side head.	4	4	3	54	39	32	3	2	2	Same
o12	Loop through seats.	4	4	0	54	39	32	3	2	2	Same
o13	*count[0]* not zero.	4	4	0	54	39	32	3	2	2	Same
o14	Print average for seat 1.	4	4	0	54	39	32	3	2	2	Same
o12–15	Continue through seat loop.	4	4	3	54	39	32	3	2	2	Same
o16	Drop to next line, return, and end.										

Output

```
Enter row, seat: 1,3
Enter score: 17
Enter row, seat: 4,2
Enter score: 19
Enter row, seat: 3,3
Enter score: 15
Enter row, seat: 3,2
Enter score: 20
Enter row, seat: 0,0
Seat        1     2     3
Row 1      20          17
    2      18
    3      16    20    15
    4            19

Avgs      18.0  19.5  16.0
```

SUMMARY

In C, as in algebra, we can use **subscripted variables**. The notation is slightly different, but the concept is the same. A subscripted variable may be used any place an ordinary variable may be used, and in the same manner. Sets of subscripted variables are called **arrays**. Although we can refer to the set, in our programs we must work with each variable individually.

Arrays are declared as a set by putting the prefix and the number of variables in a declaration statement. Initializations can accompany declarations by putting the values in braces.

The main advantage of using subscripted variables is that the subscript may be any expression. In other words, the actual variable is determined by the value of the expression, meaning that the variable name can be changed by changing the value of the expression.

Common applications of values in arrays are **inserting**, where we add a value to an ordered list, and sorting, as in a **selection sort**, where a list in no particular order is put in order.

C guarantees that the variables in an array will be of the same data type and stored contiguously in memory. The variable prefix in C is a constant pointer to the **base address** of the array. The subscript is an **offset** from that base address. The offset in bytes is the subscript times the number of bytes in a single array variable. This is also the basis of **pointer arithmetic**. Using this concept, array variables can be referred to using either array notation or pointer notation.

Values of subscripted variables may be passed to functions just like values of normal variables, but more commonly we send functions the address of the array base (using the constant prefix) so that the function can access any variable in the array. This technique sends only the address of the beginning of the array to the function. Keeping track of the end of the array is up to us.

The `sizeof` operator used with the array prefix will give us the number of bytes in the entire declared array.

Variables are not limited to single subscripts; they may have many. They can be viewed as arrays of arrays, stored in an order that reflects the last subscript varying first. A notation that does not include all the subscripts indicates a constant pointer to that section of the array. Multisubscripted arrays are declared with sets of brackets containing the number of subscripts in each position. They can be initialized by putting values in braces in the declaration. By using nested braces, we can tell the compiler specifically which values belong to which subarray. When multiple subscripts are use in the formal parameters of a function declaration, all subscripts except the first are explicitly stated.

KEY TERMS (in order of appearance)

Subscripted variable

Array

Insert

Selection sort

Base address

Offset

Pointer arithmetic

REVIEW QUESTIONS

1. How does a subscripted variable differ from a normal variable? How are the two similar?

2. What is an array?

3. Why do we use arrays?

4. What is the lowest subscript value for any subscripted variable in C?

5. In an array declaration, what does the number in braces signify?

6. What notation do we use in the declaration to initialize array variables?

7. What happens if we don't provide enough values to initialize the entire array?

8. What is allowed within the brackets of a subscripted variable in statements other than declarations?

9. How does an insert differ from a sort?

10. The array prefix is a pointer to what? Can we assign a value to the array prefix?

11. In terms of addresses, what does the value within the brackets indicate?

12. What would be the pointer notation for x[6]?

13. How does pointer arithmetic differ from ordinary arithmetic? How do we know whether we are performing pointer or ordinary arithmetic?

14. In what two ways can we effectively "pass an array to a function?"

15. What does the `sizeof` operator applied to an array prefix evaluate in a function in which the array is visible? In some other function?

16. If we pass the base address of an array to a function, how can we tell in the function where the end of the array is?

17. Can we set up an array of arrays?

18. How can we use nested braces to initialize multisubscripted arrays?

19. If we leave off subscripts from the right of a multisubscripted array, what does that indicate?

EXERCISES

1. How many addressable variables has each of the arrays declared in the following?

a. `int x[5][2];`

b. `long double f[5][2][4][3];`

c. `short a[] = {4, 2, 3, 8};`

d. `float z[5] = {3.1, 2.8};`

2. Write appropriate array declarations for the following:

    a.   The *prices* of products 1 through 10.

    b.   A *customer_data* array that stores height, weight, and shoe size of 10 customers.

    c.   A *scores* array for students by row and seat in three different classes.

    d.   An array to store *sales* for 10 product numbers sold in 4 sales regions over a 5-year period.

3. Find the error in the following code segment and tell what error indication will be given.

```
int array[5] = {1, 2, 3, 4, 5}, count;
for (count = 1; count <= 5; ++count)
    printf("%i\n", array[count]);
```

4. Given the declaration char array[10],

    a.   What is the sizeof array?

    b.   What is the sizeof array[4]?

    c.   Show a reference to *array[2]* using pointer notation.

5. Given the following declarations, which statements are invalid and why?

```
double one[10], two[5][5], *ptr, value = 1.0;
```

    a.   two[3][0] = 25;

    b.   ptr = &one;

    c.   ptr = two[2];

    d.   value = two[3][5];

    e.   printf("%f\n", two[1]);

    f.   one = ptr;

    g.   one[2] = two[3][4];

6. Show the output from this program:

```
#include <stdio.h>

void main(void)
{   short *ptr;
    short array[4] = {1,2,3,4};

    for (ptr = array + 3; ptr >= array; --ptr)
        printf("%hi  ", *ptr);
    printf("\n");
}
```

7. Show the output from this program:

```
#include <stdio.h>

void main(void)
{   int array[3][2] = {{6, 2},
                       {3, 5},
                       {1, 7}};
    int r, c;

    for (r = 0; r < 2; ++r)
    {   for (c = 0; c < 3; ++c)
            printf("%i  ", array[c][r]);
        printf("\n");
    }
}
```

PROGRAMS

1. Write a program that accepts input of five values from the keyboard and prints out the values and their difference from the mean (average) value.

   Variables

   ```
   value[]
   mean        Also use for the total
   count
   ```

   Output

   ```
   Enter 5 values separated by whitespace.
   46.2 12.6 32.654 6 25.44
   Number   Value  Difference
        1   46.20       21.62
        2   12.60      -11.98
        3   32.65        8.08
        4    6.00      -18.58
        5   25.44        0.86
   ```

2. Write a program that accepts keyboard entry of 5 values and prints out the maximum and minimum. Both the maximum and minimum should be calculated in a separate function and printed out in main().

   Functions and Variables

   ```
   main()                    min_max()
      values[]                  array[]
      smallest                  min
      largest                   max
      count                     count
   ```

   Output

   ```
   Enter 5 values separated by whitespace.
   5.74 2.6 18 -3.65 14.2
   Minimum: -3.65, Maximum: 18.
   ```

3. Write a program that adds two four-variable arrays together. The first array should be initialized with values 1, 2, 3, and 4; the second, with values 5, 6, 7, 8. Both arrays should be passed to the function *add_arrays()*, which adds corresponding variables of each array together and leaves the results in the second array. The second array should then be printed out by the main() function.

   Functions and Variables

   ```
   main()                    add_arrays()
      array1[]                  a1[], a2[]
      array2[]                  counter
      counter
   ```

   Output

   ```
   Resultant array: 6 8 10 12
   ```

4. Modify the *RANDOM* program from Chapter 6 to replace the accumulators with an array of accumulators. The program should be much shorter, but the output should be similar.

   Variables and Functions

   ```
   numbers[]    Accumulators
   count        Loop counter
   rnd()        Integer between 1 and 5
   ```

5. Write a program that will initialize an array of characters to *ABCDE* and allow you to shift, in circular fashion, those characters to the right any number of

places you specify. The shifting should be done in the function *shift()* but all the printouts should be from `main()`.

Functions and Variables

```
main()              shift()
   chrs[]              chrs[]
   places             places
   count              count
                      temp[]     To store a copy of the array
```

Outputs

```
Before shifting: ABCDE
Shift how many places? 2
After shifting: DEABC

Before shifting: ABCDE
Shift how many places? 8
After shifting: CDEAB

Before shifting: ABCDE
Shift how many places? 5
After shifting: ABCDE

Before shifting: ABCDE
Shift how many places? 41
After shifting: EABCD
```

6. Write a program that deals a hand of five cards. In order to make it accurate, you will have to start with a deck (an array) of 52 cards and shuffle the deck. In a *shuffle()* function, set up your deck numbered from 0 to 51 and another deck with numbers randomly assigned. Sort the random deck and with each swap in the sort, also swap corresponding cards in the real deck. Do the swap in a separate *swap()* function. When the random deck is in order, the real deck will be random. Use the function *show_card()* to print the suit and number of each card.

Functions and Variables

```
main()               shuffle()               show_card()          swap()
   cards[]  The deck     cards[]                 card   The card      a, b
   card     Counter      rand_deck[]             number
                         card, i, j  Counters    suit
```

Outputs

```
Your hand: Queen-Diamonds Queen-Hearts 8-Clubs 4-Clubs 7-Spades

Your hand: 5-Spades Ace-Hearts 10-Clubs King-Diamonds 4-Hearts
```

7. Skewed Opinion Research, Inc., sent out survey questionnaires with three questions. Each question was to be answered on a 1 to 5 scale, 1 meaning "awful" and 5 meaning "fantastic." Write a program that will allow input of the data, store it in a two-dimensional array, and print out the average response to each question. The program should handle any number of questionnaires (up to 20). Entry of a sentinel value, such as the letter *q*, should end the input loop.

Suggested Variables

```
response[ ][ ]     To store responses to the questionnaires
question           Question number (0, 1, or 2)
questionnaire      Questionnaire number
total[ ]           Accumulators for figuring question averages
```

Output

```
Input three responses for each:
Questionnaire 1? 4 2 5
Questionnaire 2? 1 4 1
Questionnaire 3? 3 5 2
Questionnaire 4? 3 1 2
Questionnaire 5? 3 3 4
Questionnaire 6? 2 2 3
Questionnaire 7? 5 2 1
Questionnaire 8? 3 2 4
Questionnaire 9? q

Average response for question 1 is: 3.000
Average response for question 2 is: 2.625
Average response for question 3 is: 2.750
```

STRINGS

PREVIEW   Most of our programming up to this point has been with numeric values. Here we will discuss character values and strings. After studying this chapter you should know

1. How C stores and interprets string values.
2. How we accomplish variable storage of strings.
3. Ways to input and output strings.
4. Different ways of manipulating strings.
5. Two different methods of storing strings in arrays.
6. How to convert between strings and numbers.
7. How to classify characters and convert from one classification to another.
8. Methods of separating strings into component parts.
9. How to use strings typed in at the command line.

A string is a set of characters, any characters as long as they are part of the coding scheme used on your computer. The computer itself attaches no special significance to the characters in the string; in fact, we saw in Chapter 2 that the computer can't even tell the difference between characters and numbers. It is only our instructions that tell it what to do with a set of bits in storage.

STRING VALUES

We have used string values before in the control strings of both `scanf()` and `printf()`. They were sets of characters enclosed in quotes. Let us examine how these characters are actually stored in memory. We know, of course, that the characters are stored as sets of bits, and that each character takes up one byte. Each character, then, is data type `char`. Putting a string value in our source code directs C to allocate memory for those characters—an array of `chars`.

Like any other array, the string is identified by its base address, the address of the first value (character, in this case). Also, like any other array, once the memory is allocated, we are left with the problem of how to tell where the string ends in memory. C solves the problem by putting a null character (\0) in the memory location immediately following the last character of the string. When we ask C to return the string to us, it starts at the base address and reads characters until the last one read was a null. In most cases the null is not returned with the string, just the characters.

But where is this base address? As with variables, we will probably never know, nor do we care as long as C can keep track of it. At least we can refer to the address of a variable using the address operator, `&`. The address of the `int` variable *stuff* is `&stuff`.

The notation for the address of a string value is the string value itself—the characters in quotes. The string value "Algonquin" is the address where C has chosen to store the string—compatible with data type pointer to `char`. The statement

```
printf("%p\n", "Algonquin")
```

prints the address value (00AC in one version of C).

As with any other address value, we can print the contents at a particular address.

```
printf("%c\n", *("Algonquin" + 3))
```

Since "Algonquin" is the address of *Algonquin*, the contents at "Algonquin" + 3 is the letter *o*. The following program segment,

```
void main(void)
{  char *letter;

   letter = "Algonquin";
   while (*letter != '\0')
   {  printf ("%c", *letter);
      ++letter;
   }
   printf("\n");
}
```

prints out the characters

```
Algonquin
```

We declared the variable *letter* as a pointer to `char` and then set its value equal to "Algonquin", which is, of course, the address of the characters *Algonquin\0* in memory. In the `while` loop, we moved the pointer from character location to character location until the character at the current location was null (`\0`), C's indicator for the end of the string. As a result, we printed out all the characters in the string.

The initialization of *letter* also could have been done in the declaration:

```
char *letter = "Algonquin"
```

The data types agree—both are type pointer to `char`.

String Values Versus Character Values

In Chapter 2 we were introduced to character values such as `'A'`, `'f'`, and `'\t'`. These, we saw, were simply numbers—the ASCII (or EBCDIC) values of the character codes. In fact, they were of type `int`, although we could certainly store them in `char` variables if we wanted.

There is a significant difference between the character `'A'` and the string `"A"`. The former is an integer with the value 65 (in ASCII) that takes up two or four bytes depending on the size of an integer in a particular C. The latter is an array of two `char`s, the first with the value 65 (*A* in ASCII), and the second with the value zero (the null character, `\0`).

STRING VARIABLES

As we mentioned before, there aren't any string variables. But we have seen that a string value is stored as an array of `char`s, that is, beginning at some address in memory and continuing in contiguous memory locations. Let us follow that pattern, then, and store our string in an array of `char` variables.

Declaration and Initialization

In deciding on a declaration of a `char` array, we must consider the largest string we might have to store in it, because C will allocate the space and then probably allocate something else right next to it. Also, C will not prevent us from overwriting what we consider the end of the string; in other words, write into the space allocated for the next variable or whatever.

If we are declaring a `char` array for names and most of them are "John", "Mary", "Edna", and such, but one person might be named "Cadwallader", then we must allocate at least twelve characters of space for the string. Twelve? There are only eleven characters in "Cadwallader". Remember that C considers a string as starting at some memory address and ending in a null character. We must leave an extra space for the null character.

```
char name[12];
```

This allocates twelve variables, *name[0]* through *name[11]*. They have no meaningful values yet, but we can initialize them at the time of their declaration.

```
char name[12] = {'Z', 'e', 'l', 'd', 'a'};
```

We have assigned values to the first five variables of the array. The rest of the variables in the array, since we have initialized the first few, will be assigned the value zero, which, not entirely coincidentally, is the null character.

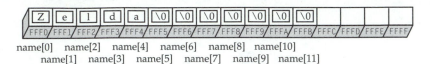

name[0]   name[2]   name[4]   name[6]   name[8]   name[10]
    name[1]   name[3]   name[5]   name[7]   name[9]   name[11]

We now have a string value in memory beginning at the address *name*, FFF0 in the example, and ending at the first null at FFF5.

The same declaration could have been accomplished this way:

```
char name[12] = {90, 101, 108, 100, 97};
```

using the ASCII values for the characters, but it is a bit easier to understand using the former method.

The same declaration and initialization could also be accomplished this way:

```
char name[12] = "Zelda";
```

C would interpret the quoted string as five character values and store them in the first five variables of *name*, setting the rest to null.

Almost the same thing could be accomplished using pointer notation instead of an array.

```
char *nom = "Zelda";
```

There are subtle differences here. The declaration in array notation finds twelve bytes of available space, allocates them to *name[0]* through *name[11]*, assigns the five character values, and sets the rest to null. Because it is an array declaration, the value in quotes is not interpreted as the address of a string, but as five values to be initialized at the locations reserved in the declaration.

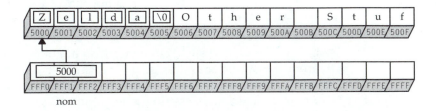

nom

The declaration in pointer notation allocates one pointer variable, *nom* (*name* in French). C has copied *Zelda* from the source code, put it in memory somewhere with a trailing null, and initialized *nom* with that address. At *name*, we can safely assign up to eleven characters because C has allocated twelve variables. At *nom* there are only six characters allocated. Assigning more than a five-character string there might be disastrous.

Another difference is that *nom* is a variable, *name* is not. Either can have the values at their addresses changed (within the allocated limits, of course), but the variable *nom* can be made to point to another place in memory while the constant *name* cannot.

We should mention that a declaration could also be made this way:

```
char name[] = "Zelda";
```

leaving out the number of variables in brackets. This would differ from the previous declaration of *name* because only six variables, *name [0]* through *name[5]*, would be allocated (remember the null; C does).

STRING ASSIGNMENTS

Since strings are sets of separate variables for each character, we can assign them one character at a time.

```
void main(void)
{  char name[12];

   name[0] = 'Z';
   name[1] = 'e';
   name[2] = 'l';
   name[3] = 'd';
   name[4] = 'a';
   name[5] = '\0';
}
```

We have been careful to include the null character at the end of the string, especially in this case where the automatic declaration of *name* leaves garbage in each of the variables.

We could not have done this:

```
name = "Zelda";
```

even though it looks like our earlier declaration. Both are data type pointer to char, but *name* is a constant; it cannot be assigned.

Also, we could not safely do this:

```
void main(void)
{  char *nom;

   *nom = 'Z';
   *(nom + 1) = 'e';
   *(nom + 2) = 'l';
   *(nom + 3) = 'd';
   *(nom + 4) = 'a';
   *(nom + 5) = '\0';
}
```

because *nom* points nowhere in particular, so we would be making assignments in unallocated, unsafe locations.

We can, however, do this:

```
nom = "Zelda";
```

because both data types are pointer to char, and *nom* is a variable. As a result of this statement, *Zelda\0* is put in memory and the base address, the address of *Z*, is assigned to *nom*.

STRING INPUT

We have used the scanf() function to input numbers and individual characters. We can also use it to input strings through the %s conversion code. In its arguments, scanf() expects to find addresses. The prefix for a character array is an address, and it is typically used to provide an argument for %s, with, of course, no need for a & to convert it to an address.

```
scanf("%s", name);
```

The function will take a set of characters from the input stream and assign them beginning at the address *name*. It will also add a null at the end of the characters to maintain C's concept of a string. If our previous assignment to *name* had been *Zelda* and we typed in *Al*, memory would look like this:

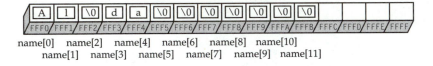

name[0]   name[2]   name[4]   name[6]   name[8]   name[10]
    name[1]   name[3]   name[5]   name[7]   name[9]   name[11]

Part of *Zelda* is still lying around, but it makes no difference because C's string ends at the first null, in FFF2.

In the ➡️Program 9–1, scanf() is used to input both a number and a string.

➡️Program 9–1

```
#include <stdio.h>

void main(void)
{  char product[10], *ptr;
   float price;

   printf("Enter price and product: ");
   scanf("%f %s", &price, product);
   printf("The price of a ");
   ptr = product;          /* Begin the pointer at the beginning of string */
   while (*ptr != '\0')            /* Null indicates the end of the string */
   {  printf("%c", *ptr);                     /* Print contents at pointer */
      ++ptr;                     /* Move the pointer to the next character */
   }
   printf(" is %.2f.\n", price);
}
```

Outputs

```
Enter price and product: 12.98 widget
The price of a widget is 12.98.

Enter price and product: 12.98, widget
The price of a , is 12.98.
```

To print out the value of the string we set a pointer to the beginning of the string and kept incrementing it until the contents being pointed to were null. (This illustrates the point, but as we shall see, there are easier ways.)

In the second execution, we tried to use the comma as a delimiter between the two values input. Comma, an inappropriate character for a number, ended that conversion, but the comma was left in the input stream. Since comma is appropriate for a string, C started the string at the comma and went to the next white space, including only the comma in the string.

The *product* array has ten variables in it, meaning that we can effectively store only nine characters. What if we type in a 15-character product name? It will be assigned, overflowing the space allocated for the *product* array and messing up something else. We can limit the number of characters that will be converted by putting a width modifier in front of the *s* type code—%ws.

For example,

```
scanf("%9s", product);
```

will stop conversion at the first whitespace or a maximum of nine characters. If it reaches the maximum, characters left over remain in the stream. For the string *product*, nine was appropriate because it is a ten-variable array but one must contain the null.

We can set up our own delimiters for strings in scanf(). Instead of using the *s* in the conversion code we can use characters in brackets. Only those characters will be accepted as part of the string. This statement:

```
scanf("%[abcd]", product);
```

will accept any product name as long as it is made up of any combination of those characters. As soon as the function reaches any other character in the input stream, the conversion ends. The following inputs will make the following assignments:

Input	Assignment
cabs	cab
back door	bac
automobile	a
cadillac	cad
bad cab	bad
badminton bird	bad

A more valuable variation on this is to precede the characters with a caret (^), meaning that anything *but* those characters will be converted. In this way, we can specifically state our delimiters. For example,

```
scanf("%[^,\n]", product);
```

establishes comma and newline as the two possible characters that end conversion. Nothing else—space, punctuation, or whatever—will.

This doesn't help the situation with the price and product because the comma ended the `float` conversion. The first thing in the stream for the string conversion will be the comma, with that conversion ending at the space, leaving us nothing as a product. Where it would come in handy is between a string followed by something else, perhaps another string, as in ➠Program 9–2.

➠**Program 9–2**

```
#include <stdio.h>

void main(void)
{  char category[10], product[10], *ptr;

   printf("Enter product and category: ");
   scanf("%[^,],%[^\n]", product, category);
   printf("Product ");
   ptr = product;
   while (*ptr != '\0')
   {  printf("%c", *ptr);
      ++ptr;
   }
   printf(" is in category ");
   ptr = category;
   while (*ptr != '\0')
   {  printf("%c", *ptr);
      ++ptr;
   }
   printf("\n");
}
```

Output

```
Enter product and category: widget,things
Product widget is in category things
```

The input had to be precisely what the `scanf()` expected; otherwise the results would be strange. The first conversion code, `%[^,]`, ended the conversion at the comma, leaving the comma in the input stream. The comma between the conversion codes matched this comma, making the next character in the stream the *t* in *things*. The second conversion code took all the characters from there to the newline, the end of the stream.

Now that we know something about strings, we can appreciate the full prototype for the `scanf()` function:

```
int scanf(const char *control_string, arguments)                    <stdio.h>
```

The *control_string* is a pointer to `char`. The `const` modifier guarantees that the function will not change its value—make it point somewhere else. We have been using string values in quotes for our *control_string*s, but we could also make up a control string elsewhere and use a pointer to it as the *control_string* argument. For example,

```
char control[] = "%f %c %[^:/;]";

scanf(control, x, i, s);
```

The `getchar()` function returns a single character from the input stream. It has the form

```
int getchar(void)                                        <stdio.h>
```

It has no value passed to it, but the value it returns is the next character from the input stream.

Like `scanf("%c", . . .)` all characters are accepted by `getchar()`, even the newline. If an end-of-file condition is encountered, the return value is the defined constant `EOF`.

The `gets()` function is commonly used for keyboard input because it gets the input stream up through the next newline and assigns it to a string, replacing the newline with the null character.

```
char *gets(char *string)                                 <stdio.h>
```

If the call to the function is successful, the return value is the address of the *string* that was passed to the function. If not, it returns the `NULL` pointer. `NULL` is a constant pointer value defined in `stdio.h`. Notice that it is written in all capital letters and has no relation whatsoever with the null character, which we symbolize with \0.

With the `gets()` function it is very important to know what is in the input stream before the call, especially after a call to `scanf()`. Whitespace is the default delimiter in `scanf()`, and newline qualifies as whitespace. Typically, `scanf()` leaves the newline in the input stream after it finishes. When `gets()` executes and you are expecting the program to stop while you enter the secrets of life, `gets()` sees the newline, which it interprets as an empty string—perfectly acceptable to it—and it assigns the empty string to the secrets of life, and the program goes on without stopping. To be sure that the input buffer is empty before the call to `gets()`, you may want to `fflush(stdin)`.

The `gets()` function, like `scanf()`, does not know how many characters are allocated to a string. If you declare `char s[10];` and input 40 characters in a `gets(s);` call, C will happily write beyond the end of the allocated string space, gleefully messing up anything that was there before. Also, don't forget, `char s[10];` will only accomodate a nine-character string; the last character must be a null.

STRING OUTPUT

Like `scanf()`, we have used `printf()` to work with single characters using the `%c` conversion code. The `%s` conversion code outputs an entire string. Its argument must be a pointer to `char` and it will print all the values from that address to the end of the string—the first null character. We can shorten the example program we used earlier by a considerable amount by replacing the loop in which we printed out single characters with a single `printf()` conversion.

▶▶Program 9–3

```
#include <stdio.h>

void main(void)
{ char product[10];
  float price;

  printf("Enter price and product: ");
  scanf("%f %s", &price, product);
  printf("The price of a %s is %.2f.\n", product, price);
}
```

Outputs

```
Enter price and product: 12.98 widget
The price of a widget is 12.98.
```

The string conversion code for `printf()` uses many of the same modifiers as those for numbers,

```
%flag width.precision s
```

with any of them being optional. If *precision* is used, it should always have the dot preceding it.

The *width* modifier states the minimum number of characters to be printed. If the string is too short, leading blanks are added—remember, right justification is the default. Too many characters will extend the length of the field, just as it does with numbers. The precision argument states the maximum number of characters. Long strings will be chopped off at the end. The only *flag* allowed is the minus sign (-), which, like numbers, indicates left rather than right justification.

▶▶Program 9–4 and its output are lined up so that you can see which line produced what.

▶▶Program 9–4   Output

```
#include <stdio.h>

void main(void)
{ char item[20] = "Flange";

  printf("X%sX\n", item);             XFlangeX
  printf("X%8sX\n", item);            X  FlangeX
  printf("X%-8sX\n", item);           XFlange  X
  printf("X%4sX\n", item);            XFlangeX
  printf("X%4.4sX\n", item);          XFlanX
  printf("X%4.3sX\n", item);          X FlaX
}
```

The `putchar()` function is the output counterpart of `getchar()`.

```
int putchar(int character)                              <stdio.h>
```

214   STRINGS

Its return value is the value of the *character* passed to it if it is successful; otherwise, it is EOF. The function puts a single character on the screen much like `printf("%c", character)` would.

The `puts()` function is the output counterpart to `gets()`. While `gets()` gets a single line from the input stream and stores it as a single string, `puts()` takes a single string and sends it to the output stream—the screen. The null character is replaced with newline so that the cursor will drop down to the next line after the string is printed.

```
int puts(const char *string)                                          <stdio.h>
```

The return value is nonnegative if it is successful, EOF if not.

STRING MANIPULATIONS

Now that we know how strings are stored, we can perform all kinds of operations on them—print them out, assign values to them, take them apart, reassemble them, and so forth. To make life easier for us, ANSI C includes a group of functions to do many of these manipulation for us. Common to all these functions is C's concept of a string—a group of contiguous characters starting at some address and ending with a null character. Also common to most of them is that C does nothing to stop you from assigning characters beyond the memory locations allocated for an individual string. You must take care of that yourself.

We could determine the length of a string, the number of characters in it, by starting at its base address and moving a character at a time until we found the null character. That is what the ANSI `strlen()` function does.

```
size_t strlen(const char *string)                                     <string.h>
```

Its return value is the number of characters in the *string* not including the null at the end. The `size_t` data type is implementation dependent—typically, but not always, an `unsigned int`. It is established in the `string.h` header file (and usually other header files as well).

The `strcpy()` function copies a string from one location to another.

```
char *strcpy(char *destination, const char *source)                   <string.h>
```

STRING FUNCTIONS?

Many of the things we have been presenting as string functions are not. They are really macros instead (see Chapter 13 on macro replacement). For example, `getchar()`, a function that only works with the `stdin` stream, is usually defined in `stdio.h` as

```
#define getchar() getc(stdin)
```

The `getc()` function does the same thing as `getchar()`, but will work with any stream, including data files (you will see this function in Chapter 11, "Files"), so rather than defining a new function for `getchar()`, most Cs just use a `getc()` that specifically works with `stdin`.

This function copies the *source* string, including the terminating null character, to the location of the *destination*. It is up to you to see that there is enough allocated room at the *destination* to accomodate the entire *source* string. The return value is a pointer to the *destination* string.

The strcpy() function has many uses, but one is to just assign a string value to an array. Remember, a string value is a pointer to the null-terminated string in memory—a pointer to char. So given the declaration, the following statement will assign *Algonquin* at the location *string*.

```
char string[20];

strcpy(string, "Algonquin");
```

A way to be sure that you do not overflow the space allocated at the *des tination* is to use the strncpy() function, which copies up to a stated maximum of characters.

```
char *strncpy(char *destination, const char *source, size_t max)
                                                            <string.h>
```

This function can be tricky, though. If C encounters a null in the *source* string before it reaches *max* characters, it copies all the characters up to and including the null, leaving the *destination* string with an exact copy of the *source*. Otherwise, C copies the first *max* characters from the *source* string. If those characters include the terminating null, fine. If not, no null is added. ➡️Program 9–5 shows an example of the latter situation:

➡️Program 9–5

```
#include <stdio.h>
#include <string.h>

void main(void)
{   char name1[12] = "Albemarle", name2[12] = "Ferdy";

    strncpy(name1, name2, 4);
    printf("%s\n", name1);
}
```

Output

```
Ferdmarle
```

Examine the diagram of this situation at the top of the next page.

You could ensure that your string was properly terminated by assigning a null character to the fifth character position of the first string (*name1[4]*).

```
    strncpy(name1, name2, 4);
    name[4] = '\0';
    printf("%s\n", name1);
```

Before Function

name1[0] name1[2] name1[4] name1[6] name1[8] name1[10]
   name1[1] name1[3] name1[5] name1[7] name1[9] name1[11]

name2[0] name2[2] name2[4] name2[6] name2[8] name2[10]
   name2[1] name2[3] name2[5] name2[7] name2[9] name2[11]

After Function

name1[0] name1[2] name1[4] name1[6] name1[8] name1[10]
   name1[1] name1[3] name1[5] name1[7] name1[9] name1[11]

name2[0] name2[2] name2[4] name2[6] name2[8] name2[10]
   name2[1] name2[3] name2[5] name2[7] name2[9] name2[11]

The `strcat()` function concatenates strings—puts one string at the end of another.

```
char *strcat(char *string, const char *add)                    <string.h>
```

This function copies the string at *add* to the location of the null in *string*. It includes the terminating null at the end of *add*. Be sure there is enough allocated space at the location *string* for all the characters in both strings plus the terminating null. The return value is the address of the combination string, *string*.

```
char first[20] = "Arlo ", last[] = "Bilbao";
```

The statement

```
printf("%s\n", strcat(first, last));
```

will print

```
Arlo Bilbao
```

and *first* will contain the value *Arlo Bilbao* with a terminating null. The string *Bilbao* is still at the location *last*, of course.

We can limit the number of characters copied from the *add* string with `strncat()`.

```
char *strncat(char *string, const char *add, size_t max)       <string.h>
```

The `strncat()` function does not have the problem associated with `strncpy()`; a terminating null is always added at the end of the concatenated string.

Often we must compare two strings to see which is greater. But how do we know whether *Murgatroyd* is greater than *Stella*? Let us examine how C makes the comparison. Each character value is nothing more than a number—the numeric value of its ASCII (or EBCDIC) code. C will compare these individual values character by character, beginning with the first character position (variable) in each string and moving toward the end. C makes the greater-than, less-than decision the first time it finds a difference in the character position it is currently comparing.

Murgatroyd and *Stella* are easy. C compares an *M* (ASCII 77) with an *S* (ASCII 83). The *S* is greater, so *Stella* is greater than *Murgatroyd*. Notice that the number of characters in each string is not significant. The first difference ends the comparison.

How about *Aaron* and *Aardvark*? The first three character positions in each string are the same, but in the fourth position are *o* and *d*. The *o* (111) is greater than the *d* (100) so *Aaron* is greater than *Aardvark*.

But *aardvark* is greater than *Aaron* because, in the first character position, *a* (97) is greater than *A* (65). *Bytes* is greater than *Byte* because the *s* in *Bytes* is greater than the null at the end of *Byte*.

Again, ANSI C has saved us from the necessity of writing the string comparison ourselves by providing the strcmp() function.

```
int strcmp(const char *string1, const char *string2)          <string.h>
```

The two strings are compared and the return value set to a positive value if *string1* is greater, zero if they are equal, or a negative value if *string1* is less.

```
if (strcmp(name, "Muleford") == 0) printf("We have found him!\n");
```

Like strncpy() and strncat(), the strncmp() function compares only up to *max* characters in each string.

```
int strncmp(const char *string1, const char *string2, size_t max)
                                                              <string.h>
```

ARRAYS OF STRINGS

We said that a string is an array of characters and that a double-subscripted array is an array of arrays; so we could store an array of strings in a double-subscripted char array.

```
char words[4][6] = {"zero", "one", "two", "three"};
```

The braces around the string values are necessary because they enclose a block of values. We could also declare it as

```
char words[][6] = {"zero", "one", "two", "three"};
```

leaving the first subscript out. Because of the initialization values, C knows how many arrays to set up.

This array takes up 24 bytes of memory organized like this:

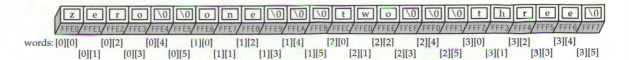

words: [0][0]   [0][2]   [0][4]   [1][0]   [1][2]   [1][4]   [2][0]   [2][2]   [2][4]   [3][0]   [3][2]   [3][4]
      [0][1]   [0][3]   [0][5]   [1][1]   [1][3]   [1][5]   [2][1]   [2][3]   [2][5]   [3][1]   [3][3]   [3][5]

Remember, when we leave the last subscript off an array identifier, it becomes the address of that array-within-an-array. In other words, *words[2]* is the address of *words[2][0]*, or *two*. Using that concept, we can access the *words* array this way:

➡️Program 9–6

```
#include <stdio.h>

void main(void)
{  char words[4][6] = {"zero", "one", "two", "three"};
   int count;

   for (count = 0; count < 4; ++count)
      printf("Digit: %i. Word: %s\n", count, words[count]);
}
```

Output

```
Digit: 0. Word: zero
Digit: 1. Word: one
Digit: 2. Word: two
Digit: 3. Word: three
```

As always, staying within the boundaries of the arrays is up to you. Let us see what happens if we change the value of *words[1]* to something greater than five characters.

➡️Program 9–7

```
#include <stdio.h>

void main(void)
{  char words[4][6] = {"zero", "one", "two", "three"};
   int count;

   strcpy(words[1], "singular");                        /* Add this line */
   for (count = 0; count < 4; ++count)
      printf("Digit: %i. Word: %s\n", count, words[count]);
}
```

Output

```
Digit: 0. Word: zero
Digit: 1. Word: singular
Digit: 2. Word: ar
Digit: 3. Word: three
```

The strcpy() function wrote *singular\0* beginning at the address *words[1]*. The printf() function printed the string beginning at *words[1]* and then the one beginning at *words[2]*, hence the strange, but explainable, output. In memory, it looks like this:

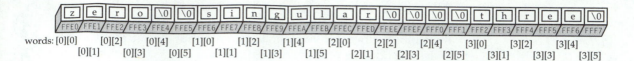

Ragged Arrays

The double-subscripted array we used above is referred to as a **rectangular array**; if you arranged the variables in a table format, each row would have the same number of columns—each string has the same number of characters, whether all those character positions are filled or not. This can lead to a great deal of unfilled memory space and execution time in moving values from one array to another. It has advantages, however, one of the greatest being its predictability—you always know exactly how large each string is so that your techniques for ensuring that you do not overflow can be simpler.

Let us look at the other possibility—**ragged arrays**. Instead of storing an array of arrays, we will store an array of pointers to strings—pointers to char. Each pointer will point to the base address of a string. In our example program, the declaration would change to

```
char *words[4] = {"zero", "one", "two", "three"};
```

or, more simply because of the initialization,

```
char *words[] = {"zero", "one", "two", "three"};
```

There are major differences between the rectangular and the ragged array. The first declares fixed, equal-length strings that reside contiguously in memory. The pointer to the whole group, *words*, and the pointers to each member of the group, *words[0]* and so forth, are constants. The second declares an array of four pointer variables. Were it not for the initialization in the declaration, these pointers would point to garbage. With this declaration and initialization, memory might look as follows:

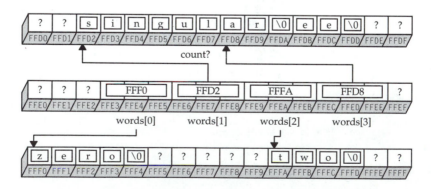

C has found places in memory to store each of the strings. The allocations for each string are not necessarily contiguous with one another and are just enough to store the string (including the null). The stuff in between the strings is anybody's guess.

(Actually, given the initialization, C probably would have stored the strings contiguously, but this is not guaranteed, and given other circumstances and other assignments of the variables in the *words* array, those strings could be all over main memory.)

Rectangular versus Ragged Arrays

A rectangular array of strings, when viewed in a table format, has the same number of columns in each row. The ragged array does not, giving the right side of the table a ragged look. (A θ represents the null character, \0.)

Rectangular Array

```
char words[4][6] = {"zero", "one", "two", "three"};
    z  e  r  o  θ  θ
    o  n  e  θ  θ  θ
    t  w  o  θ  θ  θ
    t  h  r  e  e  θ
```

Ragged Array

```
char *words[] = {"zero", "one", "two", "three"};
    z  e  r  o  θ
    o  n  e  θ
    t  w  o  θ
    t  h  r  e  e  θ
```

➡Program 9–7 could be rewritten this way:

➡Program 9–8

```
#include <stdio.h>

void main(void)
{   char *words[4]={"zero", "one", "two", "three"};
    int count;

    for (count = 0; count < 4; ++count)
        printf("Digit: %i. Word: %s\n", count, words[count]);
}
```

Output

```
Digit: 0. Word: zero
Digit: 1. Word: one
Digit: 2. Word: two
Digit: 3. Word: three
```

Adding the reassignment of *words[1]* has an unpredictable and even more disastrous effect in the ragged array. What did we wipe out by overflowing the memory allocated to *one\0*? The locations allocated to the integer *count*, perhaps?

```
        strcpy(words[1], "singular");
        for (count = 0; count <= 3; ++count)
            printf("Digit: %i. Word: %s\n", count, words[count]);
```

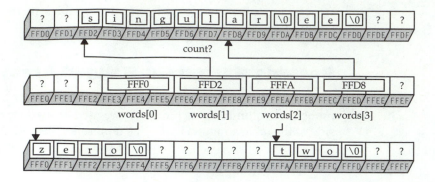

We won't even print out the results; they are apt to be total garbage!

Let us look at an example in which manipulating a ragged array is considerably more efficient than working with a rectangular array. In Chapter 7 we looked at a swap that switched the values of two variables. Here we will swap strings, first using a rectangular array (➥Program 9–9) and then a ragged one (➥Program 9–10). The programs swaps the first string with the fourth—*zero* for *three*.

In the first swap, using the rectangular array, we need the strcpy() function from the header file string.h to copy all the characters from one string to another In the second swap, using the ragged array, we leave the strings where they are and only move pointers. The first requires an extra six-byte string, an extra function, and 33 assignments, while the second requires only an extra three-byte pointer and three assignments.

➥Program 9–9 Using Rectangular Array

```
#include <stdio.h>
#include <string.h>

void main(void)
{   char words[][6]={"zero", "one", "two", "three"};
    char temp[6];                              /* Temporary string for swap */
    int count;

    /**************************************************** Print out array */
    for (count = 0; count <= 3; ++count)
        printf("Digit: %i. Word: %s\n", count, words[count]);
    /*********************************** Swap first for fourth string */
    strcpy(temp, words[3]);
    strcpy(words[3], words[0]);
    strcpy(words[0], temp);
    /**************************************************** Print out array */
    printf("\n");
    for (count = 0; count <= 3; ++count)
        printf("Digit: %i. Word: %s\n", count, words[count]);
```

```
#include <stdio.h>

void main(void)
{  char *words[]={"zero", "one", "two", "three"};
   char *temp;                                  /* Temporary address for swap */
   int count;

   /***************************************************** Print out array */
   for (count = 0; count <= 3; ++count)
      printf("Digit: %i. Word: %s\n", count, words[count]);
   /********************************* Swap first for fourth string */
   temp = words[3];
   words[3] = words[0];
   words[0] = temp;
   /***************************************************** Print out array */
   printf("\n");
   for (count = 0; count <= 3; ++count)
      printf("Digit: %i. Word: %s\n", count, words[count]);
}
```

Output for Both Programs

```
Digit: 0. Word: zero
Digit: 1. Word: one
Digit: 2. Word: two
Digit: 3. Word: three

Digit: 0. Word: three
Digit: 1. Word: one
Digit: 2. Word: two
Digit: 3. Word: zero
```

After the swaps, memory will look like this:

Rectangular Array

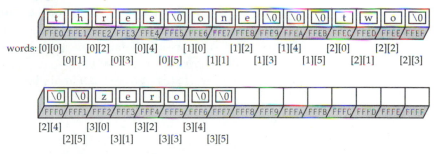

Ragged Array

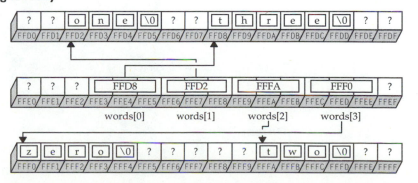

CONVERTING BETWEEN NUMBERS AND STRINGS

Something that looks like a number to us, 123.45 for example, can be stored in the computer in two very different ways—as a number, the binary IEEE notation equivalent to that value, or as a string, the seven characters *123.45\0*. Each form has its advantages. We can perform mathematics on numbers; we cannot on strings even if they look like numbers. We humans can easily understand the string; it is in familiar characters instead of weird binary notation. Also, if we store the individual characters, we have access to them. We can take the number apart and perhaps reassemble it some other way.

Because each method of storage has its unique set of advantages, it might be worthwhile to be able to convert from one notation to the other and vice versa. In fact, we have already been making conversions since Chapter 2. The printf() function converted numbers stored in memory to sets of characters and displayed them on the screen. In the other direction, scanf() converted the characters from the input stream to numbers stored in numeric variables.

Numbers to Strings

We can use a variation of printf() called sprintf() to write characters directly into memory—typically to a space allocated for a string.

```
int sprintf(char *string, const char *control_string, arguments) <stdio.h>
```

What would normally be displayed on the screen by printf() will be written to memory at the address *string*. All the formatting properties that we used with printf() are available with sprintf(). Like other string functions, sprintf() puts the trailing null at the end of the string. The return value is the number of characters written to the string, not including the null.

➡Program 9–11 stores the characters representing an amount of pay in the string array *paycheck[]*. We have used sprintf() to add other characters and round the numeric result to two decimal places.

➡Program 9–11

```
#include <stdio.h>

void main(void)
{  char paycheck[40];
   double hours = 36.7, rate = 12.36;

   sprintf(paycheck, "Pay is $%.2f.", hours * rate);
   puts(paycheck);                      /* Display so we can see result */
}
```

Output

```
Pay is $453.61.
```

Strings to Numbers

There are a number of ways of converting strings to numbers. Like `printf()`, `scanf()` has its string-in-memory counterpart `sscanf()`.

```
int sscanf(char *string, const char *control_string, arguments)   <stdio.h>
```

This function takes the characters stored at *string* instead of the input buffer, converts them according to the *control_string*, and stores them at the addresses given in the arguments. The return values are also the same—the number of assignments successfully made, or `EOF`—but in this case, if the end of the string is reached rather than the end of the file.

The `sscanf()` function is especially useful if there are extraneous characters in the string to be ignored in the conversion.

▶▶Program 9–12

```
#include <stdio.h>

void main(void)
{  char paycheck[] = "Pay is $451.63.";
   float pay;

   sscanf(paycheck, "Pay is $%f.", &pay);
   printf("%f\n", pay);                    /* Display so we can see result */
}
```

Output

```
451.630000
```

Three other functions will convert strings to numbers: `atof()` converts a *string* to type `double`; `atoi()` to `int`; and `atol()` to `long`.

```
double atof(const char *string)                              <stdlib.h>
int atoi(const char *string)                                 <stdlib.h>
long atol(const char *string)                                <stdlib.h>
```

In each case, the conversion begins at the address *string*, skips any leading whitespace, and ends at the first inappropriate character for that data type or the end of the string (the null).

OTHER ANSI CONVERSION FUNCTIONS

The ANSI functions `strtod()`, `strtol()`, and `strtoul()` allow you to do some extra things with string-to-number conversions including returning the address where the conversion stopped (the inappropriate character) and, in the latter two, allowing you to state the radix (base) of the string representation.

```
double strtod(const char *string, char **endptr)            <stdlib.h>
long strtol(const char *string, char **endptr, int radix)   <stdlib.h>
unsigned long strtoul(const char *string, char **endptr, int radix)
                                                            <stdlib.h>
```

➡️Program 9–13

```
#include <stdio.h>
#include <stdlib.h>

void main(void)
{   char string[]="123.456 is a number.";
    int intvar;
    long longvar;
    double doublevar;

    intvar = atoi(string);
    longvar = atol(string);
    doublevar = atof(string);
    printf("The string: %s\n", string);
    printf("Int: %i, long: %li, double: %f\n", intvar, longvar, doublevar);
}
```

Output

```
The string: 123.456 is a number.
Int: 123, long: 123, double: 123.456000
```

If the number represented by the characters in the string is larger than the data type can accommodate, the resulting assignment will be meaningless.

CHARACTER CLASSIFICATION

Often we are presented with a string of characters and must look inside it to interpret it. Is it a complete sentence? Does it present parameters for our program to work with? If so, what are the parameters? To examine it we must look at the individual characters. We can easily test to see if a particular character is an *A* or a comma; but usually we want to look at the type of character rather than its individual value. Is it an uppercase alpha character? Is it punctuation?

ANSI C provides us with a number of functions to classify individual characters. They all have the same format:

```
int function(int character)                                    <ctype.h>
```

For example,

```
int isalpha(int character)                                     <ctype.h>
```

returns a nonzero value if the *character* is a letter, that is, *A* through *Z* or *a* through *z*, or returns zero if it is not a letter.

➡️Program 9–14 asks for a letter from the keyboard and will loop until it gets one.

➡Program 9–14

```
#include <stdio.h>
#include <ctype.h>

void main(void)
{  int in;              /* Declare as int to save conversions in execution */

   do
   {  printf("Type a letter and <enter>: ");
      in = getchar();                      /* Assign the character to in */
      getchar();              /* Pass newline at end of input buffer */
   }while (!isalpha(in));                        /* Loop while not zero */
   puts("Finally, an alpha character!");
}
```

Output

```
Type a letter and <enter>: 4
Type a letter and <enter>: 8
Type a letter and <enter>: /
Type a letter and <enter>: g
Finally, an alpha character!
```

We can examine a string character by character by sending the character values to the isalpha() function.

➡Program 9–15

```
#include <stdio.h>
#include <ctype.h>

void main(void)
{  char *string = "23 skidoo.";

   while(*string != '\0')              /* Loop to the end of the string */
   {  if (isalpha(*string))
         printf("'%c' is alpha\n", *string);
      else
         printf("'%c' is not alpha\n", *string);
      ++string;                              /* Go to next character */
   }
}
```

Output

```
'2' is not alpha
'3' is not alpha
' ' is not alpha
's' is alpha
'k' is alpha
'i' is alpha
'd' is alpha
'o' is alpha
'o' is alpha
'.' is not alpha
```

Notice that in this particular case, by choosing to increment the pointer *string* we lose the address of the beginning of the string. If we had wanted to retain that address we could have set up another pointer or declared the string as an array and incremented the subscript.

The complete list of ANSI classification functions follows. These functions are similar to `isalpha()` in that their declarations are found in *ctype.h*, and they return nonzero if their conditions are satisfied, or zero if they are not.

`isalnum()`   Returns nonzero if the *character* is alphanumeric: 0–9, A–Z, or a–z.

`isalpha()`   Returns nonzero if the *character* is alphabetic: A–Z or a–z.

`iscntrl()`   Returns nonzero if the *character* is a control code: ASCII 1–31.

`isdigit()`   Returns nonzero if the *character* is a decimal digit: 0–9.

`isgraph()`   Returns nonzero if the *character* is printable, not including space.

`islower()`   Returns nonzero if the *character* is lowercase: a–z.

`isprint()`   Returns nonzero if the *character* is printable, including space.

`ispunct()`   Returns nonzero if the *character* is punctuation.

`isspace()`   Returns nonzero if the *character* is whitespace: space, form feed (\f), newline (\n), return (\r), horizontal tab (\t), or vertical tab (\v).

`isupper()`   Returns nonzero if the *character* is uppercase: A–Z.

`isxdigit()`   Returns nonzero if the *character* is a hexadecimal digit: 0–9, A–F.

CHARACTER CONVERSIONS

There are two simple functions, `toupper()` and `tolower()`, that convert lowercase characters to uppercase and vice versa. Their forms are:

```
int toupper(int character)                                  <ctype.h>
int tolower(int character)                                  <ctype.h>
```

If the *character* is not alpha, A–Z or a–z, it will be returned unchanged.

To illustrate the `tolower()` function, ➡Program 9–16 on the next page converts a name in all caps to the same name but in caps/lowercase.

In *MYRNA H. BALTHAZAR*, both spaces and the period are sent to the `tolower()` function but, since they are not uppercase alphabetic characters, they are returned unchanged.

TAKING STRINGS APART

Often we are faced with the task of disassembling a string into some component parts, a process referred to as **parsing** a string. Perhaps an input contains several parameters and we must separate them, or we are examining the individual words in a sentence, or a name must be divided into first, middle initial if one exists, and last. To do this we must look for clues that tell us where one part ends and another begins. The first part ends in a space; the second comes before a third, which is enclosed in parentheses.

➽Program 9–16

```
#include <stdio.h>
#include <ctype.h>

void main(void)
{   char *string="MYRNA H. BALTHAZAR";
    char *ptr;

    printf("Before: %s\n", string);
                /* ptr moves from the second chr of the string to the end */
                        /* The first character remains uppercase */
    for (ptr = string + 1; *ptr != '\0'; ++ptr)
        if (*(ptr - 1) != ' ')    /* Chr after space should remain ucase */
            *ptr = tolower(*ptr);
    printf("After : %s\n", string);
}
```

Output

```
Before: MYRNA H. BALTHAZAR
After : Myrna H. Balthazar
```

To accomplish this disassembly, we must know what the clues are and have C find them for us. The more flexible our algorithm is, the more useful it will be. For example, making it immaterial how many spaces there are between parameters allows the program to handle some possibly sloppy parameters.

The `strstr()` function returns the address of the beginning of a *search* string within a *reference* string.

```
char *strstr(const char *reference, const char *search)          <string.h>
```

If the *reference* string does not contain the *search* string, the function returns the NULL pointer constant. The code segment

```
char location[] = "Des Moines, Iowa";

printf("State: %s\n", strstr(location, ", ") + 2);
```

would print out *Iowa*. The `%s` conversion code requires an address, a pointer to `char`, which `strstr()` returns. In this case it will be the address of the beginning of the comma-space combination within *location*—the address of the comma. The name of the state begins two characters after the comma, so adding 2 to the return value of `strstr()` gives us the address of *I*. The `%s` conversion code, then, will print from there to the terminating null—*Iowa*.

Notice that if the comma were not in the *location[]* array, we would be asking `printf()` to print what was at the NULL pointer—probably nothing we would want to see displayed on our screen.

The `strstr()` function is probably the most basic of the functions that find specific characters within a string. The `strchr()` function is similar except that it finds the first occurrence of a single character instead of an entire string.

```
char *strchr(const char *reference, int character)                    <string.h>
```

If the *character* is not found in the *reference* string, the function returns the NULL pointer constant. In the strchr() function, the null character at the end of the string is a possible search character. A search for it provides a pointer to the position one beyond the last character in the string.

We could use this to find and display the dollar amount in the string given:

Program Segment   **Output**

```
char *string="Widgets cost $49.95";                    Cost: $49.95
printf("Cost: %s\n", strchr(string, '$'));
```

The %s conversion for printf() expects the address of a string—a pointer to charÑthe same data type as the return from the strchr()function. In this case the return from strchr() is the address of the $, so the string printed by printf() extends from the $ to the first null—the end of the string.

The strrchr() function is similar to strchr() except that it searches in reverse order, starting from the end of the *reference* string, finding the last occurrence of the *character*.

Another similar function is strpbrk() which finds the first occurrence of any one of the characters of the *search* string in the *reference* string.

```
char *strpbrk(const char *reference, const char *search)          <string.h>
```

For example, if we were not quite sure whether two items in a *string* were separated by a comma, a space, a dash, or a slash, we could find the separator with:

```
separator = strpbrk(string, ", -/");
```

The strtok() function is particularly useful in extracting **tokens**, sets of characters, from strings. It searches a reference string for any character from a string of delimiters (separating characters) and replaces that delimiter with a null, effectively ending the string there. The return value is the address of the reference string. The token, then, is the string at the returned address.

```
char *strtok(const char *reference, const char *delimiters)       <string.h>
```

For example, ➡Program 9–17, on the next page, extracts the characters representing the month from the date given. Notice it would not matter whether we expressed the dates as *12/6/1492*, *12-6-1492*, or *12 6 1492*. Or, for that matter, if we had a date like *9/17/96*.

After the call to strtok(), *date* still points to the same place, but the string is shortened because the null was inserted where the first slash was.

The strtok() function, however, remembers where the null was inserted. A subsequent call to strtok() with NULL (the defined NULL pointer) as the *ref erence* string argument is a signal to the funciton to make the *reference* argument the address of the character after the inserted null from the previous call. In other words strtok() will start where it left off last time. The returned value will be the new *reference* address. We can illustrate this with ➡Program 9–18 that divides a date into *month*, *day*, and *year* strings.

▶▶Program 9–17

```
#include <stdio.h>
#include <string.h>

void main(void)
{  char *date="12/6/1492";

   printf("Date: %s\n", date);
   strtok(date, "/- ");                      /* Null inserted at delimiter */
   printf("Month: %s\n", date);
}
```

Output

```
Date: 12/6/1492
Month: 12
```

▶▶Program 9–18

```
#include <stdio.h>
#include <string.h>

void main(void)
{  char *date="12/6/1492";
   char *month, *day, *year;

   printf("Date:  %s\n", date);
   month = strtok(date, "/- ");              /* Null inserted at delimiter */
   printf("Month: %s\n", month);
   day = strtok(NULL, "/- ");                /* Start where last left off */
   printf("Day:   %s\n", day);
   year = strtok(NULL, "\0");                /* Null will be replaced with null */
                                             /* in other words, no change */

   printf("Year:  %s\n", year);
}
```

Output

```
Date:   12/6/1492
Month:  12
Day:    6
Year:   1492
```

Before

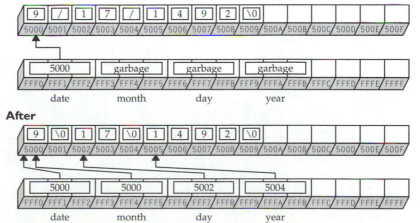

After

ARGUMENTS TO THE main() FUNCTION

With most operating systems, a program is set in operation by typing its name at the command line—at the keyboard while the operating system is waiting for a command. Often, in addition to the program name, you can type in various parameters with which the program may work. For example, the program *greeting* accepts a name from the person running the program. In the following, C:> is the operating system prompt and the person at the keyboard types the stuff in bold:

```
C:>greeting Agnes P. Schreble
```

These are known as **command-line arguments**—data passed from the command line to be used in the program. In C, command-line arguments can be accepted as arguments to the main() function. Instead of defining main() as having a void argument, we will use the following main() prototype:

```
void main(int argc, char *argv[])
```

The variable argc and array argv[] can actually have any names, but these are the traditional ones used with C that everyone recognizes. They stand for "argument count" and "argument vector" (or "argument value").

Both of these parameters are initialized as a result of the contents of the command line. The int variable *argc* is the number of command-line arguments; the first is always the program name; and the array *argv[]* is an array of pointers to char—a ragged array pointing to each individual string in the command line. Whitespace delimits strings in the command line, so our example would have four arguments, with *argc* initialized to four and *argv[0]* through *argv[3]* pointing to each of the strings with the first, *argv[0]*, pointing to *greeting*.

➡Program 9–19

```
#include <stdio.h>

void main(int argc, char *argv[])
{  int count;

   printf("The %s program welcomes", argv[0]);
   for (count = 1; count < argc; ++count)
     printf(" %s", argv[count]);
   printf("\n  Hi %s!\n", argv[1]);
}
```

Outputs

```
C:>greeting Agnes P. Schreble
The greeting program welcomes Agnes P. Schreble
  Hi Agnes!

C:>greeting Willy F. Q. Lanceford Hogworth, IV
The greeting program welcomes Willy F. Q. Lanceford Hogworth, IV
  Hi Willy!
```

PUTTING IT TOGETHER

The form of data in one place is often not what we want it to be in another place, so our programs must convert it. In this example we are given a person's first, middle, and last names, and their height and weight in various forms. We must return the last name first, height in meters, and weight in kilograms in specific-length fields. For example:

Sample Outputs

```
Enter listing: Abner Troy Brindle: 6 ft 2 in, 192 lbs
Brindle, Abner Troy  1.88 meters  87.27 kg.

Enter listing: Sheila Shirley Schildkin:1m46cm,115pds
Schildkin, Sheila Sh 1.46 meters  52.27 kg.

Enter listing: Rocky Q. Flowers: 161 cm, 85 kg
Flowers, Rocky Q.    1.61 meters  85.00 kg.
```

From the top down we can view the procedure as

> Get Listing
> Process name
> Process height
> Process weight
> Present listing

Expanding on that:

> Get Listing
> Process name
>> Extract name
>> Adjust name
> Process height
>> Extract height
>> Adjust height
> Process weight
>> Extract weight
>> Process weight
> Present listing

To adjust the name we would have to:

> Adjust name
>> Divide name into first and last
>> Build new name with last name first

To adjust the height we would have to:

> Adjust height
>> Convert first part
>>> Find digits
>>> Find units
>>> Convert digits according to units
>> Convert second part, if any
>>> Find digits
>>> Find units
>>> Convert digits according to units

To adjust the weight we would have to:

Adjust weight
    Find digits
    Find units
    Convert digits according to units

Translating all this into C we get the following program:

➡ Program 9–20

```c
#include <stdio.h>
#include <string.h>
#include <ctype.h>
#include <stdlib.h>

void adjust_name(char name[]);
float adjust_height(char *height_in);
float adjust_weight(char *weight_in);

void main(void)
{   char input[80], name[40], listing[80];
    char *height_in, *weight_in;
    float height, weight;

    /***************************************************** Enter listing */
    printf("Enter listing: ");   /* Can't use puts() and stay on same line */
1   gets(input);

    /***************************************************** Process name */
2   strcpy(name, strtok(input, ":"));                    /* Extract name */
3   adjust_name(name);

    /***************************************************** Process height */
4   height_in = strtok(NULL, ",");
5   height = adjust_height(height_in);

    /***************************************************** Process weight */
6   weight_in = strtok(NULL, "\0");
7   weight = adjust_weight(weight_in);

    /***************************************** Store and print listing */
8   sprintf(listing, "%-20.20s %4.2f meters %6.2f kg.",
            name, height, weight);
9   puts(listing);
}
                                                    void adjust_name(char name[])
/***************** Changes name from first name first to last name first */
{   char temp_name[40], *last_name;

    /********************** Divide name into first (and middle) and last */
n1  last_name = strchr(strchr(name, ' ') + 1, ' ') + 1;       /* 2nd space */
n2  *(last_name - 1) = '\0';                    /* End first and middle name */

    /***************************** Build new name with last name first */
n3  strcpy(temp_name, last_name);                        /* Put in last name */
n4  strcat(temp_name, ", ");                                  /* Add comma */
n5  strcat(temp_name, name);                             /* Add first name */
n6  strcat(name, temp_name);                      /* Copy result back to name */
}
```

—*Continued*

EXECUTION CHART — `main()`

Line	Explanation	input[] / name[]
1	Copy input stream to *input[]*, replace \n with \0.	`Abner Troy Brindle: 6 ft 2 in, 192 lbs` `?`
2	`strtok()` replaces : with \0; returns the address *input*. `strcpy()` copies string at *input* to *name*.	`Abner Troy Brindle\0 6 ft 2 in, 192 lbs` `Abner Troy Brindle\0`
3	Call *adjust_name* and pass the address *name* to *name* in *adjust_name()*.	`Abner Troy Brindle\0 6 ft 2 in, 192 lbs` `Brindle, Abner Troy\0` (after call)

Line	Explanation	input[] / At address *height_in*
4	`strtok()` starts where it left off and replaces next comma with \0. Return assigned to *height_in*.	`Abner Troy Brindle\0 6 ft 2 in\0 192 lbs` `6 ft 2 in\0`
5	call *adjust_height*, pass *height_in*. Assign return (1.8796) to *height*.	`Abner Troy Brindle\0 6 ft 2 in\0 192 lbs` `In\0` (after call)

Line	Explanation	input[] / At address *weight_in*
6	`strtok()` starts where it left off and replaces next \0 with \0. Return assigned to *weight_in*.	`Abner Troy Brindle\0 6 ft 2 in\0 192 lbs` `192 lbs\0`
7	Call *adjust_weight*, pass *weight_in*. Assign return (87.2727) to *weight*.	`Abner Troy Brindle\0 6 ft 2 in\0 192 lbs` `Lbs\0` (after call)

Line	Explanation	input[] / At address *listing*
8	Store results converted to appropriate form at *listing*.	`Abner Troy Brindle\0 6 ft 2 in\0 192 lbs` `Brindle, Abner Troy  1.88 meters  87.27 kg.\0`
9	Display string at *listing*, replacing \0 with \n.	`Abner Troy Brindle\0 6 ft 2 in\0 192 lbs` `Brindle, Abner Troy  1.88 meters  87.27 kg.\0`

EXECUTION CHART — `adjust_name()`

Line	Explanation	name[] / temp_name[]	At address last_name
n1	Inner `strchr()` returns address of first space; outer `strchr()` starts there and finds address of second space. Last name starts after that.	`Abner Troy Brindle\0` `?`	`Brindle`
n2	Put \0 before last name to end first and middle names.	`Abner Troy\0Brindle\0` `?`	`Brindle`
n3	Copy characters at *last_name* up to \0 to *temp_name*.	`Abner Troy\0Brindle\0` `Brindle\0`	`Brindle`
n4	Concatenate comma and space.	`Abner Troy\0Brindle\0` `Brindle, \0`	`Brindle`
n5	Concatenate first name.	`Abner Troy\0Brindle\0` `Brindle, Abner Troy\0`	`Brindle`
n6	Copy characters at *temp_name* to *name*.	`Brindle, Abner Troy\0` `Brindle, Abner Troy\0`	`ner Troy`

```
        float adjust_height(char *height_in)
        /************************ Changes height from almost any units to meters */
        { float height, height1;

            /*********************************** Convert first part of height */
            /***************************************************** Find digits */
h1          while (!isdigit(*height_in)) ++height_in;        /*Get to first digit */
h2          height = atof(height_in);            /* Convert until inappropriate chr */

            /***************************************************** Find units */
h3          for ( ; !isalpha(*height_in); ++height_in);        /* Beg of units */
h4          *height_in = toupper(*height_in);        /* Only first chr necessary */

            /*********************************** Convert according to units */
h5          switch (*height_in)
h6          { case 'F':                                              /* Feet */
h7              height *= .3048;
h8              break;
h9            case 'I':                                            /* Inches */
h10             height /= 39.37;
h11             break;
h12           case 'C':                                       /* Centimeters */
h13             height /= 100;
h14         }

            /***************************** Convert second part of height, if any */
            /***************************************************** Find digits */
h15         height_in = strpbrk(height_in, "0123456789");        /* Next digit */
h16         if (height_in != NULL)                    /* If there is a next digit */
h17         { height1 = atof(height_in);      /* Convert until inappropriate chr */

            /***************************************************** Find units */
h18           for ( ; !isalpha(*height_in); ++height_in);      /* Beg of units */
h19           *height_in = toupper(*height_in);      /* Only 1st chr necessary */

            /*********************************** Convert according to units */
h20           switch (*height_in)
h21           { case 'I':                                          /* Inches */
h22               height += height1 / 39.37;
h23               break;
h24             case 'C':                                     /* Centimeters */
h25               height += height1 / 100;
h26           }
h27         }
h28     return height;
        }
```
—*Continued*

In the *adjust_height()* function we have presented two different ways of finding the next digit.

```
        while (!isdigit(*height_in)) ++height_in;        /*Get to first digit */
```

moves the pointer along until isdigit() is not false; and

```
        height_in = strpbrk(height_in, "0123456789");          /* Next digit */
```

uses strpbrk() to find the next digit.

Line	Explanation	At *height_in*	*height*	*height1*
h1	Increment *height_in* while it is not pointing at a digit.	6 ft 2 in\0 6 ft 2 in\0	?	?
h2	Convert to inappropriate character—the space	6 ft 2 in\0	6	?
h3	Increment *height_in* while it is not pointing at an alpha character. This could have been done with while, like h1.	6 ft 2 in\0 ft 2 in\0 ft 2 in\0	6	?
h4	Convert what *height_in* points at to uppercase.	Ft 2 in\0	6	?
h5	Look for case 'F':, find in h6.	Ft 2 in\0	6	?
h7	Convert *height* in feet to meters.	Ft 2 in\0	1.8288	?
h8	Go past end of switch structure at h14.	Ft 2 in\0	1.8288	?
h15	strpbrk() returns address of next occurrence of any digit.	2 in\0	1.8288	?
h16	Return is not NULL.	2 in\0	1.8288	?
h17	Convert to inappropriate character—the space	2 in\0	1.8288	2
h18	Increment *height_in* while it is not pointing at an alpha character.	in\0	1.8288	2
h19	Convert what *height_in* points at to uppercase.	In\0	1.8288	2
h20	Look for case 'I':, find in h21.	In\0	1.8288	2
h22	Convert *height1* in inches to meters; add to *height*.	In\0	1.8796	.0508
h23	Go past end of switch structure at h27.	In\0	1.8796	.0508
h28	Return value of *height*.	In\0	1.8796	.0508

➡️**Program 9–20** —*Continued*

```
float adjust_weight(char *weight_in)
/***************************  Changes weight from almost any units to kg */
{   float weight;

    /*******************************************  Find digits */
w1    while (!isdigit(*weight_in)) ++weight_in;       /* Get to first digit */
w2    weight = atof(weight_in);           /* Convert until inappropriate chr */

    /*******************************************  Find units */
w3    for ( ; !isalpha(*weight_in); ++weight_in);     /* Beginning of units */
w4    *weight_in = toupper(*weight_in);          /* Only first chr necessary */

    /**************************************  Convert according to units */
w5    if (*weight_in == 'L' || *weight_in == 'P')      /* Convert if pounds */
w6      weight /= 2.2;

w7    return weight;
}
```

Line	Explanation	At *weight_in*	*weight*
w1	Increment *weight_in* while it is not pointing at a digit.	192 lbs\0 192 lbs\0	?
w2	Convert to first inappropriate character (space) and assign to *weight*.	192 lbs\0	192
w3	Increment *weight_in* while it is not pointing at an alpha character.	192 lbs\0 92 lbs\0 2 lbs\0 lbs\0 lbs\0	192
w4	Convert character at *weight_in* to uppercase.	Lbs\0	192
w5	Content at *weight_in* is 'L'.	Lbs\0	192
w6	Convert *weight* to kg.	Lbs\0	87.2727
w7	Return *weight*.	Lbs\0	87.2727

In this program there are obviously lots of input possibilities we have not accounted for. As you can see, foolproofing inputs can be a programming nightmare!

SUMMARY

A string value is a set of characters. In C we denote it by enclosing the value in quotes. The actual value of the quoted expression is the address at which C stored the characters within the quotes. C will store the value with a trailing null. In executing a program the usual interpretation of a string is a set of bytes beginning at an address and ending at the first null. This differs from an individual character value, which is simply an ASCII (or EBCDIC) code stored in a single byte in memory.

There are no string variables, but we can store string values in char arrays. Declarations and initializations can be like any other arrays, but C also understands that a quoted string can initialize a char array with C adding the trailing null. Assignment of string values is like assignment to any other array—by individual values. To make this easier for us, ANSI C has a number of functions that perform this process for various applications.

The scanf() function using the %s conversion code assigns a string from the standard input stream. The getchar() function assigns a single character from that stream, and gets() assigns the input stream up to the next newline to a single string. As with many functions that return a pointer value, gets() returns the NULL pointer if there is an error in the assignment. String output is accomplished with printf() and the %s conversion code, putchar() for single characters, or puts() for entire strings.

ANSI C has a number of functions that aid us in manipulating strings. The strlen() returns the number of characters in a string (as a size_t data type); strcpy() and strncpy() copy a string to another location; strcat() and strncat() copy one string to the end of another; and strcmp() and strncmp() compare one string to another.

Arrays of strings may be set up declaring an array of arrays—a double-subscripted array. This is called a **rectangular array** because each subarray has the same number of bytes. A **ragged array** is established by keeping an array of pointers, each pointing to a different string.

There are various functions that convert strings to numbers and vice versa. The scanf() and printf() functions convert numbers to characters and characters to numbers on input and output. The sprintf() function works similarly to printf() except that the characters are written to a designated address and a trailing null is added. The sscanf() function converts characters from a memory location rather than the input stream. The atof(), atoi(), and atol() functions convert strings to doubles, ints, and longs.

The isalnum(), isalpha(), iscntrl(), isdigit(), isgraph(), islower(), isprint(), ispunct(), isspace(), isupper(), and isxdigit() functions test characters to see if they fit into various classifications. The toupper() function converts a lowercase alpha character to uppercase, and tolower() does the opposite.

There are a number of functions that help us in **parsing** strings. The strstr() function finds one string within another, and strchr() and strrchr() find a specific character within a string. The strtok() function helps us to extract series of **tokens** from strings.

C will accept **command-line arguments** in a ragged array by defining the main() function with the variable argc to hold the number of arguments on the **command line**, and the pointer array argv[] to point to each individual argument.

KEY TERMS (in order of appearance)

getchar()
gets()
NULL
putchar()
puts()
strlen()
size_t
strcpy()
strncpy()
strcat()
strncat()
strcmp()
strncmp()
Rectangular array
Ragged array
sprintf()
sscanf()
atof()
atoi()
atol()
isalnum()
isalpha()

iscntrl()
isdigit()
isgraph()
islower()
isprint()
ispunct()
isspace()
isupper()
isxdigit()
toupper()
tolower()
Parsing
strstr()
strchr()
strrchr()
strpbrk()
strtok()
Token
Command-line argument
argc
argv[]

REVIEW QUESTIONS

1. How does C, in its standard functions, store a string value in memory? Where does the string begin and end?

2. What data type is a quoted string in a C program?

3. How does the string value "A" differ from the character value 'A'?

4. In what kind of variables do we store strings?

5. How does C ensure that we do not assign strings to unallocated locations?

6. What conversion codes can we use with scanf() for keyboard input of strings?

7. Which function is used for keyboard input of single characters?

8. Which function assigns the entire input stream to a string? What changes does it make to the input stream?

9. What functions are the output equivalents of the input functions in the three preceeding questions?

10. Which function returns the number of characters in a string?

11. Which two functions copy a string from one location into another? What is the difference between the two functions?

12. Which two functions copy a string from one location to the end of a string in another? What is the difference between the two functions?

13. Which two functions compare one string with another? What is the significance of the return values? What is the difference between the two functions?

14. Describe two different ways of storing strings in arrays. How can each type of array be initialized? How can individual strings in each type of array be referred to?

15. What function is often used to convert numbers to strings?

16. What four functions are commonly used to convert strings to numbers?

17. The text introduces 11 functions used to classify characters. Name them and tell what classifications they determine.

18. Which two functions convert a character between upper- and lowercase?

19. What function is used to find the first occurrence of one string within another?

20. Which three functions search for specific characters within a string? How do they differ?

21. Name the function used to extract tokens from a string. How is it used in its first call? In subsequent calls with the same string?

22. How may we use string arrays to receive arguments from the command line? What is the purpose of each of the variables used in command-line input?

EXERCISES

1. Which are valid declarations and initializations for strings?

   a. `char a[10] = "Alice";`
   b. `char *a = "Alice";`
   c. `char a[] = "Alice";`
   d. `char a[10] = 'A', 'l', 'i', 'c', 'e';`
   e. `char *a = {'A', 'l', 'i', 'c', 'e'};`

2. Given these declarations, which will execute without error messages, and which will produce valid data?

   `char s1[16] = "Rita", *s2 = "Al";`

   a. `scanf("%s", &s1);`
   b. `scanf("%s", s2);`
   c. `s2 = "Farley";`
   d. `s1 = "Fred";`
   e. `s1 = s2;`
   f. `s2 = s1;`
   g. `strcpy(s1, s2);`
   h. `strcat(s1, s2);`
   i   `strcat(s2, s1);`
   j. `*(s2 + 3) = s1[1];`
   k. `*(s1 + 3) = s2[1];`

3. Given the following declarations, what will be assigned at *a* and *b* as a result of the following `scanf()` operations, all with the input "Happy New Year"?

   `char a[20], b[20];`

   a. `scanf("%s %s", a, b);`
   b. `scanf("%9s %s");`
   c. `sscanf(c,"%4s %s", a, b);`
   d. `sscanf(c,"%[NHap] %s", a, b);`
   e. `sscanf(c,"%s, %s", a, b);`
   f. `sscanf(c,"%[^e]e %s", a, b);`

4. What will be the difference in output between these two statements?

   ```
   printf("%s", "Hello");
   puts("Hello");
   ```

5. What output will the following program produce?

```c
#include <stdio.h>
#include <string.h>
#include <ctype.h>

void main(void)
{   char s[] = "Algernon";

    printf("%c\n", s[2]);
    printf("%s\n", &s[2]);
    printf("%i\n", strcmp(s, "Farley"));
    printf("%i\n", strncmp(s, "Algeria", 5));
    printf("%c\n", *strchr(s, 'g'));
    printf("%i\n", strlen(s));
    printf("%i\n", islower(s[2]));
    printf("%s\n", strstr(s, "ger"));
    printf("%c\n", *strpbrk(s, "nle"));
}
```

6. What output will the following program produce?

```c
#include <stdio.h>
#include <stdlib.h>

void main(void)
{   char s[] = "123.456 and so forth";
    float f;

    printf("%i\n", atoi(s));
    printf("%f\n", atof(s));
    sscanf(s, "%f", &f);
    printf("%f\n", f);
    sprintf(s, "%i", (int) f);
    printf("%s\n", s);
}
```

7. What output will the following program produce?

```c
#include <stdio.h>
#include <string.h>

void main(void)
{   char s[] = "Steven C. Lawlor: Author, Raconteur & Scholar";

    printf("%5.5s", strtok(s, " .:"));
    printf("%s\n", strtok(NULL, ":") + 2);
    printf("%s\n", strtok(NULL, "&") + 1);
}
```

PROGRAMS

1. After giving us functions like `isalpha()` and `islower()`, how could the ANSI C committee forget the *isvowel()* function? Redeem them by writing the function to work similarly to the others mentioned. It should return nonzero if the character is a vowel (*a, e, i, o,* or *u,* upper- or lowercase), or zero if it is not a vowel. Test the function in a program that allows input of a string (`gets()`) and single character output (`putchar()`) of the characters in the string with the vowels highlighted as shown.

Variables and Functions

```
main()                          isvowel()
   string                          character
   pos    Character position in string    result
```

Output

```
Aloysius Washington
<A>l<O>ys<I><U>s W<A>sh<I>ngt<O>n
```

2. In the ASCII code, an uppercase letter has a value 32 less than the corresponding lowercase letter. Write a program that will allow you to input any string and print it in all uppercase. The function *caps()* should make the actual changes in the string. Do not use any string functions.

Functions and Variables

```
main()            caps()
   string[]          string[]
```

Output

```
Your input? What? It isn't I!
The output: WHAT? IT ISN'T I!
Your input? The cost: $2,345.67.
The output: THE COST: $2,345.67.
Your input?
```

3. The solution for Program 2 will work on either an ASCII or an EBCDIC machine, not on both. Rewrite it using string functions so that the same program will work on either machine.

4. Write a program to compare two strings without using any functions. The program should print out which string is greater or that they are equal.

Variables:

```
string1
string2
```

Outputs

```
FIRST STRING ? ABNER             FIRST STRING ? ZELDA
SECOND STRING? CRUMP             SECOND STRING? BEULAH
CRUMP IS GREATER THAN ABNER      ZELDA IS GREATER THAN BEULAH


FIRST STRING ? ROSE
SECOND STRING? ROSE
ROSE EQUALS ROSE
```

5. Good people all have last names that begin with the letters *G* through *L*; all the others are bad. Write a program that differentiates the good people from the bad.

Variable

```
name
```

Outputs

```
Name? Attila the Hun             NAME? G
Attila the Hun is a bad person.  G is a good person.


Name? M                          NAME? Lawlor
M is a bad person.               Lawlor is a good person.
```

6. Write a program with a *backward()* function that prints out a string backward. Do not use any string functions.

Functions and Variables

```
main()              backward()
   string[]             string   Address of the string
                        end      Address of the end of string
```

Output

```
Your input? This is a string.
The output: .gnirts a si sihT
Your input? backward?
The output: ?drawkcab
Your input?
```

7. Modify the *backward()* function in the Program 6 so that the function does not print out the string; it actually moves the characters in the string passed from the calling function, so that when the calling function prints out the string, it is backward. You may use a string function to find the end of the string. (Hint: Swap characters between the front and back of the string, moving the front and back points toward the center.)

Functions and Variables

```
main()              backward()
   string[]             string   Address of the string
                        temp     Use for swap of chrs from front to back
                        front    Address of current front of string
                        back     Address of current back of string
```

Output

```
Your input? This is a string.
The output: .gnirts a si sihT
Your input? backward?
The output: ?drawkcab
Your input?
```

8. Write a program that inserts line breaks in a string. The resultant lines should be 16 characters or less and should break only on whitespace (spaces, tabs, newlines). Assume that you will not encounter more than one whitespace at a time. (Or to be more robust, don't assume that.) The actual line breaks (insertion of newlines) should be done in the function *split()*.

Functions and Variables

```
main()              split()
   string               line
                        begin_line  Address of the beginning of the current line
```

Output

```
Input a string.
Now is the time for all good men to come to the aid of their party.
Now is the time
for all good men
to come to the
aid of their
party.
```

9. How many 9s can you depend on in a `double` in your C? Write a program that keeps adding 9s to a string and, to see if they are accurately held in a `double`, converts the string to a `double` and then back to a string. You should have the program stop when the original string does not match the string after conversion.

Variables

digits	Original string
number	String converted to number
digits1	Number converted back to string

Output (in a typical C)

```
               9  9
              99  99
             999  999
            9999  9999
           99999  99999
          999999  999999
         9999999  9999999
        99999999  99999999
       999999999  999999999
      9999999999  9999999999
     99999999999  99999999999
    999999999999  999999999999
   9999999999999  9999999999999
  99999999999999  99999999999999
 999999999999999  999999999999999
9999999999999999  10000000000000000
```

10. The Farfel Corporation has made a list of its salespeople and their weekly sales. Write a program to print this list in either alphabetical or sales volume order depending on your command-line argument when you invoke the program. (Hint: Set up a sort for whichever array is being sorted and "carry" the other array with it. If a swap is made in the array being sorted, make a similar swap in the other array. This is called a tandem sort.)

Partial variable list

```
names[ ]
sales[ ]
```

Data

```
Jones    8604
Smith    3716
Brown    7071
Hill     12336
Green    5004
```

Outputs

```
A>prog name

Brown      7071
Green      5004
Hill       12336
Jones      8604
Smith      3716
```

```
A>prog sales

Hill       12336
Jones      8604
Brown      7071
Green      5004
Smith      3716
```

11. Write a program that accepts any double-precision number and returns the number as a string rounded to two decimal places with commas inserted in the correct places. Use an appropriate function to convert the number to a string.

Outputs

```
Input number? 123456.789
Number with commas: 123,456.79
```

```
Input number? 12.345
Number with commas: 12.35
```

12. A company is writing form letters to a list of people. Each listing has a last name, a first name, and sometimes a middle initial. Variations of the name will appear in three places. The envelope will have the first initial and last name; the heading in the letter will have the full name (first name first); and the greeting will have only the first name. Write a program to input a name (using gets()) and return it in each of three forms.

Partial Variable List

name	Name input
envelop	Name for envelope
heading	Name for heading
greeting	Name for greeting
ref1	Location of the first space
ref2	Location of second reference point (second space or the end of the string plus one)

Sample Outputs

```
Name: Vanderklunk Ophelia T.
   O. Vanderklunk
   Ophelia T. Vanderklunk
   Ophelia

Name: Nisblinger Ted
   T. Nisblinger
   Ted Nisblinger
   Ted

Name: Phurd Agnes Q.
   A. Phurd
   Agnes Phurd
   Agnes
```

13. Write a function *word_analysis()* that receives a string and counts the number of words and sentences in the string, making these available to the calling function. A word ends in a space (or the end of the string), and a sentence ends in a period, question mark, or exclamation point. Test the function by sending it a string such as:

```
"What language?  Why, C of course!"
```

Functions and Variables

main()	word_analysis()
line[]	line
words	words
sentences	sentences

Output

```
What language?  Why, C of course!
  has 6 words and 2 sentences.
```

STRUCTURES

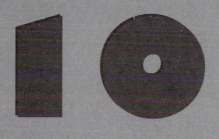

PREVIEW
When data is manipulated in records that group individual but related values, it is useful to have a mechanism that holds each record together. In this chapter we shall look at such a mechanism. At its conclusion, you should understand

1. The characteristics of C's method for accessing records (groups of data).

2. How these records are defined, declared, initialized, and accessed.

3. Using pointers to access the records.

4. How the records are used with functions.

5. A typical application of these records in maintaining ordered lists.

6. A similar concept that allows us to refer to one memory space in many ways.

Data is often stored and accessed in groups—name, address, and phone number, for example. To work with these groups in our programs, we can set up separate variables for each piece of data and make sure we process them together. Another approach is to set up the data so that it can be accessed as a single unit. We must still be able to get to the individual pieces of that unit—the address, for example—but we will also have the option of moving around the entire unit in one operation.

This is the basis of structures in C. A **structure** is a complex data type made up of other data types (including, possibly, other structures). For example, we could combine the three strings (char arrays) for name, address, and phone number into one structure, *listing*. Many times we will access the entire structure—move it into secondary storage, for example; other times we will access individual **members** of the structure—change the address, for example.

DEFINITIONS AND DECLARATIONS

The data types we have worked with previously, float, int, and so forth, have all been defined somewhere else in the language. C knows how many bytes there are in a float and its storage format. Structures are data types that we make up ourselves. Their components are existing data types, to be sure; but unless we tell C the makeup of our new data type, C cannot work with it.

Working with a structure, then, will require two preliminary steps. The first is the **structure definition**, where we tell C the makeup of the structure; the second is the **structure declaration**, where we set up variables of that structure type. Both steps can be accomplished in one struct statement or they can be separated into individual statements. The overall form is

```
struct tag {member definitions} names;
```

For example,

```
struct employee_rec
{   char name[30];
    int dependents;
    float pay_rate;
} full_time, part_time;
```

The *tag* and *member definitions* are part of the definition of the variable type. The *names* are the declarations of variables of this type. No memory space is allocated as a result of the definition. The allocations occur when variables are declared by name.

The *tag*, employee_rec in the example, is the name of the data type. It is the equivalent of float or int and is used in much the same way—we will declare variables of that data type to be used in the program. The tag is optional, but if we do not give one, all of our declarations of variables of this structure type will have to be in this one statement. By including a tag, we can define the type here and declare variables of this type elsewhere in the program—locally in a function, for example.

The visibility rules for structure definitions are the same as those for variables. Structure tags defined externally are visible globally; you can declare structure variables of that type anywhere in your program. Structure tags defined within a program block are visible only locally, within that block. Structure declarations of that type can only be in the same block. It is often a good idea to define structures externally, where they are visible to all functions. This way you can declare variables of that type locally in any of the functions. A drawback to this strategy is if you are combining code together and the same tag was used in different parts of the code.

A structure is a complex variable made up of other variable members. In the `member definitions` we will define each of the individual variables that make up the structure. Still, no memory space is allocated. These are not declarations of those variables; they only tell C what a structure will be composed of when one is actually declared. Any valid data type can be a member of a structure. In our example we have the 30 `char` variables in the array *name*, one `int`, and one `float`. Even other structures, if they are defined beforehand, can be members of structures.

When a structure of this type is actually allocated, C will store the members contiguously, in the order in which they were defined.

We shall see that by using a *tag* that has been defined beforehand, we can declare variables without having to redefine the members.

Stating variable *names* after the definition declares and allocates memory for those variables. The names are optional; if none are given, no variables are declared—presumably they will be declared sometime later. In our example, we have declared two variables of type *employee_rec*, *full_time* and *part_time*. Each of these variables will be 36 bytes long (assuming a two-byte `int` and a four-byte `float`). The `sizeof` operator would tell us that if we used an expression like

```
sizeof full_time
```

Or, we could refer to the size of the data type by saying

```
sizeof (struct employee_rec)
```

When we refer to a structure data type we must precede it with the key word `struct`. As with any other data type, when we take the `sizeof` a structure data type we must put it in parentheses.

The example definition and declaration given performs both functions within one statement. We could have accomplished the same things in any number of other ways. For example,

```
struct
{   char name[30];
    int dependents;
    float pay_rate;
} full_time, part_time;
```

would have defined the structure and allocated two variables of that type; but, since we have given the structure no *tag*, we could not declare more variables elsewhere in the program without redefining the members.

The statement,

```
struct employee_rec
{   char name[30];
    int dependents;
    float pay_rate;
};
```

defines the structure and tags it, but does not allocate any memory space for variables of that type. Notice that the semicolon after the closing brace at the end of the statement is required. At other points in our program we might have declarations such as

```
struct employee_rec full_time;
```

and

```
struct employee_rec part_time;
```

each of which declares (and allocates memory for) a variable of type *employee_rec*.

Initializations

Default initializations for structures are the same as for other variables—zero for global-lifetime variables and garbage for locals. We may also explicitly initialize structures at the time of their declarations. (Like arrays, some non-ANSI C compilers will not allow initializations of local-lifetime structures.) The important criterion for initializations is that the values are listed in the exact same order as the members in the structure.

In our last example, the structure defined as

```
struct employee_rec
{   char name[30];
    int dependents;
    float pay_rate;
};
```

could have a declaration and initialization as follows:

```
struct employee_rec full_time = {"Beulah Barzoom", 4, 12.63};
```

The entire definition, declaration, and initialization could be contained in one statement.

```
struct employee_rec
{   char name[30];
    int dependents;
    float pay_rate;
} full_time = {"Beulah Barzoom", 4, 12.63};
```

ACCESSING STRUCTURES

Structures are most often accessed—read or assigned—by accessing their individual members. Since we may have many variables of the same structure type and each of these variables will have the same member names, we must tie the member name to the specific structure variable with a **member operator**, a dot (.). The *pay_rate* member of the *full_time* structure is referred to as *full_time.pay_rate*. The second character in the *name* array member of the *part_time* structure is *part_time.name[1]* while *part_time.name* is the base address of the *name* array in *part_time*. It is, of course, constant.

The member operator is of the highest order of precedence, up there with parentheses and brackets. This high precedence assures that a member will be associated with its structure before any operations are done on it. Associativity is left to right so that members of structures which are themselves members of other structures will be evaluated correctly. The notation *three.two.one* means that *one* is a member of *two* which is a member of *three*.

Structure members can be used any place we can use any other variables. For example, we can use our *employee_rec* structure in ➡Program 10–1 that figures net pay for an employee.

➡Program 10–1

```
#include <stdio.h>

#define TAX_RATE .16                              /* General tax rate */
#define DEP_REDUCTION .02              /* Reduction for each dependent */

struct employee_rec
{  char name[30];
   int dependents;
   float pay_rate;
};

void main(void)
{  struct employee_rec employee;
   float hours, gross, tax;
   double net;

   printf("Employee name: ");
   gets(employee.name);
   while (employee.name[0] != '\0')               /* Stop at empty string */
   {  printf("Hours, pay rate, other dependents: ");
      scanf(" %f, %f, %i",
            &hours, &employee.pay_rate, &employee.dependents);
      gross = hours * employee.pay_rate;
      tax = (TAX_RATE - DEP_REDUCTION * employee.dependents) * gross;
      net = gross - tax;
      printf("   Pay to: %s   $**%.2f**\n", employee.name, net);
      fflush(stdin);                                      /* Flush stream */
      printf("Employee name: ");
      gets(employee.name);
   }
}
```

Output

```
Employee name: Maynard Freebisch
Hours, pay rate, other dependents: 36, 10.83, 2
   Pay to: Maynard Freebisch   $**350.89**
Employee name: Gilda Garfinkle
Hours, pay rate, other dependents: 44, 15.25, 4
   Pay to: Gilda Garfinkle   $**630.74**
Employee name:
```

In ANSI C an entire structure may be assigned to another structure of the same type. Given the declaration

```
struct employee_rec full_time, part_time;
```

we may have a statement in our program

```
full_time = part_time;
```

that copies the contents of all the memory locations in *part_time* to the memory locations in *full_time*. The end result is that the values of all the members of *part_time* have been assigned to the like members of *full_time*. While assigning structures may be possible, directly comparing them is not. You cannot say

```
if (full_time == part_time)
```

ARRAYS OF STRUCTURES

In our example we have seen an array, *name*, within a structure; but we can also have arrays of structures, for example,

```
struct employee_rec employee[4];
```

which declares an array of four structures. To access the pay rate of the second employee in the array we would refer to *employee[1].pay_rate*. To access the third character of the *name* member of the second employee we would refer to *employee[1].name[2]*.

The array may be initialized by putting a block of values after the declaration. The outer set of braces is required; the inner sets are not but are usually used, as in this case, to separate the values for each of the individual structures. Be sure to follow each closing brace with a comma or, for the last one, a semicolon.

```
struct employee_rec employee[4] =                 /* Last name first */
    {{"Barzoom Beulah",    5, 12.63},
     {"LaRue LeRoy",       0, 9.50 },
     {"Freebisch Maynard", 3, 10.83},
     {"Garfinkle Gilda",   5, 15.25}};
```

If your C compiler is not ANSI standard, check to make sure this initialization is allowed for local-lifetime variables.

ASSIGNING STRUCTURES

In many non-ANSI C implementations, you cannot assign a structure all at once. In such cases, the structure would have to be assigned member by member.

The following program uses a selection sort to order by name the employees in the array of structures. It then prints a report alphabetically by last name but with the first name first.

➠**Program 10–2**

```c
#include <stdio.h>
#include <string.h>

struct employee_rec
{   char name[30];
    int dependents;
    float pay_rate;
};

void main(void)
{   struct employee_rec employee[4] =                       /* Last name first */
        {{"Barzoom Beulah",    5, 12.63},
         {"LaRue LeRoy",       0, 9.50 },
         {"Freebisch Maynard", 3, 10.83},
         {"Garfinkle Gilda",   5, 15.25}};

    /****************************************************** Sort structures */
    {   struct employee_rec temp;            /* Temporary structure for swap */
        int sel, uns;                                    /* Sort counters */

        for (sel = 0; sel <= 2; ++sel)
          for (uns = sel + 1; uns <= 3; ++uns)
            if (strcmp(employee[sel].name, employee[uns].name) > 0)
            {   temp = employee[sel];
                employee[sel] = employee[uns];
                employee[uns] = temp;
            }
    }

    /*************************** Print sorted structures, first name first */
    {   char first_first[30];               /* Stores name first name first */
        char *space;                         /* Location of space in name */
        int c;                                /* Counter for employees */

        printf("Name          Dependents  Pay Rate\n");
        for (c = 0; c <= 3; ++c)
        {   /*************************** Assign name with first name first */
            space = strstr(employee[c].name, " ");
            strcpy(first_first, space + 1);
            strcat(first_first, " ");
            strncat(first_first, employee[c].name,
                    space - employee[c].name);              /* Chars to space */
            printf("%-13.13s      %3i %8.2f\n",             /*Print record */
                   first_first, employee[c].dependents,
                   employee[c].pay_rate);
```

Name	Dependents	Pay Rate
Beulah Barzoo	4	12.63
Maynard Freeb	2	10.83
Gilda Garfink	4	15.25
LeRoy LaRue	-1	9.50

POINTERS TO STRUCTURES

Since a structure is guaranteed to be stored contiguously in memory, pointers to structures would have some meaning. The definition and declaration

```
struct employee_rec
{  char name[30];
   int dependents;
   float pay_rate;
} *employee;
```

declares *employee* to be a pointer to the structure. In this case the only memory allocation is the few bytes for the pointer variable *employee*. Where it points, no one knows.

To give it a valid location to which to point, we might have declared an actual structure,

```
struct employee_rec full_time;
```

in which case we can assign the pointer variable to its address:

```
employee = &full_time;
```

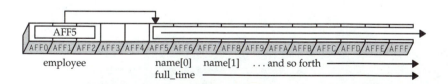

To access an individual member of a structure by its pointer we would have to refer to the contents at the location of the particular member,

```
(*pointer).member
```

For example, to access the *dependents* member of the structure pointed to by *employee* we would use the notation

```
(*employee).dependents
```

The parentheses are important because the member operator has precedence over the indirection operator, and we want *employee* to be evaluated as a pointer first and then directed to the *dependents* member.

The operation is common but the notation is somewhat clumsy so C allows this notation

```
pointer->member
```

meaning exactly the same thing. Our example could be rewritten

```
employee->dependents
```

meaning the contents of the *dependents* member of the structure pointed to by *employee*.

To assign the pay rate we could write the statement

```
employee->pay_rate = 14.25;
```

A major advantage of using pointers to structures is that when manipulating the structures, it is often not necessary to copy the entire structure from here to there, but only change pointers—a great saving in the number of operations that the CPU must execute. A perfect example is the sorting of an array of structures with all its required swaps.

Our previous example could be rewritten to swap pointers instead of whole structures, making it execute more efficiently and also work for the non-ANSI Cs that don't allow assignments of entire structures. Notice that the pointer variables in the array *employee* had to be given values of locations that were previously allocated; in this case, to the structure variables in the array *emp*. Even with that extra step execution will be quicker because there will be far fewer bytes to move.

➡️Program 10–3

```
#include <stdio.h>
#include <string.h>

struct employee_rec
{   char name[30];
    int dependents;
    float pay_rate;
};

void main(void)
{   struct employee_rec emp[4] =            /* Temp array for initialization */
        {{"Barzoom Beulah",    5, 12.63},
         {"LaRue LeRoy",       0, 9.50 },
         {"Freebisch Maynard", 3, 10.83},
         {"Garfinkle Gilda",   5, 15.25}};
    struct employee_rec *employee[4];

    /******************************** Assign pointers to valid locations */
    {   int c;

        for (c = 0; c <= 3; ++c)
            employee[c] = &emp[c];
    }
```

—Continued

```
/***************************************************** Sort structures
*/
    {  struct employee_rec *temp;        /* Temporary structure for swap */
       int sel, uns;                                      /* Sort counters */

       for (sel = 0; sel <= 2; ++sel)
         for (uns = sel + 1; uns <= 3; ++uns)
            if (strcmp(employee[sel]->name, employee[uns]->name) > 0)
            {  temp = employee[sel];
               employee[sel] = employee[uns];
               employee[uns] = temp;
            }
    }


/*************************** Print sorted structures, first name first
*/
    {  char first_first[30];            /* Stores name first name first */
       char *space;                       /* Location of space in name */
       int c;                               /* Counter for employees */

       printf("Name          Dependents  Pay Rate\n");
       for (c = 0; c <= 3; ++c)
       {  /*************************** Assign name with first name first
*/
            space = strstr(employee[c]->name, " ");
            strcpy(first_first, space + 1);
            strcat(first_first, " ");
            strncat(first_first, employee[c]->name,
                  space - employee[c]->name);        /* Chars to space */
         printf("%-13.13s          %3i  %8.2f\n",          /*Print record */
               first_first, employee[c]->dependents,
               employee[c]->pay_rate);
       }
    }
}
```

The execution will be exactly the same.

STRUCTURES AND FUNCTIONS

A member of a structure can be treated like any other variable. Its value can be passed to a function to initialize a variable of the same data type as the member's. In Chapter 6, ➧Program 6–4 calculated an employee's net pay in a function *pay()*. We can pick up that function and use it unchanged in ➧Program 10–1, shown earlier in this chapter. The result is ➧Program 10–4. In so doing, we are also illustrating modular programming and encapsulation.

```c
#include <stdio.h>

#define TAX_RATE .16                                   /* General tax rate */
#define DEP_REDUCTION .02                     /* Reduction for each dependent */

struct employee_rec
{  char name[30];
   int dependents;
   float pay_rate;
};

double pay(float hrs, float rt, int dep);           /* Function declaration */

void main(void)
{  struct employee_rec employee;
   float hours;
   double net;

   printf("Employee name: ");
   gets(employee.name);
   while (employee.name[0] != '\0')                       /* Empty string */
   {  printf("Hours, pay rate, dependents: ");
      scanf(" %f, %f, %i",
            &hours, &employee.pay_rate, &employee.dependents);
      net = pay(hours, employee.pay_rate, employee.dependents);
      printf("   Pay to: %s   $**%.2f**\n", employee.name, net);
      fflush(stdin);                                     /* Flush stream */
      printf("Employee name: ");
      gets(employee.name);
   }
}

/****************** Calculates net pay given hours, rate, and dependents */
double pay(float hrs, float rt, int dep)               /* Function definition */
{  float gross, tax;

   gross = hrs * rt;
   tax = (TAX_RATE - DEP_REDUCTION * dep) * gross;
   return gross - tax;
}
```

In ANSI C, we can also pass an entire structure to a function. The function will have to have a like structure in its argument declarations. This is a good reason to make structure definitions externally, so that they will be visible from such functions.

PASSING STRUCTURES

Many non-ANSI Cs do not allow passing entire structures to functions, nor do they allow a return of the structure from the function. All the values would have to be passed individually with the possibility of only one return value, or you could simplify things by passing a pointer to the structure.

```
#include <stdio.h>

#define TAX_RATE .16                                    /* General tax rate */
#define DEP_REDUCTION .02                        /* Reduction for each dependent */

struct employee_rec
{   char name[30];
    int dependents;
    float pay_rate;
};

double pay(float hrs, struct employee_rec worker);

void main(void)
{   struct employee_rec employee;
    float hours;
    double net;

    printf("Employee name: ");
    gets(employee.name);
    while (employee.name[0] != '\0')                        /* Empty string */
    {   printf("Hours, pay rate, dependents: ");
        scanf(" %f, %f, %i",
              &hours, &employee.pay_rate, &employee.dependents);
        net = pay(hours, employee);
        printf("   Pay to: %s    $**%.2f**\n", employee.name, net);
        fflush(stdin);                                      /* Flush stream */
        printf("Employee name: ");
        gets(employee.name);
    }
}

/******************** Calculates net pay given hours, rate, and dependents */
double pay(float hrs, struct employee_rec worker)
{   float gross, tax;

    gross = hrs * worker.pay_rate;
    tax = (TAX_RATE - DEP_REDUCTION * worker.dependents) * gross;
    return gross - tax;
}
```

In the call to *pay()*, we passed *hours* and, instead of passing the *pay_rate* and *dependents* members of *employee*, we passed the entire structure. In the function, we declared another *employee_rec* structure, *worker*, which was initialized in the call with the values from *employee*. Notice that the member names in the function have to be exactly as they were described in the structure definition near the beginning of the program.

The function never actually used the *name* member—a bit of inefficiency there. We passed 30 bytes we didn't actually need to.

In ANSI C, a structure may also be returned from a function. Suppose we add a member, *ytd*, to our example structure to store the accumulated year-to-date pay. The function can be modified to add the current net pay to that figure and return the entire structure to the main() function to be assigned to *employee*.

```c
#include <stdio.h>

#define TAX_RATE .16                                    /* General tax rate */
#define DEP_REDUCTION .02                       /* Reduction for each dependent */

struct employee_rec
{   char name[30];
    int dependents;
    float pay_rate;
    double ytd;                                              /* Accumulated pay */
};

struct employee_rec pay(float hrs, struct employee_rec worker);

void main(void)
{   struct employee_rec employee;
    float hours;
    double old_ytd;

    printf("Employee name: ");
    gets(employee.name);
    while (employee.name[0] != '\0')                        /* Empty string */
    {   printf("Hours, pay rate, dependents: ");
        scanf(" %f, %f, %i",
              &hours, &employee.pay_rate, &employee.dependents);
        printf("Pay prior to now: ");
        scanf(" %lf", &employee.ytd);
        old_ytd = employee.ytd;
        employee = pay(hours, employee);
        printf("   Pay to: %s    $**%.2f**\n",
               employee.name, employee.ytd - old_ytd);
        printf("   Total to date: $%.2f\n", employee.ytd);
        fflush(stdin);                                       /* Flush stream */
        printf("Employee name: ");
        gets(employee.name);
    }
}

/******************* Calculates net pay given hours, rate, and dependents */
struct employee_rec pay(float hrs, struct employee_rec worker)
{   float gross, tax;

    gross = hrs * worker.pay_rate;
    tax = (TAX_RATE - DEP_REDUCTION * worker.dependents) * gross;
    worker.ytd += gross - tax;
    return worker;
}
```

Output

```
Employee name: Maynard Freebisch
Hours, pay rate, other dependents: 36, 10.83, 3
Pay prior to now: 1042.57
   Pay to: Maynard Freebisch    $**350.89**
   Total to date: $1393.46

                                       Employee name: Gilda Garfinkle
Hours, pay rate, other dependents: 44, 15.25, 5
Pay prior to now: 1467.03
   Pay to: Gilda Garfinkle    $**630.74**
   Total to date: $2097.77
Employee name:
```

Again, there had to be significant changes to the program. Now that the function is returning the structure, it can no longer return a `double` value to assign to *net*. We got around this by storing the previous *ytd* value in *old_ytd*, and calculating the net pay by subtracting the *old_ytd* from the new *employee.ytd*.

In this particular case, there seem to be a number of inefficiencies by passing the entire structure. First, we have had to invent new variables and processes in the `main()` function; and second, passing and returning the entire structure forces C to move a lot of bytes around in main memory.

In Chapter 7, we skirted the problem of needing more than one return value by passing pointers to our function and having the function manipulate the contents directly. Let us again have our function return the `double` value to assign to *net*, but pass it the address of the *employee* structure. In the function, we will declare a pointer to an *employee_rec* structure to receive the address.

➥Program 10–7

```c
#include <stdio.h>

#define TAX_RATE .16                              /* General tax rate */
#define DEP_REDUCTION .02                 /* Reduction for each dependent */

struct employee_rec
{   char name[30];
    int dependents;
    float pay_rate;
    double ytd;                                   /* Accumulated pay */
};

double pay(float hrs, struct employee_rec *worker);

void main(void)
{   struct employee_rec employee;
    float hours;
    double net;

    printf("Employee name: ");
    gets(employee.name);
    while (employee.name[0] != '\0')                    /* Empty string */
    {   printf("Hours, pay rate, dependents: ");
        scanf(" %f, %f, %i",
              &hours, &employee.pay_rate, &employee.dependents);
        printf("Pay prior to now: ");
        scanf(" %lf", &employee.ytd);
        net = pay(hours, &employee);
        printf("   Pay to: %s   $**%.2f**\n",
               employee.name, net);
        printf("   Total to date: $%.2f\n", employee.ytd);
        fflush(stdin);                                  /* Flush stream */
        printf("Employee name: ");
        gets(employee.name);
    }
}
```

—Continued

```
/******************** Calculates net pay given hours, rate, and dependents */
double pay(float hrs, struct employee_rec *worker)
{  float gross, tax;

   gross = hrs * worker->pay_rate;
   tax = (TAX_RATE - DEP_REDUCTION * worker->dependents) * gross;
   worker->ytd += gross - tax;
   return gross - tax;
}
```

In the call to the *pay()* function, we passed the address of *employee*; and in the function, we declared *worker* to be a pointer to a structure of type *employee_rec*. Notice that the structure notation within the *pay()* function has changed now that *worker* is a pointer instead of a structure.

UNIONS

You can't put two things in the same place at the same time! True, but you can put one thing in that place, and call it by two different names. This is the principal behind a **union**—using different identifiers to access the data in one set of memory locations. The declaration of a union looks exactly like the declaration of a structure, except for the key word union instead of struct. The result of the declaration, however, is significantly different. A structure declares an aggregate data type, and states the accessible member variables for it. The union declares that a number of variable names of various data types may access the same space in memory.

For example, let us say that we sell two different types of products; one in bulk, by the pound or fraction thereof, and one packaged, by the package. The units of the bulk product we would want to keep in a float variable, packaged units in an int. To conserve memory space, we could store either of them at a single memory address by declaring a union variable like this:

```
union units
{  float pounds;                            /* For bulk products */
   int packs;                               /* For packaged products */
};
```

We could declare a variable (or variables) of that type by putting the name after the declaration, or in a separate declaration as in ▶▶Program 10–8. C will allocate enough space to accomodate the largest data type in the union, in this case the float.

We refer to members of the union just as we refer to members of a structure—with the member operator (.). It is important that we use the member of the union with the data type that matches the data stored in the union. In the following program, *item.pounds* is of data type float and *item.packs* is of data type int.

```
#include <stdio.h>

union units
{  float pounds;                                    /* For bulk products */
   int packs;                                       /* For packaged products */
};
void main(void)
{  union units item;
   char bulk[10];

   printf("Bulk Product (y/n)? ");
   if (*gets(bulk) == 'y')                  /* First character of input string */
   {  printf("Pounds? ");
      scanf("%f", &item.pounds);
   }
   else
   {  printf("Packages? ");
      scanf("%i", &item.packs);
   }
   printf("Pounds: %f, Packages: %i\n", item.pounds, item.packs);
}
```

Output

```
Bulk Product (y/n)? y
Pounds? 12.34
Pounds: 12.340000, Packages: 28836
```

The item Union

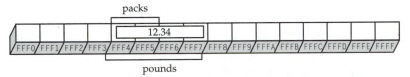

The last line of the output bears some examination. The printf() function is syntactically correct, and therefore runs without complaint from the compiler. But the output, at least the packages part, is nonsense! We stored 12.34 as a float value (four bytes in this C) in the *item* union. The second part of the printf() asked C to get a two-byte int from that space. It did, making no sense, of course. You can see that keeping track of the data types currently stored in unions is up to us. C won't do it.

Unions are often used in conjunction with structures. We might have a union of structures, or a union might be part of a structure. Let us expand our previous example to include more information about the product. If it is bulk, we want to know the product ID (a six-digit code), its form (liquid, solid, powder, and so forth), its density (pounds per cubic foot), and the number of pounds. For packaged products we want to know the brand name, type of package (box, blister, bag, and so forth), the package weight (in pounds), and the number of packages. We can declare structures for each of the types of product:

```
#include <stdio.h>

struct bulk_prods
{  char id[7];
   char form[10];
   float density;
   float pounds;
};

struct packaged
{  char brand[20];
   char pack_type[10];
   float weight;
   int packs;
};

union units
{  struct bulk_prods bulk;
   struct packaged pack;
}item;

void main(void)
{
   item.bulk.pounds = 23.45;
   printf("%f\n", item.bulk.pounds);
}
```

To access one member of the union, we use the *union.member* notation. To access a member of a structure that is a member of a union, we will extend the member notation one more level—*union.structure.member*—or, in the example, `item.bulk.pounds`.

PUTTING IT TOGETHER: LINKED LISTS

If you have a list of your friends' names and telephone numbers, you could define a structure for the data for a friend. (We have used the word *pal* in the example instead of *friend* because the latter is a key word in C++, a common extension to the C compiler.)

```
struct pal_rec
{  name[30];
   phone[12];
};
```

You could keep the data for all of your friends in an array of structures:

```
struct pal_rec pal[?];
```

How many friends do you have? After making a fool of yourself at the party last weekend, you're not sure. At any rate, you may have to drop a few from the list, but, since a few people laughed, you might pick up some new ones. So how many variables do we include in the array? It will have to accommodate the the maximum number of friends that you might ever have, not just the number you have now. After last weekend, that will mean a lot of wasted memory in blank structures.

How do you add a friend? If you keep them in alphabetical order, you will have to insert into the array as we did in Chapter 7—a routine that may, in some cases, be unavoidable, but it will take execution time to move all those structures around. You would have to drop a friend by doing the reverse, again moving a lot of structures. Storing lists in arrays, then, has some major disadvantages: allocating a fixed amount of memory, much of which may be wasted; and having to move a number of structures to add and delete.

Allocating Memory

Let us look at another method of storing lists in which we allocate only the memory we need, and no extra. First we must look at allocating blocks of memory. The `malloc()` function allocates a number of bytes in memory and returns the address of the beginning of that block.

```
void *malloc(size_t bytes)                                    <stdlib.h>
```

The return value of `malloc()` is a pointer to `void` because we are not allocating a specific data type here, just a number of *bytes*. The pointer to `void` is ANSI C's generic pointer and can be converted to any pointer type.

We could use `malloc()` to allocate space for a string, for example, when we have declared only a pointer variable rather than a `char` array.

```
char *string;

string = (char *) malloc(50);
```

After the declaration, the value of *string* is garbage and, of course, it points to garbage. In the assignment, `malloc(50)` allocated 50 bytes in memory and returns the address as a pointer to `void`. We cast that pointer to `void` as a pointer to `char`, and assign it to *string*. Now the value of *string* is changed to point to the beginning of 50 bytes of allocated memory space. (Some Cs will let you get away without casting the pointer to `void`. To maintain portability, you should cast it.)

If `malloc()` is unable to allocate memory (perhaps you have no free memory left), it returns the `NULL` pointer. You can test for that after calling the function.

```
string = (char *) malloc(50);
if (string == NULL)
   printf("Outta memory!"\n);
```

The `free()` function deallocates a block of memory previously allocated by `malloc()`—returns it to the pool of free memory that C can now allocate for some other purpose.

```
void free(void *address)                                      <stdlib.h>
```

If you have finished with the *string* variable, you can make it the *address* argument and release that memory space.

OTHER MEMORY-ALLOCATION FUNCTIONS

There are two other ANSI functions that deal with memory allocation—`calloc()` and `realloc()`. The `calloc()` function allocates a block of memory, initializing it to zero, and returning the address as a pointer to void.

```
void *calloc(size_t variables, size_t size)
```

where *variables* is the number of variables in the array, and *size* is the size in bytes of each variable. We could set up an array of 50 `float`s like this:

```
float *array;
array = (float *) calloc(50, sizeof (float));
```

The `realloc()` function changes the size of an allocated block of memory, leaving the data unchanged (except for data at the end if the size is reduced). Its return is the address of the new block, likely different from the old block, which means that it will have to move a lot of data.

```
void *realloc(void *address, size_t new_size)
```

where *address* is the address of the block to be resized (and probably moved), and *new_size* is its new size in bytes. If the value passed to *address* is NULL, then a new block is allocated, making `realloc()` act just like `malloc()`.

```
free(string);
```

When you use `free()`, be sure that the *address* argument is one that has been allocated by `malloc()`. You could get some bizarre results if this is not the case.

Structures Pointing to Structures

To avoid the time-consuming adding and deleting of structures within arrays, let us simply put our structures anywhere in memory. When we want to add one, we will just allocate another place in memory and put it there. When we delete one, we will just deallocate that memory space. How are we going to keep track of all this, and in order? We will use a **linked list**.

Each structure in memory will have, as one of its members, a pointer to the next structure in the list. To move through the list, we start at the **head** of the list, the address of the first structure; the first structure will contain the address of the second; the second the address of the third; and so forth until the last structure, at the **tail** of the list, has a NULL pointer instead of the address of another structure.

Referring to our example of the list of friends, if we were to set it up as a linked list of structures, we would define the structure as:

```
                struct pal_rec
                {   char name[30];
                    char phone[13];
                    struct pal_rec *next;
                };
```

The last member of the structure, *next*, is a pointer to the data type *struct pal_rec*. Its value will be the address of the next structure in the list.

Assuming that we had allocated space for a number of these structures and properly linked them, we could print them in order using the print() function below. For the function to work, it will have to know the head of the list—the address of the first structure. Our call to the function, then, would be

```
        print(head);
```

and the function is:

```
     /*******************************************************  Print out list */
p1   void print(struct pal_rec *pal)
     {                                         /* The first value of pal is the head */
p2       while (pal != NULL)                            /* The tail is not NULL */
p3       {   printf("%-30.30s %s\n", pal->name, pal->phone);
p4           pal = pal->next;                           /* Set pal to next address */
         }
```

For an execution sample, let us look at the first printout in the execution that follows in a few pages. After the first three insertions memory looks like this:}

Address	name	phone	next
CA3A	Deltoid, Bruce	123-456-7890	CB14
CB14	Flowers, May	111-555-1212	NULL
CCOE	Abernathy, Aloysius	111-222-3333	CA3A

EXECUTION CHART

Line	Explanation	pal	pal->name	pal->next
p1	Initialize value of *pal* from pass.	CCOE	Abernathy,	CA3A
p2	*pal* not NULL.	CCOE	Abernathy,	CA3A
p3	Print record.	CCOE	Abernathy,	CA3A
p4	Set *pal* to point to next structure.	CA3A	Deltoid,	CB14
p2	*pal* not NULL.	CA3A	Deltoid,	CB14
p3	Print record.	CA3A	Deltoid,	CB14
p4	Set *pal* to point to next structure.	CB14	Flowers,	NULL
p2	*pal* not NULL.	CB14	Flowers,	NULL
p3	Print record.	CB14	Flowers,	NULL
p4	Set *pal* to point to next structure.	NULL	?	?
p2	*pal* is NULL. Exit loop and return.	NULL	?	?

Inserting into a Linked List

To add to our list, we must first create a new structure. The *newpal()* function, which follows, allocates memory for the structure, and allows input of data for it. We pass nothing to the function, but the function returns the address of the new structure. The *next* member of the structure—the pointer to the next structure—is set to NULL. When the structure is inserted, that will change unless this new one ends up at the end of the list.

```
/*************************************************  Set up new record */
struct pal_rec *newpal(void)
{   struct pal_rec *pal;                                /* Address of new record */
                                        /* Create memory space for new record */
    pal = (struct pal_rec *) malloc(sizeof (struct pal_rec));
    if (pal != NULL)                    /* Be sure memory can be allocated */
    {   printf("Name/Phone: ");
        scanf("%[^/]/ %s", pal->name, pal->phone);
        fflush(stdin);                              /* Get rid of \n in stream */
        pal->next = NULL;
    }
    return pal;
}
```

We insert the new structure in the list by starting from the head and examining each structure in the list. When we find where we want to insert—the name, for example, is less than the name in the current structure we are examining—we change the pointer in the previous structure to point to the new one, and assign the pointer in the new structure to the address of the current one.

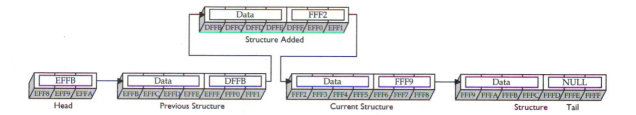

For the friends example, we can write an *insert()* function such as the one following, and call it with

```
insert(&head);                      /* Send address in case head changed */
```

Notice that we are passing the function the address of the head rather than the value of the head. It is possible that the new structure we insert will fall at the beginning of the linked list, in which case, the function will have to change the value of the head. Therefore, the function has to know where the head is, not just its value.

The *insert()* function is prototyped with *head* being a pointer to a pointer to a structure. Complicated, but necessary. Remember, *head* is a pointer to a structure. The address of *head* (&head), then, is a pointer to a pointer to a structure (**head). When we access *head* in *insert()*, we use the notation *head, meaning follow the address in the *insert()* head (EFF8 in the following diagram) to where it points (EFF8 is the address of the main() *head*), and access the value there (EFFB, which is the address of the first structure).

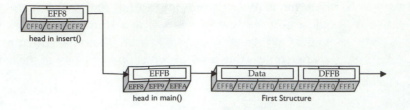

head in insert()

head in main() First Structure

Notice the three other pointers to structure declared in *insert()*. The first, *pal*, is the address of the new record. It is assigned in the `if` statement by a call to the *newpal()* function. If the record is successfully created (the return from *newpal()* is not `NULL`), the last two pointers are declared. One, *curr*, keeps track of the current record as we move from record to record; the other, *prev*, keeps track of the previous one. When we find the proper location for the new record, the pointer in the previous record is set to the new one (`prev->next = pal`), and the pointer in the new record is set to the current one (`pal->next = curr`).

For the execution example we have chosen the insertion of Ernestine Euforia.

```
     /******************************************  Insert new record into list */
i1   void insert(struct pal_rec **head)
     {  struct pal_rec *pal;                          /* Address of new record */

i2       if ((pal = newpal()) != NULL)                /* New record created */
         {  struct pal_rec *curr,          /* Record being examined for input */
                      *prev = NULL;                   /* Record before curr */

i3         curr = *head;
i4         while (curr != NULL                        /* Not at end of list */
                   && strcmp(pal->name, curr->name) > 0)    /* Name > record's */
i5         {  prev = curr;                     /* Save current record address */
i6            curr = curr->next;                      /* Go to next record */
           }
i7         pal->next = curr;                /* Insert in front of current record */
i8         if (prev == NULL)                          /* No previous record */
i9            *head = pal;                            /* First in list */
           else
i10           prev->next = pal;             /* One before points to this */
         }else                                        /* New record not created */
i11        printf("Can't create new record.\n");
     }
```

Memory Before Insertion

Address	name	phone	next
CA3A	Deltoid, Bruce	123-456-7890	CB14
CB14	Flowers, May	111-555-1212	NULL
CC0E	Abernathy, Aloysius	111-222-3333	CA3A

EXECUTION CHART

Line	Explanation	pal	pal->name	pal->next	prev	prev->next	curr	curr->name	curr->next
i1	Initialize value of *head* from pass. It points to CCOE								
i2	Call *newpal()*, assign return to *pal*. It is not NULL.	CD21	Euforia	NULL					
i3	Assign *curr* what *head* points to.	CD21	Euforia	NULL	NULL	?	CCOE	Aberna	CA3A
i4	*curr* not NULL, *pal->name > curr->name*.	CD21	Euforia	NULL	NULL	?	CCOE	Aberna	CA3A
i5	Save *curr* in *prev*.	CD21	Euforia	NULL	CCOE	CA3A	CCOE	Aberna	CA3A
i6	Set *curr* to next record.	CD21	Euforia	NULL	CCOE	CA3A	CA3A	Deltoid	CB14
i4	*curr* not NULL, *pal->name > curr->name*.	CD21	Euforia	NULL	CCOE	CA3A	CA3A	Deltoid	CB14
i5	Save *curr* in *prev*.	CD21	Euforia	NULL	CA3A	CB14	CA3A	Deltoid	CB14
i6	Set *curr* to next record.	CD21	Euforia	NULL	CA3A	CB14	CB14	Flower	NULL
i4	*curr* not NULL, *pal->name* not *> curr->name*.	CD21	Euforia	NULL	CA3A	CB14	CB14	Flower	NULL
i7	Set new record pointing to *curr*.	CD21	Euforia	CB14	CA3A	CB14	CB14	Flower	NULL
i8	*prev* not NULL.	CD21	Euforia	NULL	CA3A	CB14	CB14	Flower	NULL
i10	Set *prev* record pointing to new one and return.	CD21	Euforia	NULL	CA3A	CD21	CB14	Flower	NULL

Deleting from a Linked List

A structure is deleted by passing the pointers around it. The pointer in the structure before is changed to point to the structure after the deleted one. The memory space for the deleted structure can then be deallocated.

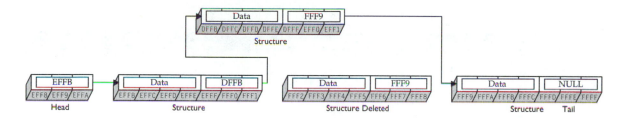

In the friends example, the *dump()* function deletes a record. As in inserting, we pass it a pointer to the head (in case the head must be modified) and examine each record in turn for the one to delete. When we find that one, we assign its pointer to the previous record (prev->next = curr->next). We can then deallocate the current record (free(curr)).

For our execution example we will delete Aloysius Abernathy.

Memory Before Deletion

Address	name	phone	next
CA3A	Deltoid, Bruce	123-456-7890	CD21
CB14	Flowers, May	111-555-1212	NULL
CCOE	Abernathy, Aloysius	111-222-3333	CA3A
CD21	Euforia, Ernestine	967-666-7777	CB41

```
                /*********************************************  Delete record from list */
d1  void dump(struct pal_rec **head)
    {
d2      if (*head != NULL)                                 /* There are names in list */
        {  struct pal_rec *curr,            /* Record being examined for deletion */
                          *prev = NULL;                   /* Record before curr */
           char dump_name[30];

           printf("Name to delete: ");
d3         gets(dump_name);
d4         curr = *head;
d5         while (curr != NULL                            /* Not at end of list */
                  && strcmp(dump_name, curr->name))       /* Name != record's */
d6         {  prev = curr;                           /* Save current record address */
d7            curr = curr->next;                          /* Go to next record */
           }
d8         if (curr == NULL)                              /* Didn't find name */
d9            printf("Name not in list.\n");
           else                                           /* Name found */
d10        {  if (prev == NULL)                           /* No previous record */
d11              *head = curr->next;                      /* First record dumped */
              else
d12              prev->next = curr->next;    /* Previous rec points to next rec */
d13           free(curr);                              /* Deallocate that memory space */
           }
        }else                                            /* List empty */
d14        printf("List empty.\n");
    }
```

EXECUTION CHART

Line	Explanation	*head	dump_ name	prev	prev-> next	curr	curr-> name	curr-> next
d1	Initialize value of *head* from pass.	CCOE						
d2	*head* does not point to NULL.	CCOE						
d3	Input name to delete.	CCOE	Aberna	NULL	?	?	?	?
d4	Assign *curr* what *head* points to.	CCOE	Aberna	NULL	?	CCOE	Aberna	CA3A
d5	*curr* not NULL, *dump_name = curr->name*.	CCOE	Aberna	NULL	?	CCOE	Aberna	CA3A
d8	*curr* not NULL	CCOE	Aberna	NULL	?	CCOE	Aberna	CA3A
d10	*prev* is NULL.	CCOE	Aberna	NULL	?	CCOE	Aberna	CA3A
d11	Change *head* to second record.	CA3A	Aberna	NULL	?	CCOE	Aberna	CA3A
d13	Deallocate space at first record and return.	CA3A	Aberna	NULL	?	CCOE	?	?

All the subsidiary functions are shown above; all that remains is to add the main() function.

➧Program 10–9

```
#include <stdio.h>
#include <stdlib.h>
#include <string.h>
#include <ctype.h>

struct pal_rec
{  char name[30];
   char phone[13];
   struct pal_rec *next;
};
```

—Continued

```
void print(struct pal_rec *pal);                        /* Print list */
void insert(struct pal_rec **head);              /* Insert new record */
struct pal_rec *newpal(void);                    /* Create new record */
void dump(struct pal_rec **head);                    /* Delete record */

void main(void)
{  struct pal_rec *head = NULL;
   int choice;

   printf("(I)nsert, (D)elete, or (P)rint: ");
   while((choice = getchar()) != '\n')             /* Return ends program */
   {  fflush(stdin);                               /* Dump end of stream */
      switch (toupper(choice))
      {  case 'I':
             insert(&head);          /* Send address in case head changed */
             break;
          case 'D':
             dump(&head);            /* Send address in case head changed */
             break;
          case 'P':
             print(head);
             break;
      }
      printf("(I)nsert, (D)elete, or (P)rint: ");
   }
}
```

Output

```
(I)nsert, (D)elete, or (P)rint: i
Name/Phone: Deltoid, Bruce/123-456-7890
(I)nsert, (D)elete, or (P)rint: i
Name/Phone: Flowers, May/111-555-1212
(I)nsert, (D)elete, or (P)rint: i
Name/Phone: Abernathy, Aloysius/111-222-3333
(I)nsert, (D)elete, or (P)rint: p
Abernathy, Aloysius            111-222-3333
Deltoid, Bruce                 123-456-7890
Flowers, May                   111-555-1212
(I)nsert, (D)elete, or (P)rint: i
Name/Phone: Euforia, Ernestine/967-666-7777
(I)nsert, (D)elete, or (P)rint: p
Abernathy, Aloysius            111-222-3333
Deltoid, Bruce                 123-456-7890
Euforia, Ernestine             967-666-7777
Flowers, May                   111-555-1212
(I)nsert, (D)elete, or (P)rint: d
Name to delete: Abernathy, Aloysius
(I)nsert, (D)elete, or (P)rint: p
Deltoid, Bruce                 123-456-7890
Euforia, Ernestine             967-666-7777
Flowers, May                   111-555-1212
(I)nsert, (D)elete, or (P)rint:
```

SUMMARY

Structures are complex data types made up of individual **members**, which can be simple or other complex data types. We state the makeup of a structure in a **structure definition** and allocate variables of that structure type in a **structure declaration**. The key word `struct` begins either a structure declaration or definition, or a statement combining both.

A structure **tag** is the name given to the new structure data type. Declaration statements using the tag can allocate structures of that type. Structure **member definitions** determine the data types of the individual members of the structure. Structures may be initialized by putting values in braces in the declaration. The `sizeof` operator will give us the number of bytes in the entire structure if we refer to the structure variable's name, or to the structure's tag in parentheses.

We can access individual members of a structure by using the structure variable's name followed by a **member operator** (a dot) and the member's name. This notation can be used any place we can use an ordinary variable. In ANSI C, we can assign one entire structure to a like one by simply using structure variables' names.

Arrays of structures are valid in C. They can be initialized using nested braces. In *structure.member* notation the structure subscript follows the structure name (before the dot) and the member subscript (if any) follows the member name. In using pointers to structures, we can access an individual member by using the (*pointer).member* notation or *pointer->member*.

Values of members of structures may be passed to functions just like values of simple data types. In ANSI C, we can pass an entire structure, or return one. More often, however, we pass a pointer to the structure and use pointer notation in the function.

A **union** is a single memory area that is accessible through different variable names. Each of these variables may have a different data type, and may even be structures. C allocates enough memory to hold the largest data type in the union. The union is accessed using the same type of notation as a structure. It is important that we access the data in the union as it was stored—using the same data type and, typically, the same variable names.

A **linked list** is a common application of structures in which order is maintained by having a pointer in each record point to the next. Using linked lists, we can easily insert into and delete from an ordered list, and the list need not occupy a large amount of allocated and available, but unused, memory. Memory for individual records of a linked list is allocated as needed by the `malloc()` function, and deallocated by `free()`. The linked list starts with a **head**, a pointer to the first structure in the list, and ends with a **tail**, the last structure in the list in which the pointer to the next structure points to `NULL` instead.

We can insert records into a linked list by making the pointer in the record before the insertion point to the new record, and making the new record point to what the one before it used to. We can delete a record by making the previous record point directly to the subsequent one. Once a record has been excluded from the list, it may be deallocated.

KEY TERMS (in order of appearance)

Structure	Member operator
Member	Union
Structure definition	`malloc()`
Structure declaration	`free()`
`struct`	Linked list
Tag	Head
Member definition	Tail

REVIEW QUESTIONS

1. What relationship does a structure bear to its members?

2. How does a structure definition differ form a structure declaration?

3. What is the purpose of a tag in a structure definition? How does the tag differ from a structure variable name?

4. What memory allocation is accomplished by a structure's memory definitions?

5. How can the `sizeof` operator be used to yield the size of an entire structure?

6. In what part of what statement can a structure be initialized?

7. What notation would access the *petunia* member of the *flower* structure?

8. In your C, how would you assign all the members of one structure to another structure?

9. How is an array of structures declared? How is it initialized?

10. How would you access the third *petunia* member of the second *flower* structure?

11. What notation would access the *petunia* member of the *flower* structure if *flower* was declared as a pointer to a structure?

12. How can a member of a structure be passed to a function? Returned from a function?

13. In your C, can you pass and return an entire structure?

14. How can you inform a function of where a structure resides in memory?

15. The declarations are similar, but how does a union differ from a structure?

16. How does C determine how much memory to allocate to a union?

17. What is the purpose of the `malloc()` and `free()` functions?

18. How does a linked list maintain order?

19. How can we insert a record into a linked list?

20. How can we delete a record from a linked list?

EXERCISES

1. Which of the following is invalid and why?

a.
```
struct
{  int a, b;
   float c;
};
```

b.
```
new_rec
{  int a, b;
   float c;
}struct rec1, rec2;
```

c.
```
struct
{  int first[2];
   char second;
}thing = {{3, 5}, 'S'};
```

d.
```
struct rec
{  int first[2] = {3, 5};
   char second = 'S';
}
```

2. Given this definition, which declarations are invalid and why?

```
struct this
{  float one;
   long two;
};
```

a. `this that, *other;`
b. `struct this those[10];`
c. `struct this it = 25.2, 6;`
d. `struct this them[];`

3. Given this definition and declaration, what notation would you use to access the following:

```
struct rec
{   char name[20];
    float salary;
}item, recs[10], *temp;
```

a.   The *name* in the *item* structure.
b.   The *salary* in the structure pointed to by *temp*.
c.   The address of *salary* in *item*.
d.   The fifth character in the *name* of the fourth *recs* structure.

4. Referring to the structure in Exercise 3, which of the following assignments are valid?

a.   `recs[4].name[2] = 'd';`   b.   `temp.salary = 1234.56;`
c.   `item.name = "Schemp";`   d.   `item.salary = 1234.56;`
e.   `temp->name[4] = 's';`   f.   `recs.salary[2] = 1234.56;`

5. Referring to the structure definition in Exercise 3, declare and initialize (with any values) a two-structure array *arr*.

6. Given the definition `struct rec record;` (referring to the *rec* structure in Exercise 3), show how you would pass its address to the function *func()* and what you would declare in the function to receive it using the identifier *recs*.

7. Referring to the situation in Exercise 6, how would you assign 4256.38 to the salary member of the structure in the function?

8. Show the declaration of a `union` *stuff* that consists of a *rec* structure (from Exercise 3) and an array of 30 characters. Choose your own member names. Define a variable *things* of that type.

9. Write the statement that assigns "Calabash" to the *name* member of the union in Exercise 8.

10. Change the declaration of the *rec* structure so that you could have a linked list of records. What other variable would you need?

11. Show the statement that would allocate space for a new record in the linked list above.

12. In the situation above, if you were adding this record to the middle of the list, what would you add to the end of the new record, and what would you change in the previous record?

13. How would you change the previous record in the situation above if you were dropping a record in the middle of the list?

PROGRAMS

1. Write a program that will accept an employee's name, wage rate, hours, and tax rate from the keyboard and print out the gross and net pay. The employee data, including gross and net pay, should be stored in a structure and the gross and net pay should be figured in a separate function. Overtime (over 40 hours) should be paid at 1.5 times the normal rate.

Suggested Variables

```
employee structure:
   name
   wage_rate
   hours
   tax_rate
   gross_pay
   net_pay
```

Output

```
Enter name, wage rate, hours, tax rate: Jones 8.25 42 .18
Gross pay for Jones is $354.75. Net is $290.90.
```

2. Rewrite the card-dealing program from Chapter 6 to store the deck in a structure array. Each structure variable should have a *value* member for the number on the card and a *suit* member, an array to hold the name of the suit.

Outputs

```
Your hand: King-Hearts Queen-Clubs Ace-Spades Queen-Hearts Ace-Clubs

Your hand: 8-Clubs 9-Hearts 2-Diamonds Ace-Hearts 4-Spades
```

3. Declare a structure tagged *month_data* to store the name of a month and its number of days (don't worry about leap year). Write it in a program that stores data for all the months and allows you to access them by number.

Variables

month_data	Structure tag
name	
days	
months[]	Array of structures
month	Month number input
abbrev[]	Month abbreviation

Outputs

```
Which month? 2
February, or Feb has 28 days.

Which month? 10
October, or Oct has 31 days.
```

4. Rewrite Program 3 so that you can input the three-character abbreviation for the month and the computer will print out the data for that month. Use the same variables.

Outputs

```
Which month? Feb
Month 2, February, has 28 days.

Which month? Nov
Month 11, November, has 30 days.
```

5. Set up a structure tagged *emp_rec* with name and Social Security number. The name member is a structure tagged *name_rec* with members for the first, middle, and last names. Put these in a program that uses a function, *emp_in()*, to input values into the entire structure. The main() function then prints out the information.

Functions, Structures, and Variables

main()			emp_in()	
employee	emp_rec structure		emp	Pointer to emp_rec
name				
s_s_no				
name	name_rec structure			
first				
middle				
last				

Output

```
First name: Barnaby
Middle name: Lance
Last name: Gildenstern
Social security number: 123-45-6789
Barnaby L. Gildenstern, 123-45-6789.
```

6. Set up a structure tagged *person_rec* and use an array of three of these to hold data for three people. Initialize the array with the data as shown below. Your program should accept a portion of a name input at the keyboard, find that person in the array, and print out the person's data as shown.

Name	Age	Height
Bilbao Arlo	28	5.92
Dalrymple Herfy	62	6.02
Greezle Eulalia	35	5.4

Structures and Variables

person[]	Array of person_rec structures
name[]	
age	
height	
name_in[]	Name to search for
space	Marks space between first and last names
count	Loop counter

Outputs

```
Enter characters for name: Dal
H. Dalrymple is 62 years old and 6.02 feet tall.

Enter characters for name: Zerch
No such name.
```

7. Set up a structure tagged *student_rec* and an array of variables of that type initialized with the data below. Your program should print out a report from that data as shown.

Name	Grade 1	Grade 2	Grade 3
Bilbao Arlo	76	92	88
Dalrymple Herfy	62	79	85
Greezle Eulalia	95	98	93

Structures and Variables

student[]	Array of student_recs
name[]	
grade[]	Three grades
stu	Counter for student array
grd	Counter for grade array
total	To figure average

Output

```
Name              1   2   3   Average
Bilbao Arlo       76  92  88  85.33
Dalrymple Herfy   62  79  85  75.33
Greezle Eulalia   95  98  93  95.33
```

8. Using Program 7 as a guide, write the program so that the main() function, for each student, calls the function *average()*, which returns the average for that student

9. Write the program for the setup referred to in Problems 7 and 8 so that the structure array is initialized in the `main()` function, but everything else is done in the function *report()*.

10. A firm uses two types of containers, boxes and cans. A box's dimensions are its height, width, and length; its volume is the product of the three. A can's dimensions are its diameter and height; its volume is $\pi \times radius^2 \times height$, where the *radius* is half the diameter. Write a program that uses the *in_pack()* function to input the type of container and *out_pack()* to display the type of container and its volume. To store the container data, set up two structures, one for each type of container. Put these two structures in a *container* union and define a *package* of that type in `main()`. Notice that the *type* is identified first in each structure. It should then be accessible at the beginning of the union, no matter which member you access. Be sure to allocate the same number of characters for *type* in each structure.

Variables and Functions

box_t	A structure for box data
type	Type of container ("Box")
height, width, length	
can_t	A structure for can data
type	Type of container ("Can")
diameter, height	
container	A union
box	Structure of type box_t
can	Structure of type can_t
package	Union of type container
in_pack()	
pack	Pointer to a container
type	'b' for box or 'c' for can
out_pack()	
pack	Pointer to a container
volume	

Output

```
(b)ox or (c)an? c
Diameter height: 2 2
Can: 6.283200 cu.in.
(b)ox or (c)an? b
Height width length: 2 2 2
Box: 8.000000 cu.in.
```

11. To keep track of your ever-changing collection of movie videos you have decided to set up a linked list. Write the program that will add to the list, delete from it, and print it out. Save the program as *VIDEOS* for future use.

Variables, Structures, and Functions

video_rec	Tag for video structure	add()	Add to list
title	Video title	head	
next	Pointer to next record	video	
main()		curr	
head		prev	
option	Add, delete, or print	delete_video()	Delete from list
print()	print out list	head	
video		curr	
new_video()	Establish new record	prev	
video		del_title	Title to delete

FILES

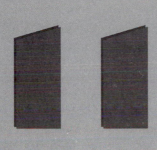

PREVIEW   Data that we wish to store permanently must be stored in files in secondary storage. After reading this chapter, you should have a working knowledge of

1. How files are identified, and how we work with sections of them at a time.

2. How C establishes its connection between a program and a file.

3. Working with files using human-readable characters.

4. Keeping track of the program's position in a file.

5. Accessing the file in bytes by directly copying between memory and the file.

6. Common applications of files including direct access and use with structures.

Most of computing is manipulating data—often large volumes of data. This data must be stored permanently, called up when needed, updated, restored, and so forth. We have, of course, used data in our previous programs. Typically we have entered it through the keyboard, processed it, and output it on the screen. Because of the nature of main memory, the data was temporary. Now we shall look at permanent retention of data in secondary storage.

Anything kept in secondary storage is considered by the operating system to be a **file**. We often separate files into two categories, program files and data files. To C it makes no difference; both are collections of bytes stored on disk. To us, though, it will probably determine how we organize and access them. The concentration here will be on data files, although the same rules and techniques apply to everything in secondary storage.

FILE IDENTIFIERS

Every block of data in secondary storage must have a unique identifier. We can't just ask the computer, "Remember that stuff I put on the disk last week?" Different operating systems have different rules for file identifiers. We will look at some general ones that will work with most systems, but you will have to get the particulars from the documentation for your own operating system.

In most operating systems, a file identifier can consist of a name and an extension. The **name** can usually be at least eight characters long and if you stick with the alpha (*A* through *Z*) and numeric (*0* through *9*) characters you should be safe. Some operating systems are case sensitive (for example, an uppercase *A* is treated as a different character from a lowercase *a*); some are not. Your file might have a name like *PAYROLL* or *lt930412*.

An **extension** is typically up to three characters of the same kinds as those allowable in a name. Extensions are often used to group files together in categories. C program source files usually have the extension *C*, executable programs often *EXE* or *COM* (for "command"). All of a company's payroll files might have the extension *PAY* and its employee files *EMP*. Extensions are usually not required, but if they exist they follow the name and are separated from it by a dot (.). Here are some typical file identifiers:

PROGRAM.C	0393Actg.Qtr
PROGRAM.EXE	X
a.out	Agnes.WHO

In addition to the identifier, most operating systems allow their secondary storage to be divided into logical storage areas called directories and subdirectories. To work with such a system, we must not only give the system the identifier but also a path to follow to find its way to the proper directory or subdirectory. In our directions to C we can give not only the file identifiers but also path directions if they are required or allowed in the operating system.

BUFFERED INPUT AND OUTPUT

As we saw in Chapter 1, we cannot access secondary storage a single byte at a time, only in blocks of bytes—perhaps hundreds or thousands of bytes per block. Our program, however, will have to work with single bytes. The solution to this apparent contradiction is to bring a block of bytes into main

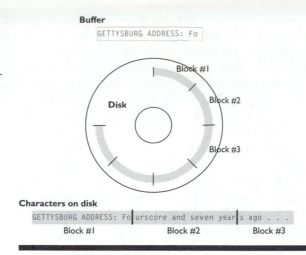

Buffer

GETTYSBURG ADDRESS: Fo

Disk — Block #1, Block #2, Block #3

Characters on disk

GETTYSBURG ADDRESS: Fo | urscore and seven year | s ago . . .

Block #1   Block #2   Block #3

Since the CPU cannot access single bytes in secondary storage, an entire block is copied into a buffer in main memory. From there, the CPU can perform the needed access.

memory where we can access each byte separately. We call the area in main memory where we temporarily store a block a **buffer**.

To access the bytes in a disk block, that particular block must be copied into a buffer in main memory. If our next access takes us into another disk block, the first one is replaced in secondary storage and the new one copied into the buffer. We may do the buffering process ourselves, but ANSI C has a number of functions that handle buffering so that it is "transparent" to us—we don't even realize that it is happening. We can access the file as if we are calling for bytes from a continuous collection of them on the disk. C will keep track of the byte position in the disk file by maintaining a **file position indicator** and automatically move things in and out of buffers when it needs to.

OPENING FILES

We must inform C of our intention to use a particular file in a program. When we do, C sets up a structure of type FILE (defined in stdio.h) in memory. This structure contains information about the file such as our current position in the file, where the end of it is, where the associated buffer is located in memory, the size of the buffer, and a number of other things.

The fopen() function directs C to set up the file description and prepare the file for use.

```
FILE *fopen(const char *file_id, const char *mode)          <stdio.h>
```

The *file_id* is the path (if any), file name, and extension (if any) of the file we intend to use. The *mode* is how we intend to use it. The return value is the pointer to the structure that holds the file description that C sets up as a result of the function call. If the file cannot be opened, the return value will be the NULL pointer. For example,

```
FILE *payfile;

payfile = fopen("\\ACCTG\\PAYROLL.D5", "rb+");
```

The first statement declares *payfile* as a pointer to a structure of type FILE. The second, through the call to fopen(), establishes a file description structure for the *PAYROLL.D5* file in the *ACCTG* directory, and assigns the pointer to this description to *payfile*. We usually refer to the pointer to the file description (*payfile*) as the "pointer to the file" or simply the "file." From this point in the program, when we access the *PAYROLL.D5* file with an ANSI function, we will pass the function the file (the address of the description that we stored in *payfile*), and it will find all the particulars of the file there.

Notice that for this operating system, the file_id in the fopen() function includes backslashes. The actual file_id above is really "\ACCTG\PAY-ROLL.D5". We used double backslashes in the string to represent a single backslash, because the single backslash is the beginning of a special character. The '\a', for example, is the audible alarm—it makes the computer beep!

File Modes

The file *mode* is a text string containing certain key characters that tell C how we are going to use the file. There are three basic modes:

"r"   Opens an existing file with the file position indicator at the beginning of the file. In the absence of further code characters, this file can only be read from. If the file does not exist, the NULL pointer will be returned.

"w"   Creates a new, empty file with the file position indicator at the beginning (which, since it is empty, is also the end). If a file with the same identifier already exists, the new, empty one will replace it. In other words, any data in the previous file will be lost! In the absence of further code characters, this file can only be written to. If the file cannot be created (no disk space or an invalid path, perhaps), the NULL pointer is returned.

"a"   Opens an existing file or, if none exists, creates a new one. The file position indicator is placed at the end (which would also be the beginning if a new file was created). In the absence of further code characters, this file can only be written to, but unlike "w", no data is lost because the writing takes place at the end of the file (the file is appended to). In most Cs, you cannot move the file position indicator to a place anywhere before the original end of the file. An error in the opening process returns the NULL pointer.

Any of these codes may be followed by a plus sign ("r+", "w+", or "a+") indicating that the file may be both read from and written to. However, before changing from reading to writing or vice versa you must call one of four functions that access the file buffer—fseek(), rewind(), fflush() (from Chapter 3), or fsetpos(). We will look at those functions shortly.

Binary versus Text Files

Programmed correctly, C will work with almost any type of file you can dream up. However, for its own workings it divides files into two types, binary and text, the principal differences being in the line endings in the file and the detection of the end of the file.

The file modes we referred to above have all been those of **text files**. Text files try to match the internal storage of data in C to the typical formatting of text for the operating system in use. The possible adjustments are in the line endings and end-of-file indications. Internally, C stores line endings with the single newline character (\n), typically referred to as a line feed (ASCII 10). A text file in UNIX uses the same character at the end of a line, so no change is made when going between main memory and secondary storage.

MS-DOS and some other operating systems, however, consider a line ending to be the combination of a return (\r, ASCII 13) and a line feed—a two-character combination. Single-character newlines in main memory, then, are translated into two-character, return/line feed combinations when written to a file, and vice versa going from a file to main memory. (Whether this is really typical of MS-DOS text files might be questionable; a good many DOS text editors and most word processors use just the line feed character. It is up to you to find out what is in your files and how to treat them in your programs.)

Some MS-DOS files use a control Z character (ASCII 26) as an end-of-file indicator. If this character is encountered in a text file, the program will get an end-of-file indication. UNIX and many other systems, MS-DOS included, track the end of a file by knowing where the file position indicator is and the number of bytes in the entire file. The control Z will be treated like any other character by a UNIX C implementation, but it will be interpreted as the end of the file by an MS-DOS C.

Binary files are the most straightforward. They assume nothing about the operating system and don't make any special adjustments or translations. What is in the program or main memory will be written to the file verbatim, and vice versa. We can declare our file mode to be binary by including a *b* in the *mode* string in either the second or last position. (For example, "r+b" or "rb+", or "wb", and so forth.)

What all this really means is that you must know the makeup of the file you are trying to access and whether it fits the standard for your operating system. Many files won't have line endings in them at all, making the difference between the types moot. We will work with these files as binary. In fact, when in doubt, use binary. You can always work with the return character (\r) as just another character if it exists at the end of the line.

CLOSING A FILE

The act of closing a file writes the contents of the current buffer, if it has changed, into the appropriate place in secondary storage, making changes permanent, and deallocates the memory space for both the file buffer and the file description structure. The fclose() function closes a file.

```
int fclose(FILE *file)                                        <stdio.h>
```

The *file* is the pointer to the file description that was established when the file was opened. The function returns a zero if successful, EOF if not. We would close *ACCTG\PAYROLL.D5* by referring to its description pointed to by *payfile*.

```
fclose(payfile);
```

Files are automatically closed at a normal program termination, including the execution of an `exit()` function, but they are not closed when the program crashes. An abnormal ending to the program, then, leaves the buffers forgotten in main memory, not updating secondary storage, and possibly losing data.

Most programmers are careful to close any file they open as soon as the file is no longer required by the program. The practice saves memory space and possible data loss if something unexpected should happen.

CHARACTER ACCESS TO FILES

We will look at two different ways of accessing files. One, **character access** (or *formatted access*), reads and writes files much as we did with the keyboard and the screen—strictly in characters. If we printed a floating-point number, for example, we used `printf()` to convert the E-notation storage into the characters that represent its value. The second is **byte access** (or *unformatted* or *binary*), in which we store sets of bytes on the file without regard to what they represent. The E-notation floating-point number, for example, would be copied from its location in memory and written on the file in exactly the same form—virtually unreadable to humans. We assume, however, that when we read it back from the file, our program will again store it in a floating-point variable so that it makes sense to C.

Formatted Access

We have used the `printf()` function to write characters to the screen, and we can use the `fprintf()` function in almost exactly the same way to write characters to a file.

```
int fprintf(FILE *file, const char *control_string, arguments)   <stdio.h>
```

For example,

```
fprintf(payfile, "Name: %s, Pay rate: %6.2f\n", name, pay)
```

The `fprintf()` arguments, except for the first, have the same meaning as they would for `printf()`. The difference is that instead of the characters appearing on the screen at the location of the cursor, they will be written to the file at the location of the file position indicator. The file, of course, is the one referred to in the first argument, the pointer to a file description established in an `fopen()` function.

The file must be opened in some mode that will allow writing to it—`"w"`, `"wb"`, `"a"`, `"ab"`, or anything with a plus sign in it such as `"rb+"`.

▶Program 11–1 will accept any number of inputs from the keyboard and write them to a file.

We open the file in the `if` structure, which tests the return value stored in *employee*. If the return value was `NULL`, there must be a problem so we would have printed the error message and made an orderly exit from the program. In the `while` loop condition we flush the input stream to get rid of the newline left over from the last input, and then use `gets()` to input the string *name*. The test in the `while` loop checks the character at address `name`—the first character of the string. If it is null, it means that we pressed only the enter key and the string is empty. Therefore, we would exit the loop.

➡Program 11–1

```c
#include <stdio.h>
#include <stdlib.h>

void main(void)
{   FILE *employee;
    int dependents;
    float pay_rate;
    char name[40];

    /********************************************* Go from keyboard to file */
    if ((employee = fopen("EMP.DAT", "w")) == NULL)        /*Check for error*/
    {   printf("Cannot open file\n");
        exit(EXIT_FAILURE);
    }
    printf("Names should be Last, First or <Enter> key to quit.\n");
    printf("Enter name: ");
    gets(name);
    while (*name != '\0')                /* Loop while name string not empty */
    {   printf("Enter pay rate, dependents: ");
        scanf("%f,%i", &pay_rate, &dependents);
        fprintf(employee, "%-10.10s/%6.2f/%2i\n",          /* Write to file */
                name, pay_rate, dependents);
        fflush(stdin);                                     /* Flush stream */
        printf("Enter name: ");
        gets(name);
    }
    fclose(employee);
}
```

Output

```
Names should be Last, First or <Enter> key to quit.
Enter name: Quibble, Marvin
Enter pay rate, dependents: 12.34, 2
Enter name: Jones, Hatshepset
Enter pay rate, dependents: 9.38,8
Enter name: Montmorrissey, Clyde
Enter pay rate, dependents: 23.98,1
Enter name:
```

File Contents

```
Quibble, M/ 12.34/ 2
Jones, Hat/  9.38/ 8
Montmorris/ 23.98/ 1
```

The input counterpart of printf() was scanf(). The input counterpart of fprintf() is fscanf().

```
int fscanf(FILE *file, const char *control_string, arguments)    <stdio.h>
```

Both scanf() and fscanf() have the same arguments, parameters, and return values except for the extra argument for the pointer to the file description.

Let us expand our program above to read the data from the file after having put it there. Notice that the file was closed and reopened for reading ("r"). The fscanf() function is somewhat easier to use than was scanf() because we probably know the exact format of the data on the file, and we don't have to depend on the keyboarder to type things with absolute precision.

➠Additional Program (11–1a)

```
/********************************************  Go from file to screen */
if ((employee = fopen("EMP.DAT", "r")) == NULL)
{  printf("Cannot open file\n");
   exit(EXIT_FAILURE);
}
printf("Name        Pay Rate  Dependents\n");
while (fscanf(employee, "%[^/]/ %f/ %i\n", name, &pay_rate, &dependents)
       != EOF)
   printf("%s     %6.2f          %2i\n", name, pay_rate, dependents);
fclose(employee);
```

Additional Output

```
Name        Pay Rate  Dependents
Quibble, M    12.34        2
Jones, Hat     9.38        8
Montmorris    23.98        1
```

In the fscanf() function, we had to make sure that we anticipated the format of the characters in the file. When we wrote to the file, we set up a slash (/) as a delimiter between values. The default delimiter of whitespace would not have worked because some of the names were written with a space between the first and last names. It would have worked between the numbers, but we wanted to be consistent. The string, then, we specifically delimited with a slash ([^/]). That would stop the string conversion, but the slash would be left in the buffer. We passed it in the buffer by putting a matching slash in the control string immediately following the brackets. A space was left before each number to match any whitespace that might be in front of either. The second slash would have stopped the conversion of the floating-point number, so it also had to be matched (%f/). The final match was that for the newline at the end of each line of the file.

The while loop that reads from the file continued until the fscanf() encountered the end of the file, at which time its return value was the defined constant EOF.

Single-Character Access

Single-character access from the keyboard and to the screen is performed by getchar() and putchar(). Their counterparts with files are getc() and putc().

```
int getc(FILE *file)                                    <stdio.h>
int putc(int character, FILE *file)                     <stdio.h>
```

Like their counterparts, getc() returns the next character from the file buffer and putc() returns the character written. Both return EOF if an error occurs.

String Access

The fgets() and fputs() are the file counterparts of gets() and puts().

```
char *fgets(char *string, int max, FILE *file)          <stdio.h>
int fputs(const char *string, FILE *file)               <stdio.h>
```

The return values are the same as for their counterparts. For fgets() the return is the pointer to the *string* if it is successful, the NULL pointer if not. For fputs() the return is nonnegative if successful, EOF if not.

Although the intent is the same, there are some significant differences between gets() and fgets(). The latter has the *file* argument, of course, but while gets() stops reading characters only at the newline in the input stream, fgets() has three different criteria for stopping its read:

1. It gets to the end of the file.

2. It encounters a newline. If this happens, unlike with the gets() function, the newline is retained as part of the string.

3. It takes *max* - 1 characters from the file buffer. The reason for one less character here is to save room for the null at the end of the string when it is written to the array in memory. If you declared an array as string[40], you could safely say fgets(string, 40, employee) because it would only take a maximum of 39 characters from the file buffer. If fgets() reaches *max* - 1 characters, any leftover characters will still be in the buffer; the file position indicator will not move to the next newline or the end of the file or wherever.

In any case, like gets(), fgets() will always add a null at the end of the characters it writes in memory.

The fputs() function is very similar to its counterpart except that a newline is not added to the string on output. The two functions, fputs() and fgets(), are typically used on the same files. If a string was read by an fgets(), it would usually have a newline at the end of it, which would be written to the string array. If the same string were written by an fputs(), that newline would be put back in the file.

The first time you write to a file that is meant to be read line by line by an fgets(), you will have to be sure that the newline is included in whatever string you write, whether it is from an fputs() or an fprintf().

MOVING THE FILE POSITION INDICATOR

The data we want from a file is not always at the beginning. We may have to reach into the middle or go toward the end to get it. One method of moving the file position indicator is by accessing the file. Whenever we read or write, the file position indicator is moved to a position just beyond our last access. There are more efficient ways, however.

The rewind() function moves the file position indicator to the beginning of the file. Where the file position indicator was before the rewind() is irrelevant; after it, the file position indicator will be at the beginning.

As usual, the *file* argument is the pointer to the description of the file whose file position indicator we want to move.

In our previous example program, we moved the file position indicator back to the beginning of a file to which we just wrote by closing and opening the file.

```
fclose(employee);
employee = fopen("EMP.DAT", "r");
```

The same thing could have been accomplished by

```
rewind(employee);
```

with a lot more efficiency. We also said that we should not switch from writing to reading or vice versa without executing one of four functions. The rewind() function was one of them.

This function will only bring us to the beginning of the file, however. We may want to jump directly into the middle somewhere. In that case we should use the more general fseek() function.

```
int fseek(FILE *file, long offset, int origin)                   <stdio.h>
```

The return value is zero if the move was successful, or nonzero if there was a problem.

The *offset* argument is the number of bytes to move in the file. It may be positive for a forward move, or negative for a backward move. It may also be large enough to move the file position indicator beyond the end of the file or before the beginning; C will not check for that or stop it. Any data you read there would be meaningless, and writing there could be disastrous. Be sure you know where the end of the file is before moving the file position indicator.

The *offset* argument is a long integer and many Cs will not convert what you have to that data type; so be sure you cast your argument as (long) if it is not already. For example, to move 10 bytes you should pass the value 10L.

The *origin* is where the move should start—the beginning, the current file position indicator location, or at the end. The *origin* argument can take one of three values, all defined constants from stdio.h.

SEEK_SET   The *origin* is the beginning of the file. An *offset* from here, naturally, should not be negative, although C will not check it for you.

SEEK_CUR   The *origin* is at the current file position. The *offset* can be either positive or negative.

SEEK_END   The *origin* is the end of the file. The *offset* should not be positive, although C will not check it for you.

Like rewind(), this is one of the functions that will allow you to change from reading to writing or vice versa, if the opening mode allows it.

The rewind() function for the *EMP.DAT* file could be rewritten as

```
fseek(employee, 0L, SEEK_SET)
```

Either one would do the job, but the former is probably simpler and more straightforward.

If we had a file made up of records of exactly *rec_len* size, we could set the file position indicator at the *record* record as follows:

```
fseek(file, (long)((record - 1) * rec_len), SEEK_SET);
```

If *rec_len* was 10 and we were looking for the third record, the *offset* would evaluate to 20, moving the file position indicator 20 bytes. That would put it past the first two records to the 21st byte position, the first position in the third record.

We can find out where the file position indicator currently is by using the `ftell()` function.

```
long ftell(FILE *file)                                    <stdio.h>
```

The return value is the current position of the file position indicator stated as an offset from the beginning of the file. It returns -1 if there is a problem. This function is particularly useful when we want to remember where we were in a file so that we may return there later.

```
previous_position = ftell(employee);
```

saves our current position, and

```
fseek(employee, previous_position, SEEK_SET);
```

will return us there later.

FINDING THE END OF A FILE

If we know exactly what is in the file and how many bytes it occupies, then we can always determine where the end of the file is and ensure that we do not pass it unexpectedly. But often we add to or delete from files, changing their lengths and the location of their ends. There are a number of techniques in C that we can use to tell whether we are at the end of the file.

OTHER FILE-POSITION-INDICATOR ACCESS

Two other ANSI functions can be used to access the file position indicator. The `fgetpos()` stores the file position indicator position in a specified memory location, and `fsetpos()` sets the file position indicator to the position stored in a specified memory location.

```
int fgetpos(FILE *file, fpos_t *position)                 <stdio.h>
int fsetpos(FILE *file, fpos_t *position)                 <stdio.h>
```

The data type `fpos_t` is system dependent, but defined in `stdio.h`.

Function Error Returns

We can test the return value of a function we are using to access the file to see if it returns the expected value or not. The `fscanf()` function returns the defined constant EOF if it encounters the end of the file; `getc()` returns EOF on any error, including the end of the file; and `fgets()` returns the defined NULL pointer on any error. Each of these functions, except `fscanf()`, lumps all error conditions, including attempting a read at the end of the file, into the same category. Usually, the error condition truly is the end of the file, but we cannot be absolutely sure.

The End-of-File Error Function

The `feof()` function is a way to test to see if an end-of-file error has occurred.

```
int feof(FILE *file)                                        <stdio.h>
```

This function returns a nonzero value if an end-of-file error has occurred, or zero if it has not. This is an after-the-fact function. It only returns nonzero if something else has created the error. We could not set up a program segment like this and expect it to work acceptably:

```
while (feof(file) == 0)          /* or, more simply, while ( !feof(file)) */
{  fgets(string, 50, file);
   and so forth
}
printf("Yup, we're at the end of the file.\n");
```

because just being at the end of the file will not make `feof()` return nonzero. It is the `fgets()` function that will eventually create the error, and we do not want to perform the "and so forth" with an invalid *string*. We should rewrite it this way:

```
while (fgets(string, 50, file) != NULL)
{  and so forth
}
if (feof(file))
   printf("Yup, we're at the end of the file.\n");
else
   printf("Something weird happened!\n");
```

or:

```
fgets(string, 50, file)
while ( !feof(file))
{  and so forth
   fgets(string, 50, file)
}
printf("Yup, we're at the end of the file.\n");
```

The end-of-file error condition must be specifically cleared for it to go away. This can be accomplished by a call to `rewind()`.

FILE HOUSEKEEPING

There are a number of little chores that we must accomplish to keep our files clean and up to date. One of these is deleting files from secondary storage, which we do with the remove() function.

```
int remove(const char *filename)                              <stdio.h>
```

The `filename` is the file identifier, including any path names necessary to find it in secondary storage. For example,

```
remove("C:\\RECORDS\\STUDENT.DAT")
```

in an MS-DOS system, deletes the file *STUDENT.DAT* from the *RECORDS* directory on the *C* disk.

UNIX does not typically use the remove() function because a single file can be referenced in several directories via links to the file. These UNIX systems use the related function, unlink(),

```
int unlink(const char *filename)                              <stdio.h>
```

which removes the file from the directory. For example,

```
unlink("/records/student.dat")
```

When there are no more surviving links to the file, then the file will actually be removed.

The file must exist to be deleted, and it must not be open. A successful deletion returns zero. The return is nonzero otherwise.

We can change the name of a file in secondary storage with the rename() function.

```
int rename(const char *oldname, const char *newname)          <stdio.h>
```

This function will change the `oldname` to the `newname`. The `oldname` file must exist and must not be open, and there may not already be a file with the `newname`.

```
rename("STUFF", "JUNK")
```

will rename the file *STUFF* in the default directory to *JUNK*.

Like remove(), full pathing may be included, and a successful operation returns zero, whereas a nonzero indicates failure.

BYTE ACCESS TO FILES

Many of our files are made up of combinations of character and numeric data. The *EMP.DAT* file is a good example. To store the employee data, we converted the numerics into characters with the fprintf() function and filled the file with characters. A distinct advantage of this approach is that we humans can read both the character and the numeric data on the file.

If only our programs and not humans were going to read the file, we would probably want to store the data in the most efficient form in terms of both the amount of storage space and the processing required for reading and writing. Converting the numeric data to characters and vice versa takes processing time and usually requires more bytes for storage. For example, the value 12345 stored as characters takes five bytes. Stored as a short it takes only two.

Instead, let us take a direct copy of the bytes in memory and put those on the file—no translation, minimal storage.

The fwrite() function does just that. We tell it the space in memory, and it writes the contents on the file.

```
size_t fwrite(const void *location, size_t bytes, size_t items,
              FILE *file)                                        <stdio.h>
```

Starting at *location* in memory, fwrite() takes a number of *items* of *bytes* length, and writes them to the file described at *file*. The return value is the number of items or partial items written. It should be the same as *items* if everything goes right. For example, given the declaration,

```
float beans[10];
```

either

```
fwrite(beans, 4, 10, beanfile);
```

assuming a four-byte float, or

```
fwrite(beans, sizeof (float), 10, beanfile);
```

will write the entire *beans* array on the file described at *beanfile*, and return 10.

The *location* argument was declared as a **pointer to** void. This is an ANSI pointer type that stores a memory address without regard to the data type to which it points. The fwrite() function must work with all data types. In fact, the function doesn't care which data type is stored at the address; it simply copies the prescribed number of bytes to the file. If *location* was the address of a structure, for example, we might have a mixture of data types beginning at the address.

The number of bytes written to the file is always the product of *bytes* times *items*. The example statement above could just as well have been written

```
fwrite(beans, sizeof beans, 1, beanfile);
```

or, for that matter,

```
fwrite(beans, 1, sizeof beans, beanfile);
```

That is, one item consisting of the number of bytes in the entire array *beans*. Remember, the sizeof an array prefix is the number of bytes in the entire array, as long as the declaration of the array is in the same program block.

This might even be a safer way to write the entire array to the file because it allows C to figure the total bytes.

The last construction has some things to recommend it. If there is some problem in writing, running out of disk space for example, a partial write will be counted in the return value. If the value given for *items* is the exact number of bytes, even one less byte written to the file would show up in the return value.

```
if (fwrite(beans, 1, sizeof beans, beanfile) != sizeof beans)
    printf("We've got problems!\n");
```

The fread() function does exactly the opposite; it takes a number of bytes from a file and writes them at an address in main memory. You must be very sure that there is enough allocated space at that memory location; C gives you no help there.

```
size_t fread(const void *location, size_t bytes, size_t items,
             FILE *file)                                        <stdio.h>
```

The arguments are exactly the same.

Given the declaration

```
float beans[10];
```

any of these statements would read 40 bytes from the file and assign them to the array *beans*.

```
fread(beans, 4, 10, beanfile);
fread(beans, sizeof (float), 10, beanfile);
fread(beans, sizeof beans, 1, beanfile);
fread(beans, 1, sizeof beans, beanfile);
if (fread(beans, 1, sizeof beans, beanfile) != sizeof beans)
    printf("We got problems!\n");
```

Wouldn't it be embarrassing if those 40 bytes in the file did not represent floats? Only to you, though, not to C.

➡Program 11–2 allows input of any number of days' production of axle grease in tons and stores the data on a file. Then it prints the data from the file on the screen.

Each of the file operations has an error check to see if everything is going to plan. The file is opened in the "wb+" mode so that a new file would be created, it could be both written and read, and there would be no translations for line endings. In the input loop, the criterion tested for is whether the current input, *grease[day - 1]*, is -1.

The number of items to be written on the file, *day*, is put on the file first; then the items themselves by specifying the sizeof (float) as the number of bytes and *day* as the number of items. Reading from the file is in exactly the same order—the integer *day* first and then *day* sets of bytes for the array *grease*. The principle of contiguous storage for arrays becomes very important in cases such as this.

➡Program 11-2

```c
#include <stdio.h>
#include <stdlib.h>

void main(void)
{   FILE *goo;
    float grease[60];/* No more than 60 days */
    int count, day=1;

    /*********************************************************** Open file */
    if ((goo = fopen("PRODUCT", "wb+")) == NULL)
    {   printf("Can't open PRODUCT file.\n");
        exit(EXIT_FAILURE);
    }
    /********************************************************* Input values */
    while (printf("Tons for day %2i (-1 to quit): ", day),
            scanf("%f", &grease[day - 1]),
            grease[day - 1] != -1)
        ++day;
    --day;                              /* Last input (-1) doesn't count */
    /********************************* Write number of values on file */
    if (fwrite(&day, sizeof (int), 1, goo) != 1)
    {   printf("Error writing file.\n");
        exit(EXIT_FAILURE);
    }
    /*********************************************** Write values on file */
    if (fwrite(grease, sizeof (float), day, goo) != day)
    {   printf("Error writing file.\n");
        exit(EXIT_FAILURE);
    }
    rewind(goo);       /* Reset pointer and allow change from write to read */
    /******************************** Read number of values from file */
    if (fread(&day, sizeof (int), 1, goo) != 1)
    {   printf("Error reading file.\n");
        exit(EXIT_FAILURE);
    }
    /********************************************** Read values from file */
    if (fread(grease, sizeof (float), day, goo) != day)
    {   printf("Error reading file.\n");
        exit(EXIT_FAILURE);
    }
    /***************************************************** Print report */
    printf("\nDay  Tons\n");
    for (count = 1; count <= day; ++count)
        printf(" %2i %5.1f\n", count, grease[count - 1]);
    fclose(goo);
}
```

Output

```
Tons for day  1 (-1 to quit): 36.4
Tons for day  2 (-1 to quit): 25
Tons for day  3 (-1 to quit): 42.38
Tons for day  4 (-1 to quit): -1

Day  Tons
  1  36.4
  2  25.0
  3  42.4
```

BYTE ACCESS AND PORTABILITY

Byte access to files may speed up the process, but it puts limits on the portability of both the files and the programs. We have already mentioned the fact that most of the ANSI standard data types are not standard in the number of bytes in the data type. If an int were put on a file as two bytes, but then the program was recompiled on another system that used four-byte ints, the data coming back from the same file would be garbage. Systems also differ in the order in which they store bits. Some put the most significant bit on the left, others on the right. Be sure you know the system particulars before you try to move either programs or files from system to system.

FILES AND STRUCTURES

A structure can be viewed as a fixed-length object stored at an address in memory. This kind of description fits perfectly with the operation of fread() and fwrite(). We can easily move structures to and from files by giving either function the address of the structure, the number of bytes in the structure (which we can get using sizeof), and the number of structures.

In ▶Program 11–3 we have modified ▶Program 10–1 that accepted employee data and calculated pay. Instead of calculating pay, we will put the data for each employee on a file *EMPLOYEE.DAT* to be used later. The file was opened for mode "wb" so that we would start with an empty file on which to write, and no special translation of our bytes would be made. Each time we input data for an employee, we write the structure to the file.

▶Program 11–3

```
#include <stdio.h>
#include <stdlib.h>

struct employee_rec
{   char name[30];
    int dependents;                          /* Does not include employee */
    float pay_rate;
};

void main(void)
{   struct employee_rec employee;
    FILE *employ;

    if ((employ = fopen("EMPLOYEE.DAT", "wb")) == NULL)      /* Open file */
    {   printf("Cannot open file.\n");
        exit(EXIT_FAILURE);
    }
    while (printf("Employee name: "),                /* Input and write to file */
           gets(employee.name),
           employee.name[0] != '\0')                       /* Empty string */
    {   printf("Pay rate, other dependents: ");
        scanf(" %f, %i", &employee.pay_rate, &employee.dependents);
        fwrite(&employee, sizeof employee, 1, employ);
        fflush(stdin);
    }
    fclose(employ);
}
```

Output

```
Employee name: Maynard Freebisch
Pay rate, other dependents: 10.83, 2
Employee name: Gilda Garfinkle
Pay rate, other dependents: 15.25, 4
Employee name: Beulah Barzoom
Pay rate, other dependents: 12.63, 4
Employee name: LeRoy LaRue
Pay rate, other dependents: 9.50, -1
Employee name:
```

Notice the different way of controlling the while loop between ➡Program 11–3 and ➡Program 10–1.

Showing the file contents as a result of this program would make little sense. We could see the characters in the strings, but the numbers were written just as they were stored in memory, in binary notation, so those bytes translated as characters would be meaningless.

We could do this week's payroll by reading the employee data from the file, inputting the number of hours for each, and printing the results. Both the structure definition and the arguments in the fread() call are exactly the same as in the last program (except that it was a call to fwrite()), ensuring that the data will be read from the file and written to the structure in exactly the same manner that it was read from the structure and written to the file in the last program.

➡Program 11–4

```c
#include <stdio.h>
#include <stdlib.h>

struct employee_rec
{   char name[30];
    int dependents;                         /* Does not include employee */
    float pay_rate;
};

void main(void)
{   struct employee_rec employee;
    float hours, gross, tax;
    double net;
    FILE *employ;

    if ((employ = fopen("EMPLOYEE.DAT", "rb")) == NULL)       /* Open file */
    {   printf("Cannot open file.\n");
        exit(EXIT_FAILURE);
    }
    while (fread(&employee, sizeof employee, 1, employ) == 1)      /* Pay */
    {   printf("Hours for %s: ", employee.name);
        scanf(" %f", &hours);
        gross = hours * employee.pay_rate;
        tax = (.16 - .02 * (employee.dependents + 1)) * gross;
        net = gross - tax;
        printf("   Pay to: %s   $**%.2f**\n", employee.name, net);
    }
    fclose(employ);
}
```

Output

```
Hours for Maynard Freebisch: 36
   Pay to: Maynard Freebisch   $**350.89**
Hours for Gilda Garfinkle: 44
   Pay to: Gilda Garfinkle   $**630.74**
Hours for Beulah Barzoom: 39
   Pay to: Beulah Barzoom   $**463.02**
Hours for LeRoy LaRue: 3
   Pay to: LeRoy LaRue   $**23.94**
```

DIRECT ACCESS TO FILES

There are two fundamental types of file access: sequential and direct. In a **sequential access**, you start from the beginning of the file and move toward the end. A novel is accessed sequentially, as is an audio or video tape. In **direct access**, you go directly to a particular point in the file. A phone book can be accessed directly, as can a CD audio disk or video disk. Going to a particular point in a file can be accomplished using the `fseek()` function as long as we know the byte position in the file.

In ➠Program 11–5 we will change the pay rate of one of the people in the *EMPLOYEE.DAT* file using both sequential and direct access to the file. We will use sequential access to find the employee in the file. Once we have found the employee's record—matched the name from the file record with the one input from the keyboard—the file position indicator will be beyond that record in the file. We will have to use direct access to return the file position indicator to the byte position of the beginning of the record, so that we may rewrite the record on the file. The record, of course, will be stored in memory as a structure.

➠Program 11–5

```c
#include <stdio.h>
#include <stdlib.h>
#include <string.h>

struct employee_rec
{  char name[30];
   int dependents;                          /* Does not include employee */
   float pay_rate;
};

void main(void)
{  struct employee_rec employee;
   char person[30];
   long record = 0;                 /* long to avoid casting in fseek */
   FILE *employ;

   if ((employ = fopen("EMPLOYEE.DAT", "rb+")) == NULL)     /* Open file */
   {  printf("Cannot open file.\n");
      exit(EXIT_FAILURE);
   }
```

—Continued

```
        printf("Employee's name: ");              /* Input person to change */
        gets(person);
        while (fread(&employee, sizeof employee, 1, employ) == 1   /* Search */
              && strcmp(person, employee.name) != 0)
          ++record;                                      /* Count record */
        if (feof(employ))                          /* Input name not on file */
        { printf("%s not on file.\n", person);
        }else                                     /* Change pay rate and rewrite */
        { printf("Pay rate for %s: ", employee.name);
          scanf(" %f", &employee.pay_rate);
          fseek(employ, record * sizeof employee, SEEK_SET);
          fwrite(&employee, sizeof employee, 1, employ);
        }
        rewind(employ);                                  /* Print changed file */
        printf("\nName          Dependents  Pay Rate\n");
        while (fread(&employee, sizeof employee, 1, employ) == 1)
          printf("%-13.13s         %3i  %8.2f\n",
                employee.name, employee.dependents, employee.pay_rate);
        fclose(employ);
      }
```

Output

```
Employee's name: LeRoy LaRue
Pay rate for LeRoy LaRue: 4.65

Name          Dependents  Pay Rate
Maynard Freeb         2     10.83
Gilda Garfink         4     15.25
Beulah Barzoo         4     12.63
LeRoy LaRue          -1      4.65
```

Output

```
Employee's name: Ebenezer Bargle
Ebenezer Bargle not on file.

Name          Dependents  Pay Rate
Maynard Freeb         2     10.83
Gilda Garfink         4     15.25
Beulah Barzoo         4     12.63
LeRoy LaRue          -1      4.65
```

We could also have done the search and change without using the variable *record*. Instead of moving a certain number of bytes from the beginning of the file, we could have moved the pointer backward one record in the file. The changed section of the program would be:

```
        while (fread(&employee, sizeof employee, 1, employ) == 1   /* Search */
              && strcmp(person, employee.name) != 0);           /* New ; */
          /* ++record;                                Don't need this */
        if (feof(employ))                          /* Input name not on file */
        { printf("%s not on file.\n", person);
        }else                                     /* Change pay rate and rewrite */
        { printf("Pay rate for %s: ", employee.name);
          scanf(" %f", &employee.pay_rate);
          fseek(employ, -(long)(sizeof employee), SEEK_CUR);   /*Change this*/
          fwrite(&employee, sizeof employee, 1, employ);
        }
```

When we moved backward in the file, the offset expression was `-(long)(sizeof employee)`. The result of the `sizeof` operator is data type `size_t`, a defined data type. It is different in various Cs, but it is typically an unsigned integer. The *offset* argument requires a signed long integer value so we must use the cast. Using just `-sizeof employee` would have been a disaster! The value of that expression, instead of being -36, would be some positive garbage number, 65500 in a C where `size_t` was a two-byte unsigned integer. C would attempt to move the file position indicator and write there, but where is that?

PUTTING IT TOGETHER

Esoteric Toys, Inc. sends letters to customers listing the products Esoteric thinks they might be interested in. Esoteric's product data is stored in a binary file, *PRODUCTS.DAT*, from which Esoteric will choose certain products. The chosen products will have to be stored in a text file, *PRODUCTS.LST*, for import into the word-processed document. When a product is chosen, its status in the *DAT* file is changed from open to listed. The overall structure of Esoteric's program is:

```
Open files
Choose products
Print list for confirmation
Close files
```

Choosing the products to list is set up as a separate module.

```
[Choose products]
    While more choices
        While not at end of file and no match yet    [Search DAT file]
            Read next record from DAT file
        End loop
        If at end of flle
            Print error message
        Else
            Add to LST file
            Change status in DAT file
        End if
    End loop
```

Esoteric does not want to print a list if nothing has been added to the list, and it wants to delete the *LST* file, so that section of the process combines the printing and closing of the *LST* file.

```
If no listings      [Print list for confirmation]
    Print error message
    Close LST file
    Delete LST file
Else
    Print listings
    Close LST file
End if
```

Printing the *LST* file is handled in a separate module.

```
[Print listings]
    Set LST file to beginning
    While more listings
        Read listing
        Print listing
    End loop
```

In ➡️Program 11–6, we have left in the function used to create a new *DAT* file for testing the program. In this function you can see the data in the *DAT* file as well as going from an array of structures to a file.

➡️Program 11–6

```c
#include <stdio.h>
#include <stdlib.h>
#include <string.h>

struct product_rec
{  char name[20];
   float price;
   char status;                              /* "o" for open, "l" for listed */
};

void new_file(void);                         /* Create new file for testing */
int add_to_list(FILE *prod, FILE *list);            /* Transfer to LST file */
void print_list(FILE *list);                             /* Print LST file */

void main(void)
{  FILE *prod, *list;
   int no_of_listings;                       /* Number of records in LST */

   new_file();                               /* Establish file for testing */

   /*********************************************************** Open files */
1  if ((prod = fopen("PRODUCT.DAT", "rb+")) == NULL)
2  {  puts("Can't open file.");
3     exit(EXIT_FAILURE);
   }
4  if ((list = fopen("PRODUCT.LST", "w+")) == NULL)
5  {  puts("Can't open file.");
6     exit(EXIT_FAILURE);
   }
   /************************************** Transfer listings to LST file */
7  no_of_listings = add_to_list(prod, list);

   /***************************************************** Print listings */
8  if (no_of_listings)
9  {  print_list(list);
10    fclose(list);
   }else
11 {  puts("No listings on file.");
12    fclose(list);
13    remove("PRODUCTS.LST");
   }
14 fclose(prod);
}
```
—*Continued*

EXECUTION CHART — `main()`				
Line	**Explanation**	**no_of_listings**	***prod**	***list**
1	Open *PRODUCT.DAT* file for read and write.	?	*DAT* file description	?
4	Create *PRODUCT.LST* file for read and write.	?	*DAT* file description	*LST* file description
7	Call *add_to_list()*.	?	*DAT* file description	*LST* file description
7	Assign return to *no_of_listings*.	2	*DAT* file description	*LST* file description
8	*no_of_listings* nonzero.	2	*DAT* file description	*LST* file description
9	Call *print_list()* to print *LST* file.	2	*DAT* file description	*LST* file description
10	Close *LST* file.	2	*DAT* file description	?
14	Close *DAT* file.	2	?	?

```
                /********************************  Add records from DAT file to LST file */
                int add_to_list(FILE *prod, FILE *list)
                {   struct product_rec product;
                    char search[20];
                    int listings = 0;                          /* Number of records added to LST */

                    printf("Add to list: ");
        a1          while (gets(search), *search != '\0')            /* No entry stops loop */
                    {
                        /**************  Search through DAT file until end of file or match */
        a2              rewind(prod);                     /* Make sure at beginning of DAT file */
                                                          /* and EOF error reset */
        a3              while (fread(&product, 1, sizeof product, prod) == sizeof product
                                && strcmp(search, product.name));
        a4              if (feof(prod)) /********************  Last read was at end of file */
        a5                 puts("Product not on file.");
                        else /*******************************************  Put on LST file */
        a6              {   fprintf(list, "%-20.20s %5.2f\n", product.name, product.price);
        a7                  ++listings;
        a8                  fseek(prod, -1L, SEEK_CUR);          /* Set file ptr back to status */
        a9                  fwrite("l", 1, 1, prod);            /* Change status to "l" */
                        }
                        printf("Add to list: ");
                    }
        a10         return listings;
                }
```

—*Continued*

EXECUTION CHART — add_to_list()

Line	Explanation	DAT position	search[]	product. name[]	listings
a1	Input *search* string. It is not blank.	Whizzit …	Ringle	?	0
a2	Call to rewind() also clears any EOF error condition.	Whizzit …	Ringle	?	0
a3	Read first record. It is not equal to *search[]*.	Doowop …	Ringle	Whizzit	0
a3	Read second record. It is not equal to *search[]*.	Beedler …	Ringle	Doowop	0
a3	Read third record. It is not equal to *search[]*.	Ringle …	Ringle	Beedler	0
a3	Read fourth record. It is equal to *search[]*.	End of file	Ringle	Ringle	0
a4	End-of-file error not set because no read attempted there.	End of file	Ringle	Ringle	0
a6	Write name and price on *LST* file in characters.	End of file	Ringle	Ringle	0
a7	Add one to *listings*.	End of file	Ringle	Ringle	1
a8	Move file position indicator back one byte.	oEnd of file	Ringle	Ringle	1
a9	Write an *l* there.	End of file	Ringle	Ringle	1
a1	Input *search* string. It is not blank.	End of file	Whatzit	Ringle	1
a2–a3	Search entire file. Last read is at end of file. Error condition set.	End of file	Whatzit	Ringle	1
a4	feof() true.	End of file	Whatzit	Ringle	1
a5	Print error message.	End of file	Whatzit	Ringle	1
a1	Input *search* string. It is not blank.	End of file	Whizzit	Ringle	1
a2	Call to rewind() clears the EOF error condition.	End of file	Whizzit	Ringle	1
a3	Read first record. It is equal to *search[]*.	Doowop …	Whizzit	Whizzit	1
a4	No end of file error.	Doowop …	Whizzit	Whizzit	1
a6	Write name and price on *LST* file in characters.	Doowop …	Whizzit	Whizzit	1
a7	Add one to *listings*.	Doowop …	Whizzit	Whizzit	2
a8	Move file position indicator back one byte.	oDoowop…	Whizzit	Whizzit	2
a9	Write an *l* there.	Doowop …	Whizzit	Whizzit	2
a1	Input *search* string. It is blank.	Doowop …		Whizzit	2
a10	Return value of *listings*.	Doowop …		Whizzit	2

Program 11–6 —*Continued*

```
#define LIST_LEN 27
/****************************************  Print listings from LST file */
void print_list(FILE *list)
{  char listing[LIST_LEN];              /* Complete listing from LST file */

p1    rewind(list);
p2    puts("\nProduct              Price");
p3    while (fgets(listing, LIST_LEN, list) != NULL)
p4       printf("%s", listing);
}
```
                                                              —*Continued*

<table>
<tr><td colspan="3">EXECUTION CHART — <code>print_list()</code></td></tr>
<tr><td>Line</td><td>Explanation</td><td>listing[]</td></tr>
<tr><td>p1</td><td>Set LST file back to beginning. Prepare for read.</td><td>?</td></tr>
<tr><td>p2</td><td>Print headings.</td><td>?</td></tr>
<tr><td>p3</td><td>Read to first \n in LST file.</td><td>Ringle …</td></tr>
<tr><td>p4</td><td>Print listing.</td><td>Ringle …</td></tr>
<tr><td>p3</td><td>Read to second \n in LST file.</td><td>Whizzit …</td></tr>
<tr><td>p4</td><td>Print listing.</td><td>Ringle …</td></tr>
<tr><td>p3</td><td>Attempt to read in LST file. At end of file. Return.</td><td>Whizzit …</td></tr>
</table>

Program 11–6 —*Continued*

```
/****************************************  Create file to test program */
void new_file(void)
{  struct product_rec product[4] = {{"Whizzit", 4.95, 'o'},
                                    {"Doowop",  6.50, 'o'},
                                    {"Beedler",  .98, 'o'},
                                    {"Ringle",  8.49, 'o'}};
   FILE *prod;
   int rec;

   if ((prod = fopen("PRODUCT.DAT", "wb")) == NULL)
   {  puts("Can't open file.");
      exit(EXIT_FAILURE);
   }
   for (rec = 0; rec < 4; ++rec)                    /* Put records on file */
      fwrite(&product[rec], 1, sizeof (product[0]), prod);
   fclose(prod);
}
```

Output

```
Add to list: Ringle
Add to list: Whatzit
Product not on file.
Add to list: Whizzit
Add to list:

Product          Price
Ringle           8.49
Whizzit          4.95
```

SUMMARY

Any entity in secondary storage is referred to as a **file**. It must be identified by a combination of a **name**, an optional **extension**, and possibly a path. A program cannot work directly with individual bytes in a file, so a portion of the file is brought into main memory in a **buffer**. C will keep track of its byte position in a file by maintaining a **file position indicator**.

The fopen() function establishes in main memory a description of the file that includes, among other things, the file identifier and its mode. The address of the description is returned by the function. The file's mode tells whether C should look for an existing file, or a new one should be created; whether the file can be read from, written to, or both; and whether it is a **binary file** or a **text file**. The fclose() function writes the contents of the current buffer, if it has changed, into the appropriate place in secondary storage, making changes permanent, and deallocates the memory space for both the file buffer and the file description structure.

Character access to a file refers to storing all data on the file in readable characters (converting numbers to strings), whereas **byte access** copies bytes from main memory (storing numbers in binary numeric form). Formatted character access is accomplished using fprintf() for writing and fscanf() for reading. Single-character access uses getc() and putc(), and string access uses fgets() and fputs().

The **file position indicator** may be reset to the beginning of the file using rewind(). The fseek() function moves the pointer a stated number of bytes from one of three origin positions: SEEK_SET, indicating the beginning of the file; SEEK_CUR, indicating the current file position; and SEEK_END, indicating the end of the file. The ftell() function returns the current byte position of the file position indicator.

A read attempted at the end of the file will cause an end-of-file error condition to be set. We can test for that with feof(). The error condition can be cleared using rewind(). A file may be deleted from secondary storage by remove() (or the related unlink() for some UNIX systems), or have its name changed by rename().

The fread() and fwrite() functions perform byte access to files, shifting data between a file and a specific location in main memory. The memory location is stated as a **pointer to** void, meaning that a given number of bytes will be stored there regardless of the data type. Structures are often used in byte access to files. The contents of a structure may be written as a series of bytes to a file, and later those bytes may be copied to a similar structure, maintaining their meaning.

In working with files, we can use **sequential access**, starting from the beginning and moving toward the end, or **direct access**, moving forward or backward between specific points in a file.

KEY TERMS (in order of appearance)

File	fputs()
Name	rewind()
Extension	fseek()
Buffer	SEEK_SET
File position indicator	SEEK_CUR
fopen()	SEEK_END
Text file	ftell()
Binary file	feof()
fclose()	remove()
Character access	unlink()
Byte access	rename()
fprintf()	fwrite()
fscanf()	Pointer to void
getc()	fread()
putc()	Sequential access
fgets()	Direct access

REVIEW QUESTIONS

1. What is meant by the term *file*?

2. What three elements can be part of a file identifier?

3. How does buffering work with files?

4. What does the file position indicator keep track of?

5. What is the purpose of the file description?

6. In file modes, what do the characters *r*, *w*, and *a* mean? What if + is added? What if *b* is added?

7. How does a binary file differ from a text file on your system?

8. Which functions do we use to open and close files?

9. How does character access differ from byte access to files?

10. Which functions do we use for formatted access to files? For single-character access? For string access?

11. Outline the differences between the functions that perform string access to files and those that perform string access to the keyboard and screen.

12. Which function moves the file position indicator to the beginning of a file?

13. How may we set the file position indicator to a particular byte position in a file? This function uses three defined constants for an origin reference. What are they and what do they mean?

14. Name the function that returns the byte position of the file position indicator.

15. Under what conditions will the return from the feof( )function be true?

16. How can we delete a file from secondary storage? Change its name?

17. Which two functions are used for byte access to files?

18. What is meant by a *pointer to void*?

19. Why is byte access to files commonly used with structures?

20. How does direct access to files differ from sequential access?

EXERCISES

1. Show the proper file mode for opening a file in each case.

   a. Read from an existing text file but ensure that the program can make no changes.
   b. Create a new binary file for both read and write access.
   c. Read and write any part of an existing text file.
   d. If a file doesn't exist, create it; otherwise allow reads and writes anywhere beyond the end of the original binary file.

2. Point out the problems in the following program segment.

```
char string[50];
FILE stuff;

if (fopen(stuff, +bw, MYFILE) == EOF)
{  puts("Can't open file.");
   exit(EXIT_FAILURE);
}
fscanf("%s", string, MYFILE);
fgets(string, MYFILE);
fclose(MYFILE);
```

3. The file position indicator is positioned at the beginning of the following characters in a file. Show the `fscanf()` function control string needed to read the data into a string and two floats.

```
Farley, 46.5 / 7.1
```

4. Show the statement needed to put the file position indicator back to the position prior to the following read.

```
fread(mem, 25, 2, file);
```

5. Why won't this work?

```
fgets(data, 50, file);
fputs(data, file);
```

6. Why won't this stop at the end of the file?

```
while ( !feof(file))
{   statements
}
```

7. Show the proper statement to write the following structure on the file pointed to by *file*.

```
struct
{  float yes[14];
   char words[50];
}goods;
```

8. Show the proper statement to move the file position indicator in the file pointed to by *file* to the beginning of the sixth record if the records are each *length* bytes long.

9. Show the `while` statement that will read 20-byte records from *file* to *loc* in memory until the end of the file is reached.

PROGRAMS

1. Write a program that allows input of names and ages from the keyboard and stores them, in characters, on the file *PEOPLE.DAT*. After the input is finished, the program should print out what is on the file as well as the average age. Enter the names in alphabetical order so that the file may be used in later programs.

Variables

`people`	Pointer to file description
`name[]`	
`age`	
`total, count`	To calculate average age

Output

```
Enter name/age: Freebisch, Lance/72
Enter name/age: Jones, Abner/45
Enter name/age: Smith, Melvin/26
Enter name/age:
Name        Age
Freebisch,  72
Jones, Abn  45
Smith, Mel  26
Average age: 47.67
```

2. Write a program that searches the file *PEOPLE.DAT* (from the problem above) sequentially for a name (last name only) input from the keyboard.

Variables

```
people                                    Pointer to file description
name_in[], last_name[], first_name[]
age
```

Output

```
Enter last name: Jones
Jones, Abner  45
Enter last name: Freebisch
Freebisch, Lance  72
Enter last name:
```

3. Write a program that will allow you to input a last name and change any last or first name or age in the file *PEOPLE.DAT* referred to in the Problem 2.

4. Write a program that will allow you to add a record, in alphabetical order, to the file *PEOPLE.DAT* referred to in Problem 3.

5. Write a program that will allow you to input a last name and delete the record with that last name from the file *PEOPLE.DAT* referred to in Problem 4.

6. A real estate firm keeps track of houses available to sell on a computer. They regularly publish two sets of listings, one of smaller houses, less than 2000 square feet, and houses 2000 square feet and over. The individual listing contains the listing date, address, price, and square footage. The date should be in six-digit fashion with year, month, and day (for example, May 4, 1995, would be 950504). Write a program that will accept listings from the terminal and enter them in either of two files, *SMALL* or *LARGE*. After entry is complete, both sets of listings should be printed out.

Variables

```
small, large   File description pointers
date
address
price
sq_feet
```

Output

```
Date, address, price, sq. feet? 950122,14 Walnut,174550,2250
Date, address, price, sq. feet? 950128,345 Oak,143990,1450
Date, address, price, sq. feet? 950205,22 Elm,156450,1700
Date, address, price, sq. feet? 950213,988 Maple,204550,3300
Date, address, price, sq. feet? 950301,76 Apple,172500,1900
Date, address, price, sq. feet?

HOUSES LESS THAN 2000 SQ. FT.
List date    Address      Price     Sq. Feet
950128       345 Oak      143990    1450
950205       22 Elm       156450    1700
950301       76 Apple     172500    1900

HOUSES 2000 SQ. FT. OR MORE.
List date    Address      Price     Sq. Feet
950122       14 Walnut    174550    2250
950213       988 Maple    204550    3300
```

7. Write a program that works with two files (*EMPLOY* and *WEEKLY*). *EMPLOY* should store the employee's name, wage, retirement, and tax rate, and should be filled by inputs from the terminal. Input is stopped by pressing just the enter key, at which time the user is asked for the hours worked for each employee. Hours worked and net pay are stored in *WEEKLY*.

   After all the data is input, a payroll report is generated using data from both files. If *EMPLOY* is filled, the user should be able to run the program with the word *weekly* on the command line, enter the *WEEKLY* data, and get a payroll report. In this case no new *EMPLOY* will be generated and the program will work with the old *EMPLOY*. Save the program as *PAY* for use later.

   Suggested Variables

emp, week	File description pointers
name	Employee name
wage	
ret	Retirement rate
tax	Tax rate
hours	
net	Net pay (hours x wage - hours x wage x tax - ret)

   Output

   ```
   Employee name, wage, ret, tax? Jones 3.5 5.5 .16
   Employee name, wage, ret, tax? Smith 4.75 6.35 .21
   Employee name, wage, ret, tax? Brown 4.25 5.75 .17
   Employee name, wage, ret, tax?

   Hours worked for Jones? 34.5
   Hours worked for Smith? 38
   Hours worked for Brown? 45


   NAME     WAGE      RET       TAX       NET PAY
   Jones    $3.50     $5.50     16%       $ 95.93
   Smith    $4.75     $6.35     21%       $136.25
   Brown    $4.25     $5.75     17%       $152.99
   ```

8. Write a program that will allow input and maintenance of the company's employee file (*EMPLOY*) as described in the *PAY* program in Problem 7. Your program should allow you to add or delete employees, or change any part of an employee's record.

9. Write a program that keeps track of student grades. It builds a new *GRADE* file by asking for a name for each of three students and three grades for each student. After all the grades are put in, a grade report is printed giving the total points and the average.

   Variables

   Structure array for student names and 3 grades

   Output

   ```
   Name and grades? Jones 68 97 24
   Name and grades? Smith 76 94 78
   Name and grades? Brown 91 56 78

   NAME    GRD    GRD    GRD    TOT    AVERAGE
   Jones   68     97     24     189    63.0
   Smith   76     94     78     248    82.7
   Brown   91     56     78     225    75.0
   ```

10. Write a program that counts the number of words and sentences in a text file. Words end at a space or punctuation, and sentences end at periods, exclamation points, and question marks. You can use a text editor or your C environment to type in a sample text file.

   Output

   ```
   File to scan: WORDS.TXT
   WORDS.TXT has 173 words and 19 sentences.
   ```

11. The BraneDed Corporation has run out of storage space, so the president, N.O. Smarts, has directed you to implement a new file-compression scheme he has cooked up—it eliminates every other character in the file. Now as long as you don't have to write the program to decompress it . . .

   Output

   ```
   File to compress? JUNK
   Now is the time for all good men to come to the aid of their party.
   After compression is:
   Nwi h iefralgo e ocm oteado hi at.
   ```

12. Write a program to store the entire linked list referred to in the *VIDEOS* program in Chapter 10 in the file *VIDEOS.DAT*.

13. Write a program to take the data from *VIDEOS.DAT* created in Problem 12 and reform a linked list.

BITWISE OPERATIONS

![chapter number 12]

One of the characteristics of C that makes it valuable for both system programming and writing programs that execute efficiently is its capability of operating on the bits within a byte. After digesting this chapter you should understand

1. The operators that operate on bits.

2. Using these operators to read and change individual bits.

3. Shifting bits to the left or right.

4. Referencing sets of bits as part of structures.

We talked about language levels in Chapter 1. C is usually considered to be a high-level language, but some call it a low-level high-level language (or a high-level low-level language) because it is capable of accessing the machine in great detail—more than most high-level languages. For this reason it is often used to write system software and software that must execute rapidly, such as word processors, graphic programs, and computer-aided design packages. One of C's low-level features is its capability of operating

Hex	Binary
0	0000
1	0001
2	0010
3	0011
4	0100
5	0101
6	0110
7	0111
8	1000
9	1001
A	1010
B	1011
C	1100
D	1101
E	1110
F	1111

▶▶TABLE 12–1
Hex–Binary Conversion

Each hex digit represents four binary digits.

on the individual bits in a byte. It is these operations that we will focus on here.

If we are to operate on individual bits, we will have to refer to values using some notation that makes the bits evident. Straight binary notation might be ideal, but it is not supported by ANSI C. The most common compromise is to use hexadecimal notation, which we introduced in Chapter 2. It is convenient because one hex digit represents four bits. Two hex digits is an even byte. We can group our binary number into groups of four bits and substitute the appropriate hex digit for each of the groups. ▶▶Table 12–1 shows the binary equivalents of all the hex digits.

Following are two numbers shown both in binary and hexadecimal notation.

```
1011 0101          0011 1100  1001 1101
  0xB5                   0x3C9D
```

We must also have a way of referring to the individual bit positions, other than "that bit somewhere in the middle." The typical method is to picture the bits as they would appear in a straight binary number—from the most significant on the left to the least significant on the right. In an eight-bit binary number, for example, the leftmost bit is the **most significant bit (MSB)** because a 1 in that position has a value of decimal 128. The rightmost is the **least significant bit (LSB)** because a 1 there has a value of 1. We usually consider the least significant the first bit, and refer to it as bit zero. The second bit is bit one, and so forth. The leftmost bit is also often called the **sign bit** because, in a value with a signed integral data type, this bit is always 0 if the value is positive, and 1 if it is negative.

```
Most significant bit              Least significant bit
                    1 0 1 1 0 1 0 1
        Sign bit    7 6 5 4 3 2 1 0   First bit
                     Bit Numbers
```

BITWISE LOGICAL OPERATIONS

We looked at the logical operators, NOT (!), AND (&&), and OR (||), in Chapter 4. These worked with variables and values of the standard data types. Here we shall look at similarly named operators, but these operators work bit by bit on the individual bits in a value. They can only be used with integral data types, and, though the names are similar, the operations they perform are quite different.

Bitwise Complement

The **bitwise complement**, ~, also called the *ones complement* or *bitwise NOT*, is a unary operator—it acts on only one value—with precedence and associativity the same as the other unary operators. The bitwise complement reverses each bit in the data addressed. It makes all the zero bits ones and all the one bits zeros.

For example, ▶Program Segment 12–1 (in a C with a 16-bit `int` and 32-bit `long`) would produce the output shown.

▶Program Segment 12–1

```
void main(void)
{  unsigned int i = 0x4BD3;
   unsigned char c = 'q';
   unsigned long l = 0x12345678L;

   printf("%X complemented is %X.\n", i, ~i);
   show_bits(i, sizeof i);
   show_bits(~i, sizeof ~i);
   printf("%lX complemented is %lX.\n", l, ~l);
   show_bits(l, sizeof l);
   show_bits(~l, sizeof ~l);
   printf("%X complemented is %X.\n", c, ~c);
   show_bits(c, sizeof c);         /* sizeof tells how many bits to print */
   show_bits(~c, sizeof ~c);       /* Minimum of int will be complemented */
}
```

Output

```
4BD3 complemented is B42C.
   4BD3   0100101111010011
   B42C   1011010000101100
12345678 complemented is EDCBA987.
   12345678   00010010001101000101011001111000
   EDCBA987   11101101110010111010100110000111
71 complemented is FF8E.
   71   01110001
   FF8E   1111111110001110
```

▶TABLE 12–2
Bitwise Operators

Operator	Explanation	Symbol	Example
Expression — Left-to-right associativity			
Unary — Right-to-left associativity			
Complement	Change 1 bits to 0 and 0 to 1.	~	~var
Multiplicative — Left-to-right associativity			
Additive — Left-to-right associativity			
Shift — Left-to-right associativity			
Left shift	Shift bits in first to left by number of bits in second.	<<	6 << 4
Right shift	Shift bits in first to right by number of bits in second.	>>	6 >> 4
Relational — Left-to-right associativity			
Equality — Left-to-right associativity			
Bitwise AND — Left-to-right associativity			
	AND values bit by bit.	&	x1 & x2
Bitwise XOR — Left-to-right associativity			
	Exclusive OR values bit by bit.	^	x1 ^ x2
Bitwise OR — Left-to-right associativity			
	OR values bit by bit.	|	x1 | x2
Logical AND — Left-to-right associativity			
Logical OR — Left-to-right associativity			
Conditional — Right-to-left associativity			
Assignment — Right-to-left associativity			
Sequential Evaluation — Left-to-right associativity			

The *show_bits()* function prints an integral number in binary notation. We will show the actual function later in the chapter. Notice that all the variables were declared as unsigned. When working with individual bits, signs or even the actual value of the number are usually irrelevant. Bit manipulations on signed values often produce unpredictable, implementation-dependent results.

Complementing the int and the long values was straightforward. The char value, 8 bits, produced a 16-bit complement—an expected result because C performs mathematical operations on nothing less than an int, which has 16 bits in this C.

Bitwise AND

The other bitwise logical operators, AND included, are binary operators—they act based on two values. They are all left-to-right associative, and each has its own place in the precedence hierarchy. ➡Table 12–2 shows the bitwise operators in their relative positions in the precedence table. The complete table is in Appendix B.

The **bitwise AND** (&) examines each bit position of both values in turn. The result in that bit position is 1 if the bits in that bit position of both of the values is one. If either (or both) is zero, then the resultant bit will be zero. With the given values, the expression value1 & value2 would produce the result shown:

```
value1       10110011
& value2     01101010
= Result     00100010
```

➡Program Segment 12–2 illustrates this operation.

➡Program Segment 12–2

```
void main(void)
{   unsigned int i1 = 0x4BD3, i2 = 0x18DF;
    unsigned long l1 = 0x12345678L, l2 = 0xFEDCBA98L;
    unsigned char c1 = 'q', c2 = 182;

    printf("%X anded with %X is %X.\n",    i1, i2, i1 & i2);
    show_bits(i1, sizeof i1);
    show_bits(i2, sizeof i2);
    show_bits(i1 & i2, sizeof (i1 & i2));
    printf("%lX anded with %lX is %lX.\n", l1, l2, l1 & l2);
    show_bits(l1, sizeof l1);
    show_bits(l2, sizeof l2);
    show_bits(l1 & l2, sizeof (l1 & l2));
    printf("%X anded with %X is %X.\n",    c1, c2, c1 & c2);
    show_bits(c1, sizeof c1);
    show_bits(c2, sizeof c2);
    show_bits(c1 & c2, sizeof (c1 & c2));
}
```

Output

```
4BD3 anded with 18DF is 8D3.
    4BD3  0100101111010011
    18DF  0001100011011111
     8D3  0000100011010011
12345678 anded with FEDCBA98 is 12141218.
    12345678  00010010001101000101011001111000
    FEDCBA98  11111110110111001011101010011000
    12141218  00010010000101000001001000011000
71 anded with B6 is 30.
    71  01110001
    B6  10110110
    30  00110000
```

In this example, the char result did not appear to be promoted to int. It would be difficult to tell, because all the leftmost bits as a result of the promotion would be zeros, which, when ANDed together would produce zeros, and leading zeros don't print. The *show_bits()* function, however, prints the exact number of bits dictated by the sizeof the value sent to it. As we are beginning to find out, much of how the C language works with individual bits is implementation dependent. Be sure you know how your C acts.

The bitwise AND is often used to examine specific bit positions in a value. If we AND the examined value with a **mask** that has 0s in the bit positions we are not interested in, and 1s in those we are, only the positions we are interested in can show values other than 0 in the result. This acts as a **filter** to allow only specific bit positions to show through. For example, if we are interested in only the second and fourth bit positions (bits one and three counting from the right), we can mask a char value with 00001010 (0x0A) and only those positions can possibly be 1s.

```
Value     11011001    01001110    11110011
& Mask    00001010    00001010    00001101
= Result  00001000    00001010    00000001
```

A standard IBM-compatible parallel port (typically a printer connection) has a status byte that can be accessed by a program. Before sending characters to this port, the program should see if it has the proper status. The bits in the status byte are interpreted as in ➡Table 12–3, which shows the required bit values for sending a character. To check the status, then, we AND the status byte with 11111001 (0xF9) and make sure the result is 11010000 (0xD0). If the status is not correct, we can test individual bits to determine the problem. The ➡Program Segment 12–3 uses the *check_status()*

➡**TABLE 12–3**
Parallel Port Status Byte

Bit	7 6 5 4 3 2 1 0	Meaning
	X	1 = Printer not busy.
	. X	1 = Receive mode.
	. . X	0 = Not out of paper.
	. . . X	1 = On line.
	. . . . X . . .	0 = No transfer error.
	. . . . . X X .	Not used.
	 X	0 = no time-out error.

function either to return a ready status, or to print error conditions and return a nonready status.

➡️Program Segment 12–3

```c
#include <stdio.h>

int check_status(char status);
void show_bits(long value, int bytes);

void main(void)
{
    if (check_status(0xFF))
        puts("  OK to print");
    if (check_status(0xD6))
        puts("  OK to print");
    if (check_status(0x54))
        puts("  OK to print");
}


int check_status(char status)
{   unsigned char mask = 0xF9                             /* 11111001 */
    unsigned char result = 0xD0;                          /* 11010000 */

    printf("Status: ");
    show_bits(status, sizeof status);
    printf("Mask:   ");
    show_bits(mask, sizeof mask);
    printf("Result: ");
    show_bits(status & mask, sizeof (status & mask));
    if ((status & mask) != result)
    {   if (status & 0x01)                                /* 0000000X = 1 */
            puts("  Time-out error");
        if (status & 0x08)                                /* 0000X000 = 1 */
            puts("  Transfer error");
        if ( !(status & 0x10))                            /* 000X0000 = 0 */
            puts("  Off line");
        if (status & 0x20)                                /* 00X00000 = 1 */
            puts("  Out of paper");
        if ( !(status & 0x40))                            /* 0X000000 = 0 */
            puts("  No receive mode");
        if ( !(status & 0x80))                            /* X0000000 = 0 */
            puts("  Printer busy");
        result = 0;                                       /* Error result */
    }else
        result = 1;                                       /* Success result */
    return result;
}
```

Output

```
Status:     FF  11111111
Mask:       F9  11111001
Result:     F9  11111001
  Time-out error
  Transfer error
  Out of paper
```

```
Status:        D6   11010110
Mask:          F9   11111001
Result:        D0   11010000
 OK to print
Status:        54   01010100
Mask:          F9   11111001
Result:        50   01010000
 Printer busy
```

We can also use AND to turn off (set to 0) specific bits. For example, to set bits 3 and 4 to zero and leave the others unchanged, we would AND the value with 0xE7 (11100111).

Value	11011001	01001110	11110011
& Mask	11100111	11100111	11100111
= Result	11000001	01000110	11100011

This would also be a good time to look at the *show_bits()* function, since it uses the AND operator:

```
void show_bits(long value, int bytes)
{  long filter = 1;                 /* Start with 1 bit in rightmost position */
   int bit;
   char bits[33] = "                                ";    /* Output space*/

   for (bit = 0; bit < bytes * 8; ++bit)
   {  if (value & filter)                          /* Bit makes it through filter */
         bits[31 - bit] = '1';
      else
         bits[31 - bit] = '0';
      filter *= 2;                                /* Shift filter one bit to left */
   }
   printf("    %*lX  %s\n", bytes * 2, value, &bits[32 - bytes * 8]);
}
```

In this function, we create a filter to pass only the bit in a single position at a time. In other words, the filter has only one 1 bit. In a loop, we move the 1 bit from the zero (rightmost) position leftward, and test to see if that bit in the examined value is set (1). The *filter* is initialized to one. After each pass through the loop, *filter* is multiplied by two, moving its 1 bit a position to the left. It starts at one (00000001), becomes two (00000010), then four (00000100), and so forth. When ANDed with the *value*, it passes only a single bit. If the bit is 1, the result will be nonzero, the test in the if statement true, and the character *1* will be put in the proper place in the string at *bit*. If the result is zero, a *0* character will be put there.

The second function parameter, *bytes*, receives the result of a sizeof operation on the *value* before it is passed to the function. It keeps track of the number of bytes in the value, so that the bit-writing operation can proceed the proper number of times, and so that the output string will be the right length. Since we are filling the string from the right side, the address passed to the printf() function for the %s conversion is not the beginning, at *bits*, but starting at the proper number of bytes from the right side of the string. That is, 32 minus the number of bits (*bytes * 8*) in the *value*.

Be careful when applying binary bitwise logical operators to two values with different data types. When a smaller signed data type is promoted to a larger one, the leftmost bit (the sign bit) is copied to fill in the extra bit positions, yielding a number with the same numeric value and sign. When the char value 0xB5 (10110101) is promoted to a 16-bit short, it becomes 0xFFB5 (11111111 10110101). This may not be your intent when used as a mask. Unsigned data types are filled in with zeros. The unsigned char value 0xB5, when promoted to unsigned short, becomes 0x00B5 (00000000 10110101). In general, you should use unsigned data types with bit manipulations because signs are meaningless when you are working with individual bit settings, and portability will be enhanced.

Bitwise OR

The **bitwise OR** (|), or the *bitwise inclusive OR*, like the bitwise AND, compares two values bit by bit. A bit position in the resultant value is set to 1 if either or both of the bits in the corresponding position of the examined values are 1. Given the expression value1 | value2, the following results would be produced:

value1	00110100	10111000	11000010
| value2	01000110	00001100	10001100
= Result	01110110	10111100	11001110

We used the bitwise AND to check for certain bits set to 1, or to set certain bits to 0. We can use the bitwise OR to check for certain bits set to 0, or to set certain bits to 1 no matter what they were before. Let us imagine that we were on the printer end in our printer port example. If we wanted to tell the port that the printer was out of paper, and there was a time-out error (the person who was supposed to load the paper was out to lunch), we would want bits zero and five set to 1. Since any of the binary bitwise operators may be used in an accumulation operation, we could use the expression status |= 0x21, which ORs *status* with 0x21 (00100001) and stores the result in *status*. No matter what the *status* was before, bits zero and five would be set to 1.

status (before)	10001001	01100100	10011100
| 0x21	00100001	00100001	00100001
= status (after)	10101001	01100101	10111101

Bitwise Exclusive OR

Using the *bitwise exclusive OR*, or **bitwise XOR** (^), the resultant bit is 1 if either, but not both, of the examined bits are 1. In other words, if the bits are different, the result will be 1. Sample results from value1 ^ value2 are:

value1	00110100	10111000	11000010
^ value2	01000110	00001100	10001100
= Result	01110010	10110100	01001110

The XOR has three interesting properties. First, any value XORed with itself (value ^ value) will result in zero.

```
value       00110100    10111000    11000010
^ value     00110100    10111000    11000010
= Result    00000000    00000000    00000000
```

This can be used in a test for equality; value1 ^ value2 is zero if the values are equal. Assembly language programmers sometimes use this as a method of setting a value to zero, because it is slightly more efficient than a straight assignment. Since program clarity is, in most cases, more important than small increases in efficiency, we should probably use value = 0 rather than value ^= value.

A second property is that a value XORed twice with a specific value returns to its original value. The expression value1 ^ value2 ^ value2 always equals *value1*:

```
value1      00110100    10111000    11000010
^ value2    01000110    00001100    10001100
=           01110010    10110100    01001110
^ value2    01000110    00001100    10001100
= Result    00110100    10111000    11000010
```

This is sometimes used as part of a simple (but not very safe) encryption routine. To encrypt data (store it in an unreadable form) each byte is XORed with a specific encryption byte. To decrypt it, the data is put through the same process.

Carrying this a step further, the following can be used to swap two values without the need for a temporary variable:

```
value1 ^= value2;
value2 ^= value1;
value1 ^= value2;
```

(Remember the accumulation operators as they were discussed in Chapter 2. The statement value1 ^= value2; is the same as writing value1 = value1 ^ value2;.)

A third property is that any bit XORed with a 1 bit will be reversed. This is used to **toggle** bits—set them to 0 if they were 1, or 1 if they were 0. The following examples toggle bits two and six (remember, we count from zero on the right):

```
value       10010100    00111011    11001010
^ toggle    01000100    01000100    01000100
= result    01010000    01111111    10001110
```

Table 12–4 shows all the bitwise logical operators and the results they produce with the various possible combinations of bits.

TABLE 12–4
Bitwise Logical Operator Truth Tables

First Value	Second Value	AND Result	OR Result	XOR Result
0	0	0	0	0
0	1	0	1	1
1	0	0	1	1
1	1	1	1	0

SHIFT OPERATORS

The shift operators, **left shift** (<<) and **right shift** (>>), move all the bits in a value a designated number of positions to the left or right. A shift expression takes this form:

```
value >> shift   or   value << shift
```

where *value* is the value to be operated on—have its bits shifted—and *shift* is the number of positions to shift the bits. In `fleeder >> 4`, the bits in *fleeder* will be shifted four places to the right.

The *shift* value should be a nonnegative integer with a value less than the number of bits in the *value* data type. Right-shifting a 16-bit `short` -3 places or 18 places would not make much sense. With most binary operators, the result is the data type of the highest data type on either side of the operation. With the shift operators, however, the result is the data type of the *value*. For portability, the *value* should be an unsigned integral data type. Results of shift operations on signed integers are implementation dependent.

In a left shift, as bits are shifted to the left they drop off, and zeros fill in at the right. As examples:

```
value      10011011    01110110    11010110 10011011
<< shift   1           3           6
= Result   00110110    10110000    10100110 11000000
```

In a right shift, bits drop off the right, but what fills in at the left is implementation dependent. Some Cs perform a **logical right shift**, which is just like a left shift—zeros fill in at the left. Others perform an **arithmetic right shift**, where the leftmost bit before the shift (the sign bit) is copied to fill in all the left positions.

```
value              10011011    01110110    11010110 10011011
>> shift           1           3           6
= Result (logical)    01001101    00001110    00000011 01011010
= Result (arithmetic) 11001101    00001110    11111111 01011010
```

Test your C to see which it does.

We can use the left shift operator in our *show_bits()* function to move the filter bit leftward by replacing

```
filter *= 2;                        /* Shift filter one bit to left */
```

with

```
filter <<= 1;                       /* Shift filter one bit to left */
```

SHIFTS AND ARITHMETIC

Although the shift operators were not intended for extensive arithmetic use, the left shift operator has the effect of multiplying a value by 2^n, where n is the number of places to shift. For example, $4 << 3$ is equal to 4×2^3 or 4×8 or 32.

Likewise, the right shift operator, at least with unsigned or positive numbers, has the effect of dividing by 2^n, truncating to the nearest integer, of course. For example, $75 >> 4$ is equal to $75 \div 2^4$, or $75 \div 16$, or 4.6875. Since we are dealing with integers, however, the result will be 4.

Compacting Data

One of the operations for which we use bit manipulations is to store the most amount of data in the least amount of space. In many cases, many of the bits that make up our data are either redundant or simply not used. The standard ASCII code, for example, uses only seven bits of the eight-bit byte. We could fit eight characters where we once stored seven by using the extra bit. All numeric characters (in ASCII) begin with the bits 0011. Since numeric characters all have the same most significant bits, if we knew we were dealing only with numeric characters, we could drop those four bits and store two characters in one byte. The ➠Program 12–4 does just that.

➠Program 12–4

```c
#include <stdio.h>

void show_bits(long value, int bytes);

void main(void)
{   char a = '4', b = '7';
    char pack;

    puts("Operation   Hex   Binary");
    pack = a;
    printf("pack = a   ");
    show_bits(pack, sizeof pack);
    pack <<= 4;
    printf("pack <<= 4");
    show_bits(pack, sizeof pack);
    b &= 0x0F;
    printf("b &= 0x0F ");
    show_bits(b, sizeof b);
    pack |= b;
    printf("pack |= b ");
    show_bits(pack, sizeof pack);
}
```

Output

```
Operation    Hex    Binary
pack = a      34    00110100
pack <<= 4    40    01000000
b &= 0x0F      7    00000111
pack |= b     47    01000111
```

BIT FIELDS

We can address the individual bits in a value using the bitwise logical operators, as we have just shown, but C provides us with an easier way for some applications—naming bits or sets of bits as variables. These are called **bit fields**. We looked at structures and their members in Chapter 10. A bit field can be a member of a structure. The bit field is a collection of one or more contiguous bits, and it acts as a miniature int. In fact, it must be defined as an int, either signed or unsigned, in the structure definition. Much of individual bit work, as we have seen, is implementation dependent, so, to enhance portability, we should specifically state `signed` or `unsigned`, not just `int`.

A bit field definition in a structure has this general form:

```
type name : bits;
```

For example

```
unsigned area : 4;
```

which defines *area* as an `unsigned int` taking up four bits.

Bit fields have some limitations, the main one being their implementation dependence. In addition, we cannot define an array of bit fields, nor, in most systems, can we define a bit field that is larger than the natural word size of the machine. That typically means no larger than the number of bits in an `int`. We cannot access a bit field by indirection, that is, set up a pointer to a bit field. That makes sense; pointers point to bytes (or words) in memory. A bit field is a part of a byte. Lastly, bit fields must be parts of structures.

For our earlier example concerning the parallel-port status byte, we might define a structure of bit fields as follows:

```
struct parallel
{  unsigned time     : 1;                    /* 1 = time out */
   unsigned          : 2;                      /* Not used */
   unsigned transfer : 1;               /* 1 = transfer error */
   unsigned line     : 1;                    /* 1 = on line */
   unsigned paper    : 1;                 /* 1 = out of paper */
   unsigned receive  : 1;                /* 1 = receive mode */
   unsigned busy     : 1;                   /* 1 = not busy */
}
```

We can declare two structures of that type:

```
struct parallel LPT1, LPT2;                    /* Two parallel ports */
```

The second bit field has no name, meaning that it is not accessible. That is perfectly acceptable; those two bits are not used, but we must still allocate room for them to maintain the same pattern as the status byte.

A bit field can be used like any other integer. We can say,

```
LPT1.busy = 0;                                 /* Set printer to busy */
```

or

```
if (LPT1.paper)                                /* Is printer out of paper? */
```

Let us rewrite our *check_status()* function to work with the status data assigned to bit fields. Externally, at the beginning of the program, we define the *parallel* structure as we have shown. Assuming we assign the status information correctly in the `main()` function, *check_status()* can be written as follows:

```
        int check_status(struct parallel LPT1)
        {   int result = 1;                               /* Success result */

            if (LPT1.time)
            {   puts("  Time-out error");
                result = 0;                                /* Error result */
            }
            if (LPT1.transfer)
            {   puts("  Transfer error");
                result = 0;
            }
            if ( !LPT1.line)
            {   puts("  Off line");
                result = 0;
            }
            if (LPT1.paper)
            {   puts("  Out of paper");
                result = 0;
            }
            if ( !LPT1.receive)
            {   puts("  No receive mode");
                result = 0;
            }
            if ( !LPT1.busy)
            {   puts("  Printer busy");
                result = 0;
            }
            return result;
        }
```

Alignment in Bit Fields

Are bits stored right to left or vice versa? If a bit field extends beyond a word
boundary, what happens? Almost everything about the alignment of bits
and bytes in bit fields is implementation dependent. Left-to-right or right-to-
left alignment is up to the implementation. If bit fields are mixed in with
nonbit fields in the same structure, such as

```
struct
{   float whatever;
    unsigned bits : 4;
    char bunch[20];
}stuff;
```

the char array, *bunch*, will begin on a byte (or word) boundary, leaving at
least the four bits after *bits* empty. But, on a 16-bit machine, if we define

```
struct
{   int this : 12;
    int that : 8;
}stuff;
```

some implementations will start *that* in the next 16-bit word, leaving 4
empty bits in the first word; others will overlap the *that* member between
the first and second words.

We can force word alignment by defining the proper number of bits for a particular implementation:

```
struct
{  int this : 12;
   int      : 4;
   int that : 8;
}stuff;
```

That doesn't help if we move our program from a 16- to a 32-bit machine.

Defining a bit field with a zero size instructs C to start the next bit field at an "appropriate" spot. That could be the next byte or the next word, depending on the implementation. So:

```
struct
{  int this : 12;
   int      : 0;
   int that : 8;
}stuff;
```

might help our move from a 16- to a 32-bit machine. It might not. Again, know your C.

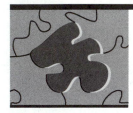

PUTTING IT TOGETHER

Let us say that we are writing the programs to keep track of books in our corporate library. All of the data on a particular title can be fit into a record with the following pattern:

Title
Author
Copy (1 through 4)
Condition (1 = perfect through 5 = junk)
Replacement code (1 = replace when tossed out)
Availability (1 = checked out)
Check-out period (1 = 1 day, 2 = 1 week, 3 = 2 weeks)
Shelf (0 = stacks, 1 = new books)

As a test, let us write a program that processes a specific book being checked in. We want to do the following to the record:

If third or fourth copy
    Set replacement code so that it won't be replaced
End If
Change its condition to 1
Check it in
If it is a day check-out book
    Change it to a week check-out book
End If
Be sure it goes in the stacks

```
#include <stdio.h>

struct book_rec
{  char title[40];
   char author[30];
   unsigned copy      : 2;              /* 0 = copy 1, 3 = copy 4 */
   unsigned condition : 3;                   /* 0 = new, 5 = junk */
   unsigned replace   : 1;              /* 1 = replace when tossed */
   unsigned char status;     /* .......X - 0 = checked out        */
                             /* .....XX. - 00 = day,   01 = 1 week */
                             /*            10 = 2 weeks, 11 = month */
                             /* ..XXX... - not used              */
                             /* .X...... - 0 = stacks, 1 = new books */
                             /* X....... - not used              */
};

void main(void)
{  struct book_rec book = {"Troglodyte Etiquette", "Van Manners, Abigail",
                           3, 0, 1, 0x40};
```

```
1    if (book.copy + 1 > 2)                     /* Third or fourth copy */
2        book.replace = 0;                  /* Do not replace when tossed */
3    book.condition = 1;                      /* Somebody dog-eared it */
4    book.status ^= 0x01;                   /* Check it in (xxxxxxx1) */
5    if ( !(book.status & 0x06))              /* Day book (xxxxx00x) */
6    {  book.status |= 0x02;             /* Make week book (xxxxxx1x) */
7       book.status &= 0xFB;              /*               (xxxxx0xx) */
     }
8    book.status &= 0xBF;                   /* Put in stacks (x0xxxxxx) */

}
```

EXECUTION CHART

Line	Explanation	copy	cond	repl	status
1	Greater than 2nd copy? Yes.	2	0	1	01000000
2	Don't replace.	2	0	0	01000000
3	Set condition.	2	1	0	01000000
4	Set check-in status by toggling first bit.	2	1	0	01000000
					^ 00000001
					= 01000001
5	See if day book. It is.	2	1	0	01000001
					& 00000110
					= 00000000
6	Change bit 1 to 1.	2	1	0	01000001
					| 00000010
					= 01000011
7	Change bit 2 to 0. (It already was.)	2	1	0	01000011
					& 11111011
					= 01000011
8	Change bit 6 to 0	2	1	0	01000011
					& 10111111
					= 00000011

SUMMARY

The C language contains facilities for working on the bits within bytes. To do this we must have some way to reference the individual bits. When referring to individual bits, we call the leftmost bit the **most significant bit**, or the **sign bit**, and the rightmost the **least significant bit**. We count bits from the right, calling the rightmost the zero bit; the second is the one bit, and so forth. Since C does not allow direct binary notation, we usually resort to hexadecimal notation in our code.

The bitwise logical operators are significantly different from the logical operators we looked at previously. The **bitwise complement** (~), a unary operator, reverses all the bits in the value referenced—the ones become zeros and the zeros ones. The **bitwise AND** (&) is a binary operator that examines each bit position in two values. The resulting bit for each position is one only if both the bits in that position of each of the values is one. We often use this operator in **masks** or **filters**, ANDing a value with a mask with one bits only in the positions in which we are interested or zero bits in the positions we want to assure are zero.

The **bitwise OR** (|) is similar to the bitwise AND in that it does a bit-by-bit operation on two values, but the result in each position in a bitwise OR is one if either or both of the bits are ones. This operator is often used to check if certain bits are zeros or to force certain bits to one. Using the **bitwise XOR**, if either but not both bits are ones, the resultant bit will be one. Any value XORed with itself will be zero; a value XORed twice with a specific value will return to its original value; and a bit XORed with a one bit will be reversed, making it a way of **toggling** bits in a value.

The **left shift** (<<) and **right shift** (>>) operators will move the bits in a value a specified number of positions to either the left or the right. A particular C implementation will either perform a **logical right shift** where zeros fill in at the left, or an **arithmetic right shift**, where the sign bit fills in at the left.

Bit fields, which address a specific set of bits, can be part of a structure. They act like small `int`s and must be declared as such in the structure definition. Bit fields are assigned and read just like any other integer member of a structure. Alignment of bits within a structure containing bit fields is implementation dependent, but declaring an unnamed bit field of zero bits will force the next bit field to start at the next byte or word, depending on the C.

KEY TERMS (in order of appearance)

Most significant bit (MSB)	Bitwise XOR
Least significant bit (LSB)	Toggle
Sign bit	Left shift
Bitwise complement	Right shift
Bitwise AND	Logical right shift
Mask	Arithmetic right shift
Filter	Bit field
Bitwise OR	

REVIEW QUESTIONS

1. Which is the most significant bit in a value? The least significant? The sign bit?
2. Are bits numbered from left to right or vice versa? Which is the zero bit?
3. What is the result of a bitwise complement on the individual bits in a value?
4. What is the resultant bit of a bitwise AND on the individual bits of two values?
5. How can the bitwise AND be used to examine specified bits in a value?
6. How can the bitwise AND be used to turn off specified bits in a value?

7. What is the resultant bit of a bitwise OR on the individual bits of two values?

8. How can the bitwise OR be used to examine specified bits in a value?

9. How can the bitwise OR be used to turn on specified bits in a value?

10. What is the resultant bit of a bitwise XOR on the individual bits of two values?

11. What is the result of a value XORed with another equal value?

12. What is the result of a value XORed twice with a specific value?

13. How do we use the bitwise XOR to toggle bits?

14. What determines the resultant data type of a shift operation?

15. In a left shift, what happens to the bits that drop off the left, and what bits are filled on the right?

16. What is the difference between a logical and an arithmetic right shift?

17. What is the data type of a bit field?

18. How do we force alignment in bit fields? Will the next bit field be aligned at a byte or word boundary?

EXERCISES

1. What are the values of the following expressions?

   a. ~0x4D
   b. 0x4D & 0xE7
   c. 0x4D | 0xE7
   d. 0x4D ^ 0xE7

2. What is the value of the following expression? Be sure to account for precedence.

   0x4D | 0xE7 ^ ~0x48 & 0xC2

3. What are the values of the following expressions?

   a. 0xE7 >> 3
   b. 0xE7 << 3
   c. 0xFD & 0xE7 >> 3

4. What mask or filter value would you use, and what operation would you perform to:

   a. Pass through only the second and fourth bits of a value?
   b. Reverse the second and fourth bits?
   c. Make the second and fourth bits one no matter what they were before?
   d. Make the second and fourth bits zero no matter what they were before?

5. Employees in the Ace Company are represented by their name (30 characters), department (0–6), job code (0–3), location (0–2), and exempt status (0 or 1). Design a structure, *emp_rec*, using bit fields that will store all this data in 32 bytes (don't forget the null required at the end of the name).

6. What is wrong with the following code segment?

```
struct rec
{  int       a;
   float     b;
   unsigned c:    4;
   float     d:    6;

   unsigned  :    0;
   int       e[5]: 2;
}something;
int f: 4;

f = c - e[2];
```

PROGRAMS

1. Using the bit-complement operation, determine the largest value of an `unsigned char`, `unsigned int`, and `unsigned long` in your C.

2. ASCII is a seven-bit code. Often the eighth bit (the leftmost or MSB) is used to create one of the many "extended" ASCII codes. Write a program that will take a string from the keyboard and set the eighth bit (ensure that it is a one) for each character as it is printed to the screen. The output depends on the screen circuitry and the extended ASCII code it uses, if any. Send the same characters to the printer. This can usually be accomplished by writing to the `stdprn` output stream, `putc(character, stdprn)`.

3. Often, word-processing programs add an eighth bit to the seven-bit ASCII code to indicate special formatting of that character (underscore, bold, and so forth). This becomes a pain in the neck when you are trying to work with just the characters in the file. Write a function *strip_high_bits()* that will take a string and return it with all the eighth bits as zeros no matter what they were before. Test it with a `main()` function that generates a string consisting of "Here it is: " and the `chars` whose values are 193 to 218, sends it to the function, and prints the result.

Output

```
Here it is: ABCDEFGHIJKLMNOPQRSTUVWXYZ
```

4. Write your own *toupper()* function. Examine the ASCII (or EBCDIC) code to see which bit is different in lower- versus uppercase characters and mask or filter that bit. Be sure your function converts only the alphabetic characters. Test the function using an initialized string in `main()`, printing that string, and then printing the characters returned from the function for each characters of the string. Do **not** include `string.h` in your program.

Output

```
The Date Today: 7/14, a Tuesday, is it not?
THE DATE TODAY: 7/14, A TUESDAY, IS IT NOT?
```

5. Devise an *odd_even()* function that accepts an integer value and returns a 1 if it is odd and a 0 if it is even. Use an appropriate mask on the value and return the result of the masking operation. Test it in a `main()` function that accepts keyboard input of an integer and prints the function's result.

Output

```
Integer: 4628
Returns: 0
```

Output

```
Integer: 37
Returns: 1
```

6. Write a program that shows whether the right shift in your C is arithmetic or logical.

7. Using two shift operations, ensure that any integer becomes even (the LSB is zero).

8. Using two shift operations, multiply an integer by 2 and then divide it by 2. For large numbers, do positive values become negative or vice versa? Why?

9. Write a program that allows input of a four-digit number as four `chars` at the keyboard and has a function, *pack()*, that packs the digits into an `unsigned short` integer, and another function, *unpack()*, that expands it into four `chars` again.

Output

```
Type a four-digit number: 7364
The value of the packed number is 29540
Here's your number back 7 3 6 4
```

10. Write a program to accept a date in the form m,5/14 (meaning Monday, May 14), pack it into a single integer, and unpack it, printing *Monday, 5/14*. Write the func-

tion *pack_date(day_name, month, day)* to pack the date, and the function *print_packed_date(packed_date)* to print out the packed date in unpacked form. The abbreviations for the days of the week beginning with Sunday are *u, m, t, w, h, f, s*, either caps or lower-case. The five least significant (rightmost) bits of the packed date should contain the day, the next four the month, and the next three the number of the day (Sunday is one). Use the `switch` statement to determine the number of the day and the printing of the full day during unpacking.

Suggested Variables

```
day_name
day_num
day
month
packed_date
error_flag
```

Output

```
Type day,M/D: t,4/12
Packed date: 1676
Date is: Tuesday, 4/12
```

Output

```
Type day,M/D: d,13/6
Invalid date
Packed date: 0
```

THE PREPROCESSOR
AND OTHER FEATURES

13

PREVIEW

The C language has a number of facilities that make the programming process easier. We have collected some of them together in a self-contained unit here, but everything in this chapter can be addressed at some earlier time. After each module, we have listed a chapter number. That particular module may be addressed concurrently with, or any time after, that chapter. The modules are:

1. The Preprocessor. (Chapter 3)
2. The Preprocessor—File Inclusion. (Chapter 3)
3. The Preprocessor—Macro Replacement. (Chapter 3)
4. The Preprocessor—Conditional Compilation. (Chapter 3)
5. The Preprocessor—Error Messages. (Chapter 3)
6. The Enumeration Data Type. (Chapter 2)
7. Renaming Data Types with `typedef`. (Chapter 2)
8. Nonstructured Program Flow. (Chapter 5)

THE PREPROCESSOR

We introduced compiler directives and the preprocessor in Chapter 3. In this section, we will discuss them much more fully. When you compile a program, the first part of the compiler to execute is a segment called the *precompiler* or **preprocessor**. (With some compilers, especially in the UNIX realm, this is actually a separate program, cpp, run first.) This part of the process operates on the source code, making changes in it, but the end result is still source code. The changes, of course, are not permanent; they only affect the source code that is passed on to the rest of the compiler.

We will look at a number of preprocessor or compiler **directives**, but no matter what is in the middle, they all start and end in the same way. The beginning of a directive is the # symbol. It must be the first nonwhitespace character on the line. (In some non-ANSI compilers, it must be the first character of any kind on the line.) The end of the directive is the first newline character—in other words, the end of the line:

```
#compiler directive
```

An exception to the ending rule is that we are permitted to continue a directive on the next line (after the newline) by putting a backslash (\) at the end of the line:

```
#compiler directive    \
    more directive      \
    more directive      \
    last of directive
```

The preprocessor will strip out the backslash and the newline that follows. The backslash must be the last thing on the line, including comments. Most compilers will choke on this:

```
#compiler directive    \    /* Beginning of directive */
    more directive
```

but will have no problem with this:

```
#compiler directive    /* Beginning of directive */    \
    more directive
```

FILE INCLUSION

We looked at file inclusion and the #include directive fairly completely in Chapter 3. Throughout the text we have used the #include directive to embed the header files provided by C into our source code. This freed us from having to define standard constants (EOF, for example) and declare standard functions (printf(), for example). We can use #include to embed anything we want in our source code—the Declaration of Independence, for example. It had better be enclosed in a comment, however, because the compiler will try to compile it. It made sense to the Founding Fathers, but it won't to the C compiler.

The #include directive is often used with header files that we have created. These often contain comments, lists of defined constants, and function declarations that we normally add to our programs. #includes may be nested, typically to about five levels. In other words, we may embed an include file that has an #include directive in it. The second include file will be embedded in position in the first include file, which is embedded in position in the original source code. For example, our include file might contain #include <stdio.h>.

An include file may also contain sections of code—entire functions, for example. This code should be thoroughly tested and debugged before being put in an include file. Remember, the include file is not part of the source code that is visible to us, only to the compiler. To fix problems in this section of code, you would have to go back to the include file itself.

MACRO REPLACEMENT

We also looked at the #define directive in Chapter 3, but only briefly and only to establish defined constants. Here we will examine its many capabilities. Basically, the #define directive tells the preprocessor to replace one set of characters with another. We refer to this replacement as a **macro**. The macro is established in a #define directive:

```
#define macro_name replacement
```

Whitespace is used to divide the keyword from the *macro_name*, and that from the *replacement*.

The macro is used by putting the *macro_name* in some subsequent spot in the program. Almost any spot will do, except that the *macro_name* in a quoted string value or a comment will not be replaced. In Chapter 3, we set up the defined constant *PI*,

```
#define PI 3.14
```

If the statement

```
printf("Area (PI * r * r) = %f\n", PI * r * r);   /* PI defined earlier */
```

appeared later in the program, it would be compiled as

```
printf("Area (PI * r * r) = %f\n", 3.14 * r * r); /* PI defined earlier */
```

The *replacement* need not be just a single word; it can be anything after the whitespace following the *macro_name*. For example,

```
#define PI 3.14
#define AREA PI * r * r

a = AREA;
```

At compile time, the statement would become

```
a = 3.14 * r * r;
```

Remember also that C concatenates quoted strings that appear together. The code

```
"this " "and " "that."
```

would be compiled as

```
"this and that."
```

By using that feature, we can replace strings using macros. For example,

```
#define COMPANY "Ajax Corp"

printf("The earnings for " COMPANY " are %f.\n", earnings);
```

would compile the statement as

```
printf("The earnings for Ajax Corp are %f.\n", earnings);
```

Parameterized Macros

We can define macros with parameters in them that will take on the values of similar parameters in the code when the replacement is made. **Parameterized macros** have one or more parameters in parentheses immediately following the *macro_name*:

Nuts & Bolts

RESCANNING MACROS

When a macro is replaced, the compiler rescans the replacement text to see if there are any more macros. If there are, it replaces them and rescans again. For example, we might have these definitions at the beginning of our program:

```
#define FOUR 2 * TWO
#define TWO 2
```

At first glance, it would appear that the macro replacement for FOUR would not be made, because TWO was defined after FOUR. This is actually true of the text in the #define directive. If we put the macro FOUR in a statement later on, however, such as

```
printf("%i\n", FOUR);
```

the preprocessor will first translate it to

```
printf("%i\n", 2 * TWO);
```

and then to

```
printf("%i\n", 2 * 2);
```

This is useful when using a number of macros from various sources—different include files, perhaps—and the order of the #defines is not evident.

```
#define macro_name(parameter_list) replacement
```

The `parameter_list` is any number of identifiers separated by commas. The open parenthesis must immediately follow the `macro_name`, with no space in between. The `replacement` should reference those parameters in their desired positions within the `replacement`. For example, given the following:

```
#define area(r) PI * r * r
```

```
surface = area(radius);
```

the macro in the statement would have `radius` substituted for `r` and would be compiled as:

```
surface = PI * radius * radius;
```

When using macros, we must be sure we understand the order in which things are done. The substitution is made before the program is run. If our statement was:

```
surface = area(radius + 3);
```

we would get some surprising results because, after translation, our statement would be:

```
surface = PI * radius + 3 * radius + 3
```

Because of operator precedence, the order of evaluation would be

```
(PI * radius) + (3 * radius) + 3
```

instead of

```
PI * (radius + 3) * (radius + 3)
```

A common way to eliminate that problem is to always put the parameters in the macro definition in parentheses, so that whatever is substituted for them will always be in parentheses:

```
#define area(r) (PI * (r) * (r))
```

when substituted in the statement becomes:

```
surface = (PI * (radius + 3) * (radius + 3))
```

Other problems may confront the haphazard macro user. For example, if you set up variable names (other than the macro's parameters), will they conflict with local variables in the code? Will braces, brackets, or other symbols conflict with the control structures in the code? Be sure you are aware of what the final substitution will be with each use of a macro.

One major advantage of macros is that they can usually be considered as typeless. Data of any type can be substituted in the previous macro and it will still work. That carries its own disadvantage. The compiler cannot type-check macro code. In addition, such code usually does not find its way into the elements used by various external debuggers, making debugging difficult.

We can use any number of parameters in a macro as long as we separate them with commas

```
#define min(x, y) (((x) < (y)) ? (x) : (y))   /* Parentheses to be safe */

lowest = min(east, west);
```

The macro call in the statement would have east substituted for x and west substituted for y, making the statement (discarding the unneeded parentheses):

```
lowest = (east < west) ? east : west;
```

Both of our example parameterized macros look very much like functions. In fact, they are used like functions. Many of the things that we introduced as functions were really macros. The getchar() "function" is typically a macro defined in *stdio.h* like this:

```
#define getchar()  getc(stdin)
```

The string classification "functions" in *ctype.h* are usually macros. We might define isupper() this way:

```
#define isupper(c) ((c) >= 'A' && (c) <= 'Z')
```

By tradition, C programmers use uppercase names for unparameterized macros (symbolic constants, such as PI), but for parameterized macros, they use lowercase identifiers to make them look just like functions.

Stringizing and Token Pasting

Let us set up a macro, *print*, that will print the value of a variable of whatever data type, as well as the name of the variable. To use printf(), we must have the correct conversion code character or characters, so we will have to call the macro with both the value and the code characters:

```
print(value, code);
```

For example,

```
print(weight, f);
```

If we #define our macro like this:

```
#define print(v, c) printf("v: %c\n", v)
```

when the replacement was made, it would end up like this:

```
printf("v: %c\n", weight)
```

The *weight* and *f* were never substituted for the *v* and the *c* in the control string because the control string was in quotes and not subject to replacement.

We can solve this problem by **stringizing**—turning into a quoted string—the replacement, and using C's string concatenation to assemble the control string. The stringizing operator is # and it belongs just before the symbol we want stringized. We will rewrite the #define, show the call, and show the replacement in two steps:

```
#define print(v, c) printf(#v ": %" #c "\n", v)
print(weight, f);                                      /* Call */
printf("weight" ": %" "f" "\n", weight);          /* Replacement, step 1 */
printf("weight: %f\n", weight);                    /* Replacement, final */
```

The **token-pasting** operator, ##, allows us to put together two *tokens* or sets of characters. For example, if in some part of our code we wanted to refer to the variable *factor_min*, or *factor_max*, or *factor_avg*, depending on the situation at that point in the program, we could

```
#define factor(x) factor_ ## x
```

and call it like this:

```
result = 0.2762 * factor(max);
```

The replacement would be:

```
result = 0.2762 * factor_max;
```

MACRO OR FUNCTION?

Should you define your routine as a macro or a function? If it's long, it will probably be a function. But if it's short, you may have a choice. Macros have some advantages. When you call a function, passed values must be put on the stack, return addresses kept, execution moved to another part of memory, return values passed back, execution moved again, and so forth. None of this really accomplishes the task of the routine. It is all *overhead*. A macro, on the other hand, is placed directly in line in the code at compile time, so that at run time this overhead is avoided. As a result, macros execute more quickly.

Another advantage of macros is that values passed to functions must be of specific data types. Those used in macros don't; the data type is determined in the substitution or the calculations that follow. For example, with

```
#define square(x) ((x) * (x))
```

the value substituted for x could be 4 or 78.2874 or a char or long double variable. The mathematics will accommodate the data type. If *square()* were a function, a value of a specific data type would have to be passed to it. Different data types would require different functions, as exist with the abs(), labs(), and fabs() functions.

A disadvantage of macros is that if they are used repeatedly in a program, they are copied into the code many times. Function code exists only once. Macros, then, could make the executable program longer and take up much more memory.

Stringizing and token pasting are in the ANSI standard, but non-ANSI Cs may not support these features.

A Macro's Lifetime

Since a macro is replaced before the program is actually compiled, the program's block structure is immaterial in the lifetime of a macro. Macros exist from the point at which they are defined in the source code to the end of the source code, or when they are undefined using the #undef directive:

```
#undef macro_name
```

For example,

```
#undef area
```

Macros may not be redefined unless the redefinition of the macro is the same as the existing definition. This allows, for instance, a macro such as NULL or EOF to be defined in more than one header file without conflict. To change a macro's definition, we would have to #undefine it and #define it again.

```
#define PI 3.14
    . . .                       /* PI is 3.14 in this section of the program */
#undef PI
#define PI 3.14159              /* PI changes to 3.14159 at this point */
```

CONDITIONAL COMPILATION

The compiler doesn't necessarily have to consider all the code that you have written. You can direct the preprocessor to skip some. Skip some? After all the time you spent typing the code, why would you want some skipped? There are a number of valid reasons. Often when debugging a program we put in extra statements to see what is happening at a certain point—some printf() functions, perhaps. We do not want these executing after the debugging, so we erase them. And then find a bug or two more, so we retype them. Instead, let's just leave them in the code, and tell the compiler to ignore them when we are not debugging.

We might be writing a program that will eventually run on more than one type of computer, or be destined for a number of slightly different users. A few lines of code will have to be different for each application. We could leave all the code in the source file, but tell the preprocessor that if this is the Acme Company, compile these lines; if it's Baker, compile those; and so forth.

To accomplish this we use directives that work much like the if and else statements—the #if and #else directives. Since the preprocessor does not use the C block structure, we end the #if structure with an #endif:

```
#if condition
    Compile these statements
#else
    Compile these statements
#endif
```

The #if, #else, and #endif directives work only with the preprocessor, so the *condition* can only react to those things that are active in the preprocessing stage—the results of other proprocessor directives such as #define. For example, we may want to declare a variable differently depending on how many records the program might process:

```
#define MAX_RECORDS 45000
   . . .
#if MAX_RECORDS <= 32767
    int records;
#else
    long records;
#endif
```

We do not need parentheses around the condition here as we do in the if statement. They are, of course, acceptable.

An #else branch is not required. We might need an extra variable if we have a lot of records, so we could write

```
#define MAX_RECORDS 45000
   . . .
int records;
#if MAX_RECORDS > 32767
    int record_set;
#endif
```

We might use a multibranch structure as we saw in Chapter 4. An #if structure may be nested within another #if structure branch, or, more commonly, we use the multibranch structure where we combined the if on the same line as the else to make a kind of else if statement. For the preprocessor, we don't have to make up one; there is one—#elif, meaning *else if*. If we had three possibilities for the maximum number of records, we might write

```
#define MAX_RECORDS 45000
   . . .
#if MAX_RECORDS <= 127
    char records;
#elif MAX_RECORDS <= 32767
    short records;
#else
    long records;
#endif
```

We can, of course, use as many #elifs as we need.

The keyword defined can be used in a *condition* to test to see whether a symbolic constant has been defined. It is always followed by the constant name being tested.

```
if defined name      often written      if defined(name)
```

The value of the constant is immaterial. All that counts is whether it has been defined.

For example, let us say that we are testing a program and have inserted debugging statements throughout. Near the beginning of the program we can have the directive

```
#define DEBUG
```

The value of *DEBUG* is nonexistent, empty, but as far as the proprocessor is concerned, it has been defined. Later in the program, we can put

```
#if defined DEBUG
    [debugging statements]
#endif
```

The #ifdef directive combines #if and defined(). We could write the first line of the previous segment as

```
#ifdef DEBUG
```

The only advantage of the long form is if you need a *condition* with two or more tests, such as

```
#if defined(DEBUG) and MAX_RECORDS > 500
```

We can test for a constant not having been defined using either the logical not or the #ifndef directive.

```
#if !defined(DEBUG)      or      #ifndef DEBUG
```

COMMENT OUT OR CONDITIONALLY COMPILE?

One popular method of not compiling code segments that exist in the source is to comment them out—enclose the code in /* */:

```
/*
    printf("Test value at step 4 is %f\n", test);
    printf("At iteration %i\n", count);
*/
```

This works fine unless one of the statements also has a comment. Most Cs do not support nesting of comments (although some are starting to), so in the following, the second statement would be compiled.

```
/*
    printf("Test value at step 4 is %f\n", test);      /* Should increase */
    printf("At iteration %i\n", count);
*/
```

Conditional compilation avoids such problems. In addition, using conditional compilation, many sections of code can be turned off or on with a single #define, whereas each commented-out section will have to be dealt with separately.

PREPROCESSOR ERROR MESSAGES

Errors may be introduced just as easily in the preprocessor code as in the rest of the program. You can set up debugging aids in the rest of the program by putting in `printf()` or `puts()` functions at critical points to print out values, error messages, or whatever. You can do a limited amount of that in the preprocessor code with the `#error` directive:

```
#error message
```

where the *message* is any quoted string. The `#error` directive stops the compile process and prints the *message*. Since the directive stops the compile, it is typically within an `#if` structure as a "we shouldn't be here" type of thing. In order for it to be useful, you must anticipate possible errors and place `#error` directives appropriately. For example,

```
#if PARSNIP = 1
    #define TURNIP 3
#elif PARSNIP = 2
    #define TURNIP 0
#else
    #ifndef PARSNIP
        #error "PARSNIP undefined."
    #else
        #error "PARSNIP must be 1 or 2."
    #endif
#endif
```

RENAMING DATA TYPES

Using `typedef` we can change the name of an existing data type to something else.

```
typedef old_name new_name;
```

where the *old_name* is the name of an existing data type—`long double`, `int`, a structure tag that we had defined earlier, or even a *new_name* defined earlier. The *new_name* can be used anywhere a data-type name is valid—declaring variables and functions, casts, `sizeof` operations, and so forth. For example,

```
typedef int INTEGER;
typedef float REAL;
typedef char STRING[MAX_CHRS];
```

establishes three new names for data types, the third being a `char` array of *MAX_CHRS* length. *MAX_CHRS*, of course, must have been `#define`d previously. Later in the program we may declare variables using these new names:

```
INTEGER x, y, z = 45;
REAL ity;
STRING names[10];
```

In the third statement, we declared an array of 10 *STRINGS* of *MAX_CHRS* each. The declaration without the `typedef` would have been

```
char names[10][MAX_CHRS];
```

A convenient way of viewing the `typedef` process is to substitute the declared variable or array for the *new_name* in the `typedef`. In our last example, substituting `names[10]` for `STRING` in `typedef  char  STRING[MAX_CHRS]` yields `char names[10][MAX_CHRS]`.

Notice the semicolons after `typedef`. It is a statement and so must have them. Traditionally, new names for data types are in capitals, like defined constants, to make them easily recognizable. A `typedef`ed name must be a complete data type; it cannot be modified by things like `signed` or `unsigned`. Given the previous `typedef`, this is illegal:

```
unsigned INTEGER q;                                        /* Illegal */
```

Now that we know how to rename a data type, why do it? One reason is for portability. We know that data types can have different sizes in different implementations of C. Let us say that we are working with a Midget computer as well as a SuperMax. On the Midget, an `int` has 16 bits; a `long`, 32; a `float`, 32; and a `double`, 64. The SuperMax has a 32-bit `int` and a 64-bit `float`. If we want our program to work with 32-bit integers and 64-bit real numbers, no matter which implementation of C we use, we can set up the following near the beginning of our code:

```
#define MACHINE 0                          /* 0 = Midget, 1 = SuperMax */

#if MACHINE = 0
   typedef long INTEGER;
   typedef double REAL;
#else
   typedef int INTEGER;
   typedef float REAL;
#endif
 . . .
REAL function(INTEGER this, REAL that);
 . . .
INTEGER i, j, k;
REAL x, y, z;
```

By changing the `#define` near the beginning of the code, we can compile the program for either computer.

Another reason to use `typedef` is for clarity and consistency. Suppose that we are working with various arrays of pointers to a specific structure:

```
struct specific
{ char name[40];
   int age;
};
 . . .
struct specific *array1[20], *array2[20];        /*Similar declarations
                                                   elsewhere*/
```

We could `typedef` the data type to make the declarations both more clear and more consistent.

```
typedef specific *ARRAY[20]
    . . .
struct ARRAY array1, array2;              /*Similar declarations elsewhere*/
```

PUTTING IT TOGETHER (The Preprocessor and `typedef`)

We are involved in a computer project for a U.S. senator. The senator would like a quick way of estimating the amount of federal funds needed to cover financial losses from natural disasters—earthquakes in California, volcanic eruptions in Northwest, blizzards in the Rockies, tornadoes in the Midwest, hurricanes in the East, laryngitis in Washington, D.C.—name your disaster. The calculations are quite complicated and the program is huge, but we will concentrate on the final formula:

$$loss = devastation \times population \times case$$

where *loss* is the dollar amount of the losses, *devastation* is the percent of complete loss in the area, *population* is the number of people in the area adjusted by a factor calculated by dividing the number of people registered in the senator's party by the number registered in the other party, *percapita* is the average loss per person if the devastation was total, and *case* is a factor based on whether the disaster is in the senator's home state (worst case, highest losses) or someone else's state (best case, lowest losses).

We want to make the program as flexible as possible, so the important parameters are defined in the beginning of the program. The senator wanted the program to work not only for estimating the need for funds in the senator's home state but also in some other state. Naturally, the calculations would be different. We couldn't remember whether the senator was a Republican or a Democrat, so we allowed for stating a party affiliation prior to compiling.

Only a few of the actual program statements are shown, but let us examine the preprocessor manipulations:

➡ Program 13–1

```
1  #include <stdio.h>                 /* Standard input/output header file */

2  #define DEMOCRAT                      /* If Republican, leave this out */
3  #define PER_CAPITA 25000       /* Loss per person if total devastation */
4  #define DETAIL                        /* Print details, not just result */
5  #define HOMESTATE               /* Change to OTHERSTATE if appropriate */
6  #define BEST_CASE 0.65               /* Least possible amount of loss */
7  #define WORST_CASE 1.35            /* Greatest possible amount of loss */

8  #ifdef OTHERSTATE
9     #define STATE "your"
10    #define CASE BEST_CASE                   /* Apply least loss factor */
11 #elif defined HOMESTATE
12    #define STATE "my"
13    #define CASE WORST_CASE               /* Apply greatest loss factor */
   #else
14    #error "Must define either HOMESTATE or OTHERSTATE."
   #endif
```

—Continued

```
15  #ifdef DEMOCRAT                    /* Adjust by percent of population in party */
16      #define population(total, demo, repub) ((total) * (demo) / (repub))
    #else
17      #define population(total, demo, repub) ((total) * (repub) / (demo))
    #endif

18  #if PER_CAPITA > 20000
19      typedef long double LOSSES;        /* Larger data type for high losses */
20      #define CODE "Lf"                    /* Conversion code for data type */
    #else
21      typedef double LOSSES;
22      #define CODE "f"
23  #endif

    void main(void)
24  {   LOSSES loss, devastation;      /* Force final calculation to LOSSES type */
        /* . . . */
25      #ifdef DETAIL
26          printf("Case factor: %g\n", CASE);
27          printf("Adjusted population: %g\n", population(pop, dem, gop));
    #endif
28      loss = devastation * population(pop, dem, gop) * PER_CAPITA * CASE;
29      printf("Funds needed in " STATE " state are %.2" CODE "\n", loss);
    }
```

EXECUTION CHART

Line	Explanation
1	Insert source file *stdio.h*.
2–7	Initial defines.
8	*OTHERSTATE* was not defined.
11	*HOMESTATE* was defined in line 5.
12	Define *STATE* as "my".
13	Define *CASE* as *WORST_CASE*, which was defined in line 7 as 1.35.
15	*DEMOCRAT* was defined in line 2.
16	Define *population* macro.
18	*PER_CAPITA*, defined in line 3, is greater than 20000.
19	Set up data type LOSSES as `long double`.
20	Define conversion code Lf to handle `long doubles`.
24	Declare 2 variables of type LOSSES (`long double`) as defined in line 19.
25	*DETAIL* was defined in line 4.
26	Print case factor *CASE*, defined in line 13.
27	Print result of *population* macro, defined in line 16.
28	Calculate *loss* using *population*, defined in line 16, *PER_CAPITA*, line 3, and *CASE*, line 13.
29	Substitute "my" for STATE and "Lf" for CODE, giving: "Funds needed in " "my" " state are %.2" "Lf" "\n", and finally: "Funds needed in my state are %.2Lf\n".

THE ENUMERATION DATA TYPE

The enumeration data type (enum) sets up a different use of the int data type. The enum definition establishes a data type that can hold one integer value from a defined set of possible integer values. A group of constants is established in this definition that are used to represent these values. Variables declared to be of this data type should hold only those values. The general form of an enum definition is:

```
enum tag {constant [= value], constant [= value], . . .};
```

where the *tag* is the new data type and *constant* is the name of an allowed constant. If a *value* is not stated, the first value is zero and each value is one greater than the previous one. For example,

```
enum boolean {false, true, off = 0, on, no = 0, yes};
```

defines the data type *boolean* and its possible values: *false*, *off*, and *no* are zero, and *true*, *on*, and *yes* are one.

A declaration of variables of an enum data type are made following this form:

```
enum tag variable [= value], variable [= value], . . .;
```

For example,

```
enum boolean status, indicator = false;
```

Definitions and declarations can be made in the same statement; for example:

```
enum
    {sun = 1, mon, tue, wed, thu, fri, sat}
    day, first_work_day = mon;
```

In this example of the combination statement, however, no *tag* is defined. We could not set up another variable, *start_week_end*, using the same defined values, because we cannot defined more than one value with the same name:

```
enum {hot, cold} temp;
enum {hot, cold} degrees;                          /* This causes an error */
```

will not be accepted by the compiler, but

```
enum warmth {hot, cold} temp;
enum warmth degrees;                               /* No problem */
```

will be accepted.

enum VALUES

An ANSI C standard compiler actually does not require that an enum variable hold only one of the declared values. The variable may hold any value as long as it is consistent with the int data type. Newer offshoots of C, particularly C++, however, do enforce the rule. Since the enum was designed to hold only specified values, and to enhance the portability of the code, most programmers follow the rule.

NONSTRUCTURED PROGRAM FLOW

The C language offers the programmer a number of ways to approach programming tasks. C is designed to be an all-purpose language and is applicable to the programming style of almost anyone. Structured programming is a style that has been adopted by a number of programmers, but it is neither universally accepted nor universally followed. C makes allowances for this by allowing program flow control that does not demand structure. The following concepts are not structured, but are part of the language. Carefully used, they are even accepted in some structured environments.

Labels

A **label** identifies a specific place in a program. The identifier is a set of characters following the same naming rules as variables. In fact, label names may even duplicate variable names without interference, but it is considered bad form to have the same name for both a label and a variable. The following are legal label names:

```
Here              NewProcedure
instance1         analysis_section
```

The label should always be the first thing on a line and is followed by a colon. For example:

```
    printf("Preliminary analysis completed.\n");
FinalAnalysis:                          /* Entry point for final analysis */
    Result += SecondSample;
    Adjust = Result / (1 - FudgeFactor);
```

or

```
    x = y * y * 4.7;
action: q = x + 9;
    printf("Percentage: %5.2%%\n", q / 100);
```

Unconditional Transfers

The goto statement causes a computer to transfer execution of the program to some specific location, marked by a label. Presumably, this spot in the program is someplace other than the next one in line. In other words, using goto you can jump around from place to place in a program. This kind of jumping about makes structured programmers shudder because it allows you to jump out of the middle of one section into the middle of another, severely affecting the program's structure. You won't find goto statements in structured programs, but they are part of the language, so we will address them here:

```
goto label;
```

When a goto statement is encountered in a program, the next statement to execute will be the one immediately following the *label*. The following program segment shows gotos in use:

```
{
     . . .
    if (total == 0)
    {  printf("Error, no total.\n);
       goto end;
    }
    if (total < 0)
    {  printf("Error, negative total.\n");
       goto end;
    }
     . . .
end:
    printf("The program has been terminated because of this error\n");
                                /* Some statement needed here */
}
```

When the *label* is used as a reference in the goto statement (as opposed to the label marking a location in the program), there is no colon following the label. The semicolon, of course, denotes the end of the statement.

The goto statement must have a place to go to; in fact, the label has to be in the same function as the goto statement.

Jumping to the End of a Loop

There are two C statements that will disrupt the normal flow of a loop. *Disrupt* is a significant word here because the normal structure of the loop is not maintained. Neither of these statements would be found in a strictly structured program, but sparingly used and well commented, they are often accepted as part of a well-formed C program.

The break statement was introduced in Chapter 4. It causes execution to jump beyond the end of a switch structure. The break statement may also be used in loops—either while, do, or for—for exactly the same purpose. The program segment below would never execute statements 3 or 4; nor would it go through the loop a second time no matter what the value of *x* was:

```
while (x > 9)
{   statement 1;
    statement 2;
    break;
    statement 3;
    statement 4;
}
```

It would be reasonable to ask, "Why even write the program with the break and statements 3 and 4 in it?" You probably wouldn't. However, the break statement can be used in an if statement within a loop rather productively. Remember, the break only jumps beyond the end of loops and switches, not ifs, so if the if is within a loop, the break will jump beyond the end of the loop.

▶Program 13–2

```
#include <stdio.h>

void main(void)
{  float price;
   float total = 0;
   short quantity;

   while (1)                              /* Always true, loop exit at break below */
   {  printf("Enter 'price,quantity': ");
      scanf("%f,%hi", &price, &quantity);

      if (price == 0) break;                      /* Exit point for the loop */
      printf("The total for this item is $%6.2f.\n", price * quantity);
      total += price * quantity;
   }
   printf("Your total is $%6.2f.\n", total);
}
```

Output

```
Enter 'price,quantity': 6.35,8
The total for this item is $ 50.80.
Enter 'price,quantity': 2.50,10
The total for this item is $ 25.00.
Enter 'price,quantity': 0,0
Your total is $ 75.80.
```

This program is a nonstructured version of the sentinel-value controlled loop ▶Program 5–4 from Chapter 5. The statements used to input the *price* and *quantity* did not have to be repeated, but neither the exit point of the loop nor the conditions for the loop are at the beginning or end of the loop. Instead, the loop conditions are stated in the if and the loop is made to continue by setting the while condition to 1 which is always true. When a price of 0 is input, the if condition is true and execution jumps to the statement following the closing brace.

If the while statement had a condition that might be false, such as while (quantity > 0), the loop would have two possible exit points, the while statement and the break statement. Remember that in Chapter 1, we stated that in structured programming, any structure should have only one entry point and one exit point.

The continue statement is similar to break except that continue does not work with switch and it jumps to the end of the loop, not beyond it. In other words, the loop will continue given that the condition is still true:

```
while (x > 9)
{  statement 1;
   statement 2;
   continue;
   statement 3;
   statement 4;
}
```

This will execute differently from the last example with the break statement. Statements 3 and 4 will still be skipped; but continue will send the execution to the end of the loop, from which point it will go back to the test in while and perhaps back through the loop again.

We have modified ➡️Program 13–2 to warn the user if the total is getting too high.

➡️Program 13–3

```
#include <stdio.h>

void main(void)
{   float price;
    float total = 0;
    short quantity;

1   while (1)                                      /* Loop exit at break below */
    {   printf("Enter 'price,quantity': ");
2       scanf("%f,%hi", &price, &quantity);
3       if (price == 0) break;                     /* Exit point for the loop */
4       printf("The total for this item is $%6.2f.\n", price * quantity);
5       total += price * quantity;
6       if (total < 100) continue;                 /* Goes to end of loop */
7       printf("Your total is getting high.\n");
        printf("It now stands at $%.2f.\n", total);
8   }
9   printf("Your total is $%6.2f.\n", total);
}
```

Output

```
Enter 'price,quantity': 14.25,6
The total for this item is $ 85.50.
Enter 'price,quantity': 9.98,3
The total for this item is $ 29.94.
Your total is getting high.
It now stands at $115.44.
Enter 'price,quantity': 0,0
Your total is $115.44.
```

EXECUTION CHART

Line	Explanation	price	quantity	total
1	Sets up infinite loop. The value 1 is always true.	?	?	0
2	Input *price* and *quantity.*	14.25	6	0
3	See if *price* is sentinel value. It isn't.	14.25	6	0
4	Display total for the item.	14.25	6	0
5	Accumulate item total in *total.*	14.25	6	85.50
6	The *total* is less than 100, so jump to end of loop at 8.	14.25	6	85.50
8	Go back to while at 1.	14.25	6	85.50
1	Still true, of course.	14.25	6	85.50
2	Input *price* and *quantity.*	9.98	3	85.50
3	See if *price* is sentinel value. It isn't.	9.98	3	85.50
4	Display total for the item.	9.98	3	85.50
5	Accumulate item total in *total.*	9.98	3	115.44
6	The total is not less than 100. Don't continue.	9.98	3	115.44
7	Display the warning message.	9.98	3	115.44
8	Go back to while at 1.	9.98	3	115.44
1	Still true, of course.	9.98	3	115.44
2	Input *price* and *quantity.*	0	0	115.44
3	See if *price* is sentinel value. It is, so break to beyond loop at 9.	0	0	115.44
9	Display *total* and quit.	0	0	115.44

SUMMARY

The precompiler or **preprocessor** segment of the compiler makes changes in the source code. Preprocessor **directives** start with a # symbol and end at the end of a line (or set of lines if each is continued with a backslash). The #include directive temporarily inserts a file of source code lines at that point in the source code.

The #define directive tells the preprocessor to replace one set of characters with another. The replacement is called a **macro**. The replacement can be any set of characters—single words, quoted string, formulas, or whatever. Quoted strings are often used to concatenate a set of characters into another quoted string.

We can also use **parameterized macros**—sets of characters, typically expressions, into which other parameters will be substituted at run time. These macros can act just like functions. In fact, many of those things that were previously presented as functions are actually macros.

In macro replacement, the **stringizing** operator, #, turns the replacement value into a quoted string, typically so that it can be concatenated into another quoted string. The **token-pasting** operator, ##, tells the preprocessor to attach the sets of characters on each side of the operator directly together. This is typically used to create a single word, such as a variable name, out of a combination of tokens.

Macros exist from the point in the source code in which they are defined to the end of the code, or until they are **#undef**ined. A macro must be undefined before it can be defined again unless the new definition is exactly the same as the old.

Not all of the source code need be compiled. We often write statements in our programs that we only use for special purposes such as debugging or compiling for different implementations. Using the #if, #elif, #else, and #endif directives, we can test for certain conditions and only those statements in the indicated branches will be compiled. The condition often includes a test to see whether a constant has been defined. For this purpose, we can use the key word defined after the #if, or the key word #ifdef. To test if a constant has not been defined, we can use the key word #ifndef.

We can direct the preprocessor to stop the compile process and print an error message by directing the process to a branch with an #error directive.

Using the typedef statement, we can change the name of an existing data type to a name of our own choosing. This is often done to make a program listing clearer, to enhance portability, or to simplify the description of complex data types.

The enum key word established a data type that can hold any one of a number of predefined integer values.

A number of statements in C allow program flow that does not strictly follow the rules of structure, but, given the proper situation, can be handy in programming. The goto statement directs the computer to jump the processing to a place in the program identified by a **label**. Two unstructured but valid statements can be used with loops. The break statement sends execution beyond the end of the loop; and the continue statement sends execution to the end of the loop but keeps the program within the loop.

KEY TERMS (in order of appearance)

Preprocessor	#undef	#error
Directive	#if	typedef
#include	#else	enum
#define	#endif	**Label**
Macro	#elif	goto
Parameterized macro	defined	break
Stringizing	#ifdef	continue
Token-pasting	#ifndef	

REVIEW QUESTIONS

1. What is the function of the preprocessor and when does this function take place?

2. What is the general form of a preprocessor directive and how does it differ from a statement?

3. What does the #include directive do?

4. How can you see what is inserted by the #include directive?

5. In what parts of a program will a macro be replaced?

6. Why are parentheses important in parameterized macros?

7. Can we use existing variable names as macro parameters? Can this cause problems?

8. How can we perform a macro replacement in the middle of a string?

9. How can we put two strings together during a macro replacement?

10. What defines the beginning and ending of a macro's lifetime?

11. Show the pattern, along with the key words, for a three-branch conditional compilation.

12. How is the key word defined used in a conditional compilation?

13. How can we test for a constant definition in a conditional compilation without using the defined key word?

14. What preprocessor directive do we use to send an error message?

15. Can we create a new data type using typedef?

16. Can we use modifiers such as long or unsigned with the typedef directive?

17. Describe some proper situations for the use of an enumeration data type.

18. How do goto and labels work together?

19. Why is goto not considered entirely proper in a structured program?

20. If a break statement is executed from within a loop, where does execution go?

21. If a continue statement is executed from within a loop, where does execution go?

22. Why are break and continue not considered entirely proper in a structured program?

EXERCISES

1. What will the output be from the program below?

```
#include <stdio.h>

#define SQUARE(x) ((x) * (x))

int square(int x)
{
   return x * x;
}

void main(void)
{   int a = 2, b=2;
    printf("SQUARE %i, square %i\n", SQUARE(a++), square(b++));
}
```

2. Why won't this program give the expected results?

```
#include <stdio.h>
#define volume(length, height, width) length * height * width

void main(void)
{   float a = 1, b = 2, c = 3;

    printf("The volume is %f\n", volume(a + 1, b - 1, c - 2));
}
```

3. Show the statements after substitution using the following defined macro:

```
#define cost(a, b) (a + (b) / 6 * 100)
```

   a.   `result = cost(z + 25, 100)`
   b.   `result = cost(f, b * 5)`

4. Given the following macro definitions, show the substitutions made for the following macro calls:

```
#define output(a) printf("At " # a ": %s\n", a)
#define string(a) str ## a
```

   a.   `output(46);`
   b.   `string(ing);`

5. Take a previously written program (or several) and rewrite it (them) so that if *DEBUG* is defined, the program prints out the name and value of each variable as soon as it is assigned or reassigned.

6. Define the data type *four_byte* as a four-byte, unsigned integral data type in your C.

7. Using `typedef`, define a single data type, *info*, that is a structure consisting of an array of three product names, each with an array of sales for the last four quarters. Information for each product should be `typedef`ed as *product*, and sales for each product should be `typedef`ed as *sales*.

8. Rewrite the first example program in Chapter 5 using the `break` and/or `continue` statements.

PROGRAMS

1. Referring to Chapter 3, Program 4, the Ajax Company plans to use the defined constants in other programs as well. Write an include file, *PAYCONST.INC*, that contains those constants, properly commented. Test the include file by using it in the program.

2. Write a macro that will swap the values of two variables of a specified type. The call should be similar to `swap(a, b, float)`. Your macro will have to declare a temporary variable of the appropriate type. Put it in a program that initializes two variables and displays their values before and after the swap.

Output

```
Before: a=5.3. b=3.6.
After:  a=3.6. b=5.3.
```

3. Write a macro, *abso()*, that will return the absolute value of any value given the value and its data type. Test it in a short program.

4. Write a macro the gives the smallest of three values. Test it in a short program.

5. Write a *trace* macro that will allow you to print out the name and the value of a variable or expression during the debugging of your program. It should work with any data type—remember casts. Validate it with the following program.

Program

```
#include <stdio.h>

#define trace                                          /* Your macro */

void main(void)
{   int a = 15;
    float b = -3.123;

    trace(a);
    trace(b);
    trace(a + b);
}
```

Output

```
a: 15
b: -3.123
a + b: 11.877
```

6. Depending on certain conditions, a calculation in your program might use one of a number of different variables (*var0a*, *var0b*, *var1a*, and so forth with the number and the last letter varying independently). Write a VAR macro with two parameters that specify the number and letter. Validate it in in the following program.

Program

```
#include <stdio.h>

#define VAR                                            /* Your macro */

void main(void)
{   float x1a = 1.1, x2d = 2.4;

    printf("x1a: %g, x2d: %g\n", VAR(1, a), VAR(2, d));
}
```

Output

```
x1a: 1.1, x2d: 2.4
```

7. Write a macro, *concat(string, number)*, that will concatenate a given number of strings (in a ragged array) together at the address of the first string.

8. Set up a partial program that conditionally compiles according to the defined constant *DEBUG*. It should show the following outputs with various values of this constant:

Output

```
DEBUG on.
DEBUG level 1, a=1

DEBUG on.
DEBUG level 2, a=1, b=2

DEBUG on.
DEBUG level>2, a=1, b=2, c=3
```

9. Rewrite the program from Chapter 5 that plays the game Totals, using `break` and/or `continue`.

10. Using `break` and/or `continue`, rewrite the program in Chapter 5 that translates numeric scores into letter grades.

ASCII CODES

Dec	Hex	Ctrl	Code	Dec	Hex	Char	Dec	Hex	Char	Dec	Hex	Char
0	00	^@	NUL	32	20	sp	64	40	@	96	60	`
1	01	^A	SOH	33	21	!	65	41	A	97	61	a
2	02	^B	STX	34	22	"	66	42	B	98	62	b
3	03	^C	ETX	35	23	#	67	43	C	99	63	c
4	04	^D	EOT	36	24	$	68	44	D	100	64	d
5	05	^E	ENQ	37	25	%	69	45	E	101	65	e
6	06	^F	ACK	38	26	&	70	46	F	102	66	f
7	07	^G	BEL	39	27	'	71	47	G	103	67	g
8	08	^H	BS	40	28	(	72	48	H	104	68	h
9	09	^I	HT	41	29	)	73	49	I	105	69	i
10	0A	^J	LF	42	2A	*	74	4A	J	106	6A	j
11	0B	^K	VT	43	2B	+	75	4B	K	107	6B	k
12	0C	^L	FF	44	2C	,	76	4C	L	108	6C	l
13	0D	^M	CR	45	2D	-	77	4D	M	109	6D	m
14	0E	^N	SO	46	2E	.	78	4E	N	110	6E	n
15	0F	^O	SI	47	2F	/	79	4F	O	111	6F	o
16	10	^P	SLE	48	30	0	80	50	P	112	70	p
17	11	^Q	CS1	49	31	1	81	51	Q	113	71	q
18	12	^R	DC2	50	32	2	82	52	R	114	72	r
19	13	^S	DC3	51	33	3	83	53	S	115	73	s
20	14	^T	DC4	52	34	4	84	54	T	116	74	t
21	15	^U	NAK	53	35	5	85	55	U	117	75	u
22	16	^V	SYN	54	36	6	86	56	V	118	76	v
23	17	^W	ETB	55	37	7	87	57	W	119	77	w
24	18	^X	CAN	56	38	8	88	58	X	120	78	x
25	19	^Y	EM	57	39	9	89	59	Y	121	79	y
26	1A	^Z	SIB	58	3A	:	90	5A	Z	122	7A	z
27	1B	^[	ESC	59	3B	;	91	5B	[	123	7B	{
28	1C	^\	FS	60	3C	<	92	5C	\	124	7C		
29	1D	^]	GS	61	3D	=	93	5D	]	125	7D	}
30	1E	^^	RS	62	3E	>	94	5E	^	126	7E	~
31	1F	^_	US	63	3F	?	95	5F	_	127	7F	DEL

B OPERATORS

Operator	Explanation	Symbol	Example
Expression — Left-to-right associativity			
Parens	To change the order of evaluation.	`( )`	`4 * (6 + 2)`
Subscript	Subscript of array. Offset in variables from base address.	`[ ]`	`array[4]`
Member	Identifies member of structure.	`.`	`structure.member`
Member pointer	Content at location of member of a pointer to a structure.	`->`	`ptr_to_str->member`
Unary — Right-to-left associativity			
Negate	Reverse the sign of an expression.	`-`	`-4`
Add	Specify a positive value. (This is the default, anyway.)	`+`	`+4`
Increment	Add one to variable in expression.	`++`	`++var or var++`
Decrement	Subtract one from variable in expression.	`--`	`--var or var--`
Complement	Change 1 bits to 0 and 0 to 1.	`~`	`~var`
Logical NOT	Make false expression (0) true (1); make true (nonzero) false (0).	`!`	`!(time > present)`
Indirection	Contents of location in expression.	`*`	`*(array + 3)`
Address	Address of variable.	`&`	`&var`
Size	Size of expression or (data type) in bytes	`sizeof`	`sizeof var`
Cast — Right-to-left associativity			
	Convert to data *type*.	`(type)`	`(int)4.2`
Multiplicative — Left-to-right associativity			
Multiply	Multiply expressions on either side.	`*`	`6 * 4`
Divide	Divide expressions on either side.	`/`	`6 / 4`
Remainder	Remainder of first divided by second.	`%`	`6 % 4`
Additive — Left-to-right associativity			
Add	Add expressions on either side.	`+`	`6 + 4`
Subtract	Subtract expressions on either side.	`-`	`6 - 4`
Shift — Left-to-right associativity			
Left shift	Shift bits in first to left by number of bits in second.	`<<`	`6 << 4`
Right shift	Shift bits in first to right by number of bits in second.	`>>`	`6 >> 4`
Relational — Left-to-right associativity			
Greater	First greater than second?	`>`	`x+y > z-19`
Less	First less than second?	`<`	`cost < maximum-100`
Greater or equal	First greater than or equal to second?	`>=`	`load >= limit`
Less or equal	First less than or equal to second?	`<=`	`TestValue <= Norm`
Equality — Left-to-right associativity			
Equal	First equals second?	`==`	`Count+1 == EndCount`
Not equal	First not equal to second?	`!=`	`CheckSum != NewSum`
Bitwise AND — Left-to-right associativity			
	AND values bit by bit.	`&`	`val1 & val2`
Bitwise XOR — Left-to-right associativity			
	Exclusive OR values bit by bit.	`^`	`val1 ^ val2`
Bitwise OR — Left-to-right associativity			
	OR values bit by bit.	`|`	`val1	val2`
Logical AND — Left-to-right associativity			
	First and second true?	`&&`	`val1 && val2`
Logical OR — Left-to-right associativity			
	First or second or both true?	`||`	`val1 || val2`
Conditional — Right-to-left associativity			
	If test true, perform first expression, otherwise perform second.	`? :`	`x > 4 ? p + 9 : p - 14`
Assignment — Right-to-left associativity			
Simple	Assign value of expression on right to variable on left.	`=`	`x = y * 22.4`
Accumulation	Perform arithmetic operation on variable to left and value of expression on right. Assign result to variable on left.	`*= /= %=` `+= -=` `<<= >>=` `&= ^= |=`	`a *= x`
Sequential Evaluation — Left-to-right associativity			
Comma	Dump value of previous operation, perform next.	`,`	`while(gets(x), *x!=0)`

C FUNCTIONS

CHARACTER CLASSIFICATION

```
int isalnum(int character)
```
    `<ctype.h>`
> **Purpose.** Test if `character` is alphanumeric: 0–9, A–Z, or a–z.
> **Return.** True: Nonzero. False: Zero.

```
int isalpha(int character)
```
    `<ctype.h>`
> **Purpose.** Test if `character` is alphabetic: A–Z or a–z.
> **Return.** True: Nonzero. False: Zero.

```
int iscntrl(int character)
```
    `<ctype.h>`
> **Purpose.** Test if `character` is a control code: ASCII 1–31.
> **Return.** True: Nonzero. False: Zero.

```
int isdigit(int character)
```
    `<ctype.h>`
> **Purpose.** Test if `character` is a decimal digit: 0–9.
> **Return.** True: Nonzero. False: Zero.

```
int isgraph(int character)
```
    `<ctype.h>`
> **Purpose.** Test if `character` is printable, not including space.
> **Return.** True: Nonzero. False: Zero.

```
int islower(int character)
```
    `<ctype.h>`
> **Purpose.** Test if `character` is lowercase: a–z.
> **Return.** True: Nonzero. False: Zero.

```
int isprint(int character)
```
    `<ctype.h>`
> **Purpose.** Test if `character` is printable, including space.
> **Return.** True: Nonzero. False: Zero.

```
int ispunct(int character)
```
    `<ctype.h>`
> **Purpose.** Test if `character` is punctuation.
> **Return.** True: Nonzero. False: Zero.

```
int isspace(int character)
```
    `<ctype.h>`
> **Purpose.** Test if `character` is whitespace: space, \f, \n, \r, \t, or \v.
> **Return.** True: Nonzero. False: Zero.

```
int isupper(int character)
```
    `<ctype.h>`
> **Purpose.** Test if `character` is uppercase: A–Z.
> **Return.** True: Nonzero. False: Zero.

```
int isxdigit(int character)
```
    `<ctype.h>`
> **Purpose.** Test if `character` is a hexadecimal digit: 0–9, A–F.
> **Return.** True: Nonzero. False: Zero.

CHARACTER CONVERSION

```
int tolower(int character)
```
    `<ctype.h>`
> **Purpose.** Convert uppercase `character` to lower.
> **Return.** If `character` uppercase letter, lowercase equivalent, otherwise no change.

```
int toupper(int character)
```
    `<ctype.h>`
> **Purpose.** Convert lowercase `character` to upper.
> **Return.** If `character` lowercase letter, uppercase equivalent, otherwise no change.

DATA CONVERSION

double atof(const char *string)   <stdlib.h>
    Purpose. Convert *string* to double.
    Return. Success: Converted number. Error: Meaningless assignment.

int atoi(const char *string)   <stdlib.h>
    Purpose. Convert *string* to int.
    Return. Success: Converted number. Error: Meaningless assignment.

long atol(const char *string)   <stdlib.h>
    Purpose. Convert *string* to long.
    Return. Success: Converted number. Error: Meaningless assignment.

FILES

FILE *fopen(const char *file_id, const char *mode)   <stdio.h>
    Purpose. Open a *file_id* file for *mode,* and establish a description and stream for it.
    Return. Success: Pointer to *file* description. Error: NULL.

int fclose(FILE *file)   <stdio.h>
    Purpose. Flush *file* stream (if open for write) and deallocate *file* description.
    Return. Success: Zero. Error: EOF.

int feof(FILE *file)   <stdio.h>
    Purpose. Determine whether end-of-file indicator for *file* is set.
    Return. Nonzero if end-of-file indicator set.

int fflush(FILE *file)   <stdio.h>
    Purpose. Empty *file* stream and return data to storage if necessary.
    Return. Success: Zero. Error: EOF.

char *fgets(char *string, int max, FILE *file)   <stdio.h>
    Purpose. Read a line (up to *max* - 1 characters) from the *file* into the *string.*
    Return. Success: *string.* Error: NULL.

int fprintf(FILE *file, const char *control_string, arguments)   <stdio.h>
    Purpose. Writes on *file* values of arguments in format specified in *control_string.*
    Return. Success: number of characters written. Error: negative value.

int fputs(const char *string, FILE *file)   <stdio.h>
    Purpose. Write the *string* onto the *file.*
    Return. Success: Nonnegative. Error: EOF.

size_t fread(const void *location, size_t bytes, size_t items, FILE *file)   <stdio.h>
    Purpose. Read *bytes* × *items* bytes from *file* to *location.*
    Return. Success: *items.* Error: Something other than *items.*

int fscanf(FILE *file, const char *control_string, arguments)   <stdio.h>
    Purpose. Assigns values from *file* to argument variables according to *control_string.*
    Return. Success: number of assignments made. Error: EOF if end of file.

int fseek(FILE *file, long offset, int origin)   <stdio.h>
    Purpose. Set the *file* pointer at *offset* bytes from *origin.*
    Return. Success: Zero. Error: Nonzero.

long ftell(FILE *file)   <stdio.h>
    Purpose. Obtain current position of *file* pointer.
    Return. Success: Bytes from beginning of *file.* Error: -1L.

size_t fwrite(const void *location, size_t bytes, size_t items, FILE *file)   <stdio.h>
    Purpose. Write *bytes* × *items* bytes from *location* to *file.*
    Return. Success: *items.* Error: Something other than *items.*

```
int getc(FILE *file)                                                        <stdio.h>
```
Purpose. Reads single character from the *file*.
Return. Success: ASCII (or EBCDIC) value of character read. Error: EOF.

```
int putc(int character, FILE *file)                                         <stdio.h>
```
Purpose. Write the *character* on the *file*.
Return. Success: ASCII (or EBCDIC) value of *character* written. Error: EOF.

```
int remove(const char *filename)                                            <stdio.h>
```
Purpose. Delete the file *filename* from secondary storage.
Return. Success: Zero. Error: Nonzero.

```
int rename(const char *oldname, const char *newname)                        <stdio.h>
```
Purpose. Change the name of the file *oldname* in secondary storage to *newname*.
Return. Success: Zero. Error: Nonzero.

```
void rewind(FILE *file)                                                      <stdio.h>
```
Purpose. Return the pointer to the beginning of *file*.
Return. None.

```
int unlink(const char *filename)                                            <stdio.h>
```
Purpose. Remove link to the file *filename* from secondary storage, or remove file if last link.
Return. Success: Zero. Error: Nonzero.

MATH

```
int abs(int expression)                                                     <stdlib.h>
```
Purpose. Obtain absolute value of int *expression*.
Return. Absolute value of int *expression*.

```
double fabs(double expression)                                              <math.h>
```
Purpose. Obtain absolute value of double *expression*.
Return. Absolute value of double *expression*.

```
long labs(long expression)                                                  <stdlib.h>
```
Purpose. Obtain absolute value of long *expression*.
Return. Absolute value of long *expression*.

```
double pow(double expression, double exponent)                              <math.h>
```
Purpose. Raise *expression* to the power of *exponent*.
Return. Result of the exponentiation.

```
int rand(void)                                                              <stdlib.h>
```
Purpose. Obtain next in a series of random numbers.
Return. Value between zero and RAND_MAX.

```
double sin(double angle)                                                     <math.h>
```
Purpose. Obtain sine of *angle* stated in radians.
Return. Sine of *angle*.

```
double sqrt(double expression)                                              <math.h>
```
Purpose. Obtain the square root of the *expression*.
Return. Square root of the *expression*.

```
void srand(unsigned seed)                                                   <stdlib.h>
```
Purpose. Set the *seed* for generation of random numbers.
Return. None.

```
time_t time(NULL)                                                           <time.h>
```
Purpose. Used as shown to give a different seed for random-number generation.
Return. Random-number seed.

MEMORY ALLOCATION

void free(void *address)   <stdlib.h>
> **Purpose.** Deallocate a block of memory allocated by malloc(), calloc(), or realloc().
> **Return.** None.

void *malloc(size_t bytes)   <stdlib.h>
> **Purpose.** Allocate a block of memory
> **Return.** Success: Address of allocated block. Error: NULL.

PROGRAM CONTROL

void exit(int status)   <stdlib.h>
> **Purpose.** Terminate program in orderly fashion indicating *status* of termination.
> **Return.** None.

void main(int argc, char *argv[])
> **Purpose.** Control function of C program. Puts argc strings from command line into *argv[].
> **Return.** None.

STRINGS

int sprintf(char *string, const char *control_string, arguments)   <stdio.h>
> **Purpose.** Stores at *string* the values of arguments in format specified in *control_string*.
> **Return.** Success: Number of characters printed. Error: negative value.

int sscanf(char *string, const char *control_string, arguments)   <stdio.h>
> **Purpose.** Assigns values from *string* to argument variables according to *control_string*.
> **Return.** Success: Number of assignments made. Error: EOF if end of string.

char *strcat(char *string, const char *add)   <string.h>
> **Purpose.** Put *add* string at the end of *string*.
> **Return.** *string*.

char *strchr(const char *reference, int character)   <string.h>
> **Purpose.** Find the first occurrence of a *character* in a *reference* string.
> **Return.** Success: Address of the *character* in the *reference* string. Error: NULL.

int strcmp(const char *string1, const char *string2)   <string.h>
> **Purpose.** Compares two strings.
> **Return.** Positive value if *string1* greater, negative if *string2*, zero if equal.

char *strcpy(char *destination, const char *source)   <string.h>
> **Purpose.** Copy *source* string to *destination*.
> **Return.** *destination*.

size_t strlen(const char *string)   <string.h>
> **Purpose.** Find number of characters at *string*.
> **Return.** Number of characters at *string*.

char *strncat(char *string, const char *add, size_t max)   <string.h>
> **Purpose.** Put up to *max* characters of *add* string at the end of *string*.
> **Return.** *string*.

int strncmp(const char *string1, const char *string2, size_t max)   <string.h>
> **Purpose.** Compares up to *max* characters of two strings.
> **Return.** Positive value if *string1* greater, negative if *string2*, zero if equal.

char *strncpy(char *destination, const char *source, size_t max)   <string.h>
> **Purpose.** Copy up to *max* characters of *source* string to *destination*.
> **Return.** *destination*.

```
char *strpbrk(const char *reference, const char *characters)                    <string.h>
```
Purpose. Finds first occurrence of any of *characters* in *reference*.
Return. Success: Address of occurrence. Error: NULL.
```
char *strrchr(const char *reference, int character)                             <string.h>
```
Purpose. Find the last occurrence of a *character* in a *reference* string.
Return. Success: Address of the *character* in the *reference* string. Error: NULL.
```
char *strstr(const char *reference, const char *search)                         <string.h>
```
Purpose. Find a *search* string in a *reference* string.
Return. Success: Address of beginning of search string in reference string. Error: NULL.
```
char *strtok(const char *reference, const char *delimiters)                     <string.h>
```
Purpose. Extract and mark end of tokens in *reference* string.
Return. Success: Address of beginning of *reference* string. Error: NULL.

TERMINAL INPUT/OUTPUT

```
int printf(const char *control_string, arguments)                              <stdio.h>
```
Purpose. Prints values of arguments in format specified in *control_string*.
Return. Success: number of characters printed. Error: negative value.
```
int scanf(const char *control_string, arguments)                               <stdio.h>
```
Purpose. Assigns values from input stream to arguments according to *control_string*.
Return. Success: number of assignments made. Error: EOF if end of file.
```
int getchar(void)                                                              <stdio.h>
```
Purpose. Read one character form keyboard.
Return. Success: ASCII (or EBCDIC) value of character read. Error: EOF.
```
char *gets(char *string)                                                       <stdio.h>
```
Purpose. Read a line from the the keyboard into the *string*.
Return. Success: *string*. Error: NULL.
```
int putchar(int character)                                                     <stdio.h>
```
Purpose. Display the *character* on the screen.
Return. Success: ASCII (or EBCDIC) value of *character* displayed. Error: EOF.
```
int puts(const char *string)                                                   <stdio.h>
```
Purpose. Display the *string* on the screen.
Return. Success: Nonnegative. Error: EOF.

INDEX